LIVING AND WORKING

IN

NEW ZEALAND

A SURVIVAL HANDBOOK

by

Mark Hempshell

SURVIVAL BOOKS • LONDON • ENGLAND

First published 1999

Survival Books Limited, Suite C, Third Floor
Standbrook House, 2-5 Old Bond Street
London W1X 3TB, United Kingdom
Tel. (44) 171-493 4244, Fax (44) 171-491 0605
E-mail: survivalbooks@computronx.com
Internet: www.computronx.com/survivalbooks

British Library Cataloguing in Publication Data.
A CIP record for this book is available from the British Library.
ISBN 1 901130 05 3

Printed and bound in Great Britain by Page Bros. (Norwich) Ltd., Mile Cross Lane, Norwich, Norfolk NR6 6SA, UK

ACKNOWLEDGEMENTS

My sincere thanks to all those who contributed to the successful publication of this book, in particular the many people who took the time and trouble to read and comment on the draft versions, including Ron & Pat Scarborough, Joe Laredo, David Hampshire (for chapter 19, 20 & Appendices), Karen Verheul (proof-reader), New Zealand Outlook, New Zealand News UK and everyone else who contributed in any way and whom I have omitted to mention. Also a special thank you to Jim Watson for the superb cover, fantastic cartoons and map.

By the same publisher:

Buying a Home Abroad
Buying a Home in Florida
Buying a Home in France
Buying a Home in Ireland
Buying a Home in Italy
Buying a Home in Portugal
Buying a Home in Spain
Living and Working in America
Living and Working in Australia
Living and Working in Britain
Living and Working in France
Living and Working in Spain
Living and Working in Switzerland

What Readers and Reviewers Have Said About Survival Books

When you buy a model plane for your child, a video recorder, or some new computer gizmo, you get with it a leaflet or booklet pleading 'Read Me First', or bearing large friendly letters or bold type saying 'IMPORTANT – follow the instructions carefully'. This book should be similarly supplied to all those entering France with anything more durable than a 5-day return ticket. It is worth reading even if you are just visiting briefly, or if you have lived here for years and feel totally knowledgeable and secure. But if you need to find out how France works then it is indispensable. Native French people probably have a less thorough understanding of how their country functions. – Where it is most essential, the book is most up to the minute.

Living France

We would like to congratulate you on this work: it is really super! We hand it out to our expatriates and they read it with great interest and pleasure.

ICI (Switzerland) AG

Rarely has a 'survival guide' contained such useful advice This book dispels doubts for first-time travellers, yet is also useful for seasoned globetrotters – In a word, if you're planning to move to the USA or go there for a long-term stay, then buy this book both for general reading and as a ready-reference.

American Citizens Abroad

It's everything you always wanted to ask but didn't for fear of the contemptuous put down – The best English-language guide – Its pages are stuffed with practical information on everyday subjects and are designed to complement the traditional guidebook.

Swiss News

A complete revelation to me – I found it both enlightening and interesting, not to mention amusing.

Carole Clark

Let's say it at once. David Hampshire's *Living and Working in France* is the best handbook ever produced for visitors and foreign residents in this country; indeed, my discussion with locals showed that it has much to teach even those born and bred in *l'Hexagone*. – It is Hampshire's meticulous detail which lifts his work way beyond the range of other books with similar titles. Often you think of a supplementary question and search for the answer in vain. With Hampshire this is rarely the case. – He writes with great clarity (and gives French equivalents of all key terms), a touch of humour and a ready eye for the odd (and often illuminating) fact. – This book is absolutely indispensable.

The Riviera Reporter

The ultimate reference book – Every conceivable subject imaginable is exhaustively explained in simple terms – An excellent introduction to fully enjoy all that this fine country has to offer and save time and money in the process.

American Club of Zurich

What Readers and Reviewers Have Said About Survival Books

What a great work, wealth of useful information, well-balanced wording and accuracy in details. My compliments!

Thomas Müller

This handbook has all the practical information one needs to set up home in the UK – The sheer volume of information is almost daunting – Highly recommended for anyone moving to the UK.

American Citizens Abroad

A very good book which has answered so many questions and even some I hadn't thought of – I would certainly recommend it.

Brian Fairman

A mine of information – I may have avoided some embarrassments and frights if I had read it prior to my first Swiss encounters – Deserves an honoured place on any newcomer's bookshelf.

English Teachers Association, Switzerland

Covers just about all the things you want to know on the subject – In answer to the desert island question about *the one* how-to book on France, this book would be it – Almost 500 pages of solid accurate reading – This book is about enjoyment as much as survival.

The Recorder

It's so funny – I love it and definitely need a copy of my own – Thanks very much for having written such a humorous and helpful book.

Heidi Guiliani

A must for all foreigners coming to Switzerland.

Antoinette O'Donoghue

A comprehensive guide to all things French, written in a highly readable and amusing style, for anyone planning to live, work or retire in France.

The Times

A concise, thorough account of the DO's and DON'Ts for a foreigner in Switzerland – Crammed with useful information and lightened with humorous quips which make the facts more readable.

American Citizens Abroad

Covers every conceivable question that may be asked concerning everyday life – I know of no other book that could take the place of this one.

France in Print

Hats off to Living and Working in Switzerland!

Ronnie Almeida

IMPORTANT NOTE

New Zealand is a diverse country with many faces; a number of ethnic groups, religions and customs; and continuously changing rules, regulations (particularly regarding social security, education and taxes) and prices. Note that a change of government in New Zealand, which can occur every three years, can have far-reaching repercussions for many important aspects of daily life in New Zealand.

I cannot recommend too strongly that you check with an official and reliable source (not always the same) before making any major decisions, or taking an irreversible course of action. However, don't believe everything you're told or read (even, dare I say it, in this book). Useful addresses and references to other sources of information are included in all chapters and in Appendices A and B, to help you obtain further information and verify details with official sources. Important points have been emphasised, in bold print, some of which it would be expensive, or even dangerous, to disregard. Ignore them at your peril or cost. Unless specifically stated, the reference to any company, organisation or product in this book doesn't constitute an endorsement or recommendation. Any reference to any place or person (living or dead) is purely coincidental.

CONTENTS

12. HEALTH 173

13. INSURANCE 185

14. FINANCE 201

15. LEISURE 219

APPENDICES   **297**

INDEX   **309**

SUGGESTIONS   **317**

ORDER FORM   **320**

AUTHOR'S NOTES

- All times are shown using am (ante meridian) for before noon and pm (post meridian) for after noon. Most New Zealanders don't use the 24-hour clock. All times are local, so check the time difference when making international telephone calls (see **Time Difference** on page 282).

- All prices shown are in New Zealand dollars unless otherwise noted (e.g. £ = GB£sterling). Prices should be taken as estimates only, although they were mostly correct at the time of publication.

- His/he/him also means her/she/her (please forgive me ladies). This is done to make life easier for both the reader and (in particular) the author, and *isn't* intended to be sexist.

- Most spelling is (or should be) English.

- Warnings and important points are shown in bold type.

- Lists of Useful Addresses and Further Reading are contained in **Appendices A** and **B** respectively.

- For those unfamiliar with the metric system of weights and measures, Imperial conversion tables are shown in **Appendix C**.

- A map of New Zealand is contained in **Appendix D**.

INTRODUCTION

Whether you're already living or working in New Zealand or only thinking about it – this is THE BOOK for you. Forget about all those glossy guide books, excellent though they are for tourists, this amazing book was written especially with you in mind and is worth its weight in kiwi fruit. *Living and Working in New Zealand* is designed to meet the needs of anyone wishing to know the essentials of New Zealand life including immigrants, temporary workers, businessmen, students, retirees, long-stay tourists, holiday home owners and even extra terrestrials. However long your intended stay in New Zealand, you'll find the information contained in this book invaluable.

General information isn't difficult to find in New Zealand, where a wide range of books are available on every conceivable subject. However, reliable and up-to-date information specifically intended for foreigners *Living and Working in New Zealand* isn't so easy to find, least of all in one volume. Our aim in publishing this book is to help fill this void and provide the comprehensive *practical* information necessary for a relatively trouble-free life. You may have visited New Zealand as a tourist, but living and working there is a different matter altogether. Adjusting to a different environment and culture, and making a home in any foreign country can be a traumatic and stressful experience, and New Zealand is no exception.

You need to adapt to new customs and traditions, and discover the New Zealand way of doing things, for example finding a home, paying bills and obtaining insurance. For most foreigners in New Zealand, finding out how to overcome the everyday obstacles of life has previously been a case of pot luck. But no more! With a copy of *Living and Working in New Zealand* to hand, you'll have a wealth of information at your fingertips. Information derived from a variety of sources, both official and unofficial, not least the hard won personal experiences of the author, his family, friends, colleagues and acquaintances. *Living and Working in New Zealand* is a comprehensive handbook on a wide range of everyday subjects and represents the most up-to-date source of general information available to foreigners in New Zealand. It isn't, however, simply a monologue of dry facts and figures, but a practical and entertaining look at life in New Zealand.

Adapting to life in a new country is a continuous process and although this book will help reduce your learner's phase and minimise the frustrations, it doesn't contain all the answers (most of us don't even know the right questions). What it *will* do is help you make informed decisions and calculated judgments, instead of uneducated guesses and costly mistakes. Most important of all it will help you save time, trouble and money, and repay your investment many times over!

Although you may find some of the information a bit daunting, don't be discouraged. Most problems occur once only and fade into insignificance after a short time (as you face the next half a dozen). Most foreigners in New Zealand would agree that, all things considered, they love living there. A period spent in New Zealand is a wonderful way to enrich your life, broaden your horizons, and hopefully please your bank manager. I trust this book will help you avoid the pitfalls of life in New Zealand and smooth your way to a happy and rewarding future in your new home.

Good Luck!

David Hampshire (Editor)
October 1998

1.

FINDING A JOB

Although New Zealand is one of the few countries in the world which is keen to attract new workers from abroad – most countries positively discourage them – it doesn't mean that it's necessarily easy to find a job there. New Zealand has a relatively small labour market and there's a lot of competition for the best paid jobs, although there are certain industries where skilled staff can literally pick and choose from a surfeit of vacancies, this is very much the exception rather than the rule. In common with most other developed countries, New Zealand has suffered the ravages of unemployment in recent years and its economy went into a deep recession during the early '90s which resulted in the wholesale closure of businesses throughout the country. In 1992, unemployment reached a peak of around 11 per cent, virtually the worst on record. In the last few years, however, the economy has picked up and the unemployment rate fell to around 6 per cent before increasing again in late 1998 to over 7.5 per cent (it's as high as 25 per cent in some cities such as Dunedin).

Anyone arriving in New Zealand who's looking for a job should expect to find stiff competition from the locals: the New Zealand workforce is well educated, well trained and well motivated (the new system whereby you don't get the dole if you don't seek work helps) and you shouldn't expect employers to favour you just because you've shifted yourself and your family halfway round the world. Even well-qualified local graduates can no longer expect to walk into a job (as used to be the case) and a recent survey found that as many as 60 per cent still didn't have a job (or the job for which they studied) one year after graduation. It's also important to note that many young (and not so young) people leave the country each year in search of better employment opportunities overseas, mainly bound for the UK, the USA and Australia (a country which, if it wasn't for the enhanced career opportunities, many New Zealanders wouldn't be seen dead in). If a New Zealander cannot find a job in his place of birth it's bound to be more difficult for a foreigner.

This gloomy state of affairs, however, disguises the true employment situation in New Zealand to a great extent. The fact is, although there are a few stories of failure, only a small number of new migrants with good job skills fail to find a job and most who are prepared to work hard and adapt to the New Zealand way of doing things find that they do better in their job or career here than they would have at home (the unemployment rate among skilled migrants is much lower than the national average). Nevertheless, it's essential to have a plan of action, do your homework before arrival and (if necessary) be prepared to change your plans as you go along.

Over the last decade there has been a major shift in the economy towards services rather than manufacturing. Many manufacturing industries have disappeared altogether and others (such as car assembly) don't exactly have the brightest of futures. On the other hand, the service sector is expanding fast and some estimates claim that up to 75 per cent of the workforce is involved directly or indirectly in service industries. Job vacancies in the business and financial services industries have increased considerably in recent years, making it the fastest growing employment sector in the country. Although some workers have been retrained, however, not all have been able to make the move from manufacturing to service jobs. The result of this economic transition means that there's often a surplus of manufacturing skills, but a shortage of service industry skills.

Many employers have something of a haphazard approach to recruitment and are often reluctant to plan ahead, with the result that they're slow to retrench surplus staff during periods of recession and are equally slow to recruit new employees (and pay sufficient attention to skills and training) when business picks up. They do, however, appreciate 'old-fashioned' values such as hard work (particularly yours) and a willingness to 'muck in' and get things done. Therefore, anyone who arrives in New Zealand with a strong work ethic will have something of a head start in the jobs market.

QUALIFICATIONS

The most important qualification you need to find a job in New Zealand is a good level of spoken and written English. All employers expect their staff to have adequate English, which depends on the type of job you're after – the more skilled the position the better your English must be. When you apply in the business investor or general skills categories (see **Chapter 3**) you'll need to prove that you have a high standard of English. You will also need to show that you come from an English-speaking background or pass a test set by the International English Language Testing System (IELTS).

As regards more formal qualifications, it's a condition of employment for most jobs in New Zealand that overseas qualifications must compare with New Zealand's standards and be accepted by local employers. An organisation named The New Zealand Qualifications Authority (NZQA) assesses foreign qualifications to determine whether they are equivalent to New Zealand qualifications. The New Zealand Immigration Service can provide you with the forms you can contact NZQA, PO Box 160, Wellington.

For some jobs you must be registered with the appropriate New Zealand professional organisation. The registration process includes an assessment of your professional or trade qualifications and leads to membership of the appropriate body, thus allowing you to work in New Zealand. If your trade or profession is one where registration is required, you should contact the relevant body well in advance as you may need to take an examination or undergo a period of retraining, for which you must pay. In some cases courses can be taken in other countries, although they may be held on only one or two dates a year. Since January 1996 it has been necessary to obtain registration (where applicable) before applying for permanent residency. Professions and trades requiring registration are listed below (new trades and professions are gradually being added to the list):

Architects: Architects Education and Registration Board, PO Box 438, Wellington (☎ (04) 473 5346).

Dentists: Dental Council of New Zealand, PO Box 10 448, Wellington (☎ (04) 499 4820).

Electricians: Electrical Works Registration Board, PO Box 10 156, Wellington (☎ (04) 472 3636).

Engineers: Institution of Professional Engineers (IPENZ), PO Box 10 156, Wellington (☎ (04) 472 3636).

Lawyers: New Zealand Law Society, PO Box 5041, Wellington (☎ (04) 472 7873).

Midwives and Nurses: Nursing Council of New Zealand, PO Box 9644, Wellington (☎ (04) 385 9589).

Pharmacists: Pharmaceutical Society of New Zealand, PO Box 11 640, Wellington (☎ (04) 385 9708).

Plumbers, Gasfitters and Drainlayers: Plumbers, Gasfitters and Drainlayers Board, PO Box 11 422, Wellington (☎ (04) 384 2751).

Real Estate Agents: Real Estate Agents Licensing Board, PO Box 5570, Wellesley Street, Auckland (☎ (09) 520 6949).

Teachers: Teachers Registration Board, PO Box 5326, Wellington (☎ (04) 471 0852).

Veterinarians: Veterinary Council of New Zealand, PO Box 10 563, Wellington (☎ (04) 473 9600).

Chiropractors, Dieticians, Dispensing Opticians, Medical Laboratory Technologists, Medical Radiation Technologists, Occupational Therapists, Optometrists, Physiotherapists, Podiatrists, Psychologists: Registration Boards Secretariat, PO Box 10 140, Wellington (☎ **(04) 499 7979.**

Degrees from universities in most western countries are considered equivalent to degrees from New Zealand universities and most school qualifications are considered equivalent to New Zealand school qualifications, at least so far as employers and university admissions staff are concerned.

GOVERNMENT EMPLOYMENT SERVICE

The New Zealand Employment Service (NZES) is a government agency operated by the Department of Labour that provides a job-finding (or 'vacancy-filling') service to employees and employers. You will find an NZES office in every town of any size and in major cities there are several. It's usually necessary to call into an NZES office in person – they cannot help you find a job from abroad. The service is free of charge, but you must be a citizen or a permanent migrant or, at the very least, a working holidaymaker with a working holiday visa. The only exception to this is Australians, who don't need to fulfil the above criteria in order to use the NZES services. The official line is that the NZES provides a service to the unemployed (not necessarily those looking to change jobs) and that it will 'help you look for a job, not find you one'. Vacancies handled are mostly in the local area and are for unskilled, semi-skilled and skilled jobs, including casual and temporary vacancies.

Unemployed people registering with the NZES and claiming social security must make a 'Job Seeker Commitment' to look for full-time work or training. If they break this commitment their unemployment benefits can be progressively reduced: by 20 per cent for the first 'offence' and subsequently by an additional 20 per cent and finally by a further 40 per cent. There are exceptions for those with children under 14 or anyone caring for a disabled or dependant relative. In future, NZES services will be combined with other government services working with the unemployed, such as social security and training, with the aim of ensuring that everyone who's unemployed has access to help with finding a job or training (or, as the more cynical may say, that everyone claiming benefits is found a job as soon as possible!). The head office of the NZES is

6th Floor, Aurora House, 62 The Terrace, PO Box 3705, Wellington (☎ (04) 473 7800). The main local NZES offices are listed below:

Auckland: PO Box 5227, Auckland (☎ (09) 377 2967).
Christchurch: PO Box 22495 Christchurch (☎ (03) 365 3133).
Dunedin: PO Box 900, Dunedin (☎ (03) 477 0399).
Hamilton: PO Box 3033, Hamilton (☎ (07) 838 1144).
Invercargill: PO Box 157 Invercargill (☎ (03) 214 4919).
Wellington: PO Box 27149 Wellington (☎ (04) 801 9900).

In some areas a scheme called the Career Action Programme (CAP) is run by the government-funded organisation, Careers NZ. CAP consists of a 12-week, part-time course which can be taken during the evenings and weekends covering such areas as goal setting, decision making, networking, time management, how to analyse newspaper advertisements, job interviews, preparing CV.s, writing job application letters and other useful job hunting skills.

RECRUITMENT AGENCIES

There are many organisations in New Zealand that can find you a job (or at least try to) which can be broadly divided into recruitment consultants and employment agencies. Recruitment consultants tend to specialise in skilled, professional and executive jobs, while employment agencies handle all kinds of jobs, but particularly skilled, unskilled and temporary jobs. You can find local recruitment consultants and employment agencies by looking in the yellow pages, available at major libraries and in the reading rooms of some New Zealand Consulates and High Commissions. Some immigration consultants can also arrange an introduction to agents. Employment agencies are also listed on the New Zealand Immigration Services internet site (www.immigration.govt.nz).

Usually an employment agency cannot help you unless you're physically present in New Zealand, although they're normally willing to provide general information about local job prospects over the phone. Once you arrive in New Zealand they will ask to see your visa or migration papers before they will help you. In the past, agencies were lax about enforcing this requirement (some may still be), but severe penalties for employing illegal immigrants have prompted them to obey the law. If you're working for a temporary employment agency, you may find that you're in fact employed by the agency.

Both recruitment consultants and employment agencies are engaged by employers to fill vacancies and therefore don't charge you for finding you a job (they are finding an employee for the employer, not vice versa). Other services such as compiling CVs and counselling may be offered for which you may be charged, so check in advance. Some recruitment consultancies have offices abroad and if you plan to use them it pays to make a few simple checks before doing so. For example, the law of your home country may permit them to make a charge for finding you a job or even for simply registering your details. Also check exactly what they will do for you. A recruitment consultant who merely mails your CV to prospective employers is unlikely to find you a job, whereas a consultant with employers on his books in the industry in which you want to work (ask for proof) could prove to be a useful contact.

TEMPORARY, CASUAL & SEASONAL JOBS

Temporary, casual and seasonal jobs that last for either a few days, weeks or months are available throughout the year in New Zealand, particularly during the summer and early autumn when the largest employers, the tourist and farming industries, are at their busiest. If you aren't already a New Zealand citizen or migrant, it's important to make sure that you're eligible to work in New Zealand on a casual basis before you arrive. Most nationalities (with the exception of Australians who may work in New Zealand under the 'Closer Economic Relations' agreement), aren't permitted to work in New Zealand, at least not without wading through a mountain of red tape first. There are special working holiday schemes for young people from Canada, Japan, the Netherlands and the United Kingdom, whereby you're entitled to look for seasonal, temporary and casual employment. Students from the USA can spend up to six months working in New Zealand under the 'Work in New Zealand Program' operated by the Council On International Educational Exchange (CIEE). Other nationalities can obtain visas for temporary jobs only if there's no New Zealander or permanent migrant available to do a job (see **Chapter 3**).

In common with other countries, pay and conditions for casual and temporary jobs are usually poor. You may be paid less than the minimum wage (or payments for food and accommodation may effectively reduce it below this level) and you may not be entitled to benefits such as holiday pay. Jobs obtained through reputable, well-known agencies are likely to be better in this regard than jobs obtained through small ads. or word-of-mouth. A recent change in the taxation regulations has also made casual working by temporary visitors less attractive financially. Casual workers have a flat rate deduction of 20.7 per cent taken from their wages by employers to cover income tax and ACC contributions (see page 189). Any extra tax due or refundable is made following the filing of an income tax return at the end of the tax year, which is easy in theory but difficult if you're no longer in New Zealand. Some casual workers have doubts about whether less scrupulous employers pay the tax over to the Inland Revenue Department at all!

If you're seeking a casual or seasonal job, you should be prepared to be persistent and compete with the local casual labour force. Many jobs of this kind are the preserve of Pacific Islanders, particularly Samoans and Pitcairn Islanders, who the New Zealand authorities allow to look for work in recognition of the fact that there are precious few job opportunities in the Pacific Islands (every country has its source of cheap labour and New Zealand is no exception). These migrants tend to be at the bottom of the jobs heap and are willing to do almost anything for almost any wage. Opportunities for temporary, casual and seasonal jobs include:

Tourism: New Zealand attracts tourists year-round, particularly during the summer (November to March), with a tourist boom over the Christmas and New Year period. Jobs are available in shops, at tourist attractions, and on boats and beaches throughout the country. In winter (April to October) the tourist industry mainly centres around skiing, when Queenstown in the South Island is the busiest resort town.

Hotels and Catering: hotels, motels, lodges, restaurants and bars normally have a demand for waiters and waitresses, barmen and barmaids, chambermaids, receptionists and handymen throughout the year. Employment agencies such as Kelly Recruitment (which specialises in this kind of work) usually have vacancies. If you want to go-it-alone, there's nothing to stop you approaching hotels and restaurants directly, although it's advisable to telephone and ask about vacancies before travelling to the back of beyond looking for work.

Farming: there are thousands of farms, small and large, in New Zealand which usually need help, particularly during busy periods such as harvest times or sheep-shearing. The work is likely to be hard and the hours long, but in addition to wages (around $300 a week, which is the so-called 'award rate', or piece rate where you're paid according to how much produce you pick) you may receive free accommodation and food (all the lamb and kiwi fruit you can eat!). Good places for fruit picking are Nelson, Motueka, Blenheim, Kerikeri, the Wairu Valley, Gisborne, Tauranga, Te Puke, Otago and the Christchurch area. The soft fruit picking season (apples, strawberries, grapes, peaches and – need we say – kiwi fruit) starts in December and lasts until April or May. You don't need to go far to find a sheep farm (sheep station) in New Zealand, but the far north-east and south of the North Island, and the Otago and Canterbury regions of the South Island are the main centres for this industry. If you think you would enjoy the experience of working on an organic farm (low or no pay, but free accommodation and plenty of organic food), an organisation called Willing Workers On Organic Farms (WWOOF, PO Box 1172, Nelson) can arrange placements on almost 500 farms throughout New Zealand (a fee of $20 is charged for the list of members).

Business: employment agencies specialise in temporary and casual job vacancies in offices and shops in most parts of the country, though principally in Auckland and Wellington. It's obviously an advantage if you have some experience, and if you have a qualification in a profession such as banking, finance, insurance, accountancy or law, you could walk into a well paid job as these industries frequently have short-term staff shortages. Hundreds of New Zealand professionals leave the country each year to spend 6 or 12 months working in London on the traditional overseas experience, therefore qualified staff are needed from abroad to balance the equation.

Industry: as in most countries, there are often casual jobs available in factories and warehouses cleaning, labouring, portering, driving or in security. Particularly numerous are casual, temporary and seasonal jobs in some of the massive plants which process and pack meat, fish, fruit, vegetables and dairy products. This kind of work is notoriously unreliable and plants which may be working flat out one week, stand idle the next after the season is over or the market has slumped. Jobs of this kind can be found through employment agencies, in local newspapers or simply by turning up at the factory gate (very early!).

There are many books for those seeking holiday jobs including *Summer Jobs Abroad* by David Woodworth and *Work Your Way Around The World* by Susan Griffith (both published by Vacation Work).

JOB HUNTING

When looking for a job in New Zealand it's best to use every possible route available, as the more applications you make the better your chance of finding something suitable. Contact as many prospective employers as possible, either by writing, telephoning or calling on them in person. Naturally it's easier to find a job after you've arrived in New Zealand, although you should start preparing the ground before you arrive by doing research into potential employers and contacts.

The way you market yourself is also important and depends on the kind of job you're seeking. For example, the recruitment of executives and senior managers is handled almost exclusively by recruitment consultants or positions are obtained as a result of networking (i.e. through contacts). At the other end of the scale, manual jobs requiring no previous experience may be advertised at NZES offices, in local newspapers and on notice boards, or may simply be passed around by word of mouth (a less posh name for networking). When job hunting you may find the following resources useful:

New Zealand Newspapers: obtain copies of as many New Zealand newspapers as possible, all of which contain positions vacant sections. Situations vacant are advertised most days, the most popular days being Wednesday and Saturday. New Zealand's main newspapers are regional rather than national and include *The Dominion* (Wellington), *The Evening Post* (Wellington), *The New Zealand Herald* (mainly Auckland based news and vacancies with some national coverage), *The Otago Daily Times* (Dunedin) and *The Press* (Christchurch). It's also worth checking capital and city central libraries abroad as they sometimes have New Zealand newspapers. If you live near a New Zealand Consulate or High Commission, or a New Zealand Immigration Service information office, you may find they have a reading room containing recent copies of New Zealand newspapers. Most New Zealand newspapers will also mail you a copy on subscription, although it will take at least a week for it to reach you in Europe or the USA, by which time the vacancy may have been filled several times over.

Most newspapers also carry a 'Situations Wanted' column, although unless you're exceptionally well qualified or have a skill that's in short supply, you cannot expect much of a response when placing an advertisement of this kind.

Foreign Newspapers: if you're seeking an executive or professional position you'll find that vacancies are sometimes advertised in the national newspapers of other countries. For example, the UK's *Times Higher Education Supplement* and the *Sydney Morning Herald* occasionally carry vacancies for jobs in New Zealand. However, local employers usually go to the trouble of advertising jobs abroad only when vacancies are proving hard to fill locally or when they require unusual or exceptional skills and qualifications.

Trade Journals: there aren't a great many trade journals in New Zealand, although those that exist carry a range of vacancies for qualified and experienced people. The main journals include *Business Magazine* (PO Box 92316, Auckland, ☎ (09) 379 4233), *Education Gazette* (PO Box 12418, Thorndon, Wellington, Engineering, PO Box 12241, Wellington, ☎ (04) 473 9444), *Management Magazine* (PO Box 93218, Auckland, ☎ (09) 379 4233) and *New Zealand Farmer* (PO Box 4233, Auckland, ☎ (09) 579 1124).

Opportunities in New Zealand, usually at the executive and professional level, are also advertised in trade journals in other English-speaking countries, mainly Australia, the UK and the USA.

Employment Offices: visit local NZES offices in New Zealand (see page 22). Jobs on offer are mainly non-professional, skilled, semi-skilled and unskilled.

Recruitment Consultancies and Employment Agencies: if you're looking for an executive or professional position, you can apply to recruitment consultancies in New

Zealand and abroad specialising in the kind of position you're seeking. (They will usually be pleased to help and advise you, whether or not you have applied for permission to live in New Zealand.) On the other hand, employment agencies can usually help you only if you're already in New Zealand and have been granted permanent residence (or exceptionally, a working holiday visa).

Professional Organisations: if you're a professional, it may be worthwhile contacting professional organisations in New Zealand. Although they cannot find you a job, they can often help with advice and provide the names of prospective employers. For addresses see **Qualifications** on page 58.

Government Departments: if you're considering a position or career with a government department or another public body, it's worth contacting the relevant organisation directly. It isn't necessary to be a New Zealand citizen to apply for many official positions, particularly in areas where there's a shortage of skills. For many years the New Zealand Ministry of Education has welcomed, lured and enticed teachers to fill vacancies in schools in order to combat a serious shortage of teachers. Vacancies are advertised through its own recruitment agency, NZ Teach, which operates in English-speaking countries world-wide. The New Zealand police are also suffering a shortage of experienced officers, as several Australian forces (particularly Queensland) have a habit of poaching experienced New Zealand officers with the lure of a 20 to 30 per cent pay rise. Your local New Zealand Consulate or High Commission will put you in touch with the relevant government department.

Unsolicited Job Applications: apply to companies directly in New Zealand, whether or not they are advertising vacancies. Needless to say, it's a hit-and-miss affair, but the great advantage is that you aren't competing directly with hundreds of other applicants as with an advertised job vacancy. This approach can be particularly successful if you have skills, experience and qualifications which are in short supply in New Zealand. When writing from abroad, enclosing an international reply coupon may help elicit a response. Useful addresses can usually be obtained from trade directories (such as *Kompass New Zealand*) which are available at major libraries and New Zealand Chambers of Commerce abroad or the New Zealand Chamber of Commerce, PO Box 11043, Wellington (☎ (04) 472 3376).

Networking: networking (which originated in the USA) is basically making and using business and professional contacts. You should make use of contacts both in New Zealand and any New Zealanders you come into contact with abroad, including friends, relatives, colleagues and business contacts. If you're already in New Zealand, seek out expatriate links such as clubs, pubs and churches. Generally people who have moved to another country are interested to get to know those from the same place and are happy to pass on job tips or leads.

WORKING WOMEN

New Zealand has a long history of women doing traditionally male jobs dating back to the pioneering days when women had to run the house, prepare the food, look after the children and work on the farms (in some cases they still do). Consequently it isn't unusual to find women doing traditionally male jobs such as truck driving, factory work or even politicking. At least a quarter of New Zealand politicians are female and the country has a female Prime Minister, although given the uncertain nature of New Zealand politics no one knows for how long!

Just over 50 per cent of women work in New Zealand, a high figure made possible in part by the country's excellent system of early childhood education. There's no reason why women shouldn't take jobs in almost any industry although as in other countries, women tend to take jobs in certain industries, such as the caring professions and education. The growth in service industries, always a popular career choice with women, has created more career opportunities. Women have also made good progress in professions such as law and medicine (even if few have reached the top levels).

All members of the workforce are entitled to equal pay for equal work under the Equal Pay Act 1972. In practice the average wage tends to be marginally lower for both female and ethnic minority workers. A recent survey by Statistics New Zealand revealed that women's wages were, on average, around $220 a week lower than men's. This is partly because women and ethnic minorities are more likely to do unskilled or semi-skilled work, and, in the case of women, because they often work part-time. A 1998 UN report criticised New Zealand's free market policies, saying they're to blame for unequal pay and an appalling maternity leave policy. Discrimination in the workplace is illegal in New Zealand under the Human Rights Act 1972, which protects employees against discrimination on grounds that are irrelevant to the performance of the job including sex, ethnic group, age or disability. However, this doesn't extend as far as the home, where male chauvinism is alive and well and the country's reputation as a land of 'rugby, racing and beer' is still largely deserved (although generally not quite as marked as in Australia).

SALARY

It's usually quite easy to determine what sort of a salary you should command in New Zealand, as wages and salaries are normally quoted in job advertisements. There's a marked difference between salaries in the major cities of Auckland and Wellington and the rest of the country (often up to as much as 20 per cent). This reflects the fact that not only are living costs higher in these cities, but that jobs here also often carry more responsibility (i.e. stress). New Zealand employers can be rather coy when quoting salary figures using terms such as 'salary to'. For example, 'salary to $55,000' usually means you're highly unlikely to receive $55,000 and the employer is probably thinking in terms of paying $40,000. The term 'negotiable', e.g. 'salary $55,000 negotiable', is frequently used in job advertisements and means that you'll need to work hard to convince the employer that you're worth $55,000! If you have qualifications or skills that are in short supply you may be able to negotiate a higher salary. For example, the wool industry was recently thrown into turmoil when shearers began flocking to Australia in their hundreds in search of higher pay and the Shearing Contractors' Organisation was forced to raise pay rates by 20 per cent to persuade shearers to stay.

A national minimum wage applies in New Zealand and is $6.88 per hour. This doesn't, however, apply to those under 20 years of age who receive the 'youth minimum wage' of $4.20 an hour. A recent survey carried out by Statistics New Zealand revealed that some 40,000 adult employees received less than the legal minimum wage (it didn't say how this was possible!), but that most (over 1 million) earned at least 30 per cent more than the legal minimum wage. The average hourly earnings in May 1998 was over $17.

As few wages nowadays are negotiated on a collective basis, there's often a huge variation in wages in different industries and areas. As a rough guide, average weekly wages in the manufacturing sector are between around $460 in Auckland (the highest) and $400 in Dunedin (the lowest). In the business sector, average weekly wages in the major cities are highest in Wellington (just over $600) and lowest in Christchurch (around $500).

Executive and professional salaries are typically lower than other developed countries such as Australia, France, Germany, Japan, the UK and the USA, although a lower cost of living, particularly housing costs, compensates. The average salary for top company bosses is around $175,000. According to Price Waterhouse, executive salaries rose by 10 to 12 per cent in 1997, while the average rise in wages was just 2.5 per cent. New Zealand employers don't traditionally shower executives with fringe benefits on top of their basic salary package, but may be willing to offer them depending on how much they want to employ someone. Nevertheless, company cars are widespread at executive level as are health insurance benefits (55 per cent of executives have them) and superannuation or pension schemes (60 per cent). Productivity bonuses and profit sharing may also be offered. Relocation costs and a contributions towards housing expenses are usually offered only to employees with particularly desirable skills (but it's worth asking).

SELF-EMPLOYMENT & STARTING A BUSINESS

The idea of becoming self-employed or starting a business in New Zealand is appealing and often considered by those planning to live there. New Zealanders don't traditionally have a 'wheeler-dealer' personality and there isn't an ingrained enterprise culture. Most people work from nine-to-five for a large company and going-it-alone, which often involves working from five (am) to nine (pm), isn't seen as an attractive proposition. However, since the mid '80s a more adventurous attitude has spread throughout the country with people opening a wide range of small businesses.

Generally speaking, it isn't wise to start or buy a business in New Zealand in which you don't have previous experience. Setting up a smallholding or a bungee jumping business may seem like a good idea at the time, particularly if your only experience of New Zealand is a holiday, but it's rarely as simple as it appears. That said, many experts consider that New Zealand is something of a 'virgin' market for many business ideas which are commonplace in the USA or Europe. There have also been many cases of business ideas being transplanted from Australia and successfully taking root over the Tasman.

Professional Advice: before embarking on a business project in New Zealand ensure that you take advice regarding the legal and financial aspects from a good lawyer and accountant. A useful guide for anyone going into business in New Zealand is Ernst & Young's book *Doing Business In New Zealand*, available from their offices world-wide. It's also essential to check your visa status (see **Chapter 3**). It's possible to migrate to New Zealand under the business investor category where your investment funds, business experience, qualifications and age are assessed under the points system. If you haven't any business experience or substantial investment funds, you may not be eligible under this category. However, there's little to stop anyone migrating under the general skills category and initially taking employment and then buying or starting a business. This can, in fact, be a good course of action as it allows you to test the water before taking the plunge with a new venture.

Government Help: the Ministry of Commerce operates the Small Business Agency (SBA), the purpose of which is to help and advise those wishing to run their own business (whether by starting or buying a business) and also to help small businesses grow. They can help with planning and preparation, the law regarding business names, taxation and other financial regulations, locating premises, marketing, finding staff and management. As with free government services in any country, the help provided is limited, but they can direct you to other sources of help. For more information contact your local SBA office or the SBA head office (Small Business Agency, PO Box 11012 Wellington, ☎ (04) 472 3141). The Ministry of Commerce also funds local Business Development Boards which provide small grants (usually up to $20,000), subject to certain conditions, to those wishing to start or buy a small business. They also publish a monthly magazine, *Business Development News* which contains valuable advice for small business owners and would-be entrepreneurs. For information contact the Ministry of Commerce, Ministry of Commerce Building, 33 Bowen Street, PO Box 1473, Wellington (☎ (04) 472 00300, internet: http://www.govt.nz:80/ps/min/com). If you know the type of business you want to start, it's also advisable to contact the local trade association (the Small Business Agency can help you).

Finance: you should usually reckon on having at least 50 per cent of the cost of a business purchase or start-up. New Zealand banks look more favourably upon an application for a loan if you have a substantial lump sum of your own to invest, not to mention good business experience and a well thought out business plan. As with banks elsewhere, they will also expect security for your loan, preferably in the form of property in New Zealand.

Buying An Existing Business

As anywhere it's much easier to buy a going concern in New Zealand than to start a new business. The bureaucracy is reduced considerably if you buy a going concern, as is the risk. It isn't entirely risk-free, however, and every precaution must be taken to ensure that you don't buy a going-nowhere concern. You can find businesses for sale through local estate and commercial agents, and also through ads. in local and regional newspapers. However, it's vital to inspect a business personally (never rely solely on the glowing description you're given by an agent) before agreeing to buy it, to shop around and compare it with similar businesses, and to gain independent advice regarding its true market value and future prospects.

One of the most important aspects to consider when buying a business in New Zealand is its location, particularly if what appears to be a thriving concern is offered for quick sale at a temptingly low price. One thing to look out for is a situation where a town centre has been left as a ghost town (or shortly will be) by the opening of a new out-of-town shopping mall or the building of a new road which will take passing trade right past your new business – at 100kmh!

Starting A New Business

Most people are far too optimistic about the prospects for a new business, whether in their home country or abroad. Be realistic or even pessimistic when estimating your income and overestimate the costs and underestimate the revenue (then reduce it by up to 50 per cent!). While hoping for the best, plan for the worst and make sure that you have enough money not only to set up the business, but to keep it going until it's established. Bear in mind that while New Zealand is a virgin market with many new business opportunities yet to be exploited, it's also a small and relatively conservative market. In the good times fortunes certainly have been made by shrewd entrepreneurs, but when the economy takes a nose-dive (as it did in the early '90s) they have been lost just as easily. While there's always room for the entrepreneur in New Zealand, it makes sense to play it safe and hedge your bets to some extent and not choose anything too risky. Newcomers tend to have an idealistic view of starting a business, which is all very well, but try to be practical and also look at the downside of your proposed 'dream' business. For example, jet-boating, scuba diving, yacht charter businesses, café-bars and smallholdings are great business ideas, but hard work and often only seasonal.

Location: choosing the location for a business is even more important than choosing the location for a home. Depending on the kind of business, you may need to be near a housing development, have good access to roads or be close to a tourist resort. Don't forget that future development plans can effect the desirability of the location. Plans regarding new roads or shopping developments are usually available from the local town authorities.

Employees: if you're starting a new kind of business or one which requires specialist skills, you should check that these skills are available in the local workforce. The New Zealand workforce is well educated and trained, but certain sectors have grown so fast in recent years that it's difficult to find skilled and qualified staff in some areas and trades or professions. When you do find staff, you may find that they command sky-high salaries. Make enquiries with the NZES (see page 22) regarding unskilled and skilled staff, and with a recruitment consultant if you're going to need executives and specialist staff.

Restrictions: there are few restrictions on the kinds of business that can be started (or purchased) by new migrants in New Zealand. Foreign involvement in telecommunications and transport used to be heavily restricted, but is no longer, and as a result American investors raced to snap up New Zealand companies the minute ownership controls were relaxed. Restrictions have also been eased in the last area to be protected by law, broadcasting. Government approval via the Overseas Investment Commission (OIC) is required only in the case of foreign investments in excess of $10 million. The main point to bear in mind is that if your business involves practising a trade or profession that must be registered in New Zealand, then you'll need to register before you can start a business (see **Qualifications** on page 58).

Business Entities: the simplest form of trading entity in New Zealand is an individual trading on his own, which involves unlimited liability. However, there are no accounting, auditing or reporting requirements other than the need to keep accounts for the Inland Revenue Department (IRD). You can also form a partnership, which is governed by the Partnership Act 1908, when it's usual to have a formal written agreement between the parties. This doesn't need to be drafted by a lawyer and the rights and responsibilities of each partner are governed by the agreement rather than the law. A partnership can be either special, in which some partners (who cannot be involved in the management of the business) may have limited liability, or general, in which all partners have unlimited liability.

A limited company or corporation can be established under the Companies Act 1993. Registration of a company is a relatively simple procedure which is made upon application to the Registrar of Companies giving details of the directors, the registered address and the company's constitution. It isn't necessary, however, to have a constitution as the Companies Act serves as a ready-made constitution for companies without their own. Registration takes one day and costs $300 plus $60 to register the name. Under the Companies Act there's no longer a distinction between a public and a private limited company, and no requirement to appoint a secretary. Directors can be held personally liable for the debts of their company if they are found not to have carried out their duties properly.

Taxation: the usual financial year for companies in New Zealand ends on 31st March, although it's possible to adopt an accounting year which doesn't correspond to the financial year (but permission is required from the Commissioner of the IRD). Businesses must prepare and file their income tax return with the IRD by the following 7th July and are required to make interim 'provisional' tax payments on the seventh day of the fourth, eighth and twelfth months of their income tax year, based on an estimate of the tax due. The final balance (terminal tax) is payable on the eleventh month following the balance date. Resident companies pay income tax at a rate of 33 per cent on their world-wide taxable income. Employers are also required to make contributions to the Accident Compensation Corporation (ACC) scheme (see page 189).

Goods & Services Tax (GST): if the turnover (or expected turnover) of your business exceeds the GST threshold limit, which is $30,000, then you'll need to register for GST (see page 212). This means you'll need to levy GST (at 12.5 per cent) on your goods and services, although you'll also be able to claim GST paid on anything you buy for your business. To register for GST, simply apply to your local IRD office. Once registered you must file a GST return every two months, although smaller businesses with a turnover of less than $250,000 are usually permitted to make a return every six months. There are substantial penalties if you don't register for GST or file late returns.

Customs: if you're moving to New Zealand with the intention of becoming self-employed or buying or starting a business and want to bring any specialist tools, equipment, machinery or stock with you, you must prepare an inventory and obtain permission from the Collector of Customs. You may be permitted to bring some tools and business equipment with you free of customs duty, otherwise you'll be required to pay GST at 12.5 per cent and customs duty on their value. Note that you can bring any household items (which can include those with a combined work and household use) to New Zealand free of GST and duty when you first settle there. For further information contact the Collector of Customs Offices at one of the following offices: PO Box 29, Auckland (☎ (09) 377 3520), PO Box 2098, Christchurch (☎ (03) 371 5000) or PO Box 2218, Wellington (☎ (04) 473 6099).

TRAINEES & WORK EXPERIENCE

New Zealand is a participant in an international trainee programme designed to give young people the opportunity for further education and occupational training, and to enlarge their professional experience and knowledge of other countries. The participant countries include Austria, Belgium, Canada, Denmark, France, Finland, Germany, Ireland, Luxembourg, Netherlands, Norway, Spain, Sweden, Switzerland, the United Kingdom and the USA. If you're aged between 18 and 30 (USA 21 to 30) and have completed a minimum of two years' vocational training, you may be eligible for a trainee's position in New Zealand. The trainee agreement covers many professions and must be in the occupation for which you were trained. Positions are usually granted for one year and can sometimes be extended for a further six months. Information about the trainee programme can be obtained from the Department of Employment/Labour (or similar) in the participating countries.

Technical and commercial students who wish to gain experience by working in industry and commerce in New Zealand during their holidays can apply to the International Association for the Exchange of Students for Technical Experience (IAESTE), which has over 60 member countries. A good knowledge of English is essential and applicants must be enrolled at a college or university and be studying engineering, science, agriculture, architecture or a related subject.

Young people who are studying or working in agriculture, horticulture or home management can participate in an exchange programme operated by the International Agricultural Exchange Association (IAEA). This programme provides between six and fourteen months work experience on a farm in New Zealand. A fee is charged but the programme provides a placement, wage, and free board and lodging. For information contact the local IAEA office in your home country or write to IAEA, Parklane Arcade, The Strand, PO Box 328, Whakatane.

ILLEGAL WORKING

New Zealand developed a reputation as something of a 'soft touch' when it came to illegal working, particularly among immigrants who had been turned away by countries such as Australia, Canada and the USA which have stricter immigration regulations. New Zealand's work regulations and enforcement were lax in comparison and a blind eye was often turned to those working without the necessary visa. Many people who work illegally have been refused a permit or didn't bother applying at all and simply settled in New Zealand as a permanent visitor. Asylum seekers have also become a serious problem. While New Zealand has always provided a refuge for victims of oppressive regimes, the number of applicants during the early '90s created a major strain on the social security budget, when officials struggled to process a never-ending stream of asylum claims and appeals against refusal which took many months or even years to come to court. Note that it's perfectly legal to arrive in New Zealand on a tourist visa, find a job and then apply for residence (most other countries don't permit this).

In the last few years the New Zealand authorities have become increasingly concerned about the country becoming an immigration 'dustbin' for those refused by other countries, particularly the unskilled from poor Asian countries who have tended to regard the country (particularly its relatively generous social security system) as the promised land. It's estimated that illegal immigrants claim at least $8 million in social security payments annually. High unemployment in the early '90s meant that a blind eye could no longer be turned to illegal workers, even those doing unpleasant and poorly paid jobs, which in the past New Zealanders wouldn't entertain. As a result new laws were introduced providing stiffer penalties for illegal workers (including fast-track deportation) and also fines for employers who employed them. The police and immigration authorities have also begun to enforce the regulations, mounting periodic 'dawn raids' on companies likely to employ illegal workers, such as fruit farms and large factories.

Despite tougher immigration regulations, many employers still won't ask to see your visa or immigration papers before taking you on. They will, however, usually expect to see your IRD number. This can be obtained from the nearest IRD office simply by producing your immigration papers and proof of your permanent address in New Zealand, such as a utility bill or driving licence.

LANGUAGE

A good knowledge of English is an essential pre-requisite for living and working (or even holidaying) in New Zealand. If you cannot speak and write English well, not only will you find it extremely difficult to find a job, but you probably won't qualify for a work visa in the first place. You will, however, be relieved to hear that you won't be required to speak Maori (which was made an official language in 1974) as well! Although New Zealand is officially bilingual and there have even been proposals to replace some English place names in favour of Maori names (hopefully shorter than Taumatawhatatangihangakoauauotamateapokaiwhenuakitanatahu – ``the place where Tamatea, the man with big knees, who slid, climbed and swallowed mountains, known as 'landeater', played his flute to his loved one.``), English is still the major language of business and spoken by all. New Zealanders aren't generally adept at speaking foreign languages; when your nearest neighbours are hundreds of miles away and even they speak English (of a sort), there's little opportunity to practice French, German or Italian. Some shrewd New Zealanders with an eye to the future have made great strides in Japanese and other Asian languages, but don't bank on it. If you don't speak English well in New Zealand, you'll be sunk!

Don't be fooled into thinking that New Zealand English is more or less the same as Australian English. As any New Zealander will tell you, New Zildish is the proper antipodean version of English and it's the Australians who have corrupted it. Many Australian words and phrases aren't used in New Zealand and the same applies to American, Canadian and other versions of English. The use of 'proper' English often comes across as rather snobbish or superior in New Zealand, where people at all levels of society use New Zealand's own dialect, even at work. The main distinguishing characteristic of the New Zealand dialect is to shorten words so that they end in 'o', 'y' or 'ie'. For example, 'arvo' for 'afternoon' or 'kindy' for kindergarten. Like accents in any country, a New Zealand accent can vary from slightly difficult to understand to completely unintelligible!

2.

WORKING CONDITIONS

Employees in New Zealand generally enjoy good working conditions and terms of employment. Working conditions in New Zealand are somewhere between those in the UK and USA, where they are relatively lightly regulated, and France and Germany, where they are extensively regulated. New Zealand industry suffered a large number of trade union disputes and strikes during the '70s and early '80s, but the situation became more conciliatory in the '90s, with employers and employees more willing to discuss and even avoid problems. However, working days lost to strikes have increased in the last couple of years and in 1997/98 there were around 70 major industrial stoppages at a cost to employees of some $8.5 million in lost wages and salaries (the highest figure for some years).

The cornerstone of modern industrial relations in New Zealand is the Employment Contracts Act 1991, which gave employees the freedom to decide whether or not they wished to belong to a trade union and outlawed 'closed shops' (where all employees were required to belong to a union). Most importantly, it gave employees the right to negotiate their terms of employment and raise any problems directly with their employers, rather than comply with agreements negotiated by trades unions or other bodies. This has allowed both employers and employees to tailor their working terms and conditions to suit their individual circumstances, and therefore avoid unnecessary disputes. As a result, working conditions have improved in many industries, although in others they have become less favourable. For example, many unskilled and part-time workers in service industries feel that their pay and working hours have suffered as a result of the decline in union 'muscle'. Many companies have taken advantage of the opportunity to negotiate individual agreements, with the result that working hours, holidays, pay and other benefits are no longer standard throughout the country for a particular industry. Consequently working conditions vary considerably between employers and among individual employees.

Equal Rights: New Zealand has a relatively good record on equal rights and the participation rate of both women and ethnic minorities in the workplace is favourable when compared with countries at a similar level of economic development. It is also one of the few countries where a woman has been able to reach the highest office in the land (prime minister). As childcare provision is relatively good, substantial numbers of women are able to go out to work, although there are frequent calls for free childcare to be made more widely available to enable more women to work full-time. All members of the workforce are entitled to equal pay for equal work under the Equal Pay Act 1972. In practice, however, average wages tend to be marginally lower for both female and ethnic minority workers. This is often due to the fact that they are more likely to do unskilled or semi-skilled work, or, in the case of women, because they frequently work part-time.

Discrimination in the workplace is illegal under the Human Rights Act 1972, which protects employees against discrimination on any grounds that are irrelevant to the performance of their job, including sex, ethnic group, sexual orientation, age or disability.

TERMS OF EMPLOYMENT

When negotiating your terms of employment for a job in New Zealand, the checklists on the following pages will prove invaluable. The points listed under **General**

Positions (below) apply to most jobs, while those listed under **Executive Positions** (see page 41) usually apply to executive and senior managerial appointments only.

General Positions

- Salary:
  - Is the salary adequate, taking into account the cost of living? Is it index-linked?
  - Is the total salary (including expenses) paid in New Zealand dollars or will the salary be paid in another country in a different currency, with expenses for living in New Zealand?
  - When and how often is the salary reviewed?
  - Does the salary include an annual or end-of-contract bonus?
  - Is overtime paid or time off given in lieu of extra hours worked?
- Relocation Expenses:
  - Are removal expenses or a relocation allowance paid?
  - Does the allowance include travelling expenses for all family members?
  - Is there a limit and is it adequate?
  - Are you required to repay the relocation expenses (or a percentage) if you resign before a certain period has elapsed?
  - Are you required to pay for your relocation in advance? This can run into thousands of dollars for normal house contents.
  - If employment is for a limited period only, will your relocation costs be paid by the employer when you leave New Zealand?
  - If you aren't shipping household goods and furniture to New Zealand, is there an allowance for buying furnishings locally?
  - Do relocation expenses include the legal and agent's fees incurred when moving home?
  - Does the employer use the services of a relocation consultant (see page 77)?
- Accommodation:
  - Will the employer pay for a hotel or pay a lodging allowance until you find permanent accommodation?
  - Is subsidised or free, temporary or permanent accommodation provided? If so, is it furnished or unfurnished?
  - Must you pay for utilities such as electricity, gas and water?
  - If accommodation isn't provided by the employer, is assistance provided to find suitable accommodation? If so, what sort of assistance?
  - What will accommodation cost?
  - Are your expenses paid while looking for accommodation?

- Working Hours:
  - What are the weekly working hours?
  - Does the employer operate a flexi-time system? If so, what are the fixed working hours? How early must you start? Can you carry forward extra hours worked and take time off at a later date, or carry forward a deficit and make it up later?
  - Are you required to clock in and out of work?
  - Can you choose whether to take time off in lieu of overtime or be paid for it?
- Leave Entitlement:
  - What is the annual leave entitlement? Does it increase with length of service?
  - What are the paid public holidays? Must you take them on the due day or can they be 'moved' to another day either at your or the employer's request?
  - Is free air travel to your home country or elsewhere provided for you and your family, and if so, how often?
- Insurance:
  - Is extra insurance cover provided besides obligatory insurance (see **Chapter 13**)?
  - Is free life insurance provided?
  - Is free health insurance provided for you and your family?
  - For how long will your salary be paid if you're sick or have an accident?
- Company Pension:
  - Is there a pension scheme and what percentage of your salary must you pay?
  - Are you required or able to pay a lump sum into the pension fund in order to receive a full or higher pension?
  - Is the pension transferable to another employer?
- Employer:
  - What are the employer's future prospects?
  - Does he have a good reputation?
  - Does he have a high staff turnover?
- Is a travel allowance (or public transport) paid from your home to your place of work?
- Is free or subsidised parking provided at your place of work?
- Is a free or subsidised company restaurant provided? If not, is an allowance paid or are luncheon vouchers provided? Some companies provide excellent staff restaurants which save employees both money and time.
- Will the employer provide or pay for professional training or education, either in New Zealand or abroad?

- Are free work clothes or overalls provided? Does the employer pay for the cleaning of work clothes?
- Does the employer provide any fringe benefits, such as subsidised banking services, low interest loans, inexpensive petrol, employees' shop or product discounts, sports and social facilities, and subsidised tickets to local events?
- Do you have a written list of your job responsibilities?
- Have your employment conditions been confirmed in writing? For a list of the possible contents of your employment conditions, see page 42.
- If a dispute arises over your salary or working conditions, under the law of which country will your employment contract be interpreted?

Executive & Managerial Positions

The following points generally apply to executive and top managerial positions only:

- Is private schooling for your children financed or subsidised? Will the employer pay for a boarding school in New Zealand or abroad?
- Is the salary index-linked and protected against devaluation? This is particularly important if you're paid in a foreign currency that fluctuates wildly or could be devalued. Are you paid an overseas allowance for working in New Zealand?
- Is there a non-contributory pension fund? Is it transferable and if so, what are the conditions?
- Are the costs incurred by a move to New Zealand reimbursed? For example the cost of selling your home, employing an agent to let it for you, or storing household effects.
- Will the employer pay for domestic help or towards the cost of it?
- Is a car provided? With a driver?
- Are you entitled to any miscellaneous benefits, such as membership of a social or sports club or company credit cards?
- Is there an entertainment allowance?
- Is there a clothing allowance? For example if you arrive in New Zealand in the winter you could find it distinctly chilly, particularly in the south.
- Is extra compensation paid if you're made redundant or fired? Standard redundancy or severance payments are usually quite small, but executives often receive a generous 'golden handshake' if they're made redundant, e.g. after a take-over.

EMPLOYMENT CONTRACT

All employers are entitled to an employment contract when their employment commences. This can be either written or oral, although it's obviously an advantage to have a written contract. The terms of the contract can be either collective or individual, i.e. they apply to all employees in the same company (or the same industry) or just to one employee. Collective contracts are less common than they used to be, particularly as trade union power and membership has decreased. If your employer has a collective contract with his employees, and both you and the employer agree, you can be issued with a collective contract of employment. Alternatively it's up to you to negotiate an individual contract of employment with an employer. If you wish you can appoint a trade union or another person as your agent to negotiate your contract for you. A contract of employment must, by law, cover certain areas, e.g. wages and holiday provision. The provisions of the contract in this regard mustn't be less than the minimum statutory provisions governed by law. The contract must also specify the procedure to be followed in the case of disputes.

EMPLOYMENT CONDITIONS

Employment terms and conditions contain an employer's general rules and regulations regarding working conditions and benefits that are applicable to all (or most) employees, unless stated otherwise in your employment contract. Employment conditions are explained in this chapter or a reference is given to the chapter where a particular subject is covered in more detail.

Validity & Applicability

Employment conditions usually contain a clause stating the date from which they take effect and to whom they apply.

Salary & Benefits

Your remuneration may be quoted either as a salary, payable monthly, or a wage payable weekly or fortnightly. It's more usual to have your salary paid into a bank account by direct credit transfer. If you wish, you're entitled to ask for a cheque (e.g. a cashier's cheque or bank draft), although you aren't entitled to receive cash. A national minimum wage of $6.88 per hour applies in New Zealand, although it doesn't apply to those under 20 years of age who receive the youth minimum wage of $4.20 an hour. A recent survey by Statistics New Zealand revealed that some 40,000 adult employees receive less than the legal minimum wage, but that most (over 1 million) earn at least 30 per cent more than the legal minimum wage. New Zealand employees don't receive an automatic annual bonus (the so-called 13th month payment) as is found in some countries, although some industries operate productivity and performance bonus schemes.

Working Hours & Overtime

There aren't any standard working hours in New Zealand. Traditionally the workforce worked a 40-hour week, commencing at 8.30am and finishing at 5pm, Monday to Friday, with a half-hour break for lunch. However, since the Employment Contracts Act took effect employers and employees have been free to set the length of their own working week and start and finish times. The majority of employees still work around 38 or 40 hours over five days a week, although some companies (mainly larger organisations and manufacturing companies) have introduced different working patterns in agreement with their employees. Some large factories, for example, work four ten-hour shifts spread over seven days. Generally workers in New Zealand expect to have Saturdays and Sundays off, although this is changing as more organisations (particularly service industries) operate at weekends.

Overtime is traditionally paid at a rate of 'time and a half', although in many industries it has effectively been abolished as employers have agreed with employees (or have insisted) that they take time off in lieu of being paid overtime.

Flexi-Time Rules

Some New Zealand employers operate flexi-time working hours, the conditions and rules of which vary depending on the employer. They are most common in public service and are more likely to apply to those in administrative, managerial and professional positions. However, many employees can work flexible hours if they need to and working parents are usually permitted to leave work for a short period at any time for personal reasons. A flexi-time system usually requires all employees to be present between certain hours, known as the core or block time. For example 9 to 11.30am and from 1.30 to 4pm. Employees may make up their required working hours by starting earlier than the required core time, reducing their lunch break or by working later. Many business premises are open from around 7am until 6pm or later, and smaller companies may allow employees to work as late as they wish, providing they don't exceed the safe maximum permitted daily working hours.

Travel & Relocation Expenses

Travel and relocation expenses depend on what you have agreed with your employer and are usually included in your employment contract or conditions. Given the expense of moving people and goods to New Zealand, even from Australia, let alone from Europe or the USA, employers usually pay expenses only for executives or key employees with specialist skills. It's worth asking, however, and even if the entire cost of travel and relocation isn't forthcoming your prospective employer may be prepared to make a contribution. Currently, for example, New Zealand is so short of qualified teachers that the Ministry of Education makes a contribution towards the relocation of foreign teachers and New Zealanders wishing to return home.

If you're hired from outside New Zealand, your air ticket and other travel costs are usually booked and paid for by your employer or his representative. In addition you can usually claim any extra travel costs, for example the cost of transport to and from airports and hotel expenses en route. Most employers pay your relocation costs to New Zealand up to a specified amount, although you may be required to sign a contract stipulating that if you leave the employer before a certain period (e.g. five years), you must repay a percentage of your removal costs.

An employer may pay a fixed relocation allowance based on your salary, position and size of family, or he may pay the total cost of removal. The allowance should be sufficient to move the contents of an average house, and you must usually pay any excess costs (such as insurance for valuable items) yourself. If you don't want to bring your furniture to New Zealand or have just a few belongings to ship, it may be possible to obtain a grant towards the purchase of furniture locally up to the limit of your allowance. Check with your employer. When they're liable for the total cost, a company may ask you to obtain two or three removal estimates. Depending on the employer, they may expect you to settle the remover's bill and then claim reimbursement, or may instruct a New Zealand remover with agents in your home country to handle the removal and bill them directly. If you change jobs within New Zealand, your new employer may pay your relocation expenses when it's necessary for you to move house. If you're moving from the country to either Auckland or Wellington you should also ask for a pay rise to cover the extra cost of buying or renting a home!

Social Security

As social security contributions are largely non-contributory in New Zealand, the official line is that neither employees or employers make contributions. In practice, however, both parties must contribute to the Accident Compensation Corporation (ACC) scheme which provides compensation in the event of an accident, either at work or elsewhere. It's important to note, however, that receiving any sort of government benefits, which are collectively known as 'government transfers', isn't conditional upon having contributed to the scheme. Unemployment and sickness benefits, for example, are available to all New Zealanders and permanent residents regardless of their employment history, although there may be other eligibility criteria and means testing.

Health Insurance

Some companies and professional organisations have their own supplementary health insurance schemes that pay out for medical expenses, such as doctors' consultation fees, prescription charges, and hospital out-patient charges that aren't covered under the national healthcare scheme. Some even provide for exclusive private medical treatment. These schemes may be either contributory or non-contributory. In cases where they are non-contributory, they should be considered as part of your salary rather than a 'freebie' from your employer and the value of the benefits will depend on the employer's individual scheme. If the scheme is contributory it isn't usually obligatory to contribute, although as schemes usually take advantage of bulk insurance rates it's unlikely that you would be able to purchase similar cover for less independently. For more information, see page 193.

Company Pension Fund

Many employers offer either a contributory or non-contributory pension scheme which provides you with an additional private pension upon retirement. It isn't obligatory to join although schemes usually offer a good deal that's difficult to match when buying the same pension independently. See page 193 for more information.

Annual Holidays

Holiday entitlement in New Zealand is governed by the Holidays Act and cannot be changed by a contract of employment. It is, however, the biggest area of dispute between employers and employees. A recent report by the Labour Department revealed that over 900 complaints about breaches of annual holiday entitlement and some 350 complaints about breaches of public holiday entitlement were investigated in 1997. Employees are entitled to three weeks' paid annual holiday after they have completed 12 months employment, on average less than any developed country other than the USA. They're entitled to take two of these weeks as an unbroken period. Holidays must usually be booked and agreed with your employer at the start of a calendar year. As the peak summer holiday period in New Zealand is December to February, this means that you need to plan well in advance to obtain your preferred holiday dates.

There are innovative proposals in New Zealand to introduce legislation which will allow employees to 'sell' their unused holiday back to their employer. Many employees and trade unions are against this, believing that employees will come under pressure to sell most or all of their annual leave back to their employer, whether they wish to or not.

Public Holidays

New Zealand has 11 statutory annual public holidays on which employees cannot be required to work unless it's stipulated in their contract of employment. In practice, many employees in essential services are required to work on public holidays, for which they are offered additional pay or, more usually nowadays, time off in lieu. In some cases employers and employees have opted to take their public holidays on a different day from that on which they occur, which is perfectly legal. There are, however, two public holidays, Waitangi Day and Anzac Day, which cannot (by law) be moved and on which employees cannot be compelled to work. New Zealand's statutory public holidays are as follows:

Date	Holiday
1st January	New Year's Day
2nd January	New Year Holiday
6th February	Waitangi Day
Late March/early April	Good Friday
Late March/early April	Easter Monday
25th April	Anzac Day
First Monday In June	Queen's Birthday
First Monday in October	Labour Day
25th December	Christmas Day
26th December	Boxing Day

Different parts of the country also have a provincial Anniversary Day, which varies according to the region and has the status of an official public holiday in that region.

Maternity & Paternity Leave

New Zealand employment legislation provides for an extensive period of leave for mothers, both before and after the birth of a child. In a recent survey by the Equal Employment Opportunities Trust (EEOT), however, one-third of New Zealand employers said they were unaware of this legislation. The leave entitlement begins once an employee has worked for an employer for 12 months, whether full or part-time (providing she works for more than ten hours a week). All periods of maternity and paternity leave are unpaid, although the regulations provide extensive employment protection and you cannot be dismissed for applying for or taking parental leave. The impact of this is that many expectant mothers, and to a greater extent fathers, don't take their entire leave entitlement. Although rare, some employers provide paid maternity/paternity leave.

Mothers are entitled to take up to ten days leave during pregnancy for antenatal care and pregnancy-related illnesses, and are also entitled to take up to 14 weeks' maternity leave which can begin up to six weeks before the birth. Fathers can take up to two weeks' leave around the period of the birth (but aren't entitled to time off for pregnancy-related illnesses!). In some circumstances it's possible for mothers to take up to 52 weeks' leave after a birth, although an employer isn't necessarily obliged to keep a job open for this period.

No Smoking Rules

It's common in New Zealand to find that many workplaces don't permit smoking on the premises. These can be identified by groups of furtive-looking people gathering around the entrance for the mid-afternoon or mid-morning 'smoko' or tea break. Such rules are taken seriously and people usually *never* smoke in a no-smoking building. Although there's no legislation against smoking (yet) in health-conscious New Zealand, you may be asked whether you smoke when applying for a job and be discriminated against if you answer 'yes' (although not usually officially).

Drug & Alcohol Testing

An increasing number of employers in New Zealand require employees to undergo drug testing, both at the outset of employment and at other times on a random basis. This is perfectly legal and if applicable will usually be stated in your contract of employment. It's particularly found in occupations where you're required to drive or operate heavy machinery. Urine samples are tested for the use of cannabis, morphine, heroin, cocaine, amphetamines and benzodiazepine, and breath tests are also carried out for alcohol. Positive testing can lead to instant dismissal.

Paid Expenses

Expenses paid by your employer are usually listed in your employment contract and may include travel costs from your home to your place of work. This is more likely for Auckland and Wellington commuters than residents of other towns, where employers may provide employees with a rail or bus pass or, alternatively, free car parking at or near their place of work. Larger employers provide an employee restaurant or canteen, whereas smaller employers may provide employees with luncheon vouchers.

Part-Time Job Restrictions

There's usually a clause in your contract of employment to the effect that you cannot work part-time or on a freelance basis for a company in the same line of business as your employer. However, there isn't usually a restriction on taking other kinds of part-time work.

Retirement

The usual retirement age in New Zealand is 65 for both men and women. However, the country is moving away from the concept of a fixed national retirement age and allowing employees to retire earlier or later depending on their and their employer's preferences. You should, therefore, check your employment contract to see at what age you'll be expected to retire. It isn't unusual for people to go on working beyond the usual retirement age (65), particularly in family businesses or small companies.

Dismissal and Disputes

The situations under which you can be dismissed will be specified in your employment contract and include incompetence, embezzlement and absenteeism. There's also no general right to strike. Employees who fail to work on the terms agreed with their employer (e.g. by initiating a go-slow or a work-to-rule) are occasionally locked-out, although they haven't actually withdrawn their labour (lock-outs are the result of many industrial disputes in New Zealand). Disputes with your employer can be referred to the local Employment Tribunal. More serious issues, together with appeals against the decision of a Tribunal, are heard by the Employment Court. There are proposals to abolish the Employment Court and have disputes related to employment and breaches of employment contracts heard by civil courts.

Union Membership

There are numerous trade unions in New Zealand, most of which are members of the Council of Trade Unions which presents (or at least attempts to) a united front to the government on employment issues. Union power and influence has declined considerably since the '70s, particularly since the Employment Contracts Act took away their rights to negotiate terms and conditions of employment on behalf of their members. Membership of trade unions stands at around 400,000, down from a peak of 700,000 in the early '80s. Unions remain strongest in the older industries, such as engineering and motor manufacturing, but have little influence in the newer service industries.

Under New Zealand law, trade unions are permitted to organise on any company premises although closed shops are banned. Trade unions are permitted to negotiate employees' working conditions only if they are authorised by an employee to act as his agent. Employers must recognise this, but aren't obliged to negotiate or settle with the union (although most do so where unions are active, if only to simplify the whole procedure), but they *are* obliged to negotiate and settle with the individual employees.

3.
PERMITS & VISAS

Before making any plans to live or work in New Zealand, you must ensure that you have a valid passport and the appropriate permit or visa. Only nationals of Australia can live and work in New Zealand with no more official documentation than their passport. All other nationalities (with a few exceptions) must apply for permission to stay in New Zealand, either temporarily or permanently, before their arrival. New Zealand makes a distinction between those staying temporarily, who must apply for a visa or permit, and those wishing to stay permanently, who must apply for residence.

Immigration is a contentious issue in New Zealand, with some politicians and individuals wishing to increase immigration (they claim that the South Island could continue to absorb immigrants almost indefinitely) and others wishing to cut it sharply (they obviously wish to keep New Zealand's many charms and delights to themselves). This can result in confusing messages being sent to prospective migrants. It's probably true to say that New Zealand warmly welcomes immigrants of the 'right type': in the words of the official literature New Zealand welcomes people who 'will contribute to New Zealand, by bringing valuable skills or qualifications to the country, setting up a business or making a financial investment'. You should 'intend to live there for a long time, be easily able to adapt to New Zealand's lifestyle, obey New Zealand's laws and have no previous criminal convictions'. In the past, New Zealand took a rather lax approach to immigration, although procedures have become more rigorous in recent years and illegal immigration and overstaying is taken much more seriously than previously. The country sets an annual immigration quota, which was 38,000 in the financial year 1998/99 (but was expected to be increased to around 50,000 in 1999).

Immigration is a complex subject and the rules are constantly changing. You shouldn't base any decisions or actions on the information contained in this book without confirming it with an official and reliable source. Residence regulations are taken seriously by the New Zealand authorities and if your application isn't in order it can easily result in rejection. The authority responsible for controlling entry to New Zealand is the New Zealand Immigration Service (NZIS), or *Te Ratonga Manene* in Maori, a service of the Department of Labour. A list of NZIS offices, branches and agencies in New Zealand and world-wide is provided in **Appendix A**. New Zealand embassies, consulates and high commissions can also provide information on immigration.

Immigration Consultants: New Zealand immigration consultants operate in several countries (such as the Netherlands and the UK) and can advise you on your chances of being accepted for residence in New Zealand under the various categories, and assist with your application. However, it isn't necessary to use an immigration consultant and there's no evidence to suggest that applications for residence made through consultants stand any better chance of being accepted than personal applications. Undoubtedly using a consultant can save you a lot of work, but it's debatable whether it's worth the (often considerable) fees. If you use an immigration consultant to make your application, ensure that you know exactly what you'll be charged as fees aren't regulated. The names of some immigration consultants can be found in the publications listed in **Appendix A**.

VISITOR'S VISAS

If you plan to visit New Zealand for a short period (e.g. for a holiday, business trip or to assess the country before applying for residence), the residency rules don't apply. Instead, you'll need to apply for a visitor's visa (if applicable) and a visitor permit on arrival, which allow you to stay temporarily. A visitor's visa is an endorsement in your passport which allows you to travel to New Zealand and to be granted a visitor permit on arrival. The visa may be for a single journey or multiple entries and allows you to visit New Zealand as a tourist, to see friends or relatives, study, take part in sporting and cultural events, undertake a business trip or have medical treatment. It doesn't state on the permit that you can use it to look for a job or visit New Zealand with a view to living there, although many people use it for this purpose (and it's perfectly legitimate).

The only people who don't need a visa to travel to New Zealand are Australian citizens and nationals of countries who are exempt from the need to obtain one. Everyone else needs a visitor's visa to travel to New Zealand and you won't even be allowed to board a plane to New Zealand without one. Nationals of certain countries can use a 'visa waiver scheme' which allows you to travel to New Zealand without a visitor's visa and obtain a visitor permit on arrival. Nationals of the following countries can use the visa waiver scheme: Austria, Belgium, Brunei, Canada, Denmark, Finland, France, Germany, Greece, Iceland, Indonesia, Italy, Japan, Korea (South), Kiribati, Liechtenstein, Luxembourg, Malaysia, Malta, Monaco, Nauru, the Netherlands, Portugal, Singapore, Spain, Sweden, Switzerland, Thailand, Tuvalu, the United Kingdom and the USA (except for nationals from American Samoa and Swains Island).

Applicants under the visa waiver scheme must have a valid return ticket, sufficient money to support themselves (usually around $1,000 per month or $400 if staying with friends or relatives), a passport valid for three months beyond the date they intend to leave New Zealand, and must plan to visit New Zealand only for the time granted on arrival. If you comply with these rules you can travel to New Zealand and should be granted a visitor permit on arrival, which will usually be valid for three months (six months for UK nationals). Visitor permits can be extended on application to the NZIS, but this is at their discretion, and visitors may stay for a total of nine months in an 18-month period. If you have been in New Zealand for a total of nine months (which can be made up of a number of visits) during any period of 18 months, you're required to remain abroad for nine months before returning to New Zealand as a visitor. You can apply for a further stay of three months if you're able to support yourself financially without working.

Those who travel to New Zealand with a visa or visa waiver must complete an arrival card on their outgoing journey, which serves as an application for a visitor permit and is processed on arrival. You can be refused a visitor permit (and also a visitor's visa) if you don't meet the entry requirements or are someone to whom section seven of the Immigration Act 1987 applies. This includes those who:

● have committed a criminal offence which resulted in imprisonment of 12 months or more;

● are the subject of a New Zealand 'removal order';

● have been deported from any country;

- are believed to have criminal associations or are suspected of being likely to constitute a danger to New Zealand's security or public order.

The above rules also apply to Australians who don't need prior consent to travel to New Zealand.

Visitor's visas can be applied for at NZIS offices and New Zealand diplomatic missions. Like Australia, New Zealand operates a system whereby applications for visas in major cities such as London and New York can be cleared almost instantly via an electronic link with the NZIS computer in New Zealand.

Fees are usually charged for visas and permits, and vary depending on the country where you apply. They must be paid in local currency by bank cheque (draft), money orders or cash (if you're applying in person). Personal cheques and credit cards aren't usually accepted. Fees aren't refundable irrespective of whether a visa is granted or not! Citizens of certain countries (mainly Austria, Finland, Iceland and Japan) aren't charged for certain kinds of visa.

TRANSIT VISAS

Those from certain countries wishing to pass through New Zealand on their way to another country require a transit visa. If you're a citizen of Afghanistan, Bangladesh, Bulgaria, China (PRC), Ethiopia, Ghana, India, Iran, Iraq, Libya, Myanmar (Burma), Pakistan, Somalia, Sri Lanka, Syria, Turkey or Zaire travelling between New Zealand and the Cook Islands, Fiji, New Caledonia, Solomon Islands, Tahiti, Tonga, Vanuatu and Western Samoa, you'll need a transit visa. This allows you to stay in New Zealand for no more than 24 hours and remain within the transit area of the airport. If you wish to stay in New Zealand for more than 24 hours and/or leave the transit area of the airport, you'll need a visitor's visa.

WORKING HOLIDAY VISAS

There are special working holiday schemes for young people from Canada, Japan, the Netherlands and the United Kingdom, under which you're entitled to look for seasonal, temporary and casual employment. Students from the USA can also spend up to six months working in New Zealand under the 'Work in New Zealand Programme' operated by the Council On International Educational Exchange (CIEE). Applicants must be aged between 18 and 30, possess a return travel ticket and have a minimum of $4,200 for living expenses. Applicants don't need an offer of employment and can take any casual job on arrival. You must apply for the visa from your local New Zealand Consulate or High Commission before your arrival in New Zealand. The number of visas available to each country is limited (usually around 2,000 per country) therefore it's advisable to enquire well in advance, e.g. autumn of the year prior to the year in which you plan to work.

WORK VISAS

In New Zealand terms, a work visa is issued for a period of temporary work in New Zealand. It isn't usually suitable for those intending to take up permanent residence in the country and applies mostly to contract workers and other short-term employees. A work visa is only granted to foreigners where no suitable New Zealand citizen or resident is available to do a job. Their issue isn't based on a points system and each case is treated on its merits taking into account the availability of local labour. To obtain a work visa you must have a firm offer of a job in writing and apply to the NZIS, which can be done outside or within New Zealand (if, for example, you arrived as a visitor and then wish to work). The visa fee is around $150 (depending on where it's issued) and isn't refundable, even if your application is rejected. If successful, a working visa applies only to one job for a specified period of time, usually a maximum of three years (but often for a much shorter period).

STUDENT VISAS

Those wishing to study in New Zealand on a course lasting longer than three months require a student visa. Like a work visa, this is a temporary visa and applicable only for the course and duration for which it applies. Before applying for a student visa you must have an offer of a place from a New Zealand educational institution confirmed in writing. You must also have paid the course fees or have proof that you're able to do so, and have evidence of sufficient funds to support yourself during your course of study. Sufficient funds usually means at least $1,000 per month for short courses and a minimum of $7,000 per year for longer courses. This isn't to say that you'll be able to live on this sum and you'll almost certainly require more. If you don't have the money yourself, it's acceptable to be sponsored by someone (either in New Zealand or abroad), but you'll need to produce evidence of your sponsorship.

A student visa doesn't allow you to work to supplement your funds. However, if you can find a suitable job you can apply for a work visa on the same terms as any other non-resident (see **Work Visas** above). If a period of work experience is part of your course then (in most cases) the NZIS will grant a work visa to undertake this work.

SPECIAL VISITOR CATEGORIES

Certain categories of visitors to New Zealand require special visas or must meet certain conditions when visiting New Zealand. These include the following:

Business Visitors: if you intend to visit New Zealand to discuss and negotiate business arrangements and plan to stay no longer than three months in any one year, you'll need a visitor's visa or visitor pass and to meet the normal visitor requirements. This permits you to undertake business discussions and negotiations, although it doesn't permit you to work in an employed or self-employed capacity.

Conference Delegates: if you're attending a conference in New Zealand you should check with the organiser to see whether special arrangements have been made for conference cards to replace visitor visas. Conference organisers must make arrangements for these in advance of the conference.

Dependent Children: a single parent travelling with a child may need to provide evidence (e.g. custody or guardianship papers) that the child has the right to leave his country of residence.

Group Visitors: if you're travelling in a group, e.g. an organised tour or educational exchange, the group may qualify for a group visa. To qualify the group must be travelling for the same purpose, have the same travel arrangements and have a leader who's responsible for travel, visa and arrival arrangements.

Medical Treatment: if you're travelling to New Zealand for medical treatment and consultation, you must apply for a visitor's visa and complete an 'Intended Medical Treatment' form. If this isn't possible due to an emergency, you should contact the NZIS who may be able to make special arrangements for you. Note that unless you're a citizen of a country with which New Zealand has a reciprocal agreement (see page 183) or hold a temporary permit valid for two years or more, you aren't entitled to receive publicly-funded medical treatment in New Zealand and must pay the full cost yourself.

Occupational Registration: if you have applied for residence and require New Zealand registration to work in your profession, you may undertake practical or educational training for up to three months on a visitor permit. If you need more time to obtain your registration you must apply for either a student or work visa before travelling to New Zealand.

Returning Residents: a returning resident's visa is required by anyone who has been granted residence in New Zealand and then leaves the country (e.g. for a holiday in their home country) with the intention of returning at a later date. If you wish to do this you should apply for a visa from the NZIS *before* leaving New Zealand in order to guarantee that you'll be readmitted on your return. If you don't have a visa the immigration officer is entitled to refuse you admittance and insist that you apply for residence all over again! If this happens your application will be dealt with under the regulations at that time, which may have changed from those in force when you first obtained residence in New Zealand. The only circumstance under which you don't need a returning resident's visa is if you have New Zealand or Australian citizenship.

RESIDENCE

Applying for residence is regarded as seeking the right to live and work in New Zealand permanently. Under the Immigration Act 1987, any person who wishes to immigrate to New Zealand must apply for residence, which entitles you to live, study or work indefinitely in New Zealand. The only foreigners this doesn't apply to are Australian citizens, who need only produce their passports when entering New Zealand (although they are subject to the same good character requirements as other visitors). Applications for residence are assessed by the New Zealand Immigration Service (NZIS). Under the Immigration Act 1987, the NZIS applies the country's immigration policy formulated by the Minister of Immigration and must follow the rules and isn't allowed to make exceptions. If your application is declined you can appeal to the 'Independent Residence Appeal Authority'. All applicants for residence must attain a high standard and provide the information and documentation necessary to meet the current regulations. Most people apply for residence from outside New Zealand, although it's possible to apply for residence from within the country providing you're there lawfully on a temporary permit. There's a fee for processing applications.

Categories Of Residence

The are four main categories of residence, which are listed below:

1. **General Skills Category:** the general skills category operates on a points system, where applicants score points for factors such as qualifications, work experience and age. This category is used by most foreigners wishing to live and work in New Zealand.

2. **Business Investor Category:** the business investor category operates on a points system, where applicants score points for factors such as investment funds, business experience, qualifications and age.

3. **Family Category:** the family category is available to those who are either in a genuine and stable marriage, a de facto or homosexual relationship with a New Zealand citizen or resident, or who have immediate family members who are New Zealand citizens or residents living there permanently.

4. **Humanitarian Category:** the humanitarian category is available to those who have the support of a close family member who's a New Zealand citizen or permanent resident and whose circumstances are causing serious physical or emotional harm to the applicant or a New Zealand party that can be resolved only by the applicant being granted residence in New Zealand.

Under the above categories the principal applicant is the person assessed against the immigration criteria. A spouse who's legally married to the principal applicant may be included, but a de facto partner may only be included if the principal applicant and partner have been living in a genuine and stable relationship for at least two years at the time of the application. Homosexual partners may not be included and are eligible for residence only if their partner is a New Zealand citizen or resident. Dependent children may be included in your application if they are single, aged 19 or under, have no children of their own, and are totally or substantially reliant on you for financial support. If you're divorced or separated from your children's mother or father, you must have the right to remove them from your current. country of residence and provide documentary evidence of this. Adopted children can be included on an application whether or not they have been adopted formally.

Health Requirements

You and your accompanying family members must be in good health. In official parlance this means you mustn't be a danger to public health or be likely to become a burden on the public health system. You may be required to undergo a medical examination.

Character Requirements

You and your accompanying family members must be of good character. In order to prove this you're required to provide a police certificate (for each person over 17) from your country of citizenship and any country where you have lived for 12 months or more (in total) in the previous ten years. The residence pack provided by the NZIS explains how to obtain these certificates. Section seven of the Immigration Act 1987 defines what constitutes good character. Some of those who may be refused entry include:

- Anyone who has been convicted and sentenced to imprisonment for five years or more.
- Anyone who has been convicted and sentenced to imprisonment for 12 months or more during the proceeding ten years.
- Anyone who has been deported from New Zealand or any other country.
- Anyone who it's believed may be associated with criminal groups or who may constitute a danger to New Zealand.

English Language Requirements

New Zealand's two official languages are English and Maori (*Te Reo Maori*). English is the most common language and all intending residents must have a good level of English language skills before applying for residence. This isn't just to allow you to find and perform work, but so that you can integrate into society. The New Zealand Immigration Service has a simple 'acid test' to determine whether you have a good level of English, which is as follows:

- If you can hold a conversation in English you probably have a good level of spoken English.
- If you can read and complete a job application form and write your CV in English you probably have a good level of written English.

All principal applicants and accompanying family members aged 16 years and over must meet the specified standard of English language if applying under the 'general skills' and 'business investor' categories. You must produce evidence of either of the following:

- Meeting band level five in each of the four modules of the International English Language Testing System (IELTS) general or academic module;
- Having an English language background, i.e. you must speak English as your mother tongue or have lived in a country that's wholly or substantially English speaking and used English on a daily basis.

Principal applicants must meet the English language standard, but if your other family members don't meet the acceptable standard at the time your application is approved they must pay a $20,000 bond to the NZIS. If your family members learn English to an acceptable standard the NZIS will consider reimbursing all or part of your bond on a sliding scale. If they meet the standard within three months of their arrival the entire $20,000 will be returned and if they meet the standard within one year of arrival you'll receive $14,000 back. If they don't meet the standard within one year you won't receive any money back – so it's a pretty good incentive to learn!

New Zealand Ministry of Education Management Centres can provide more information about English language standards and also details of courses in New Zealand for those whose English isn't up to the required standard. Their addresses are as follows:

Auckland: 6-10 Nugent Street, Grafton, Private Bag 92614, Symonds Street, Auckland (☎ (09) 377 7655, fax (09) 302 3020).

Christchurch: 123 Victoria Street, Private Box 2522, Christchurch (☎ (03) 365 7386, fax (03) 364 1631).

Dunedin: John Wickcliffe House, Princes Street, Dunedin (☎ (03) 474 0152, fax (03) 479 0250).

Hamilton: Cnr Grey and Bridge Streets, Private Bag 3011, Hamilton (☎ (07) 838 3705, fax (07) 838 3710).

Lower Hutt: 2nd Floor, 65 Waterloo Road, Lower Hutt (☎ (04) 566 1219, fax (04) 566 1944).

Wanganui: 116 Victoria Avenue, Private Bag, Wanganui (☎ (06) 345 5607, fax (06) 345 5817).

Fees: a settlement fee is charged to all successful principal applicants and accompanying family members in the general skills and business investor categories. The fee is $250 for each person included in your application, up to a maximum of $1,000 per application, and must be paid before residence is granted. If you're outside New Zealand, you're required to pay in the equivalent of your local currency.

Income Support: you're expected to have sufficient financial resources to maintain yourself and your dependants for at least your first 12 months in New Zealand. During this period income support (New Zealand social security payments) is unlikely to be granted except in cases of severe hardship.

Retiring To New Zealand: there's no special immigration category for those wishing to retire to New Zealand and those over 55 aren't able to apply for residence under the general skills category. Most retirees seek residence under the family category, although people with business experience and capital may qualify under the business investor category.

GENERAL SKILLS CATEGORY

The general skills category admits migrants who, in the words of the official documentation, will 'increase New Zealand's levels of human capital, enterprise and innovation and foster international linkages'. This basically means that you can qualify under this category only if you have a skill or talent that's considered beneficial to New Zealand. Whether or not you're considered 'beneficial' is calculated using a points system that allocates points for your various attributes which are totalled to give a final score. In order to be considered you must score at least 25 points and even then acceptance depends on the prevailing pass mark at the time of your application. The pass mark is calculated at the beginning of each week and available from NZIS offices or via the internet (www.immigration.govt.nz). The various areas under which you're assessed for the general skills category are listed below:

Employability Factors

Qualifications

You're allocated points for all qualifications that are comparable to a New Zealand standard, as determined by the NZIS, although you may need to obtain a qualifications assessment from the New Zealand Qualifications Authority (NZQA) before the NZIS can make a decision. You can be allocated points only for one or a series of qualifications that are comparable to a New Zealand qualification; partially completed qualifications aren't accepted. You must score a minimum of ten points to qualify (the maximum score is 12 points).

If you're claiming points for a qualification in an occupation where professional registration is required by law in New Zealand, you must gain full registration before points are awarded. Occupations where compulsory registration is required include: architects, chiropractors, clinical dental technicians, dental technicians, dentists, dieticians, dispensing opticians, electricians, electrical service technicians, enrolled nurses, environmental health officers, lawyers, line mechanics, medical laboratory technologists, medical radiation technologists, medical practitioners, midwives, nurses, occupational therapists, optometrists, pharmacists, physiotherapists, plumbers, gasfitters and drainlayers, podiatrists, psychologists (if employed in state services or a licensed institution), real estate agents, teachers (in primary and secondary schools and free kindergartens) and veterinarians. Points are scored as follows:

- New Zealand basic qualification: a degree, diploma or trade certificate of a minimum of three years training, study or work experience: 10 points.

- New Zealand advanced qualification: a minimum of one year of training, study or work experience which builds on a base qualification: 11 points.

- New Zealand masters degree or higher: 12 points.

Work Experience

You can claim up to ten points for work experience, which must be relevant to the qualification for which you're allocated points. You must score a minimum of one point for work experience and you cannot count experience which was an integral part (or a course requirement) of your training for the qualification for which you're allocated points (i.e. work experience must be entirely separate from your formal training or study). Points are allocated on the basis of work experience of 30 hours or more per week, although experience of less than 30 hours per week may be awarded points on a pro rata basis. You can claim one point for each two complete years' work experience, i.e. one point for two years experience, two points for four years experience (etc.) up to a maximum of ten points for 20 years work experience.

Offer Of Employment

You don't need to have found a job in New Zealand before you can apply for residence under this category. However, you can be allocated five points if you have a genuine offer of employment, which will substantially boost your chances of acceptance. The offer of employment must be for ongoing, full-time employment by a single employer and must be current at the time of your application. Employment must also be permanent, for an indefinite term or for at least 12 months with an option of further terms. Positions of self employment or payment by commission and/or retainer aren't acceptable. You must obtain registration if it's required by law to take up the offer of employment, and if this isn't required, employment must be relevant to the qualification for which you're allocated points.

Age

You can be allocated points for your age at the time that you lodge your application. However, if you turn 25 years of age while your application is being processed, your points for age can be increased. If you're 56 years of age or over an application for residence under the general skills category won't be considered. Points are scored for age as follows:

Age	Points
18-24	8
25-29	10
30-34	8
35-39	6
40-44	4
45-49	2
50-55	0

Settlement Factors

You can be allocated a maximum of seven points for settlement factors, which include the following:

Settlement Funds: you can be allocated a maximum of two points for settlement funds, i.e. cash, shares, stocks or other assets. These funds must be transferred to New Zealand before residence can be granted and must be free of debt. You don't need to transfer funds to New Zealand until your application has been approved in principle and have six months from the date of approval to transfer funds. You can be allocated points if the funds are wholly owned by the principal applicant or spouse or if they are owned jointly. One point is scored if you have $100,000 in funds and two points if you have $200,000.

Spouse Or Partner's Qualifications: you can be allocated a maximum of two points for your spouse or partner's fully completed qualification providing it's comparable to a New Zealand qualification. The comparability rules are the same as for the principal applicant's qualifications (see page 58) except that your spouse or partner doesn't need to be registered before your application is processed (although he or she will need to be registered if he or she wishes to work in that occupation). One point is scored for a basic qualification and two points for an advanced qualification, masters degree or higher.

New Zealand Work Experience: you can be allocated a maximum of two points for work experience gained lawfully in New Zealand, which must be relevant to the qualification for which you're hoping to be allocated points. You can be allocated points for New Zealand work experience under both this section and the work experience section (listed above under **Employability Factors**). Points are allocated on the basis of work experience totalling 30 hours or more per week, although work experience of less than 30 hours may be awarded points on a pro rata basis. You can claim one point for one year's work experience and two points for two years or more.

Family Sponsorship: you can be allocated three points for family sponsorship. Your family sponsor must be aged over 16; a New Zealand citizen or resident; lawfully and permanently living in New Zealand for at least three years; and a parent, brother, sister or child of the principal applicant or the principal applicant's spouse. If you have a family sponsor, they are responsible for providing information and advice about settling in New Zealand, and providing you with financial support and accommodation for at least your first 12 months there. Your family sponsor must complete a 'Sponsorship Form' available from NZIS offices in New Zealand.

The points from the above categories are added to find your total points score in the general skills category.

BUSINESS INVESTOR CATEGORY

The objective of the business investor category is to select business investor migrants who will 'increase New Zealand's level of human capital, enterprise and innovation, and also foster international links'. To be granted residence under the business investor category you must score sufficient points to meet the pass mark applicable at the time your application is accepted, make an acceptable investment (see below), and meet other requirements such as health and good character. Applications in the business investor category with a points score of 11 or less will be refused and those scoring 12 points or more will be approved only if they meet the relevant pass mark (those that don't score at least one point for accumulated earnings funds won't be approved). The pass mark is recalculated at the start of each week and can be obtained from NZIS offices or via the internet (www.immigration.govt.nz).

Human And Investment Capital Factors

Business Experience: you can be allocated a maximum of five points for your business experience. Business experience is defined as a minimum of two years owning or managing a lawful business enterprise (real estate agents and lawyers will be glad to hear that they aren't excluded) or senior management experience. Points are allocated on the basis of business experience of 30 hours or more per week, although business experience of less than 30 hours a week may be awarded points on a pro rata basis. You can claim one point for each four years' business experience up to a maximum of five points for 20 years' experience.

Qualifications: you're allocated points for all qualifications that are comparable with a New Zealand standard, as determined by the NZIS, although you may need to obtain a qualifications assessment from the New Zealand Qualifications Authority (NZQA) before the NZIS can make a decision. You're allocated points only for one or a series of qualifications that are comparable to one New Zealand qualification and partially completed qualifications aren't accepted. Your qualification must be relevant to the business experience for which you're claiming points. Note that occupational registration isn't required for the allocation of points. You can claim one point for a basic qualification and two points for an advanced qualification such as a masters or higher degree.

Accumulated Earnings Funds: you can be allocated a maximum of ten points for accumulated earnings funds and must score at least one point in this category. Your funds must have been earned as a result of your business experience and/or accumulated as returns on the investment of funds which have been earned by you as a direct result of your business experience. You must submit an accumulated earnings report (compiled by a recognised agency) showing the link between your business experience and your accumulated earnings, and that your business experience was in a lawful business enterprise. You aren't required to transfer funds until your application has been approved in principle. Funds must be invested in an investment capable of providing a commercial return. Points are scored as follows:

Funds	Points
$750,000	1
$1,000,000	2
$1,250,000	3
$1,500,000	4
$1,750,000	5
$2,000,000	6
$2,250,000	7
$2,500,000	8
$2,750,000	9
$3,000,000	10

Direct Investment Funds: you can be allocated a maximum of five points for direct investment funds. Accumulated earnings funds (above) can also be used to gain points for direct investment funds. When invested, direct investment funds must be used to acquire a significant influence in the management of an enterprise in New Zealand undertaking bona fide trading activities. A significant business is defined as ownership of 25 per cent or more of the business and taking an active role in its management. Points for direct investment funds are scored as follows:

Investment	Points
$750,000	3
$1,250,000	4
$1,500,000	5

Age: you can be allocated points for your age, although if you're aged 55 to 64 years points will be *deducted* (one of the few situations where this is done under the points system). If you're 65 years of age or over, an application cannot be made under the business investor category. Points for age are scored as follows:

Age	Points
25-29	10
30-34	8
35-39	6
40-44	4
45-49	2
50-54	0
55-59	minus 2
60-64	minus 4

Settlement Factors

You can be allocated a maximum total of seven points for settlement factors, which are as follows:

Settlements Funds: you can be allocated a maximum of two points for settlement funds, i.e. cash, shares, stocks or other assets. These funds must be transferred to New Zealand before residence can be granted and must be free of debt. You aren't required to transfer funds to New Zealand until your application has been approved in principle. Settlement funds must be separate from accumulated earnings funds or direct investment funds. You can be allocated points if the funds are wholly owned by the principal applicant or spouse or when they are jointly owned. One point is scored if you have funds of $100,000 and two points if you have $200,000.

Spouse Or Partner's Qualifications: you can be allocated a maximum of two points for your spouse or partner's fully completed qualification, providing that it's comparable to a New Zealand qualification. The comparability rules are the same as for the principal applicant's qualifications (see page 58) except that your spouse or partner doesn't need to be registered before your application is processed (although he or she will need to be registered if he or she wishes to work in that occupation). Points are scored as follows: one point for a basic qualification and two points for an advanced qualification, master's degree or higher.

New Zealand Business Experience: you can be allocated a maximum of two points for business experience gained lawfully in New Zealand as the owner and manager of a business or the senior manager in a business. Points are allocated on the basis of business experience of 30 hours or more per week, although experience of less than 30 hours per week may be awarded points on a pro rata basis. You can claim one point for one year's New Zealand work experience and two points for two or more years experience.

Family Sponsorship: you can be allocated three points for family sponsorship. Your family sponsor must be aged over 16; a New Zealand citizen or resident; lawfully and permanently living in New Zealand for at least three years; and a parent, brother, sister or child of the principal applicant or the principal applicant's spouse. If you have a family sponsor, they are responsible for providing information and advice about settling in New Zealand, and providing you with financial support and accommodation for at least your first 12 months there. Your family sponsor must complete a 'sponsorship form' available from NZIS offices in New Zealand.

The points from all the above categories are added to find your total points score in the business investor category.

Transfer & Investment Of Funds: if your application is approved in principle, you'll be required to transfer your funds to New Zealand within six months. If you're transferring direct investment funds, you have 12 months and can be granted a work visa so that you can come to New Zealand to decide how best to invest your funds. Your residence in New Zealand will be subject to the requirement that funds are invested in an acceptable investment for a period of not less than two years. If you don't meet this requirement your residence may be revoked and you may be required to leave New Zealand.

FAMILY CATEGORY

The objectives of the family category are to permit New Zealand citizens or residents to be joined by their eligible spouses, partners, parents, siblings or children, and to allow New Zealand citizens or residents to sponsor family members and help them settle.

Marriage, De Facto & Homosexual Relationships: you may be granted residence under this category if you're married to and living in a genuine and stable relationship with a New Zealand citizen or resident; living in a genuine and stable de facto relationship of at least two years standing with a New Zealand citizen or resident; or living in a genuine and stable homosexual relationship of at least four years standing with a New Zealand citizen or resident. You and your partner may be called to an interview with the NZIS to assess whether you're living together and that your relationship is genuine and stable (if it's suspected that you're bogus, you'll be split up and asked the same questions to see whether your answers match). If you have been in a de facto relationship (i.e. living together as husband and wife, although unmarried) for at least 18 months you can apply for residence, but your application may not be granted until you have been in the relationship for two years (the authorities obviously believe that most relationships break up between 18 months and two years). For homosexual relationships an application can be made after two years, but may be deferred until you have been together for four years.

Parent: you may be granted residence if you have an adult child aged 17 or over who's a New Zealand citizen or resident living lawfully and permanently there and who's prepared to sponsor you, and:

- If you have no dependent children and all your adult children are living permanently outside your home country, or:

- If you have no dependent children and have an equal or greater number of adult children living lawfully and permanently in New Zealand than in any other single country, including your home country, or:

- If you have dependent children and have an equal or greater number of adult children living lawfully and permanently in New Zealand than in any other single country, including your home country. The number of dependent children must be the same as, or less than, the number of adult children living lawfully and permanently in New Zealand.

If necessary, your family sponsor will be responsible for providing financial support and accommodation in New Zealand for at least your first 12 months there.

Sibling/Adult Child: You may apply for residence under this category if you have a close family member, e.g. parent, brother or sister who's a New Zealand citizen or resident living lawfully and permanently in New Zealand and who's prepared to sponsor you; you're single (including widowed or divorced) and have no children; and you have no immediate family in your home country. If necessary, your sponsor will be responsible for providing financial support and accommodation in New Zealand for at least your first 12 months there.

Dependent Child: you may apply for residence under this section if you're aged 19 years or under and:

- you're single;

- you have no children of your own;

- you're totally or substantially reliant on your parents or guardians for financial support, whether living with them or not;

- your parents live lawfully and permanently in New Zealand;

- you were born or adopted before your parents applied for residence and you were declared on your parents' application for residence; or you were born after your parents applied for residence; or you were adopted by your parents as a result of a New Zealand adoption or an overseas adoption recognised under New Zealand law.

If your parents are separated or divorced, you must provide evidence that the custody or visitation rights of a parent living outside New Zealand won't be breached by you coming to New Zealand.

HUMANITARIAN CATEGORY

You may apply for residence under this category if:

- you or a New Zealand party are suffering serious physical or emotional harm (you're required to submit medical or psychiatric reports supporting your claim of serious physical or emotional harm);

- you have a close family member who's a new Zealand citizen or resident who's prepared to sponsor you;

- the only reasonable solution to the situation is the granting of residence;

- it would not be contrary to the public interest to allow you to reside in New Zealand.

Your family sponsor must be:

- aged 17 years or over;

- either a New Zealand citizen or the holder of a New Zealand residence permit who isn't subject to requirements under section 18A of the Immigration Act 1987;

- you or your spouse's or partner's parent, adult sibling, adult child, aunt, uncle, nephew, niece, grandparent or a person who has lived with and been part of your family for many years.

Your sponsor will be responsible for ensuring accommodation is available for you for at least your first 12 months in New Zealand.

SPECIAL CATEGORIES

In addition to the four main categories already discussed, New Zealand also has special residence categories for certain national groups:

Western Samoa Quota Scheme: this scheme applies to Western Samoan citizens living in Western Samoa or American Samoa who are aged between 18 and 45 years and have an offer of employment in New Zealand. The scheme is administered by the Apia, Western Samoa, Branch of the NZIS who can provide details.

Pitcairn Islanders: this scheme operates in recognition of the fact that there are few employment opportunities on Pitcairn Island. Pitcairn Islanders are considered for residence on favourable terms if they have a firm offer of employment in New Zealand. They must complete the standard residence form and attach supporting documents (fee, two photos, birth certificate, passport, medical and X-ray examinations, and character reports).

RESIDENCE PERMITS

Once you have been granted residence you automatically have the right to live and work in New Zealand for an indefinite period and work in any job you wish. Unlike some countries, you aren't required to apply for separate work and residence permits after you have arrived in New Zealand.

New Zealand residents retain the passport of their home country and must obtain a 'returning resident's visa' before leaving New Zealand in order to be readmitted upon their return.

CITIZENSHIP

After three years' residence in New Zealand you can apply for New Zealand citizenship, which carries the right to vote in New Zealand elections and hold a New Zealand passport. It's then no longer necessary to apply for a returning resident's visa when leaving the country (see above). Children born of New Zealand residents automatically become New Zealand citizens and can hold dual nationality where this is permitted by the laws of their parents' countries of origin. Enquiries about citizenship should be directed to the Department of Internal Affairs, PO Box 805, Wellington.

4.

ARRIVAL

On arrival in New Zealand your first task will be to negotiate immigration and customs, which fortunately for most people present no problems. You may find it more convenient to arrive in New Zealand on a weekday rather than during the weekend, when offices and banks are closed. If you arrive in New Zealand by ship, customs and immigration officials may board the vessel to carry out their checks. With the exception of Australians and visitors from countries who qualify under the visa waiver scheme, all those wishing to enter New Zealand for any reason require a visa (see **Chapter 3** for information). **If you need a visa and arrive in New Zealand without one, you'll be refused entry.**

There are also a number of tasks that should be completed on arrival, which are also described in this chapter, plus suggestions for finding local help and information.

IMMIGRATION

When you arrive in New Zealand your passport and other papers will be inspected by an immigration officer and (providing everything is in order) you'll be given leave to enter and remain for the purpose and the period for which you have applied. It's worth noting that visitors can be refused entry (even with a valid visa) if an immigration officer believes that they could be a threat to public security or health, i.e. a visa doesn't grant an automatic right of entry. Visitors arriving from countries that come under the visa waiver scheme (see page 51) can apply for a visitor permit on arrival using the form provided on the aircraft or ship. Bear in mind that you may be expected to produce other documents to support your claim for entry, such as a return ticket and evidence of funds. New Zealand immigration officials are usually fairly amiable although certain Asian visitors and young people on working holidays (who rank highly as potential illegal immigrants) may be subjected to greater scrutiny.

If you arrive in New Zealand at a location which isn't an authorised customs seaport or airport, you're required to report to an immigration officer within 72 hours of your arrival and must meet the usual visa requirements. The harbour master or airfield owner will tell you where to report. Special arrangements apply to yachts which arrive for the purpose of undertaking essential repairs or to wait out bad weather during the hurricane season (October to April), in which case a visitor permit may be granted for a longer period than usual.

CUSTOMS

New Zealand customs carry out checks at points of entry into the country in order to enforce New Zealand's customs regulations. Customs regulations apply to everyone entering the country, whether residents, visitors or migrants. There are no special concessions, even for visitors from Australia despite the 'closer economic agreement' with New Zealand (apparently they're not that close!). When you arrive in New Zealand you must complete a declaration stating whether you have any banned, restricted or dutiable goods (above your duty-free allowances). Most ports of entry operate a red 'goods to declare' and a green 'nothing to declare' channel basis. If you know (or think) you may have goods that should be declared, declare them on arrival. If you don't make a declaration your luggage won't be inspected as a matter of course, but you may be subject to a random check.

Apart from immediate personal effects (such as clothing) everyone entering the country aged over 17 is allowed certain duty-free allowances which include 200 cigarettes, 250g of tobacco or 50 cigars or a mixture of all three not weighing more than 250g; 4½ litres of wine or beer; and a 1.125l bottle of spirits or liqueur. You may also import other goods valued up to $700. New Zealand law allows you to purchase duty-free goods at a New Zealand airport on arrival, although if you exceed your allowances you can be charged customs duty plus GST at 12.5 per cent. If you're entering the country to take up residence you can also import your used household effects and a motor car (see page 150) although it's unlikely you'll be bringing these when you arrive at the airport! New Zealanders are also entitled to these allowances if they've been out of the country and living abroad for at least 21 months.

In addition to the usual items such as drugs, pornography, firearms and explosives (which you cannot import without special permission), New Zealand customs are particularly sensitive about the importation of anything with plant or animal origins. There are special regulations governing the following:

- Animals or items made from animal feathers, skin, fur, horns, rusks, etc.
- Equipment used with animals including riding tackle.
- Biological specimens.
- Garden tools, furniture and ornaments.
- Lawn mowers, strimmers, etc.
- Tents and camping equipment.
- Golf clubs.
- Vacuum cleaners, brooms and brushes.
- Basket, wicker and cane items.
- Bicycles.
- Walking/Wellington boots.

It isn't advisable to import any of the above items into New Zealand. However, if for some reason you wish to, you should seek advice from customs and declare them on arrival. Special inspection, cleaning and fumigation procedures are often required, for which you may be charged. Food, plants, dried flowers, seeds and potpourri mustn't be imported into New Zealand under any circumstances. You can be fined for importing an illicit apple or kiwi fruit, even if it came from New Zealand in the first place!

Pets and other animals shouldn't be imported into New Zealand without prior authorisation from customs. Should you wish to take your pet to New Zealand you should entrust the job to a specialist pet shipping service. You require a health certificate provided by a vet in your home country and your pet will need to undergo a period of quarantine after it arrives in New Zealand (limited exemptions apply to pets imported from Australia, Hawaii, Norway, Sweden and the UK). The good news is that you won't be charged duty on your pet.

If you bring prescribed drugs or medication with you, you should carry a prescription or letter from your doctor stating that the medicine is being used under a doctor's direction and is necessary for your physical well being. You should carry drugs in their original containers.

If you have any doubts about whether anything you wish to import into New Zealand is banned or restricted, you should make enquiries with a New Zealand Embassy, Consulate or High Commission, or directly to one of the following New Zealand customs offices: PO Box 29, Auckland (☎ (09) 377 3520), PO Box 2098, Christchurch (☎ (03) 371 5000) or PO Box 2218, Wellington (☎ (04) 473 6099).

EMBASSY REGISTRATION

Nationals of some countries are required to register with their local embassy or consulate after taking up residence in New Zealand. Registration isn't usually mandatory, although most embassies like to keep a record of their country's citizens resident in New Zealand (it helps to justify their existence).

FINDING HELP

One of the biggest difficulties facing new arrivals in New Zealand is how and where to find help with day-to-day problems, for example, finding accommodation, schooling, insurance and so on. This book was written in response to this need. However, in addition to the comprehensive information provided in this book, you'll also require local information. How successful you are at finding help will depend on your employer, the town or area where you live (e.g. residents of cities are better served than those living in rural areas) and your nationality.

There's an abundance of information available in English, but little in other foreign languages. An additional problem is that much information isn't intended for foreigners and their particular needs. You may find that your friends and colleagues can help, as they can often offer advice based on their own experiences and mistakes. But take care! Although they mean well, you may receive as much false and conflicting information as accurate (it won't necessarily be wrong, but may be invalid for your particular situation).

Your local community is usually an excellent source of information. As anywhere it's often not what you know but who you know that can make all the difference between success or failure. String-pulling or the use of contacts is common and is invaluable when it comes to breaking through the layers of bureaucracy, when a telephone call on your behalf from a neighbour or colleague can work wonders. In fact, any contact can be of help, even a professional acquaintance, who may not even charge you for his time. Your local town hall, post office, council office, citizens advice bureau and tourist office may also be able to help. Some companies employ staff to help new arrivals or contract this job out to a relocation consultant (see page 77), although most employers are totally unaware of (or don't understand) the problems and difficulties faced by foreign employees and their families.

There are a wealth of expatriate organisations in major cities, particularly Auckland and Wellington, where foreigners are well-served by English-speaking clubs and organisations. Contacts can be found through local magazines and newspapers (see page 262) and Citizens Advice Bureaux. Women living in country areas will find a good network of support is offered by Country Women's Institutes. Most consulates provide their nationals with local information including details of lawyers, interpreters, doctors, dentists, schools, and social and expatriate organisations.

CHECKLISTS

Before Arrival

The following checklist contains a summary of the tasks that should (if possible) be completed before your arrival in New Zealand:

- Look for a job, if appropriate. Even if you intend to look for a job after you have arrived, it's advisable to make some preliminary enquiries about opportunities and possible employers.

- Obtain a visa, if necessary, for you and all your family members (see **Chapter 3**). Obviously this must be done before arrival in New Zealand.

- Visit New Zealand prior to your move to compare communities.

- Find temporary or permanent accommodation (see **Chapter 5**).

- Arrange for shipment of your household and personal effects to New Zealand (see page 88).

- Arrange health and travel insurance for your family (see pages 193 and 196). This is essential if you aren't covered by a private insurance policy and won't be covered by New Zealand's public healthcare scheme.

- Open a bank account in New Zealand and transfer funds (you can open an account with many New Zealand banks while abroad). It's advisable to obtain some New Zealand dollars before your arrival as this will save you having to queue to change money on arrival.

- Obtain an international driver's licence, if necessary.

- If you don't already have one, it's advisable to obtain an international credit or charge card, which will be invaluable during your first few months in New Zealand, where almost everyone uses 'plastic'.

Don't forget to bring all your family's official documents including birth certificates; drivers licences; marriage certificate, divorce papers or death certificate (if a widow or widower); educational diplomas, professional certificates and job references; school records and student ID cards; employment references; medical and dental records; bank account and credit card details; insurance policies; and receipts for any valuables. You may also need the documents that were required to obtain your residence visa in the first place, and also for other purposes such as to enrol your children at school. It's also worthwhile taking numerous passport-size photographs (students should take at least a dozen).

After Arrival

The following checklist contains a summary of tasks to be completed after arrival in New Zealand (if not done before arrival):

- On arrival at a New Zealand airport, have your visa cancelled and your passport stamped, as applicable.

- You may wish to rent a car for a week or two until buying one locally (see page 167). Bear in mind that it's practically impossible to get around in rural areas without a car. Even if you're taking your own car, you'll be unable able to drive it until it has been cleared through customs (see **Car Importation** on page 150).
- Register with your local consulate (see page 70).
- Make courtesy calls on your neighbours within a few days of your arrival. This is particularly important in villages and rural areas if you want to be accepted and become part of the local community.
- Do the following in the few days after your arrival:
  - Check the availability of local doctors, dentists and hospitals (obtain advice and recommendations from your neighbours).
  - Open a bank account at a local bank and give the details to your employer (see page 206).
  - Arrange schooling for your children (see **Chapter 9**).
  - Obtain an Inland Revenue Department (IRD) number from your local Inland Revenue office (see page 214).
  - Arrange whatever insurance is necessary (see **Chapter 13**) including:
    * Health insurance (see page 193).
    * Car insurance (see page 156).
    * Household insurance (see page 195).

5.

ACCOMMODATION

In most areas of New Zealand, accommodation to buy or rent isn't difficult to find, depending on your requirements. There are, however, a few exceptions. For example, in Auckland, accommodation is more expensive and can be in short supply in the more popular areas. Property prices rose sharply during the '80s, although the '90s have seen more modest, steady growth. In 1998 there was evidence to suggest that prices were increasing again, with rises of almost 50 per cent reported for some unique properties in particularly desirable areas, although these tend to be isolated examples. Property prices and rents in New Zealand vary considerably between Auckland and elsewhere, often by 50 per cent or more.

There's been a return to apartment living in city centres and prices of apartments in some areas are comparable with those for houses, although most New Zealanders prefer a house with a garden. Home ownership in New Zealand is high at around 75 per cent compared with some 40 per cent in Germany and 60 per cent in the UK, and most New Zealanders prefer to own their own home rather than rent. In addition, a significant number of New Zealanders also own a holiday home (called a bach in the North Island and a crib in the South Island), although it's often quite a modest property. New Zealanders are quite mobile and tend to move home much more than people in some other countries, with around 7,500 domestic properties changing hands each month (a large number for such a comparatively small country). Over the last few years there has been a small but marked movement of people from the South to the North Island, and from throughout the country to Auckland, which has helped to fuel property shortages and accompanying higher prices in this part of the country.

TEMPORARY ACCOMMODATION

On arrival in New Zealand, you may find it necessary to stay in temporary accommodation for a few weeks or months, for instance before moving into permanent accommodation or while waiting for your furniture and other possessions to arrive. Generally you'll find it easier to move into a hotel or motel initially and then look for somewhere permanent, rather than rushing into renting or purchasing a property which later turns out to be unsuitable, e.g. in the wrong place for work or much more expensive than you could have found by shopping around on the spot.

Many hotels, motels and guest houses cater for long-term guests and offer reduced weekly or monthly rates. A motel can be a good choice as many provide a kitchenette and some even have separate living and dining areas and one or two bedrooms, making them perfectly adequate for a short stay. If you're planning to arrive during the winter (April to October), self-catering holiday apartments can be rented quite cheaply, although they're often located in remote places.

For details of suitable accommodation obtain a copy of Jason's *Motels and Motor Lodges* or *Holiday and Leisure Accommodation*, which although mainly intended for tourists contain several establishments offering long-term discounts, particularly out of season. For further information about hotels, motels, guest houses and hostels see **Chapter 15**.

RELOCATION CONSULTANTS

If you've got money to spare or you're fortunate enough to have your move to New Zealand paid for by your employer, you can arrange for a relocation consultant to handle the details. There are, however, few relocation consultants dealing with New Zealand and they mainly handle corporate clients with lots of money to pay their fat fees. They usually charge on a daily basis, plus expenses. The main service provided by relocation consultants is finding accommodation (either to rent or purchase) and arranging viewing. Other housing services include conducting negotiations, drawing up contracts, arranging mortgages, organising surveys and insurance, and handling the move. They may also provide reports on local schools, health services, public transport, sports and social facilities, and other amenities and services. Some companies provide an 'advice line' which you can call with queries and problems once you've moved in. Finding the right sort of property can take some time and you should allow up to six months between deciding to emigrate and moving into a purchased property, although a move can often be arranged in just a few weeks if you plan to rent a home.

NEW ZEALAND HOMES

Most New Zealand families live in detached homes set on their own plot of land, known as a section. This dates back to the pioneering days when the authorities divided great tracts of land into plots for house building. The sections were a quarter of an acre in size and hence the phrase 'quarter acre paradise' was coined to describe the typical New Zealand home as well as the country itself. A quarter acre section (or at least its metric equivalent) is still the standard plot size in New Zealand, although nowadays many plots have been subdivided, another property has been built in the garden, or even the original house has been demolished and several new properties built in its place. At one point this sub-division threatened to get out of hand and therefore the government imposed a new minimum plot size of 690 square metres. Most New Zealand properties are single-storey bungalows (although they are usually called houses), but two-storey houses are becoming more popular, the older wood and corrugated iron versions of which are known as villas. If a property is described as a villa don't expect a palatial property complete with columns, marble floors and a sunken bath worthy of Cleopatra, as they're usually quite modest homes (more like a wooden hut with a tin roof).

Semi-detached properties, terraced homes (known as townhouses) and apartments aren't as common as detached properties in most of New Zealand. The suburbs of most main cities have large townhouses from the Victorian area, many of which have been lovingly restored, and in recent years new small-scale townhouses have been built. Apartments are largely confined to city centres. Apartment living went out of fashion in the '80s when many people moved out to the suburbs, although it's becoming fashionable again and apartments in the central areas of Auckland and Wellington are highly sought after. There are no high-rise apartments to speak of in New Zealand. One type of housing that's unique to this part of the world is the 'unit', which is a single building containing a number (often four or six) of smaller properties set on their own land, and is part way between a house and an apartment.

New Zealand homes often aren't built to the same quality standards as is common in Europe and construction methods are similar to those used in Australia and many parts of the USA. Brick and stone are less common, except in the more expensive properties, although cheaper properties may have a single feature wall in brick or stone to add a touch of 'elegance'. Older properties are built of wooden weatherboards (most older houses were made of Kauri wood) with corrugated iron roofs (you'll be able to tell if you have a corrugated iron roof from the noise when it rains!). In newer properties, where 'real' wood is deemed to be too expensive, the construction is timber frame filled in by what are essentially plywood panels sprayed with fibre cement and painted to give the impression of rendered brickwork. Modern roofs also tend to be made of textured steel or concrete tiles rather than corrugated iron. Although new arrivals from Europe tend to regard New Zealand home construction as 'flimsy', the materials used are perfectly adequate given the climate and building materials available. The added advantage is that there's a significant cost saving over brick and stone properties, and repair and maintenance costs are also lower. In addition, New Zealand is officially situated within an earthquake belt (it has been affectionately dubbed the 'shaky isles' or 'quakey isles') and therefore 'flimsier' construction has its benefits in that it's more flexible in the event of a 'quake, easier to repair, and also less likely to cause you serious injuries if it comes tumbling down around your ears!

The design and layout of properties is pretty standard and varies little throughout the country. A typical home has a hallway, kitchen, living area, dining area (which may be combined with either the living area or kitchen), bathroom and three bedrooms. Unless you're buying an individual, architect-designed property (rare, except at the top end of the price range) the floor plan will be boringly monotonous and it often seems as if every house in New Zealand was built from the same set of plans. It will, however, be functional and quite spacious. New Zealand homes are, on average, a little smaller than American homes but roomier than properties in Britain and the rest of Europe.

Most properties, except for the very oldest unrenovated properties, are well equipped and fitted. Fitted kitchens with cupboards and built-in appliances are standard and many newer properties also have a utility or laundry room. Newer properties are also likely to have an en suite bathroom attached to the main bedroom as well as a second bathroom (often known as a family bathroom). Bedrooms frequently have fitted furniture and some homes also have large walk-in wardrobes. Some modern builders proudly boast that all you need to move into their homes is a lounge suite and a bed! If you find an older property that hasn't been renovated it will be in stark contrast to a modern home; leaky tin roofs, gaps in the windows and even holes in the weather-boarding are all fairly commonplace in such properties. It's wise to tread warily if you're offered a house at a tempting price that's described as 'needing TLC' (tender loving care), which is usually a euphemism for a dump!

BUYING PROPERTY

Buying a house in New Zealand is usually a good long-term investment and preferable to renting. Most New Zealanders prefer to own their own homes, usually with the help of a mortgage, and as mortgages have become easier to come by in recent years the demand for properties is rising, thus ensuring that the value of your home should increase annually. The latest statistics reveal that house prices are rising by an average of 6 per cent a year and the average time a home spends on the market is just 35 days – both signs of a healthy property market.

It's important to note, however, that most New Zealanders buy a house to provide themselves with a home and not as an investment, and there's little demand for properties from wealthy overseas buyers as there is in some countries. You shouldn't, therefore, expect to get rich quick when buying a home in New Zealand. It's true that in recent years there have been cases of shrewd entrepreneurs making a killing by snapping up derelict ocean-front property for renovation or buying townhouses in the 'wrong' districts of Auckland or Wellington, which then became 'yuppified' and skyrocketed in value. However, these conditions are quite rare and usually only enjoyed by well-informed speculators.

Non-residents can buy one property on less than an acre (4,047m2) of land in New Zealand without any restrictions. For property exceeding one acre, permission is required from the District Land Registrar or the Land Value Tribunal. Permission isn't required if permanent residency has been granted, in which case you can buy as much of New Zealand as you can afford!

The Cost

In general, property prices in New Zealand are slightly lower than in Europe due to the smaller population (less demand), lower cost of land and generally lower construction costs. There is, however, a huge gulf between Auckland and the rest of the country. Property is much more expensive in Auckland, mainly because most of the best paid jobs are found here and therefore demand is higher and people can afford to pay more. Auckland is also attractive as the climate is considered the best in New Zealand, at least by the people who live there, and prices are also pushed up because a majority of immigrants make Auckland their first choice. Price fluctuations are much less marked throughout the rest of the country. Figures from the Real Estate Institute of New Zealand show that the average price for a three-bedroom detached house ranges from around $80,000 in Otago to $200,000 in Auckland, with the average being around $160,000. Apartments are often as (or more) expensive as houses and townhouses, as they are invariably located in city centres, whereas most houses are located in suburbs or in the country. Advertised prices are usually around 3 to 8 per cent above the actual property value and substantially above the official government valuation for tax and statistical purposes.

Lifestyle Plots

The term 'lifestyle plot' or 'block' refers to a large plot of (often) undeveloped land, usually in the country, which is sold in a package and is what may otherwise be termed a smallholding. Buyers of lifestyle plots tend to be independent, rustic types who, while not necessarily self-sufficiency freaks, yearn for a more rural way of life. They often build their own home on the plot (or have one built), and may keep horses or ponies or a few farm animals in addition to growing their own vegetables. Lifestyle plots are available in many areas and are usually temptingly cheap. When buying a lifestyle plot the main points to check are that mains services are available nearby and the cost of connecting them, and that the land is suitable for your purpose, e.g. the quality of the soil and whether water is available for irrigation. If you plan to keep animals, good fencing (preferably post and rail) should be included, as the cost of fencing a large plot can be high. Finally, it makes sense to check any existing development plans for the area, as there have been a number of cases of buyers planning a life of seclusion, only to find some years later that their plot adjoins an industrial park or sits astride a new highway. You can expect to pay around $200,00 for a small lifestyle plot (two hectares) or $300,000 if it's within commuting distance of Auckland (the practice of working in Auckland and commuting to a 'farm' in the country has become popular in the last few years).

Buying A House Without Land

One way of buying a house that's rare outside Australia and New Zealand is that of buying a house without land! In some cases, where developers have purchased a quarter acre plot of land complete with a house, they will remove the house and put it up for sale without land. All you need to do is find yourself a plot of land and have your new home delivered to the site and installed there. This method of buying a house is by no means as common as it used to be, but it's still done and can be a way of buying a home cheaply. The main points to be aware of are not to buy a house until you have somewhere to site it and to make sure your plot has services available. Also confirm the cost of moving the house and reinstalling it, which may exceed the value of the house in the first place! The job needs to be done by specialist builders and hauliers who will literally cut the house into two or three sections and move it to your plot.

Choosing The Location

As when buying a property in any country, its location is an important factor in not only determining its value, but how pleasant a home it will make. The most popular areas of New Zealand are the major cities of Auckland (particularly), Wellington and Christchurch, mainly because the vast majority of people live and work in these cities. Popular regions for retirement and second homes on the North Island include the Coromandel Peninsula, the Bay of Islands, the Bay of Plenty and the Kapati Coast (north of Wellington). In the South Island, the Southern Alps, the Glaciers, Mount Cook, Milford Sound and the northern Marlborough region (e.g. Blenheim, Nelson and Picton, all handy for the ferry) are all popular, as is Banks Peninsula south of Christchurch.

It's important, of course, not to allow the desirability of the area to cloud your judgement, but rather choose a property in an area that's well suited to your needs. Some points you may wish to consider include:

- City or country? Few places in New Zealand, except for central Auckland and Wellington, have a truly big city feel. On the other hand, there's a considerable difference between living in a town and living in the country, several parts of which are remote. You may like the idea of living in seclusion in the country, but does the idea of hardly ever seeing anyone (except for, occasionally, the postman) really appeal to you?

- Accessibility to work. Most New Zealanders drive to work as there are few commuter railways and no underground railways. Therefore unless you plan to live in a suburb conveniently close to a bus route you'll need to check the road links to your place of work. There aren't many multi-lane motorways (expressways) in New Zealand, so journey times can be higher than you may expect.

- Ethnic areas. As is the case in other countries, people of different ethnic groups tend to prefer to live in the same area as their family and friends. Therefore you'll find some areas, particularly Auckland suburbs, predominantly occupied by certain ethnic groups.

- The climate. Broadly speaking the North Island is milder (the northern tip of the island can seem quite tropical), particularly in summer, while the South Island is chillier and can be quite cold in winter. Rainfall varies only slightly wherever you live, except that in the South Island it's more likely to fall as snow in winter.

- Physical position. New Zealanders tend to place a great deal of importance on the actual physical position of their homes. Properties in positions which catch the sun usually sell at a premium over those in shady spots because they tend to be not only brighter but also warmer in winter. In Wellington, for example, any property which is sheltered from the wind and doesn't live forever in the shadows cast by the surrounding hills is likely to be worth significantly more, and will also be more pleasant to live in. On a similar theme, bear in mind that many areas of New Zealand, particularly on the North Island, are prone to flash floods after torrential rain. It's therefore advisable to avoid properties located near rivers and streams (which can quickly become raging torrents in heavy rain) or that are situated in hollows.

- Schools. The availability of good local schooling is a major preoccupation of parents and many families have even moved house so that they are close to the best state schools. This will also affect you if you don't have children, as you'll pay a premium for a property that's within walking distance of a school with a good reputation. You can of course buy a home in an inexpensive area and send your children to a school in a more up-market area, particularly since school catchment areas have been scrapped (previously state schools had to draw their pupils from the surrounding area).

- Local services. It's important to check the local services in an area, particularly if you don't plan to drive. With the growth of supermarkets, many areas don't have many (or any) local shops and you should also bear in mind that New Zealand doctors don't usually make house calls. In the country the nearest shop may be half an hour's drive away (or more) and even many city suburbs have been built for those with cars.

- Leisure. Wherever you live in New Zealand you won't be far from various kinds of leisure activity, but you need to think about where your priorities lie. If you're into culture and dining out, then you need to be located in a large town otherwise you'll be disappointed with the choice available locally. Keen 'yachties' and other water-sport enthusiasts will find the slightly warmer waters in the north more to their taste, while the South Island is most favoured by skiers and hikers.

- Parking. Although inner city apartment living has become fashionable in recent years, such properties rarely have much (or any) secure parking, an important consideration if you own a car. Even if you don't own a car, you may find that visitors are few and far between if they cannot park nearby.

- Crime. Nowhere in New Zealand has a sky-high crime rate, although some inner city suburbs have high rates of burglary, car theft, gang troubles, muggings and even shootings. On the other hand, most rural areas have precious little crime and a car break-in may make headline news.

Conveyancing

Transferring the ownership of property (conveyancing) is relatively straightforward in New Zealand, as it's easy to establish whether the title to a property is clear (i.e. has no debts). As a result, it isn't mandatory to use a lawyer to do your conveyancing, although given the thousand-and-one other things to be done when buying a house it's unlikely you would want to do it yourself. Conveyancing by a lawyer, who's the only professionals permitted to charge for conveyancing, costs in the region of $1,000 to $2,000 plus a land transfer registration fee of $150. There's no fixed scale of conveyancing charges as this was abolished in 1984, so it's worth shopping around and haggling over the cost. It's possible to find a lawyer who will do the job for as little as $400! When calculating your budget, bear in mind that banks charge a mortgage processing fee equal to 1 per cent of the mortgage amount and require a deposit (usually $500 minimum) on application.

Purchase Contracts

As soon as you agree to purchase a property you'll be required to sign a sales contract, which basically commits you to go through with the purchase. There are usually exclusions to this (e.g. you aren't obliged to go ahead with the purchase if a new highway is about to be built through the living room), but you cannot back out because you decide that you don't like the house or cannot afford it, without paying compensation. You also cannot drop the price you've agreed to pay at a later date.

Many estate agents try to insist that purchasers sign a contract as soon as a sale is agreed, i.e. the day you view the property and say that you want it. However, it isn't advisable to sign a contract before taking legal advice and confirming that the title is clear. If you feel obliged to sign a contract before the conveyancing checks are complete, you should ask your lawyer to insert a clause in the contract to the effect that the contract is null and void if any problems arise. There's no legal requirement to sign the contract there and then, providing it's done within a reasonable time, so don't allow yourself to be pressured into signing. It's usually better to pass up a property if, for example, the agent says that another party is keen to sign, rather than buy a property that you aren't really sure about.

The advantage of this system is that the seller cannot accept a higher offer after he has signed a contract with you, although most real estate agents will try to talk up the price to the highest possible level before pressing the highest bidder to sign a contract. A deposit of 10 per cent is required when a sales contract is signed. This is usually non-refundable, but most contracts include a clause requiring its return if the title to the property isn't clear or the land is subject to government requisition (compulsory purchase). When buying a property it's the exception rather than the rule to have a structural survey carried out. The main exception is if you're borrowing more than 80 per cent of the value of the property, when the lender will usually insist that a survey and valuation is carried out to protect their interests.

Once you've instructed your solicitor to act on your behalf in a property purchase, his main task will be to conduct a title search, i.e. to established that the person selling the property is in fact entitled to sell it. This is usually carried out swiftly (the Department of Survey and Land Information is extremely efficient, unlike in some countries where they take several weeks just to open the letters) and it's rare to discover hidden horrors in New Zealand, such as dozens of relatives who all lay claim to a property. One peculiarly local concept in property purchase is cross leasing (also known as X-leasing). This usually applies in a situation where the previous owner of a section has leased part of it for the construction of another home (e.g. the one you're planning to buy). In this case your ownership of the land is leasehold rather than freehold, usually for the balance of a period such as 100 years, at a nominal rent. To all intents and purposes your title to an X-leased section is as secure as freehold. Your lawyer will explain if there are any particular conditions of which you need to be aware.

Because of the short period of time which usually exists between viewing a property and being required to sign a contract, it's advisable to have your finances arranged before you start looking. Most banks will give you an 'in principal' decision on a mortgage before you have found a suitable property and issue you with a mortgage guarantee certificate. This allows you to make an offer in the knowledge that, assuming the property is in order and your financial circumstances haven't changed, you'll be lent the money to buy the property.

Property Income: if you're interested in buying property for rental, then by and large there are no legal restrictions on letting. It's worth noting, however, that there isn't a particularly buoyant rental market for holiday property in New Zealand and, even then, it's largely seasonal during the summer only. With such a large proportion of the population owning their own holiday homes, and such a large number of hotels, motels, guest houses and campsites, the demand for such properties is modest and so you cannot expect to make a killing.

REAL ESTATE AGENTS

When looking for a house to buy you can choose between visiting the local real estate agents, looking for a private sale in the small ads. or touring the area looking for 'For Sale' signs. The easiest option is to visit a real estate agent (or a number). There are both 'family' estate agents and a number of large national chains, of which the most well known is Harcourts. If you wish to check out the market before you arrive in New Zealand, you can browse ads. from a number of agents on the internet (e.g. http://adagent.com/real/newz.html).

All real estate agents in New Zealand must be licensed and registered with the Real Estate Agents Licensing Board. Don't deal with anyone who isn't registered because if they cannot meet the standards for registration it's unlikely that they will abide by any other standards either. However, the fact that an agent is licensed shouldn't be taken as a cast-iron guarantee that he's reputable. It's illegal for a real estate agent to deliberately mislead you, but as in other countries, there are lots of little tricks of the trade which are perfectly legal, such as exaggerating the desirability of the local area or suggesting that other people are clamouring to buy a house that has been up for sale for months. In New Zealand, real estate agents' fees are entirely the responsibility of the vendor and the buyer doesn't pay anything. If anything this underlines the fact that the agent is working for the seller, not for you, so you cannot expect him to do you any favours.

Before visiting an agent, try to get an idea of the kind of property you're looking for (i.e. a house or an apartment), the price you can afford to pay and where you wish to live. The agent should then be able to give you a list of properties which fit that description. You should avoid the temptation to look at properties which are outside the areas you have chosen or that cost more than you can afford. If a property you view seems suitable you'll be pressed to make a decision quickly. The larger real estate agencies publish property newspapers or magazines allowing you to target likely properties you wish to view. For example Harcourts publish a 'Blue Book' series, which it's possible to purchase in a number of countries.

If your real estate agent suggests that you buy a property 'off plan', this means that the property hasn't yet been built. As in any country this has its risks, although it's becoming more common in New Zealand in a market where there's a keen demand for new properties, particularly those in desirable locations.

When you see a property you like don't hesitate to haggle over the price, which is standard practice, even where the seller or the agent suggests the price is firm or gives the impression that other buyers are keen to snap up a bargain. Usually an offer of between 3 and 8 per cent under the asking price would be perfectly in order and there's nothing to say you cannot offer less. To get an idea of whether asking prices are realistic you can check with Valuation NZ, a government agency that publishes monthly tables of likely minimum, maximum and average property prices on a region-by-region basis. At least one real estate agent, Bayley's, also publishes regular surveys and reports on the state of the New Zealand property market and current prices. For information contact Bayley's Real Estate Ltd., PO Box 8923, Symonds Street, Auckland (☎ (09) 377 6450).

Glossary of Property Terms

Term	Meaning
B+T	Built from brick with a tiled roof.
Bach	A holiday home (North Island)
Back section	A property built behind another with no road frontage.
Brs	Bedrooms.
Corr	Corrugated iron roof.
Crib	A holiday home (South Island).
Dbrs	Double bedrooms.
Ens	En suite bathroom.
Rumpus room	Playroom.
Sleepout	A garden room, similar in concept to a conservatory.
TLC	Tender loving care required. Real estate agent's speak for a derelict building
T/H	Townhouse.

Villa	Usually describes an older house, made of wood.
Whiteware	Domestic appliances. Often included in the price of new homes or offered for sale at an agreed price in older houses.
Section	A plot of land with a house or for building.
X-Lease	Cross lease. Home built on part of a section (usually half).
X-Leasable	A section which could be divided and partly sold or leased for another property.

Auctions

A small proportion of domestic properties in New Zealand (around 5 per cent) are offered for sale at public auction. These are usually properties whose value isn't easily determined, such as unique luxury properties and those requiring major renovation. Properties repossessed from those who have failed to meet their mortgage repayments are also sold by auction. If you have an eye for a bargain or enjoy the thrill of the auction room, you may wish to consider buying a property at auction. Before doing so you should:

- Ascertain the true market value of a property. The best way to do this is to check on the selling prices of similar properties in the immediate area. **It's wise to peg your maximum bid at least 30 per cent below the likely selling price in a private sale.**

- Pre-arrange your finance. You will probably be expected to pay a 10 per cent deposit as soon as your bid is successful and sign a contract within a day or two (if not immediately).

- Inspect the property thoroughly. Never buy sight unseen no matter how low the price. If it seems too good to be true, it probably is!

- If the property seems genuine you could consider making a pre-auction bid, starting at 30 per cent less than the likely private sale price. Auction prices are notoriously unreliable and sellers who are a little 'jittery' may agree to a deal before the auction, which is perfectly legal.

RENOVATION, RESTORATION & BUILDING

Property renovations and repairs are a major pastime in New Zealand where tens of thousands of people spend their evenings and weekends renovating, extending or redecorating their home (or when they cannot take any more do-it-yourself, building or renovating a holiday home). It may be something you wish to consider, as due to the plethora of new homes there are plenty of older properties in need of renovation in New Zealand, which are often offered at tempting prices.

It isn't particularly expensive to renovate a property in New Zealand as the basic materials (weather-boarding and corrugated iron) are plentiful and cheap. The main difficulty is likely to be finding somebody who will do the renovation for you. As most New Zealanders are avid 'DIYers' there's a shortage of people to do odd jobs and small property repairs. On the other hand, if you're keen on DIY yourself it could be the ideal solution. Another drawback is that property in need of renovation is sometimes in a serious state of decline, with a rotten wooden frame or weather-boarding and a terminally leaky tin roof. Therefore, even if you intend to do much of the work yourself, you should take advice from a surveyor or builder as to whether a house is worth saving in the first place. Don't, whatever you do, believe an agent who says that a property will 'make a charming home with a little work' without taking expert advice. Bear in mind that although you're unlikely to make a loss on your renovation project, you're also unlikely to make a huge profit.

Any new building or significant addition to an existing building must comply with town planning regulations. Consent for the work can be obtained from your local council who will send a building inspector to advise you on what you can or cannot do and monitor the works. If you intend buying an older building, it's advisable to check that it isn't registered with the Historic Places Trust, as extensions and renovations to such properties are strictly controlled. Even many timber buildings which appear to have little or no historical interest are protected in this way, as they are considered part of the country's heritage.

If you decide to build a house or renovate or extend an existing one, you should hire a builder who's a member of the Master Builders Federation (MBF), which provides the 'Master Builders Five Year Guarantee Scheme'. This guarantees the work and materials for five years with the added advantage that should your original builder go out of business, the MBF will find you another master builder to complete the work and may even contribute towards any additional cost. The same guarantee applies to new houses built by MBF members. The MBF also strongly advises customers against paying any builder before work has been completed. According to the Institute of Valuers, the cost of building a house of average quality construction is around $900 per square metre.

SELLING PROPERTY

When it comes to selling a home in New Zealand there's a choice between doing it yourself and engaging a real estate agent to handle the sale for you. If you have an attractive house in a good area and it's in the average price band, you may get a fair bit of interest simply by planting a 'For Sale' sign in your garden. If, however, your property is tucked out of the way or is a highly individual or expensive home, an agent is probably the only realistic choice. Real estate agents' charges have been rising annually in recent years and are higher than in many other developed countries, therefore many people try to sell their own homes, although most are forced to eventually admit defeat and hand the job over to an agent.

There have been no fixed real estate agent fees since the official 'Scale of Real Estate Agent's Commission' was abolished in 1985, although they are likely to be in the region of 2 to 4.5 per cent of the selling price of a property. It's wise to shop around agents and haggle over fees, as the first agent may demand 4.5 per cent while the next asks just 2 per cent (or even less) and does an equally good (or bad) job. It's common practice among New Zealand property sellers to add the agent's commission to the house value before fixing the asking price. It isn't unusual for a seller to put his property in the hands of several agents (a 'non-exclusive contract'), with the commission going only to the agent who finds the eventual buyer. Take care, however, that your agreement with each agent permits this (it usually does) and that each agent doesn't expect to be paid commission even if they don't sell the property.

RENTED ACCOMMODATION

Finding A Rental Property: you may wish to rent a property when you first arrive in New Zealand, thus allowing you more time to look around for a home to buy. Rental property of all sizes and descriptions are readily available in New Zealand, although only some 25 per cent of property is rented (including just 10 per cent of new properties). It's possible to arrange to rent a house or flat before you arrive in New Zealand and several immigration consultants (and even some travel agencies) can arrange rentals for you. Bear in mind that properties obtained through these sources are often more expensive than average market rents. Another drawback of renting through these sources is that it's difficult to picture a property accurately from thousands of miles away and the location may also be inconvenient (although it may look ideal on a map).

You can find property for rent through rental agencies, real estate agencies who mainly sell properties but who also sometimes handle rentals, and by looking at the small ads. in local newspapers. If you see anything advertised in a newspaper you should arrange to view it straight away as the best properties are snapped up quickly. Suffice to say, you should never rent anything without viewing it first. New Zealand landlords and agents are notoriously inventive in their descriptions (although legislation has been introduced to try to curb this) and they can make the shabbiest most tumbledown villa sound like the poshest place in town.

Rental Costs: the main divide in rental costs is between Auckland and Wellington and the rest of the country. In these two cities you'll pay significantly more to rent a property, particularly in the better areas. There's not a great deal of difference elsewhere, although rents in Christchurch are beginning to rise. Apart from the location, the size and facilities of a property are the main features governing the rent. The typical rental cost for a small unfurnished apartment or house in Auckland is around $300 per week, whereas in Dunedin, one of the cheaper areas, it's likely to be around $200 per week. The rent for a small apartment in the above towns would be around $200 and $125 respectively. Anything with a sea view will cost up to 50 per cent more, particularly in Auckland (there are lots of glorious views in New Zealand, but sea views are the only ones for which landlords charge extra). Cheap rental properties are at a premium in any town with a university and may actually cost more than a good quality property elsewhere. Most landlords prefer to let their properties for at least 12 months at a time and some won't let for less than this period; those who do tend to set a higher rent, particularly for lets of less than six months. If you find a rental property through a real estate agent, they usually charge a fee equal to one week's rent.

Tenancy Agreements: when renting property in New Zealand it's usual to sign a tenancy agreement. The Ministry of Housing issues a standard agreement for landlords and tenants. If your landlord uses this agreement, then providing you're happy with the details (such as the rent and so on) it isn't usually necessary to have it checked by a lawyer, as the terms and conditions are simple and written in non-legal language (other countries please take note!). Most tenancy agreements are on a periodic basis, which means that the tenancy continues indefinitely until either party gives notice. A tenant is required to give 21 days notice to end a tenancy, but a landlord must give 90 days notice except in exceptional circumstances, such as when he wishes to move into a property himself (when he must give only 42 days notice). It's also possible to have a tenancy agreement for a fixed period, in which case the tenancy lasts for the period agreed at the outset only, although it can be extended by mutual agreement.

When you take up a tenancy you must pay a bond to the landlord, which is usually the equivalent of one or two weeks' rent, although by law it can be up to four weeks. The bond isn't held by the landlord but by the 'Bond Processing Unit' of the Tenancy Services Department (Ministry of Housing). At the end of the tenancy the bond processing unit refunds your bond less the cost of any damage (for which you're responsible under the standard tenancy agreement). If you're in dispute with your landlord the Tenancy Services Department will advise you on your rights and responsibilities and help resolve the dispute. The biggest causes of disputes between landlords and tenants, apart from failure to pay the rent on time, are landlords who fail to maintain their premises (although they are legally required to) and disputes with neighbours (who may also be the same landlord's tenants) in, for example, an apartment block or units.

Inventory: although you can find both furnished and unfurnished rental properties in New Zealand, the majority are offered on an unfurnished basis. However, kitchen appliances such as a stove, refrigerator and washing machine are usually included and many bedrooms have fitted or walk-in wardrobes, therefore you'll often find that you don't need a great deal of furniture anyway. Whatever is provided with a house or apartment, it's important to obtain an inventory and check that everything that's listed in the inventory is actually provided. If appliances are included, check that they work properly and report any faults to the landlord immediately. If you don't, you may find that you're held responsible at the end of the lease. If you rent an unfurnished property and have no furniture, it's possible to rent furniture for between $250 to $400 per month for an average size house.

Public Housing: public Housing is provided in New Zealand by the Housing Corporation who build and let homes, mainly to low income individuals and families. Public housing isn't the responsibility of the local council and doesn't play a large part in housing New Zealand's population (only around a quarter of rented homes, or less than 6 per cent of all residential properties, comprise public housing).

MOVING HOUSE

Once you've found a home, permanent or temporary, you can begin to consider the question of moving your possessions to New Zealand. This should be planned well in advance as it can take anything from six weeks to six months (if moving from Europe or North America) depending on the efficiency of your shipping company and allowing for customs clearances. It's usually best to time things so that you arrive in New Zealand before your possessions, which will give you time to find a home and avoid storage costs. It also makes customs clearance easier if you're on the spot when your shipment arrives, which is essential unless you have engaged someone to do this for you.

Although it's possible to ship every last one of your belongings to New Zealand, you should consider whether it's really worth the effort and expense, given that there's little that cannot be bought locally. It's generally inadvisable to ship bulky items of furniture and large domestic appliances, which may not even work in New Zealand! On the other hand, it's probably worthwhile taking all your clothes and personal possessions, together with larger items of great value or to which you're particularly attached. Shipping the entire contents of a three bedroom house from Europe or North America to New Zealand costs at least GB£5,000/US$7,500. Many companies offer international removals, although you should choose a company that actually specialises in shipping to New Zealand. Some companies will also pack your belongings in your home country and unpack them in New Zealand, which is naturally more expensive than doing it yourself, but saves a lot of hassle if you can afford it.

It's also important to make sure that your possessions are insured, the cost of which won't usually be included in the removals quote. The cost is likely to be up to 2 per cent of their value. If you have anything that's particularly valuable (such as antiques) you should agree an insurance value separately with the insurance company, rather than accept the 'guesstimate' which they usually make based on the likely value of the contents of an average house.

Make a complete list of everything to be moved and give a copy to the removal company. Don't include anything that's illegal or restricted. As well as the usual items such as firearms and explosives, bear in mind that New Zealand customs are particularly sensitive about the import of anything with plant or animal origins (see **Customs** on page 68). This includes not only live plants and animals, but items such as seeds, bulbs, fur and wicker goods. Although you can sometimes import these, it makes it simpler if you leave them out of your shipment entirely. When packing your possessions take care not to use any packing which is made from, or includes, plant products (such as straw). If you're travelling from Europe or North America also bear in mind that your shipment must pass through the tropics on its way to New Zealand, therefore packing things in plastic is to be avoided as it will cause condensation to build up as your belongings sail through 95 per cent humidity and may lead to mildew.

ELECTRICITY

The electricity supply in New Zealand is 230 volts AC, 50Hz, which is mostly generated by hydroelectric power plants (so conservationists can consume energy to their heart's content). Electricity is supplied by local electricity companies, some of which are publicly owned, although many are privately owned after government sell-offs in the '80s and '90s. The supply is usually reliable, despite the catastrophic and well publicised cable failures in Auckland in early 1998, which left the central area of the city without full power for several weeks!

Connection & Registration: to have the electricity connected (or the bill transferred to your name when moving into a new home) simply telephone your local electricity company on the number shown in the telephone directory. You will need to pay a bond ($130) and will be billed every two months (most people pay by direct debit from a bank account). The typical bill for an average house is around $200 for two months (rates have been falling in recent years).

Power Rating: appliances from countries with a 220V or 240V system (e.g. the UK and Europe) usually work in New Zealand. However, electrical equipment rated at 110 volts AC (for example, from the USA) requires a converter or a step-down transformer to convert it to 230 volts AC, although some electrical appliances (e.g. electric razors and hair dryers) are fitted with a 110/220 volt switch. Check for the switch, which may be located inside the casing, and make sure it's switched to 220 volts *before* connecting it to the power supply. Converters can be used for heating appliances but transformers, which are available from most electrical retailers, are required for motorised appliances (they can also be purchased second hand). Total the wattage of the devices you intend to connect to a transformer and make sure its power rating *exceeds* this sum.

Generally all small, high-wattage, electrical appliances, such as kettles, toasters, heaters and irons, need large transformers. Motors in large appliances such as cookers, refrigerators, washing machines, dryers and dishwashers, will need replacing or fitting with a large transformer. In most cases it's simpler to buy new appliances in New Zealand, which are of good quality and reasonably priced. Note also that the dimensions of New Zealand cookers, microwave ovens, refrigerators, washing machines, dryers and dishwashers, differ from those in some other countries. All electrical goods sold in New Zealand must conform to local safety standards. If you wish to buy electrical appliances, such as a cooker or refrigerator, you should shop around as prices vary considerably (choose those that have a high energy efficiency rating, which are cheaper to run). You shouldn't bring a TV or video recorder from any country other than Australia, as they probably won't work due to the different transmission system in use in New Zealand.

Frequency Rating: a problem with some electrical equipment is the frequency rating, which in some countries, e.g. the USA, is designed to run at 60 Hertz and not New Zealand's 50 Hertz. Electrical equipment *without* a motor is generally unaffected by the drop in frequency to 50Hz (except TVs). Equipment with a motor may run okay with a 20 per cent drop in speed, however, automatic washing machines, cookers, electric clocks, record players and tape recorders are unusable in New Zealand if they aren't designed for 50Hz operation. To find out, look at the label on the back of the equipment. If it says 50/60 Hertz, it should be okay. If it says 60Hz, you may try it anyway, **but first ensure the voltage is correct as outlined above.** If the equipment runs too slowly, seek advice from the manufacturer or the retailer. For example, you may be able to obtain a special pulley for a tape deck or turntable to compensate for the drop in speed. Bear in mind that the transformers and motors of electrical devices designed to run at 60Hz will run hotter at 50Hz, so make sure that equipment has sufficient space around it for cooling.

Fuses: most apartments and all houses have their own fuse boxes, which are usually of the circuit breaker type in modern homes. When a circuit is overloaded the circuit breaker trips to the OFF position. When replacing or repairing fuses of any kind, if the same fuse continues to blow, contact an electrician and **never attempt to fit a fuse of a higher rating than specified, even as a temporary measure.** When replacing fuses, don't rely on the blown fuse as a guide, as it may have been wrong. If you use an electric lawnmower or power tools outside your home or in your garage, you should have a Residual Current Device (RCD) installed. This can detect current changes of as little as a thousandth of an amp and in the event of a fault (or the cable being cut), will switch off the power in around 0.04 seconds.

Plugs: unless you have come from Australia, all your plugs will require changing, or a lot of expensive adapters will be required. New Zealand (and Australian) plugs have three pins: two diagonally slanting flat pins above one straight (earth) pin, which are unique (to these two countries). Plugs aren't fused. Most appliances purchased new in New Zealand, in common with most other countries, are already fitted with plugs. Some electrical appliances are earthed and have a three-core flex – you must *never* use a two-pin plug with a three-core flex. **Always make sure that a plug is correctly and**

securely wired as bad wiring can prove fatal. Note that for maximum safety, electrical appliances should be turned off at the main wall point when not in use.

Bulbs: electric light bulbs in New Zealand are either of the Edison screw or bayonet cap type. Low-energy light bulbs are also available and are more expensive than ordinary bulbs, although they save money by their longer life and reduced energy consumption. Bulbs for non-standard electrical appliances (i.e. appliances not made for the New Zealand market) such as refrigerators, lamps and sewing machines, may not be available in New Zealand (so bring extras with you). Plug adapters for imported lamps and other electrical items can be difficult to find in New Zealand, therefore it's advisable to bring a number of adapters and extension cords with you, which can be fitted with local plugs.

Rewiring: it's illegal in New Zealand for individuals to do anything more than the most basic electrical work around their homes, such as rewiring a plug or changing a light bulb. Anything else, such as rewiring or fitting a new socket, must be done by a qualified electrician.

GAS

Mains gas is available in most cities, towns and villages in the North Island, with the exception of a few remote corners, but in the South Island it's available only in Christchurch and Dunedin. As with electricity, it's supplied by local companies, which can be found in your local telephone directory. Gas is popular for cooking (it costs less than electricity) in New Zealand, although it's less commonly used to provide heating and hot water (although gas heaters are becoming increasingly popular). Note that there may be no gas supply in older homes and modern houses may also be all electric. If you're looking for a rental property and want to cook by gas, make sure it already has a gas supply (some houses have an unused gas service pipe). In country areas without mains gas, you can buy appliances that operate on bottled gas. On payment of a deposit for the bottle and regulator, your local supplier will provide you with gas bottles and replace them when they are empty. Large users can also have a storage tank installed and have gas delivered by tanker.

If you buy a home without a gas supply, you can usually arrange with your local gas company to install a line between your home and a nearby gas main (providing there's one within a reasonable distance, otherwise the cost will be prohibitive). If a home already has a gas supply, simply contact your local gas company to have the gas supply reconnected or transferred to your name (there's a connection charge). A security deposit (e.g. $150) is usually payable. You must contact your local gas company to get a final reading when vacating a property. If you need to purchase gas appliances, such as a gas cooker or fire, you should shop around as prices vary considerably. Special controls can be fitted to many appliances to make them easier to use by the disabled and the blind or partially sighted (studded or Braille controls).

Gas central heating boilers, water heaters and fires should be checked annually. Ask for a quotation for any work in advance and check the identity of anyone claiming to be a gas company employee (or any kind of 'serviceman') by asking to see an identity card and checking with his office. **Bear in mind that gas installations and appliances can leak and cause explosions or kill you while you sleep. If you suspect a gas leak, first check to see if a gas tap has been left on or a pilot light has gone out.** If not there's probably a leak, either in your home or in a nearby gas pipeline. Ring your local gas company immediately and **vacate your home as fast as possible.** Gas leaks are extremely rare and explosions caused by leaks even rarer (although often spectacular and therefore widely reported). Nevertheless, it pays to be careful. You can buy an electric-powered gas detector which activates an alarm when a gas leak is detected.

WATER

New Zealand usually has an abundant supply of water and mains water is available everywhere apart from in the most remote areas (and even in those it sometimes shoots up in boiling form directly out of the ground!). Over the last few years some north-western parts of the North Island have suffered something of a drought, although this is rare. All tap water is drinkable although in towns it's heavily chlorinated (as in many other countries). Water is supplied and billed by your local water company, which may be a division of your local council. Usually you pay an annual water rate which is set according to the size and value of your property, although in some areas (usually in newer properties) homes have a water meter and you're charged according to use. Usually it's cheaper to pay for your water on the rated system, although modest users living in large properties will find it cheaper to have a meter fitted. Mains drainage is found throughout New Zealand with the exception of remote rural areas, where properties usually have a septic tank.

HEATING

Never assume that because the weather in New Zealand is generally mild in summer you won't need heating at other times of the year. There are few areas of New Zealand where you won't need effective heating, together with good insulation (older properties aren't usually well insulated). Only a few areas, such as Northland (the northernmost tip of the North Island), are warm enough to manage without good heating. Most newer homes in New Zealand (and many older homes also) have central heating systems, consisting of heated water systems or ducted air. These are powered by electricity or mains or bottled gas and often double as air-conditioning in summer. Many homes also have a fireplace, as much for effect as for its practical use.

Older properties may have a wood-burner, which is essentially a stove which not only heats the room but provides hot water. Note, however, that although it's attractive, a wood-burner requires a good deal of care and attention and wood is relatively expensive. Older properties often have free-standing electric or gas heaters, rather than a central heating system.

6.

POST OFFICE SERVICES

The New Zealand Post Office (known as NZ Post) is a New Zealand tradition and has a rich past, similar to the American 'Pony Express'; tales abound of how postmen in bygone days struggled through forests and mountains to ensure that the mail was delivered. Today the postal service remains a mainstay of New Zealand life, particularly for those living in remote regions. In addition to delivering (and collecting) letters and parcels, rural postmen deliver a variety of goods including milk, newspapers, bread and even animals. They also offer a haulage service and, in some cases, carry passengers in their trucks and post buses to and from villages and isolated farms. In many ways, NZ Post lives in the past and New Zealand is one of the few developed countries not to have a system of post (zip) codes, which makes life difficult for the poor New Zealand 'postie'. A lot of sorting is still done by hand and postmen need to rely on their geographical and personal knowledge of who lives in their area. Nevertheless, it's efficient enough and NZ Post manage to deliver even poorly addressed letters on time.

There are over 1,000 post offices or postal shops throughout the country, which are operated by NZ Post in major towns and cities. In small towns, post offices are called postal shops and are run by private individuals who operate the postal shop alongside another business (such as a grocers or a dairy) and are paid either a salary or a commission by NZ Post. Some 80 per cent of New Zealand post offices are operated in this way. Postal shops offer a friendly, personal service to post office standards, as well as providing a range of other goods and services such as bill payment (BillPay) and Lotto tickets, and acting as a focal point for the local community. Some postal shops provide cheque encashment and deposit services (there's usually a sign indicating the services available). This spirit of private enterprise continues through to rural postmen, who aren't post office employees but private individuals with the concession to deliver mail (they offer various other delivery and collection services to supplement their income).

Information about NZ Post services is available from post office and postal shops in a variety of leaflets, and also via the internet (www.nzpost.co.nz). Compensation is paid for loss or damage up to the limit applicable for the service used (usually $250), plus reimbursement of postage for lost mail.

NZ Post got its first real mail rival in 1998 when the Australian company Fastway launched its national private postal service (it was expected to have 400 outlets by the end of 1998). New Zealand is one of the few countries in the world that allows private companies to compete with the nationalised postal service.

BUSINESS HOURS

Business hours for main post offices in towns and cities in New Zealand are usually from 9am to 5pm, Monday to Friday, and they are closed on Saturdays and Sundays. Postal shop opening hours in small villages vary considerably, because they're usually a private business and opening hours aren't decided by NZ Post. Whatever the opening hours of the shop, however, you won't be able to obtain post office services outside the 9am to 5pm period. Most outlets with postal shops open at least from 9am to 5pm, but in some rural areas they operate shorter hours or aren't open every day.

LETTER POST

There are two categories of domestic letter post in New Zealand, ordinary post (simply called Post) for non-urgent letters, which are usually delivered the next day within a city and within two to three working days to most other areas, and FastPost, which ensures delivery the next working day between major towns and cities. The cost of posting a letter (medium envelope 1200mm x 235mm) within New Zealand is 40¢ (80¢ for extra large envelopes) for an ordinary post letter and 80¢ ($1.20 for extra large envelopes) for a FastPost letter, rising on a sliding scale according to weight.

International letters can be sent by AirPost (3 to 6 days to Australia, 6 to 12 days to the UK, 4 to 10 days to the USA) or EconomyPost (10 to 15 days to Australia and 15 to 20 days to the UK and the USA). Rates for a 20g AirPost letter are $1 to Australia, $1.50 to the USA and South Africa, and $1.80 to Europe. Postcards (which are sent by EconomyPost) and aerogrammes costs $1 to all destinations.

General Information

Note the following general information regarding New Zealand postal services:

- In addition to post offices and postal shops, stamps can be purchased from many shops (which saves time queuing at a post office).

- When using FastPost (air mail) you should affix a FastPost label or use one of the purpose made envelopes (with red and blue markings as used for air mail in many other countries) and, where available, post letters in a FastPost postbox.

- Postboxes are red, some of which are beautifully ornate cast-iron 'monuments' dating back to Victorian times. There are also special postboxes for FastPost in major cities and towns.

- There are no postal codes (zip codes) in New Zealand. Always state the name of the nearest large town when addressing mail, as there are several small places with the same name in New Zealand. It isn't necessary to state which island your mail is intended for in your address, unless this is the main way of distinguishing between two towns with the same name. Take care when writing Maori place names as an extra letter added or dropped accidentally (or bad handwriting) can send your letter speeding off to entirely the wrong place, e.g. Whangara and Whangarei are 600km/370mi apart.

- A postman is obliged to deliver your mail only as far as the roadside. If you have a long driveway you'll need to provide a mailbox, which is usually mounted on a gate post or fixed to a fence. In rural areas the postman will collect your letters and parcels for posting when delivering mail.

- Many large mail users (i.e. businesses and government departments) have their mail delivered to a post office box (also called a private bag) at the main post office of the town where they are located. This allows mail to be pre-sorted and is also quicker as mail may be collected from the box several times a day instead of delivered just once. If you're writing to a company with a PO box or private bag number, always use it even if you know the street address (which is intended for the use of personal callers only).

- The address for many isolated properties (usually farms) in New Zealand is often simply the name of the addressee, followed by RD and a number (e.g. RD9), which is an abbreviation for 'Rural Delivery', followed by the address of the nearest small town. This form of address is perfectly adequate to ensure delivery of your mail, assuming the postman knows everyone's name on his route (which he usually does).

- If you have reason to write to a government minister in New Zealand all you need do is write his name, followed by 'Wellington' on the envelope and it will reach him. You don't even need to affix a stamp if posting your letter in New Zealand.

- When you're sending mail overseas, be sure to mark it clearly with the country of destination, bearing in mind that many New Zealand places names are 'imported' from abroad. If you're sending a letter to Canterbury (UK), Canterbury (USA) or Canterbury (Australia) make sure the address makes this clear – if it doesn't, NZ Post will deliver it to Canterbury, New Zealand (where else?).

REGISTERED POST

It isn't usually necessary to send mail by registered post unless it's valuable, as you can be confident that ordinary mail will be delivered. However, NZ Post provides both recorded and registered mail services. With recorded mail a signature is obtained on delivery and it's most suitable for important documents rather than valuable items (compensation is minimal if mail is lost). With registered mail you must use a pre-paid plastic envelope (obtainable from postal shops), available in A5 ($4.45) and foolscap ($6.50) sizes, which have a weight limit of 1.5kg. An 'advice of receipt' costs an additional $1.70. Compensation is paid up to a specified amount if registered post is lost or damaged.

DOMESTIC PARCELS

Unlike letter post, parcel deliveries in New Zealand are open to much wider competition. While NZ Post provides an efficient parcel delivery service, private operators are also allowed open access to the market. Therefore, while the easiest way to send a parcel may be to go to a postal shop and send it by NZ Post, it may be cheaper or faster to use a private courier firm, particularly if you make frequent shipments. In some areas, postal shops offer a choice of either NZ Post or private couriers for parcel shipments.

NZ Post's parcel service handles parcels up to 20kg (1.05 metres in length and 2.5 metres in combined length plus girth) which are divided in four rates depending on distance: across town, short haul, within island and between islands. Rates range from $2 for a parcel weighing up to 500g across town up to a maximum of $24 for a parcel weighing 15 to 20kg between islands. Delivery times are from the next working day to a maximum of two to three working days. NZ Post also provides a FastPost parcel service for parcels weighing up to 20kg. There are three rate bands based on distance: short haul (up to 150km, same island), within island (over 150km) and between islands. Rates are from $3 for a parcel weighing up to 500g (short haul) up to a maximum of $34.40 for a parcel weighing 15 to 20kg between islands. Delivery times are next working day to all destinations with the exception of some remote rural areas.

NZ Post provides a fast CourierPost service for parcels weighing up to 3kg. Special Trackpaks must be used costing from $3.60 (including postage) for DLE size (130mm x 240mm) up to $13.75 for LF size (400mm x 440mm). Delivery is made to 180 centres nationwide and is guaranteed by 9am the next working day to local addresses, by noon (the next day) to residential addresses and within two days to rural addresses. A signature of the addresses can be collected for an additional $1.90. Compensation for loss or damage is provided up to $1,500 and additional insurance is available up to $50,000.

INTERNATIONAL MAIL

NZ Post provides no less than six options for sending international mail: CourierPost, EMS, RegisteredPost, AirPost, EconomyPost and SeaPost. In addition to NZ Post, a number of private companies (such as DHL and TNT) also offer fast (but expensive) courier services to many countries.

CourierPost International is the fastest NZ Post service and is available to around 220 countries world-wide utilising the DHL Worldwide Express service. It provides free insurance of up to $2,000 for loss or damage, plus reimbursement of postage if lost, and additional insurance is available up to $50,000. Documents must weigh less than 1kg and customs parcels up to 20kg. Special TrackBoxes are available from post shops in sizes of 5kg and 15kg. Sample rates for documents weighing up to 500g are: Australia ($14), UK ($27) and USA ($24); documents weighing from 500g to 1kg cost: Australia ($20), UK ($36) and USA ($32). To send a 5kg parcel by CourierPost costs $73 to Australia, $139 to the UK and $124 to the USA (prices for a 10kg parcel are $123, $239 and $214 respectively). CourierPost takes one to three days to most destinations.

EMS International is an express mail service for urgent letters and documents to over 120 countries. It doesn't include parcels. It provides compensation of up to $250 for loss or damage, plus reimbursement of postage if lost. The maximum weight is 500g and rates include $12 to Australia, $20 to the South Pacific, $22 to East Asia and North America, $25 to Western Europe and $29 to the rest of the world. Delivery times vary from one to ten days, depending on the destination.

RegisteredPost International is for important letters and documents weighing up 200gm and no larger than A4. Letters and documents are sent in pre-paid envelopes available in A5 ($7.50) and A4 ($10) sizes. An 'advice of receipt' costs an additional $1.70. Delivery times are the same as ordinary international letters. Compensation up to $250 is paid for loss or damage, plus reimbursement of postage if lost.

AirPost International is a fast service for letters and documents (maximum weight 200g), small parcels (maximum weight 2kg) and customs parcels (maximum weight up to 20kg). Letter and document rates are based on three envelope sizes: medium (235 x 120 x 10mm), large (325 x 230 x 10mm) and extra large (385 x 260 x10mm). The maximum value for small parcels is $620 (including GST). Compensation up to $250 is paid for loss or damage, plus reimbursement of postage if lost (additional insurance up to $1,500 is available for customs parcels for an additional $8). AirPost takes three to six days to most destinations.

Sample rates for AirPost letters are, medium letters: Australia ($1), UK ($1.80) and USA ($1.50); large letters: Australia ($1.80), UK ($3) and USA ($2.50); extra large letters: Australia ($3), UK ($6) and USA ($5). Small parcels cost from $2 (100g) to

$19 (2kg) to Australia, from $3 (100g) to $39 (2kg) to the UK, and from $2.50 (100g) to $35 (2kg) to the USA. To send a 5kg parcel by AirPost costs $37 to Australia, $108 to the UK and $88 to the USA (prices for a 10kg parcel are $67, $198 and $148 respectively). Occasionally NZ Post have special offers, e.g. between 13th and 31st July 1998 there was 25 per cent off all AirPost parcels to the UK for cash customers.

EconomyPost International is an inexpensive service when time isn't critical and offers the same services, envelopes, weights, values, compensation and insurance as AirPost International. Sample rates for EconomyPost letters are, medium letters: Australia (70¢), UK (80¢) and USA (80¢); large letters: Australia ($1.20), UK ($1.80) and USA ($1.50); extra large letters: Australia ($1.80), UK ($3) and USA ($2.50). Small parcels cost from $1.50 (100g) to $13.50 (2kg) to Australia, from $2 (100g) to $23 (2kg) to the UK, and from $1.80 (100g) to $19.50 (2kg) to the USA. To send a 5kg parcel by EconomyPost costs $33.50 to Australia, $85 to the UK and $68.50 to the USA (prices for a 10kg parcel are $53.50, $155 and $113.50 respectively). EconomyPost takes 10 to 15 days to most destinations.

SeaPost International is an economical service available only to Western Europe, East Asia and North America for small parcels and customs parcels. Weights, values, compensation and insurance are the same as AirPost International. Small parcels cost from $1.80 (100g) to $21.50 (2kg) to the UK and from $1.80 (100g) to $16 (2kg) to the USA. To send a 5kg parcel by SeaPost costs $57.50 to the UK and $50 to the USA (prices for a 10kg parcel are $102.50 and $90 respectively). There's no SeaPost service to Australia. SeaPost takes 42 to 63 days depending on the destination or around nine weeks to Europe, so it's most suitable for sending large, heavy items where speed isn't important (e.g. Christmas presents sent in October).

Note also the following when sending international mail:

● The last posting dates for Christmas (for delivery by December 24th) for letters and parcels are displayed in postal shops in October.

● International parcels require a customs declaration form (OS9 or OS9A for insured parcels) plus a commercial invoice or proforma invoice if the contents form part of a commercial transaction.

● Post shops offer a wide range of packaging materials and NZ Post publish a 'parcel packaging guide' and information on 'how to package a parcel' (see also internet: www.nzpost.co.nz).

● You're prohibited from sending certain items by mail, a list of which is available from post offices.

MAIL COLLECTION

Mail is delivered once daily in New Zealand, which can range from very early in the morning to much later in the day, depending on the area. If there's nobody at home when a large or bulky item (or something you need to sign for) is delivered, NZ Post won't leave the item, but will leave a card. The easiest way to have this mail delivered is to complete and return the card stating when and where you would like it delivered. You can have it delivered to a neighbour or another address (such as your work address) if you prefer. If you're travelling around New Zealand, mail can be sent care of the *Post Restante* service to all main city post offices and can be collected during normal business hours by presenting proof of identity (such as a passport or driving licence).

TELEGRAMS, TELEX & FACSIMILE

NZ Post no longer provides a 'traditional' telegram service where messages are delivered by hand, as nowadays almost everyone has access to a telephone. Telegrams, however, can still be sent from postal shops or by calling freephone 24-hours a day (0800) 801801. The cost within New Zealand is a flat $15.50 for up to 100 words (50 if telephoned), plus $5 for each additional 50 words. The standard delivery time to major towns is the same working day if lodged before 11.30am and the next working day if lodged after 11.30am. An urgent 2-hour delivery service is available for an additional charge of $25 Monday to Friday and $40 on Saturday. Charges can be added to your telephone bill or paid by credit card. Delivery outside main cities and towns are sent by FastPost for targeted delivery the next day (delivery to some remote areas takes longer).

International telegrams cost $30 for up to 30 words plus $1 per additional word. Addressee details are charged as words, and words of ten characters or more are charged as two words (expensive things words – use them sparingly!). As with domestic telegrams, messages are delivered with the mail rather than by special courier, and delivery times vary depending on the country.

Facsimiles (faxes) can also be sent from a variety of locations in New Zealand including postal shops, stationers, newsagents and many other businesses, who can also receive them on your behalf. NZ Post provides a FaxLink service from over 160 post offices from where a fax can be sent for a flat fee of $2.50 plus 25¢ per page within the same town or city or $1.50 per page nationwide. International charges are Australia ($1.60 per page), South Pacific ($2.50), North America ($3) and rest of the world ($4). NZ Post will also receive faxes for $2.50 when collected from a postal shop (they can be delivered by CourierPost for $5). For more information ☎ freephone 0800-501501.

Most businesses and many households also have fax machines. Machines (Groups 2/3) imported from abroad usually function okay in New Zealand, although you aren't supposed to connect them unless they are Telecom approved. Telex machines aren't widely used any longer in New Zealand although most major hotels, banks, government offices and large businesses have them.

7.

TELEPHONE

New Zealanders are enthusiastic telephone users and telephone ownership in New Zealand is among the highest in the world at around 450 lines per thousand people. It's due in part to the long distances which separate many communities, because local calls are free and the fact that many New Zealanders are immigrants with family and friends overseas. The telephone system in New Zealand has been extensively updated since 1990 and all areas are served by modern digital exchanges (the last exchange on which subscribers could only make calls via the operator was closed in 1991, making the holder of the post redundant after 55 years service).

The telecommunications industry has been extensively deregulated over the last few years. The main telecommunications operator in New Zealand is the Telecom Corporation of New Zealand (TCNZ) or Telecom (internet: www.telecom.co.nz) for short, which used to be state owned (and part of the post office), but was established as a separate company in 1987 and then privatised. In June 1990, Ameritech and Bell Atlantic of the USA purchased a 64 per cent stake in TCNZ for $2.5 billion, which was reduced to 49.6 per cent in 1993 under government direction. The chief officer and chief financial officer of the company are, however, appointed from Ameritech and Bell Atlantic. Although Telecom is essentially a private company, in effect it's the national telephone company and maintains 1.7m fixed lines and 325,000 cellular phone connections.

The deregulated environment has allowed Telecom to become much more than a telephone company and it maintains a number of other telecommunications services including cable telephone and cable TV networks. Telecom is also New Zealand's largest company and one of the country's most successful, recording profits of $550 million in 1997/98, although this was achieved with the aid of a pay freeze and numerous redundancies. After deregulation other telecommunications companies (such as Clear Communications) entered the marketplace, although they remain minnows compared with Telecom.

INSTALLING A TELEPHONE

It's difficult to manage without a phone in New Zealand and most people who can afford to have one. In fact, many households have two or more lines which enables them to connect a fax machine or modem, or to remain contactable when teenage children spend hours (and hours) gossiping to their friends (don't panic – local calls are free!). Theoretically you're free to obtain your telephone service from any company you choose. In practice, however, there's little choice as Telecom is the only company that can offer telephone services in many parts of the country. Some areas are served by alternative operators, the largest of which is Clear Communications which operates in Auckland, Wellington and Christchurch. These networks are sure to grow, but are by no means extensive and to date often serve business customers only. In Auckland and Wellington you can receive your telephone service via fibre optic cables which also provide cable TV (owned by First Media, yet another offshoot of Telecom). The easiest way to find out whether there's a choice of telephone companies in your area is to ask your neighbours. If a Telecom line and telephone are already installed in your property you can usually take over the connection, but you aren't obliged to if an alternative is available.

To have a telephone connected simply call your chosen telephone company (the number will be in your local telephone directory). Before connecting your line

Telecom (or another operator) will need your name and address; date of birth; proof of your address (such as a driving licence or other official document); details of your previous address (and proof) and employer; and the address of a relative or friend in New Zealand (if applicable) whom you can use as a reference (plus six pints of blood or your first-born as a deposit!). If you have just arrived in New Zealand your immigration documents should be acceptable as proof of identity, otherwise ask your employer (if you have one) if he will confirm your identity. Once your application has been approved your phone will be connected within 24 hours if your home has an existing line or within 48 hours if it hasn't and there are lines nearby. The connection fee is $61.88 to reconnect an existing line or $100 if a new line needs to be installed. This doesn't apply to remote areas, where you'll be quoted a price for the work involved.

Although you'll probably need to rent your phone line from Telecom, you don't need to rent a telephone from them, although some 75 per cent of consumers do (which is a hang-over from the old days when there was no choice). A basic touch-tone phone costs $4 per quarter to rent. However, you can buy a wide variety of telephones of all shapes and sizes (plus answering machines and other equipment) from telephone and electrical shops, with prices starting at around $12, which works out much cheaper than renting in the long term. Make sure that the phone you buy is a touch-tone (DTMF) phone (most are). Note that although touch-tone phones purchased abroad usually work perfectly well in New Zealand, you aren't supposed to connect them unless they're Telecom approved.

ISDN Access: if you have a computer and use it frequently it's possible, where available, to have an ISDN (Integrated Service Digital Network) line installed at your home or office. The service is available in all city and town centres and also to homes where a cable telephone or TV service is provided. The advantage of an ISDN line is that it allows data to be transmitted much faster than over a standard line (115.2 kilobytes of data per second) and you can also make and receive voice or fax calls while the modem is in use. Such lines are more expensive than standard lines (an additional $115 per year rental) and they don't provide free local calls, but are becoming popular with serious home computer users.

USING THE TELEPHONE

Using the telephone in New Zealand is simplicity itself. The numbering system was changed in 1990 and all standard telephone numbers now have nine digits. There are just five telephone regions in New Zealand, each with a two-digit regional code:

Region	Code
South Island	03
Wellington	04
South of North Island	06
Waikato/Bay of Plenty	07
Auckland and Northland	09

Telephone numbers have seven digits which include a three-digit district code and a four-digit subscriber number. When dialling to another region, dial the regional code and then the seven-digit number. When dialling within a region, just dial the seven-digit number (even when dialling within a district with the same district code). The only drawback to the system is that many people don't quote the regional code in their numbers because they expect callers to know what it is.

Telephone numbers with other codes are special in some way. Numbers prefixed with '01' usually connect you to a telephone company service, such as the operator. Mobile telephone numbers are identified by the prefix '025'. Numbers beginning with 0800 are freephone numbers, which are becoming common in New Zealand where many businesses provide an 0800 number for their customers use. When you dial a major company (such as a bank or airline) you dial the same number from anywhere in the country, rather than a local number. The telephone system then 'reads' your telephone number to find your location and routes your call, through what's known as a 'value added network', to the office dealing with your location. So, for example, when you dial an 0800 number from Christchurch you could end up speaking to someone in Christchurch or, equally, to someone in Auckland. Note that 0900 numbers are premium rate telephone numbers, where the cost of the call is inflated (typically $2.99 per minute) to pay for the service, for example, an information line.

Telephone Dials: all new telephones sold in New Zealand are of the push-button variety, although there are still many dial-operated phones around, mainly in homes (rarely payphones). One point to note is that these are numbered in reverse order compared with most other countries, i.e. the '9' is nearest the stop and the '1' farthest away.

Dialling Tones: dialling tones are the same as in some other countries (e.g. Britain) and are different from American and other European tones. The ringing tone consists of two short rings followed by a pause and the engaged (busy) tone consists of alternating beeps of the same length, each with a slightly different tone.

If you're unable to get through to the number you want, call the operator on 010. If you wish to make a reverse charge (collect) call, however, dial 010 for domestic and 0170 for international calls. For information about Telecom services dial 123.

OPTIONAL SERVICES

Telecom provides a range of optional services, which can usually be ordered individually or as part of a package deal, for which a touch-tone phone is required. They include the following:

Call Minder: call minder is a phone message service (much the same as having your own answering machine) that allows callers to leave a message when you aren't at home or your line is busy. The call is automatically answered by the call minder service with your personal recorded greeting.

Call Transfer: call transfer allows you to divert calls to another telephone number automatically, e.g. from home to office (or vice versa) or to a mobile telephone.

Call Waiting: call waiting lets you know when another caller is trying to contact you (through beeps on the line) when you're already making a call and allows you to speak to the caller without terminating your current call. You can suspend the call waiting beeps when using the internet, otherwise your internet connection is automatically broken.

Conference Calling: conference calling allows you to hold a three-way conversation, either within New Zealand or abroad.

Alarm Calls: an alarm call allows you to programme your telephone to ring at a pre-set time, for example to wake you, or remind you of an appointment or to make an important call.

Caller ID: this system allows you to check who's calling before you answer the phone. The caller's number is displayed on an LCD display which is either built into a special telephone or is a separate caller ID display unit.

Price Required: by dialling 010 before making a call and asking for this service, you'll be informed of the cost of a call shortly after it ends. Alternatively dial 013 (016 for international calls) before making a call and the cost will be listed separately on your next bill.

However, not all optional services are available in every area.

CHARGES

New Zealand has a regulatory body which rules on whether telephone charges are fair and reasonable, and leaves it to 'market forces' to keep charges competitive. However, one of the new telecommunications operators, Clear Communications, is suing the government and Telecom. It's alleging uncompetitive practices and gross overcharging by Telecom for the portion of Clear Communication's calls which pass through Telecom exchanges, thus hindering them from competing effectively with Telecom (this is a world-wide problem and how former monopolies seek to maintain their dominance).

The monthly line rental for a standard line is $35.66, which includes unlimited free local calls. The area which qualifies as 'local' is listed in your telephone directory and varies depending on the area, but doesn't cover the whole dialling code region! This arrangement is heaven for chatterboxes and also great for internet surfers who can hook up for hours at no cost, although you need to make sure that your service provider has an access number within your local calling area. One of the drawbacks, however, is that you'll often find numbers engaged for hour upon hour in the evenings and at weekends. Alternatively, if you don't make many local calls (less than 13 a week on average) you can pay a line rental of $24.75 per month plus 20¢ for each local call up to two hours in duration and 20¢ for each additional two hours or part thereof. This service isn't available in all areas.

For non-local and non-freephone (0800) calls there are ten charge bands, with rates increasing with distance (the boundary of each band is roughly every 150km/93mi). However, this is largely academic as there isn't an enormous difference between the cost of the cheapest and most expensive bands, particularly during off-peak times. The week is divided into four charging periods (which can greatly affect the cost) as follows:

Rate	Period
Peak	8am to noon, Monday to Saturday
Standard	noon to 6pm, Monday to Saturday
Off Peak	6am to 8am and 6pm to 10.30pm daily, and Sundays from 8am to 6pm
Cheap	All other times

Calls are charged per second but priced on a per minute basis. If a call lasts for less than a full minute you pay only the pro rata cost for that minute. With Telecom, a minute over the longest distance at peak rate costs $1.60 and 58¢ at off-peak rate.

Alternative Networks: although most people rent their telephone line from Telecom, there's no obligation to make all your calls via the Telecom network. Under deregulation, other companies can provide your telephone service even when you have a Telecom line. This is achieved by entering an access code before calls, which routes calls to your local exchange over Telecom lines, but uses the alternative company's lines for the long-distance part of its 'journey'. The cost is charged to your account by the alternative company (usually debited to a credit card) and doesn't appear on your Telecom bill.

The main alternative network is Clear Communications, who provide long-distance calls at up to 50 per cent cheaper than Telecom. To use the service you must register your telephone number with them and then dial 050 before a call (you can also make calls from any telephone by entering an access code). It's worth considering an alternative company to Telecom if you make a lot of international calls, as calls are usually significantly cheaper. Short distance calls cost the same, therefore don't use Clear Communications for these (unless you rent your line from them, which is possible in some areas).

BILLS

Telephone bills are issued monthly in New Zealand and you have around a week to pay before a reminder is sent. You can pay bills by post, at postal shops and some other outlets that are Telecom agencies, or pay your bill by direct debit from a bank account. All telephone bills in New Zealand are itemised, although it's possible to request a non-itemised bill if you wish. You can also decide the level at which itemisation begins, e.g. all calls over 50¢, $1 or $5. This is handy if you just want to keep an eye on the more expensive calls and don't want to receive reams of paper listing all your calls.

INTERNATIONAL CALLS

It's possible to direct dial international calls from all private and public phones in New Zealand through the ISD (International Subscriber Dialling) system. A full list of country codes is shown in the information pages of your telephone directory. To make an international call, dial the international access code of 00 followed by the country code and number you want. It's usually much cheaper to use an alternative company to make international calls (see **Charges** above). Telecom do, however, have periodic special offers, e.g. in 1998 the maximum weekend charge (6pm Friday until midnight Sunday) was $10 to Australia and $15 to Canada, Ireland, the UK and the USA, which may offer better value.

It's possible to make 'home direct' calls in New Zealand by dialling 0009 followed by the country code of the country you wish to call (e.g. '1' for the USA, 44 for the UK). You will then be connected directly to an operator in the country you're calling, who will place the call for you and charge the cost to either the number you're calling or your own home bill, assuming you have a telephone account in that country. It's quite expensive, however, and much more expensive than paying for the call yourself. Travellers visiting New Zealand from the USA and holding a calling card from a US telephone company, can use home direct and have the cost charged to their account. If you have an AT&T calling card (or a card issued by a company with which AT&T has an agreement) simply dial 000 911 from any telephone. You can then dial your call yourself and no operator intervention is necessary.

International telephone calls via Telecom are charged according to a number of zones, with Australia in the cheapest zone and the UK in one of the most expensive. Alternative companies (such as Clear Communications) levy a separate rate for each country, rather than charging per zone. For operator international assistance call 0170.

If you're travelling overseas you can use Telecom NZ's Direct service to call New Zealand. By dialling the relevant local access number you can speak to an operator in New Zealand and charge the call to your Telecom account, calling card, a credit card, or place a reverse charge (collect) call. For information and access numbers contact Telecom.

DIRECTORIES

You're entitled to a copy of the telephone directory (called telephone books in New Zealand) for your local region, which is delivered when your line is connected and annually thereafter. Directories for other regions can be ordered for a nominal cost and charged to your bill. If you live outside the Auckland region it's advisable to order the Auckland book as most important businesses (e.g. airlines, banks, etc.) are located there. Subscribers are divided into private and business customers and there's also a separate yellow pages for each region (a copy is delivered with your local telephone book). If you don't have a directory handy (or cannot be bothered to look the number up) the number for directory enquiries (known as directory assistance) is 018 for domestic numbers and 0172 for international numbers.

PUBLIC TELEPHONES

Public phones can be found in the streets of all towns and villages, and at various other locations including post offices, bus stations and airports. All payphones allow local, national and International Subscriber Dialling (ISD) calls. International calls can also be made via the operator or the home direct service. Most old-style call boxes have been replaced by new kiosks with push-button phones. Call boxes accept either coins (coloured blue), PhoneCards (coloured green) or credit cards (coloured yellow), but not a combination of these. Credit card phones are found mainly in cities. The majority of payphones (over 4,000) accept only PhoneCards. This is intended to prevent theft and save money by not having to empty coin boxes (rather than for customer convenience). When making a local telephone call from a payphone, the call isn't free (as it is when calling from a private telephone) and the standard rate is 20¢ per minute.

PhoneCard Payphones: Telecom PhoneCards are available from post offices, service stations, Telecom Centres and various shops (such as dairies) displaying a Telecom PhoneCard symbol, a green, yellow and blue illustration of a card being inserted into a telephone receiver. They are sold in values of $5, $10, $20 and $50 and have different designs, usually scenic views of New Zealand (many people collect them and some issues are valuable and much sought after). PhoneCard cards save you from having to find change or carry around lots of coins. The procedure when using a PhoneCard in most payphones is as follows:

1. Lift the receiver and check for the dial tone.

2. Insert your PhoneCard into the slot.

3. Wait (this is displayed while your card is checked).

4. Your card's remaining credit is displayed, e.g. 10 units. You can now dial your number.

5. Hang up when you're finished and remove your card.

Coin Phones: coin phones usually accept 10¢, 20¢ and 50¢ coins. You must lift the receiver and insert at least 20¢ before dialling (the minimum cost of even the shortest local call). In older coin boxes you should insert only small coins (one at a time), because if you speak for less than the time you have paid for, you won't receive any change. In newer boxes (where the amount in reserve is shown on a digital display) you can insert as much money as you like as wholly unused coins are automatically refunded at the end of the call. However, you still won't receive any change from a partly used coin, e.g. if you insert 50¢ but make only a 20¢ call. Making an international call from a coin phone can be difficult as you need to insert at least $3.30 (the minimum charge) in coins. Even if you plan to use the home direct service you must insert 20¢ (which isn't refunded) to access the service.

Credit Card Phones: in some places, mainly city centres and airports, there are payphones that accept international credit cards (e.g. American Express, Bankcard, Diners Club, Mastercard and Visa), where the cost is automatically debited to your credit card account. Credit cards cannot be used in PhoneCard payphones and vice versa.

Private Payphones: there are private payphones in hotels, bars, shops and other businesses. They are usually lightweight, portable units rather than phone kiosks and operate like any other phone, except that they don't usually give change so you should insert only the amount that you expect to spend. The main point to note is that the owner of the phone can set whatever rate he wishes, which is usually much higher than Telecom's rates (and he has no obligation to display what the charges are). The same applies to calls from hotels, which levy a surcharge that can be as high as 100 per cent above the cost of calls. When making a call from a hotel room you can usually dial direct.

Calling Cards: if you do a lot of travelling, you can obtain a Telecom calling card. Calls can be made with a calling card from any phone, public (including credit card payphones) or private (including mobile phones), and charged to your home or business Telecom account or a credit card. You can also use the card to make calls to New Zealand from overseas, using the NZ Direct service. A calling card can be limited to 20 pre-selected numbers or to numbers with a particular prefix. Additional cards can be allocated to family, friends or business associates. Although cards are free, there are high charges for the convenience of using a calling card. A Personal Identification Number (PIN) protects you against misuse of your card.

MOBILE PHONES

Given the remoteness of many parts of New Zealand, mobile (cellular) telephones are quite popular and there are some 350,000 in service with around 20 per cent of New Zealanders owning one. Coverage is surprisingly good despite the difficult terrain in many places and the country is covered by both analogue and digital networks. Recently, however, there has been a scare about the risks to health from mobile phone antennae towers and one garage owner who planned to mount a tower on his land adjacent to a primary school received death threats!

The main cellular network is operated by, you guessed it, Telecom Mobile. Although you can buy a mobile telephone directly from Telecom, there are many private operators and mobile phone shops who can connect you to the service. It's also possible to rent mobile phones by the day or week, starting at around $17 a day. Clear Communications are planning to launch a cellular network in the near future which is expected to be cheaper than Telecom Mobile. A recent development is a voice-activated mobile phone, which is ideal for use in the car. Unfortunately these machines can recognise only a New Zealand accent, so if you don't have one you'll need to dial manually (or cultivate the accent!).

EMERGENCY NUMBERS

The only emergency number you need to know in New Zealand is 111. This can be dialled free from any telephone and will connect you to the nearest emergency operator who will connect you to the police, fire or ambulance as required. You don't need any money, even when calling from a payphone, whether it accepts coins, PhoneCards or credit cards. Be ready to tell the emergency operator which service you require, your name and location. If you don't know your location it doesn't matter because the operator can pinpoint your location as the telephone from which you're calling automatically 'sends' its identity when you make a call.

8.

TELEVISION & RADIO

Broadcasting in New Zealand, as well as the ownership of TV and radio stations, used to be strictly regulated by the government, although since 1991 it has been deregulated to a certain extent. Since then a number of new companies (particularly huge, foreign media corporations) have entered the market, making the broadcasting industry extremely volatile. New companies are frequently starting up, both in radio and TV, buying up existing stations and, just as frequently, closing down. It doesn't pay to become too attached to a particular programme as you may find that the next time you sit down in front of 'the box' your favourite station has disappeared!

TELEVISION

TV Stations

There are three terrestrial national TV stations in New Zealand, imaginatively named TV1, TV2 and TV3; TV1 and TV2 are state owned and TV3 is privately owned. All stations, even those that are state owned, carry advertising, although the amount of revenue the state owned channels can raise from advertising is limited (they also receive state funding). There are also both state and privately owned regional TV stations in some areas (e.g. Christchurch TV), although TVNZ, the state owned broadcasting company recently closed its five Horizon Pacific regional channels. There are plans to set up a new youth-oriented national TV station. The government plans to sell off TVNZ in the near future (already long delayed).

Terrestrial TV is short on the New Zealanders' passion, sport, as all the major sporting events have been sold to the highest bidder, namely satellite or cable. This accounts partly for the success of cable and satellite TV in New Zealand. If you like watching sport you'll need to invest in a satellite dish or cable hook-up to watch the big matches, although you can watch them free at hotels (pubs) that show live sport on large-screen TVs.

Cable Television

Cable TV has made slow but steady progress in New Zealand and is currently available in parts of Hutt Valley, Wellington and several suburbs of Auckland. The main operator is First Media, an offshoot of NZ Telecom, who plan to provide cable TV to 400,000 homes within the next few years, although the sparse population means that universal cable coverage is unlikely. Cable TV provides exclusive cable channels as well as satellite and terrestrial TV broadcasts, and numerous foreign cable and satellite programmes such as CNN. Eventually over 50 channels will be available on cable.

The easiest way to find out whether cable TV is available in your area is to ask your neighbours. The presence of cable 'pillars' (junction boxes) and unsightly, subsiding trenches in the roadways and pavements of Auckland and Wellington's smartest suburbs are also a good indication! First Media operates a pick-and-choose menu pricing system, with a basic cable TV subscription package costing from $14.99 per month for the main sports, news and movie channels. It's also possible to choose which channels you want to receive and the days on which you wish to receive them, paying as little as $1.50 per day for one channel, which works out cheaper if (for example) you just want to watch movies at weekends. If you subscribe to cable TV, you can also obtain your telephone service via cable.

Satellite Television

Sky satellite TV is well established in New Zealand, where it's owned by a consortium of international communications and media companies (TVNZ also has a stake in the enterprise). Foreign investors have pumped millions of dollars into satellite TV, confident that it's the way ahead in a country where long distances and a sparse population have slowed the sprawling trenches of cable networks. However, Sky TVNZ remains a loss-making enterprise.

Sky TV has around a quarter of a million subscribers, which is a large number given the relatively small population of New Zealand. You can take out a subscription by calling your nearest dealer and have a dish installed within a few days. If you live in a remote or mountainous area, you may need a larger dish in order to receive transmissions. A package to receive Sky TV, including a large dish, receiver/decoder and installation costs around $650.

Sky viewers pay by monthly subscription, although an increasing number of programmes (like top sporting events) are on a pay-per-view basis, which is payable in addition to the basic cost (and can make satellite TV quite expensive). Sky TV provides three channels: Sky News, Sky Movies and Sky Sports. Sky News incorporates BBC and CNN transmissions into its programmes and, together with Sky Movies, is much the same as satellite TV in other countries. Sky Sports' main trump card has been to secure the exclusive rights to broadcast most top sporting events in New Zealand including the All Black's rugby matches. As this is something which few New Zealanders can live without (literally), it may account for the impressive following that satellite TV has made.

Television Programmes

TV in New Zealand doesn't have a particularly good reputation as most people freely admit. The small population and limited budgets mean that there are relatively few good home-made programmes (at around 20 per cent, the lowest percentage in the developed world – a growing cause for concern among certain groups), and TV stations prefer to import programmes from other English-speaking nations (mainly Australia, the UK and USA) by the planeload. Lovers of America's 'Oprah Winfrey Show' and Britain's 'Coronation Street', 'Eastenders', 'Panorama' and 'Soldier, Soldier' will be delighted to hear that they are all shown on New Zealand TV. The quality of documentary programmes is high and wildlife programmes such as 'Meet The Real Penguins' and 'Mount Cook' have won New Zealand programme makers top awards in Asia and Europe. News programmes are also presented professionally, although they tend to focus on national rather than international news, and coverage can also be quite superficial (making CNN and Sky News good value for those who wishing to know what's happening in the wider world).

TV viewing figures tend to suggest that New Zealanders have a more intelligent taste in TV than their European or North American counterparts. News or documentary programmes usually comprise the top three programmes ranked by audience figures. A TV gardening programme, 'Maggie's Garden Show', is also regularly in the top five. 'Air NZ Holiday', a travel programme (also a thinly disguised advertisement for a well-known airline) is regularly top of the TV pops. The famous British soap 'Coronation Street' usually makes the lower half of the top ten and when TVNZ bosses recently announced plans to cut the weekly showings of 'Corrie' from three to two they received an angry petition of 20,000 signatures in protest. New Zealanders also have their own home-grown soaps of which the most popular is the hospital drama 'Shortland Street', although the programme rarely appears in the top ten. Most stations and their programmes are broadcast in English, but a small number are broadcast in Maori including *Te Karere* (News in Maori).

New Zealand TV stations show more advertising and other 'promotional messages' than TV stations elsewhere in the English-speaking world, with viewers having to endure an average of 15 minutes commercials every hour (compared to around 13 minutes in Australia, 11 minutes in the USA and 7.5 minutes in the UK).

Most daily newspapers and many magazines contain TV sections giving details of programmes for terrestrial, cable and satellite stations. A magazine called *TV Guide* has the most extensive listings including in-depth features on forthcoming movies and other programmes allowing you to plan your viewing (it also happens to be New Zealand's largest-circulating weekly magazine). *The Listener* is an upmarket magazine of comment and criticism (similar to the British publication of the same name) and also contains TV programme listings.

Buying TVs and Videos

It is unlikely to be worth bringing either a TV or a video recorder with you to New Zealand as they are available locally quite cheaply. Also, a TV made for a foreign market is unlikely to be compatible with the New Zealand transmission system (a PAL variant) and voltage, particularly if it's intended for the US system (you'll be able to receive a picture or sound, but not both). Equipment imported from Australia will work, but again it's unlikely to be worthwhile shipping a TV across the Tasman.

Like a TV, a video recorder has become an essential item of equipment in the majority of New Zealand homes in the last few decades. The cheapest video recorder costs you around $300. There are video cassette rental stores in cities and towns and a night's rental of a top movie costs around $10. Videos can also be purchased, including top films and sporting events, starting at around $10 for the oldest releases.

Television Licence

If you own a TV in New Zealand you must pay an annual TV licence fee, known as the Public Broadcasting Fee, of $110 per year (for any number of TVs in a home) which can be paid by post or at a post office. There's much controversy about the fee, which provokes a mini-outcry whenever it's raised and many people are reluctant to pay it at all. You're even required to pay the fee if you live outside the range of terrestrial transmitters and don't have a satellite dish! Regular checks are made by government inspectors and thousands of people are fined each year for not paying the fee. Checks are made not so much by the use of 'detector vans', but by a process of elimination which assumes that because almost everyone has a TV, those who aren't listed as having paid the fee must be watching illegally.

The Public Broadcasting Fee raises around $95 million annually for an organisation known as New Zealand On Air, which in turn funds the state run TV New Zealand (TVNZ) and Radio New Zealand. The government has announced that TVNZ may be required to obtain more of its funding privately (from advertising and other methods) in future.

RADIO

Radio broadcasting in New Zealand follows the model established for the TV industry in that there are both state operated and commercially run radio stations. Radio New Zealand (RNZ) runs two national stations, Concert FM and the National Programme, which are both rather staid, upmarket programmes, similar to the BBC's Radio 4. They are funded from the public broadcasting fee and don't broadcast advertising. They have a good reputation for the quality of their broadcasting, although mainly have an older and declining audience. RNZ also operates a network of local radio stations throughout the country, which are partly publicly funded and partly funded from advertising. They mainly broadcast rock and pop music, easy listening, local and regional news, and sport.

National commercial radio is limited to one station, Fine Music FM, a classical music station, which isn't even a New Zealand station as it's relayed from the USA. However, there are many local commercial radio stations, with almost 100 FM stations alone plus others broadcasting on the AM frequency. Stations are closely involved with their local communities and play pop music or easy listening plus local news and sport. Because there are so many commercial stations competing for a limited amount of advertising money, stations go to extraordinary lengths to attract listeners. Recently More FM 91.8 in Auckland was criticised by police for running a 'Toot Dr. Loot' contest which encouraged motorists to cause traffic jams by stopping at green lights during the city's rush hour. A motorist who solicited an on-air 'toot' from the following vehicle was rewarded with a $10 prize. Verbal abuse was rewarded with $20! New Zealand also has a tourist radio station (Tourist Information FM) which broadcasts information on local attractions and events in areas indicated by blue Tourist Information FM signs (tune to 88.2). As the name suggests, it's mainly for tourists but also useful to others. Most radio stations broadcast in English, although there are a number of state and private radio stations broadcasting in Maori, particularly in areas with large Maori communities such as Auckland and the northwest tip of the country.

The BBC World Service is re-broadcast on a local frequency in several main cities including Auckland and Wellington. It can also be received direct. To obtain a free BBC World Service programme guide and frequency information write to BBC Worldwide, BBC World Service, PO Box 76, Bush House, Strand, London WC2B 4PH, UK (☎ 0171-752 5040). The BBC publishes a monthly magazine, *BBC Worldwide*, containing comprehensive information about BBC World Service radio and TV programmes, which is available on subscription from the above address.

9.

EDUCATION

New Zealand has always had an effective and well respected educational system, although few areas of New Zealand life have gone through more upheaval in the last ten years. In 1987, the prime minister launched a major review of education with the aim of developing a system that would improve educational opportunities and prospects for all. Prior to the '90s, education in New Zealand was highly centralised and under the control of the Department of Education. However, the review set out to achieve its objectives by creating something of a commercial market in the state educational system with schools being given increased autonomy, the freedom to set to their own rules and to spend their budget in a way that most benefits their students. To encourage each school to strive for excellence, parents have been given much more freedom of choice about which school their children attend.

Most of the changes made during the '90s have been in the primary and secondary sectors, which in the past were the responsibility of the Department of Education via regional or local authority school boards (who managed all the schools in their districts in the same way). Today these schools are mainly run by boards of trustees comprising members of staff, politicians, business people and other worthy citizens. The trustees have considerable leeway in how a school is run, but they are responsible to the Education Review Office for their actions and for meeting the standards laid down by the government. The Education Review Office monitors their progress and reports directly to the Minister of Education.

There have been many critics of educational reforms over the last ten years, although most are forced to admit that they have been largely successful. The New Zealand education system is regarded as one of the best in the world and, when ranked alongside their counterparts from other developed countries, New Zealand students often have superior levels of numeracy and literacy. Education is compulsory in New Zealand for all children between the ages of 6 and 16, although most children start school at five. The school leaving age was increased from 15 to 16 in the '80s and there are proposals to further increase it to 17. In addition to state and private school education, over 5,000 children are schooled at home, either by parents or tutors.

Enquiries about education in New Zealand should be directed to the Communications Unit, Ministry of Education, Box 1666, Wellington (☎ (04) 473 5544).

STATE OR PRIVATE SCHOOL?

If you're able to choose between state and private education, the following checklist will help you make your decision:

- How long are you planning to stay in New Zealand? If you're uncertain, it's probably better to assume a long stay. Due to language and other integration problems, enrolling a child in a New Zealand state school is advisable only for a minimum of one or two years, particularly for children who aren't native English speakers.

- Bear in mind that the area where you choose to live will affect your choice of school(s). For example, it's usually more convenient to send a child to a state school near your home, and if you choose a private day school you must take into account the distance from your home to the school.

- Do you know where you're going when you leave New Zealand? This may be an important consideration with regard to a child's language of tuition and system of education in New Zealand. How old is your child and what age will he be when you plan to leave New Zealand? What future plans do you have for his education and in which country?

- What educational level is your child at now and how will he fit into a private school or the New Zealand state school system? The younger he is, the easier it will be to place him in a suitable school.

- How does your child view the thought of studying in New Zealand? If you aren't from an English-speaking country, what language is best from a long-term point of view? Is schooling available in New Zealand in his mother tongue?

- Will your child require your help with his studies, and more importantly, will you be able to help him?

- Is special or extra tutoring available in New Zealand for other subjects, if necessary?

- What are the school hours? What are the school holiday periods? How will the school holidays and hours affect your family's work and leisure activities?

- Is religion an important aspect in your choice of school? Usually only private church-run schools offer a comprehensive religious education and are run according to religious values.

- Do you want your child to go to a co-educational or a single-sex school? New Zealand state schools are usually co-educational.

- Should you send your child to a boarding school? If so, in which country?

- What are the secondary and further education prospects in New Zealand or another country? Are New Zealand examinations or the examinations set by prospective New Zealand schools recognised in your home country or the country where you plan to live after leaving New Zealand? If applicable, check whether the New Zealand Higher School Certificate and University Bursary examinations are recognised as a university entrance qualification in your home country.

- Does a prospective school have a good academic record? Most schools provide a glowing prospectus, but also check their exam pass rate statistics.

- How large are the classes? What is the pupil-teacher ratio?

Obtain the opinions and advice of others who have been faced with the same decisions and problems as yourself, and collect as much information from as many different sources as possible before making a decision. Speak to teachers and the parents of children attending the schools on your shortlist. Finally, most parents find it pays to discuss the alternatives with their children before making a decision. See also **Choosing a Private School** on page 120120.

STATE SCHOOLS

The New Zealand state school system educates around 95 per cent of all children and is one of the government's largest expenses, consuming well over 10 per cent of the national budget. There are state schools throughout New Zealand and most children attend a day school, although around 10,000 attend state boarding schools. Many of these are children whose homes are in remote areas and for whom boarding school is the only way of receiving a full secondary education. However, state boarding schools in the cities also attract local day students due to their reputations for academic excellence. Most state schools are co-educational, including a number of single-sex schools that have opened their doors to the opposite sex in recent years, particularly in the higher grades. State schools are organised on the comprehensive system and attract students with a wide range of abilities. There's much less distinction between 'good' and 'not-so-good' schools compared to many other countries, with all schools striving to maintain and improve standards within the terms of their charter. However, as is the case in other countries, schools in wealthier areas where parents can afford to provide extra finance and support, tend to have better academic records than schools in poorer areas.

Most state schools follow a balanced curriculum based around the sciences, mathematics, the humanities, practical or vocational skills and modern languages. The study of the Maori language and culture is undertaken in all schools, although some Polynesian schools focus on this more than others. The majority of schools recognise New Zealand's strengthening links with Polynesian and Asian countries, rather than with Europe. For example, the study of Japanese (and recently Chinese) has been added to the curriculum and often replaces the study of French and German. All state schools have good sports facilities and are usually set amidst extensive sports fields, and offer a variety of sports of which (as would be expected) rugby is the most popular.

In general, the standard of teaching is high and teachers have a good reputation among their peers abroad. However, the country suffers from a shortage of qualified teachers (there are around 700 teacher vacancies at any given time) and it has been estimated that around 12,000 children in primary education don't have a permanent class teacher. The problem tends to be worse in schools in poorer areas and those with large Maori communities. To try to solve the problem the government has set up an organisation called TeachNZ offering a package of enhanced pay and benefits to tempt teachers from other countries to come and work in New Zealand, and to encourage New Zealand teachers who have gone abroad (often in search of higher salaries) to return home.

The standard of discipline is good in most state schools, although some schools in poor or ethnic areas have problems with race relations and gangs. Most schools have strict anti-violence policies where verbal or physical violence isn't tolerated, although the level of enforcement is variable. The latest threats to discipline in New Zealand schools are alcohol and drugs, which has prompted some schools to introduce drug and alcohol testing for students. Corporal punishment isn't permitted in New Zealand schools in any form (it was banned some years ago), although there have been calls to reintroduce it.

Language

To get the most out of the New Zealand educational system, students of all ages must be able to communicate in English. This is a basic requirement imposed by the government and one that's taken into account when prospective migrants apply for residence. For children whose mother tongue isn't English, most schools (at least in areas attracting a significant number of immigrants) provide extra English language tuition. However, the amount of tuition provided varies depending on the school and may be insufficient for some children. Many educationalists agree that while children in New Zealand have a similar level of ability in most subjects to children of a similar age in other English speaking countries, they are generally more advanced with regard to reading and writing than children in Australia, the UK and the USA. In many areas, children of both Maoris and other Polynesians who receive only minimal Maori tuition at school, attend Maori language 'nests' (known as *Kohanga Reo*) where they learn the Maori language and culture.

Enrolment

Parents are responsible for ensuring that their children are enrolled in the most suitable school. Finding the 'best' school is something that you'll need to do largely unaided, as there's no central body which will allocate your child to the most appropriate or best available school. Indeed, the concept of parental choice is crucial to the new 'market' that now operates in education. The Education Review Office (ERO) publishes a booklet entitled *Choosing a School for a Five Year Old*, which is available from their offices (its general principles also apply to choosing a school for older children). The ERO will also supply a list of all suitable schools in an area on request.

Parents are no longer compelled to enrol children in their nearest school, as used to be the case, and schools are now free to 'tout' for business to a certain extent. Many do this by producing a glossy prospectus and inviting prospective students and parents for an informal chat in an attempt to 'sell' their services. However, despite the freedom of choice which the system now provides, most parents find it necessary to send their children to the nearest school for the sake of convenience, and in any case in some areas there's only one primary or secondary school. There's also evidence to suggest that wealthier families have been quitting areas where schools are struggling and moving to areas with better-performing schools. The Education Review Office booklet suggests parents take into account the following criteria when choosing a school: the proximity of a school to their home, how safe it is to walk there, and where the child's siblings or friends attend school. They also suggest that parents should take into account whether a school operates individual age group or composite classes (where several age groups are taught in the same class by one teacher). Composite classes are found in some rural schools and are generally thought to be detrimental to a child's progress. Official policy apart, visiting schools and discussing their merits with parents are both highly recommended before making a decision.

School enrolments are made simply by contacting the relevant school. The Education Review Office recommends that parents take a child's last report from his current school and also examples of his work (where it's in English) to help their new teachers assess their level of ability as accurately as possible.

Details of all schools, universities and polytechnics in New Zealand are contained in a publication entitled *Excellence: NZ Education Directory*. It's published in January each year and can be purchased in bookshops in New Zealand or consulted in public libraries.

School Hours & Holidays

Schools are allowed a certain amount of freedom to set their own hours, but they are usually from 8.30 or 9am until 3.30 or 4pm, Monday to Friday. There's normally an hour's break for lunch and short breaks mid-morning and mid-afternoon. The New Zealand academic year follows the calendar year, in common with Australia, and unlike the September-July system that operates in most of Europe and North America. This system creates a frantic situation for parents and children alike, as the main school holidays, summer holiday period and the festive season are all compressed into a few short weeks. The Ministry of Education stipulate that all schools must open for a minimum period each academic year which varies from year to year, although it's usually around 394 half days for primary schools and 380 half days for secondary schools. The ministry has also declared that there must be four terms each year and sets fixed term dates for state schools throughout the country, although schools are allowed some freedom to take half-term breaks and occasional days off. Term dates vary from year to year, but are approximately:

Term	Period
1	Last week in January to the first week of April.
2	Last week in April to the first week of July.
3	Last week in July to the last week in September.
4 – Primary	Second week in October to the second week in December.
– Secondary	Second week in October to the first week in December.

Secondary schools usually close one week earlier at the end of the year, due to examinations.

Costs

Educating children can be an expensive business in any country, no less so in New Zealand. An Auckland newspaper recently reported that the cost of educating a child in New Zealand is around $25,000, assuming he starts at age five and leaves at age 16. This was considered a modest estimate for a child attending a state school where no tuition fees are charged. The cost of a private education, including tuition fees and all expenses, was reckoned to be around $180,000 for the same period. This is broadly similar to costs in other developed countries.

State schools aren't allowed to charge fees of any kind, but there are extra expenses associated with educating your children. Many schools suggest that you donate a set amount at the start of each year or term to help boost their finances. This is set by individual schools and varies from modest sums in poorer areas to larger solicitations in wealthier areas and is unlikely to be less than $150 annually. Although it's entirely voluntarily, parents may feel obligated or that they are harming their child's education if they don't contribute. If you want your child to take part in any extra-curricular activities, such as specialist sports coaching or music tuition, then you also need to allow for the cost of this. Of course schools provide a basic education in these areas, but many parents like their children to pursue extra interests. A year's tuition in a musical instrument can easily cost $1,000. In addition there are the inevitable (sometimes expensive) school trips, in which most parents wish their children to participate. Many schools organise residential trips where the entire class spends a week together studying, for example, the environment or participating in adventure sports. The cost of such a trip is likely to be at least $200 and possibly more if special clothing or equipment needs to be bought or hired.

There are some expenses which are unavoidable even in the 'free' state sector. Schools are entitled to charge for items such as text books and stationery, for which around $100 per year should be allowed (more for students studying in the higher grades). Parents are also expected to pay for school uniforms (where these are worn) and other special clothing such as sports kit. The cost of a full, new school uniform is at least $500 to $600 which, depending on how fast your child is growing, may last less than one school year. Parents on a limited budget can buy these items second-hand from local shops.

Class Grading System

With effect from the 1998 academic year, New Zealand introduced a new system of grading school years based on a 'year of schooling' system. This is similar to the system that has been used in Australia and the USA for many years and which is also becoming common in the UK. It measures the number of years a student has spent in the educational system as a whole, rather than the number of years spent in each school, as was previously the case. Students in their first year of compulsory education are classified as 'year one' and by the time they move to secondary school for their first year of secondary education, usually at age 13, they are classified as 'year nine'. Under the old system children starting secondary education were called first formers as grading was 'reset' when they moved to secondary school (or, in some cases, third formers when grading was reset when they moved to middle school two years previously at age 11). The confusion inherent in the old system is obvious and while it will take some time for the new system to settle down, it's ultimately much easier to understand. Students who start a New Zealand school after the age of six (for example those who have migrated) are allocated to the same year grade as the majority of children their age.

Students usually progress from one grade to another at the end of each academic year regardless of their level of attainment. Occasionally a student who has failed to make insufficient progress in one year may be required to repeat the previous year's study, but this is rare. If for some reason your child is absent from the New Zealand educational system for all or the major part of an academic year, the new system permits them to rejoin the same grade they were in when they left.

Early Childhood Education

A large proportion of children in New Zealand attend some kind of nursery school well before the compulsory school starting age of six, which is known as 'early childhood education'. Almost 90 per cent of four year olds attend a nursery school or similar and a smaller percentage start even earlier. Most parents expect their children to receive some sort of schooling before compulsory school age. The government has a policy of partly-funding early childhood education, which means that they subsidise the facilities but aren't committed to providing all children with free schooling. If you can afford to pay something towards the cost you can send your child to a nursery or similar school almost straight from birth and they can go to whatever establishment you choose. If you cannot afford to pay towards the cost your choice is more restricted and you may need to join a waiting list with the result that your child may not be able to begin his early childhood education until at least age four and probably not until age five.

Early childhood education is provided in various centres including kindergartens (known as 'kindys' in New Zealand), play centres, crèches, childcare centres and community playgroups. Kindergartens take children from two upwards and are usually free, although space is limited. There's a kindergarten waiting list of 10,000 in Auckland alone and it's advisable to enrol your child as soon as possible in order to secure a place. Where private kindergartens are available they are likely to charge around $700 per term. Play centres, childcare centres and community playgroups are often run by voluntary organisations or groups of parents, and are essentially free and non profit-making, but need to charge a small daily fee to cover expenses. Crèches take children at any age (from babies upwards) and tend to be more upmarket. They can, however, be quite expensive, although they are subsidised by the government providing they are registered and employ qualified staff.

Primary School

Primary schools educate children aged between five and ten. Your child is entitled to a place at primary school from age six, although many take children from age five, which is a considerable relief for parents who have been paying private kindergarten fees. Indeed, enrolling a child at age five is often the only way to ensure that by age six, when he must legally attend school, he will be able to attend the school of your choice. If you want your child to attend one of the better primary schools, it's advisable to make enquiries well in advance rather than waiting until he's almost aged six.

Primary school education in New Zealand concentrates on studying spoken and written English (reading, writing and spelling) plus maths, social studies, sciences, art, health education, music and physical education (PE). The standard of New Zealand primary reading and writing education is particularly high. Some say that this is because it still relies heavily on 'old fashioned' methods such as learning by rote and dedicating a lot of time to children reading to teachers and classroom assistants.

Primary school pupils don't wear uniforms although some schools have a school T-shirt or sweatshirt for pupils to wear on a voluntary basis, which schools sell to raise funds (try telling your kids that it's voluntary when all their friends wear them).

Intermediate School

Intermediate school caters for children aged 11 and 12 and, as the name implies, serves as a bridge between primary and secondary schools. In some country areas an intermediate school education has always been provided within the local primary school, with students not moving on to secondary school until they are almost 13. However, the latest educational trend in many areas, not just in the country, is for students to stay at primary school until age 12 and then move directly to secondary school, or even for secondary schools to take students at age 11. Whichever route is taken, students are thought to benefit as they suffer only one upheaval in their schooling in 11 years (from age 5 to 16), rather than two changes of school within two years. Students at intermediate and secondary schools wear uniforms which parents must pay for.

Intermediate school education in New Zealand concentrates on studying spoken and written languages (reading, writing and spelling) plus maths, social studies, sciences, art, health education, music and PE. The main difference compared to primary school is that subjects are taught by specialist subject teachers in their classrooms, with students rotating between them, rather than being taught all lessons by one class teacher. Also added to the curriculum are more practical skills such as wood and metalwork and domestic science.

Secondary School

At secondary school students study a core curriculum of subjects which consists of English, mathematics, social studies, general science, health and PE, music, home economics, arts and crafts. They can also choose to study other optional subjects such as history and geography, economics, and languages such as French and German or, increasingly, Japanese. Exactly what subjects a student studies is decided in conjunction with parents and teachers. There's also some variation in the range of optional subjects from school to school, with individual schools competing in the educational marketplace to offer subjects which are regarded as either beneficial to students' future careers or which are fashionable, such as information technology or Chinese. While all secondary schools must offer the balanced core curriculum, there's a tendency for some to specialise in certain areas such as business, sciences or vocational skills. This means that choosing a secondary school requires more thought and planning with regard to a child's future career than it did previously.

Examinations

The following examinations are set by schools in New Zealand:

School Certificate (SC): the school certificate is taken by most students after three years at secondary school at the age of 16. It's awarded after a written examination and students may study courses in up to six subjects, depending on their ability and interests. Surprisingly students aren't required to take the school certificate in English (although they must study it). School certificates are awarded in six grades: A1, A2, B1, B2, C1 and C2. The standard is broadly similar to Australia's School Certificate (SC), Britain's General Certificate of Secondary Education (GCSE) and the standard reached by students who graduate from tenth grade in the USA.

Sixth Form Certificate (SFC): the sixth form certificate is awarded to students after they have studied a subject at a more advanced level than school certificate for one year. Up to six subjects can be studied and English must be studied although (as for the school certificate) it isn't compulsory to take an exam in this subject. Grades are issued ranging from one to nine, with one being the highest.

Higher School Certificate (HSC): the higher school certificate is awarded to pupils who have studied an advanced course for two years in at least three subjects (the choice of subjects is decided by students). It's similar in standard to the HSC in Australia, Britain's 'A levels' and that required to graduate from twelfth grade in the USA.

University Bursaries Examination (UBE): the university bursaries examination is for students wishing to go to university, where a successful pass may provide not only a place on a student's chosen course, but also a scholarship.

PRIVATE SCHOOLS

New Zealand has a flourishing private school sector, although it serves only some 5 per cent of the school population. In recent years a number of state schools have effectively become private schools, as the government now gives greater autonomy to state schools which has encouraged them to join the commercial market and sell themselves more positively. Private schools range from nursery (kindergarten) schools to large day and boarding (high) schools, from traditional-style schools to those offering 'alternative' education such as Montessori and Rudolf Steiner schools. They include schools sponsored by churches and religious groups (parochial), educational foundations and private individuals, and schools for students with learning or physical disabilities and for gifted children. In addition to mainstream parochial (e.g. Catholic) schools, there are also schools for religious and ethnic minorities, for example Muslims, where there's a strict code regarding the segregation of boys and girls.

Most private schools are single sex, although some have become co-educational in recent years. There are also boarding schools in New Zealand, although few schools accept boarders only and many accommodate both day students and boarders. Children who board usually do so because they live too far from school to travel every day or because their parents are working overseas.

Most private schools provide a similar curriculum to state schools and set the same examinations. However, some private schools offer the International Baccalaureate (IB) examination, an internationally recognised university entrance qualification, which may be an important consideration if you intend to remain in New Zealand only for a limited period.

Fees vary considerably depending on a variety of factors including the age of students, the reputation and quality of the school, and its location (schools in major cities are usually the most expensive). Private schools receive some funding from the government, although most of their spending is financed from fees paid by parents. The average fee for borders is around $4,500 per term. Some schools offer reduced fees to parents with two or more children attending a school. To the fees must be added another $2,000 or so a year for uniforms, books, building levies, special equipment (e.g. for sports), excursion charges, computers and assorted surcharges.

The advantages of private schools are many-fold, not least their excellent academic record, which is generally better than those of state schools. Don't, however, send your child to a school with high academic standards unless you're sure that he will be able to handle the pressure. Many private schools have resolutely embraced new technology and the use of computers and the internet are widespread. Don't, however, assume that all private schools are excellent or that they all offer a better education than state schools, which isn't true.

Private schools place the emphasis on traditional teaching including hard work, good manners, consideration for others, responsibility, and not least, a sense of discipline (values which are sadly lacking in some state schools). They provide a broad-based education (aimed at developing a pupil's character) and generally provide a more varied approach to sport, music, drama, art, and a wider choice of academic subjects than state schools. Their aim is more the development of the child as an individual and the encouragement of his unique talents, rather than teaching on a production-line system (as is often the case in state schools). This is made possible by small classes (an average of around 15 to 20 pupils or as little as half that of some state schools) which allows teachers to provide pupils with individually tailored lessons and tuition. Private schools are also better equipped to cater for special needs including gifted children; slow learners or those who suffer from dyslexia; children who benefit from a single-sex school; those requiring boarding facilities; and children whose parents want them to be educated in the customs of a particular religious belief.

Make applications to private schools as far in advance as possible (before conception for the best schools). Obviously if you have just arrived in New Zealand, you won't be able to apply one or two years in advance, which is generally considered to be the best time to book a place. However, if you plan to send your children to private school, you should start planning well in advance, if possible long before arriving in New Zealand. The best and most popular schools have a demanding selection procedure and long waiting lists (perhaps many years), and parents register a child for entry at birth at some schools. Don't rely on enrolling your child in a particular school and neglect the alternatives, particularly if your preferred school has a rigorous entrance examination. When applying you're usually requested to send previous school reports, exam results and records. Before enrolling your child in a private school, make sure that you understand the withdrawal conditions in the school contract.

Choosing a Private School

The following checklist is designed to help you choose an appropriate private school in New Zealand:

- Does the school have a good reputation? How long has it been established?

- Does the school have a good academic record? For example, what percentage of students obtain good examination passes and go on to university? All the best schools provide exam pass-rate statistics.

- What does the curriculum include? What examinations are set? Are examinations recognised both in New Zealand and internationally? Do they fit in with your future education plans? Ask to see a typical student timetable to check the ratio of academic to non-academic subjects. Check the number of free study periods and whether they are supervised.

- How large are the classes and what's the student/teacher ratio? Does the stated class size tally with the number of desks in the classrooms?

- What are the classrooms like? For example their size, space, cleanliness, lighting, furniture, furnishings and equipment such as computers. Are there signs of creative teaching, e.g. wall charts, maps, posters and pupils' work on display?

- What are the qualification requirements for teachers? What nationalities are the majority of teachers? Ask for a list of the teaching staff and their qualifications.

- What is the teacher turnover? A high teacher turnover is a bad sign and may suggest inadequately paid teachers with poor working conditions.

- What extras must you pay for? For example, lunches, art supplies, sports equipment, outings, clothing, health and accident insurance, text books and stationery. Most schools charge parents for absolutely everything.
- Which countries do most students come from?
- Is religion an important consideration in your choice of school?
- What provision is available for children whose mother tongue isn't English?
- What standard and kind of accommodation is provided? What is the quality and variety of food provided? What is the dining room like? Does the school have a dietician?
- What languages does the school teach as obligatory or optional subjects? Does the school have a language laboratory? (Some private schools focus on French and German which are of minimal use in New Zealand, whereas state schools are tending to teach Asian languages which students may find more useful in their future lives.)
- What is the student turnover?
- What are the school terms and holiday periods?
- If you're considering a day school, what are the school hours? Is transport provided to and from school?
- What are the withdrawal conditions, should you need or wish to remove your child? A term's notice is usual.
- What sports instruction and facilities are provided? Where are the sports facilities located?
- What are the facilities for art and science subjects, for example, arts and crafts, music, computer studies, biology, science, hobbies, drama, cookery and photography? Ask to see the classrooms, facilities, equipment and some students' projects.
- What sort of outings and school trips are organised?
- What medical facilities does the school provide, e.g. infirmary, resident doctor or nurse? Is medical and accident insurance included in the fees?
- What punishments are applied and for what offences? Private schools are likely to be strict, although corporal punishment is forbidden.
- What reports are provided for parents and how often?
- Last but not least, unless someone else is paying, what are the fees?

Before making a final choice, it's important to visit the schools on your shortlist during term time and talk to teachers and students (if possible, also speak to former students and their parents). Where possible, check out the answers to the above questions in person and don't rely on a school's prospectus or principal to provide the information. If you're unhappy with the answers, look elsewhere. Finally, having made your choice, keep a check on your child's progress and listen to his complaints. Compare notes with other parents. If something doesn't seem right, try to establish whether the complaint is founded or not, and if it is, take action to have the problem resolved. Never forget that you or your employer are paying a lot of money for your child's education and you should ensure that you receive good value. See also **State or Private School?** on page 120.

APPRENTICESHIPS

A system of apprenticeships operates in New Zealand, where it's usually known as 'industry training'. This is an arrangement between an employee and an employer which allows the employee to undergo a period of training that meets industry standards. Currently there are some 45,000 people undertaking industry training throughout the country. There's no rigid format to industry training, which is offered by both large and small employers, but by no means all employers. Some employers provide on the job training whereas others provide training both in the workplace and at a polytechnic or other college. The range of industry training options is being widened and made more flexible in order to suit the needs of different employees and employers, e.g. the sports, fitness and recreation industry has recently introduced standards for industry training and has enrolled over 1,000 new trainees.

HIGHER EDUCATION

Higher and further education are known as post-compulsory education in New Zealand. Higher education is provided by 7 universities, 25 polytechnics and a number of colleges of education specialising in teacher training. Higher education institutions in the country are expected to operate on a 'free market' basis and compete with one another for students. They are funded partly by student fees and partly by government funding, which is allocated according to student numbers rather than on the basis of need. It's possible that direct government funding may cease entirely in future and be replaced by a student voucher scheme. Under this scheme students would receive vouchers from the government to pay for their tuition and this will be the only way in which universities and colleges would receive government finance.

Universities: universities are the most prestigious educational establishments in New Zealand. They include the University of Auckland, the University of Waikato (located at Hamilton), Massey University (at Palmerston North), Victoria University (Wellington), University of Canterbury and Lincoln University (both at Christchurch), and the University of Otago at Dunedin. All universities offer a wide choice of courses, although each tends to have certain specialities in which it's regarded as a 'centre of excellence' for that subject. For example, the University of Otago specialises in medicine, dentistry, surveying, home science, physical education (PE) and pharmacy, and Lincoln University specialises in agriculture and horticulture. The University of Auckland specialises in architecture, planning, engineering, medicine, optometry and art, and the University of Canterbury in engineering, fine art and forestry. Victoria University is the main centre for public administration and social work, whereas Massey University is well known for agriculture and horticulture, and also produces most of New Zealand's veterinary surgeons.

No university is regarded as better or worse than any other, although a degree from a university that's a centre of excellence in a subject is more highly valued than a degree from a university which isn't. Auckland is the largest university in terms of student numbers (22,000) and offers the widest range of courses. It's also more cosmopolitan whereas the others are, both geographically and intellectually, more provincial. Degree programmes last for three or four years for an honours course. Entry requirements depend on the individual course and some of the most prestigious courses such as medicine demand nothing less than the best grades. Each university handles its own admissions and most distribute an enrolment pack in the first week of September. Applications must be submitted by the end of the first week of December at the latest (the date usually coincides with the end of the secondary school term).

Student Finances: higher education in New Zealand isn't provided free and students must pay tuition fees which go towards funding their course of study and also support themselves during their studies. The fee for the least expensive standard, full-time course is around $2,500 per year, although specialist courses (such as medicine) cost substantially more. Basic living expenses (including accommodation and food) are unlikely to be less than $200 per week, in addition to the cost of books, transport and entertainment.

Very few students are fortunate enough to have parents who can afford to pay all their expenses (although most parents who can afford to help out) or are able to find jobs to finance their studies. Students whose family income (or own income if they are 25 or over) is less than $27,800 per year may apply for a grant known as a student allowance, which covers some (but not all) of the cost of their education. As this is a relatively modest income limit in New Zealand terms, most students don't qualify. As a result, most students obtain a student loan to finance the difference between their or their parents' contribution and their tuition fees and living expenses. The gap is set to increase further in the next few years, as many universities are planning to drastically increased their fees. New Zealand introduced a system of student loans in 1992 which allows students to borrow up to $10,500. Since they were introduced some 215,000 students have taken advantage of loans, with an average loan to be repaid from future income of $8,000 (although many students owe $20,000 or more). Universities offer a number of scholarships to promising students, although the number is limited and few students can depend on these to finance their studies. The government is also working on a plan which in future may see students being paid a 'wage' similar to the amount paid in unemployment benefit.

There are four elements to a student loan: a contribution towards compulsory fees, course related costs (such as books), living costs and an administration fee. To qualify for a loan, students must be studying a course that's either funded by the Ministry of Education or recognised as a qualifying course. The latter category refers to courses run by private organisations, rather than state colleges and universities, which must consist of either full or part-time study for at least one year. Students can usually take out a loan for living costs even if the course they are studying isn't funded by the Ministry of Education. Those who receive a student allowance can also apply for a student loan (indeed they usually need to), but aren't entitled to the part of the loan that applies to living costs. Factors such as age, income, parental income and credit rating don't affect your entitlement to a loan, nor is it necessary to provide security or a guarantee.

If the financial situation for New Zealand students isn't all that promising, then it's much worse for foreign students who don't qualify for a student loan (loans are restricted to New Zealand citizens or permanent residents). If you don't qualify for a loan you're also charged much higher fees by universities and colleges.

Polytechnics: while universities specialise in academic study, polytechnics tend to specialise in applied studies. They don't compete directly with universities, although some subjects (e.g. accountancy) can be studied at both university and a polytechnic. Polytechnics tend to offer diploma or certificate courses rather than degrees and provide mainly short courses or courses for those who are already in work and wish to study part-time.

The university and polytechnic academic year runs from February until November. All universities provide accommodation in halls of residence for a proportion of students, either on campus or nearby, although many students live in shared houses or live as boarders in private homes. Given their financial situation, it's much more cost-effective for students to live at home with their parents, although few choose to do so.

Postgraduate Studies: all universities offer facilities for postgraduate study, usually within their subjects of speciality only. Students ·who climb this far up the academic ladder are rewarded by much lower tuition fees for postgraduate courses than for first degrees. This reflects the contribution that postgraduate studies make towards a university's reputation and prestige. It's also common for New Zealand students to undertake postgraduate studies at foreign universities, usually in Australia, the UK or the USA, particularly when their area of expertise isn't well catered for in New Zealand. Foreign postgraduate students are also welcomed at New Zealand universities and are offered the same favourable rates as local students.

FURTHER EDUCATION

It's official government policy that New Zealanders are encouraged to study and learn at all stages of their lives. A keystone of the government's further education programme is the Adult Open Learning Service (AOLS) which is provided by The Correspondence School in Wellington. The Correspondence School was established in the 1920s and is something of a New Zealand institution. It provides correspondence courses catering for adults wishing to gain qualifications in order to get a job or those who just want to improve their academic ability, and is taken by people in towns and cities as well as those in rural areas. The school offers over 200 courses and around 7,000 students are enrolled at any one time. It's manned by a team of student advisors and clerks who offer pre-enrolment advice, course counselling and student support. Students receive tuition by means of written courses, by telephone and at seminars. There are academic, vocational and general interest courses, including the full range of secondary school subjects, as well as more practical and general interest courses. Course fees range from $40 to $80. For information contact the Adult Open Learning Service, The Correspondence School, Private Bag 39992, Wellington (fax (04) 499 4000).

LANGUAGE SCHOOLS

If you don't speak English fluently (or you wish to learn another language) you can enrol in a language course at one of the many language schools in New Zealand. Many languages are spoken in New Zealand, so there's plenty of opportunity to learn and practice foreign languages with immigrants. Obtaining a working knowledge or becoming fluent in English while living in New Zealand is relatively easy, as you'll be constantly immersed in the English language and will have the maximum opportunity to practise. However, if you wish to speak or write English fluently, you'll probably need to attend a language school or find a private tutor. Note that it's usually necessary to have a recognised qualification in English to be accepted at a college of higher or further education in Australia.

English-language courses are offered at all levels by universities; language schools; migrant education colleges; foreign and international organisations; local associations and clubs; private colleges; open learning institutions; and private teachers. Classes range from language courses for complete beginners, through to special business or cultural courses and university-level seminars leading to recognised diplomas. There are language schools in all cities and large towns in New Zealand, many equipped with computers, language laboratories, video studios, libraries and bookshops.

Most language schools offer a variety of classes depending on your current ability, how many hours you wish to study a week, how much money you want to spend and how quickly you wish to learn. Full-time, part-time and evening courses are offered by most schools, and many also offer residential courses or accommodation with local families (highly recommended to accelerate learning). Courses that include accommodation (often half board, consisting of breakfast and an evening meal) usually offer good value for money. Bear in mind that if you need to find your own accommodation, particularly in Wellington or Auckland, it can be difficult and expensive. Language classes generally fall into the following categories:

Category	Number of. hours a week
compact	10 to 20
intensive	20 to 30
total immersion	30 to 40+

Most schools offer compact or intensive courses and also provide special courses for businessmen and professionals (among others), and a wide variety of examinations, most of which are recognised internationally. Course fees vary considerably and are usually calculated on a weekly basis. Fees depend on the number of hours tuition per week, the type of course, and the location and reputation of the school. Expect to pay up to $500 a week for an intensive course providing 20 to 30 hours of language study per week and around $300 a week for a compact course.

Total immersion or executive courses are provided by some schools and usually consist of private lessons for a minimum of 30 to 40 hours a week. Fees can run to $2,000 or more a week and not everyone is suited to learning at such a fast rate (or has the financial resources). Whatever language you're learning, don't expect to become fluent in a short period unless you have a particular flair for languages or already have a good command of a language. Unless you desperately need to learn a language quickly, it's better to arrange your lessons over a long period. Don't commit yourself to a long course of study (particularly an expensive one) before ensuring that it's the correct one. Most schools offer a free introductory lesson and free tests to help you find your appropriate level. Many language schools offer private and small group lessons. **It's important to choose the right course, particularly if you're studying English in order to continue with full-time education in New Zealand and need to reach a minimum standard or gain a particular qualification.**

For an introduction to language in New Zealand see page 34

10.

PUBLIC TRANSPORT

Despite being a country with its population dispersed over a wide area, New Zealand has a good public transport service centred around road, rail and air links, plus the essential umbilical ferry link connecting the North and the South Islands. Unless you live in a remote country area you shouldn't find it too difficult to get around without your own transport. Probably the most impressive feature of public transport is that the different elements are closely integrated and if you start a journey by bus, continue by rail and then take to the air, you'll usually find that services are planned and timed to connect. However, car ownership and usage in New Zealand is still high, which shouldn't be taken as a sign that public transport is unreliable (although it does have a few shortcomings, such as finishing too early in many cases), but rather that the roads are relatively uncongested and therefore that driving still has many advantages over public transport. Even in metropolitan Auckland and Wellington, commuters travelling into the centre often drive as the relatively modest rush hour traffic hasn't induced them to let the bus or train take the strain.

Disabled Travellers: like many countries, New Zealand has only started to take access for the disabled seriously within the last decade. The law now requires that all new building and redevelopment projects incorporates 'reasonable and adequate' access for disabled people. There are, however, still a lot of old public buildings in New Zealand which cannot be modified for practical or aesthetic reasons. Commercial operators tend to be more forward thinking and most leisure attractions provide disabled access, and hotels and motels are required to provide at least a few units with wheelchair access. Domestic airlines and trains cater fully for disabled travellers, but you should tell them that you need special assistance when booking. As most taxis are simply converted saloon cars you can use them only if you can gain access to a standard car. There are wheelchair-accessible taxis in cities, although you need to book in advance (particularly for the return journey) as their number is limited. There are no special facilities for the disabled on coach and bus services.

TRAINS

New Zealand's rail network is privatised and operated by a consortium which includes American owners. It's operated by NZ Rail under the name Tranz Rail, or Tranz Scenic for the more picturesque services aimed at leisure travellers. The network is limited due mainly to the difficult terrain in many parts of the country and, of course, the fact the lines cannot cross the Cook Straits (until they build a bridge or tunnel). The service itself is modern and comfortable (part of the Auckland-Wellington line has recently been electrified), but neither frequent or fast. As a result, rail services are widely promoted as a tourist attraction rather than a day-to-day amenity. In this regard the rail service is excellent as many lines pass through native forests, past volcanic peaks and through alpine passes giving spectacular, panoramic views. NZ Rail is criticised by New Zealanders for its disorganisation and timekeeping, although foreigners rarely seem to complain. There are eight main railway routes are:

The Geyserland	Auckland-Rotorua
The Overland	Auckland-Wellington
The Northerner	Auckland-Wellington (Overnight service)
The Bay Express	Wellington-Napier
The Southerner	Christchurch-Invercargill
The Coastal Pacific	Christchurch-Picton
Tranz Alpine	Christchurch-Greymouth
The Southerner	Christchurch-Dunedin

The Tranz Rail timetable is simple as there's only one train a day on most services, with the exception of Auckland-Roturua where there are three daily return services and Auckland-Wellington where there are two. Special day return excursions run on the Tranz Alpine as it's a popular tourist trip. Most services commence their outward journey between 8 and 8.30am each morning, so if you sleep in you'll have to wait until the next day or catch the bus instead!

Fares range from $47 for the cheapest rail trip (Auckland-Rotorua) to $103 for the most expensive (Auckland-Wellington). There's only one class of travel whichever service you choose. If you're a student, an International Youth Hostel Association (IYHA) member or over 60 you qualify for a 30 per cent discount. You need an ID card, membership card, pension book or passport as proof and must book in advance.

All services provide free refreshments with a free lunch on the Overlander service, although there are also buffet cars selling more substantial meals and a bar on all services except the Northerner. All trains have guided tourist commentaries (whether you're a tourist or not). If you wish to take a bicycle on a train check when booking, as they aren't allowed on many services and only limited space is available when they are. Smokers may also have a tough time travelling by train in New Zealand as smoking isn't permitted on any train, even though some of the journeys can take ten hours or more.

Train Information: enquiries about services and a copy of the latest timetable can be obtained from travel agents, Tranz Rail travel centres or by calling freephone (0800) 802802. As the sole daily departure on most routes changes by just a matter of minutes from year to year, you'll soon have committed the timetable to memory if you're a regular train traveller. A copy of the timetable can be obtained from Tranz Rail, PO Box 12440, Wellington.

Buying Tickets: the easiest way to book a trip by train is to call Tranz Rail on freephone (0800) 802802 and pay by credit card, although you can also book at travel agents (a booking is fee is charged) or free at stations. If you 'accidentally' travel on a train without a ticket (or with an invalid ticket or pass) you must pay the full fare plus a modest surcharge, but you won't be made to get off the train in the middle of nowhere!

Season & Special Tickets: given the limited nature of the rail system, there are no season or special tickets on Tranz Rail. If you expect to do a lot of travelling you should consider buying a travelpass (see page 147) which allows you to travel on trains, coaches and the Interislander ferry. Another option used by some travellers is to purchase a YHA card costing $99 for 28 days, which although it isn't a travel pass, allows you a 50 per cent discount on all Tranz Rail services.

Sleeping Services: the only sleeping service in New Zealand is the overnight 'Overlander' service between Auckland and Wellington which operates each night except Saturday. The Wellington bound service leaves Auckland at 8.40pm each evening, arriving in Wellington at 7.35am. The Auckland bound service leaves Wellington at 7.45pm, arriving at its destination at 6.45am. It isn't a true sleeper service as there are no sleeper cars (passengers doze in the regular seats), but it's around 25 per cent cheaper than the daytime service (you aren't charged anything for the free overnight 'accommodation').

Stations: Tranz Rail stations have few facilities. This is mainly because, in many cases, there's only one arrival or departure a day and hence no call for buffets, bars and the range of other services you usually find at major railway stations. There's an enquiry office open from before the first train leaves (or at least 7.30am) until 5.30pm for information and reservations. Taxis and buses don't stop at stations throughout the day, but tend to congregate there as each train arrives. This means you may have to wait in a queue although you're unlikely to be left stranded as the thoughtful transport authorities usually arrange a connecting bus service timed to meet the last train. Stations aren't always conveniently situated for city centres, for example Auckland's is on Beach Road a 15 minute walk from the city centre, and isn't on a regular bus route. Wellington's is on Waterloo Quay on the edge of the central area, located near one of the city's bus stations and served by the city's commuter railway services (it's also connected by shuttle bus to the Interislander ferry terminal).

METRO/COMMUTER RAILWAY SERVICES

There are no underground or 'metro' services anywhere in New Zealand. There's a fast and reliable commuter rail network in Wellington known as Tranz Metro, although it doesn't run underground. One line runs from the railway station to Waiarapa and another runs to Palmerston North. Tranz Rail has recently purchased around 60 carriages from Britain which are to be refurbished and used on these and other services, although no official announcement has been made as to whether this injection of British Rail technology will make the service better or worse! Timetable and fare information can be obtained from Tranz Metro (☎ (04) 498 3000, ext. 44933).

BUSES & TRAMS

Most towns and cities have a good public bus service and some cities operate double-decker buses, with both upstairs and downstairs seating areas, which are common in Britain but rare in most other countries. Bus services have been deregulated and privatised to some extent in recent years, although in many cases the original public bus company is still the largest operator on a majority of routes. In Auckland, the main operator is Auckland Regional Council (ARC), whose buses are bright yellow. One of the drawbacks of the public bus service is that it ends early and on Saturdays and Sundays the last services leave at around 5pm. Even during the week in Auckland and Wellington you won't find a bus running after 11.30pm (many routes finish much earlier) and some routes are discontinued altogether at weekends. This is why many city dwellers have a car, which is an attractive option given that New Zealand has little serious congestion compared with most other countries.

One benefit of bus deregulation is that small private firms and taxi operators have been allowed to enter the public transport business, and many operate services late into the evening and at weekends when the main operators have suspended their services. Some services, using minibuses and cars, can be ordered by phone when required. As several companies now operate in most towns there's no centralised place to obtain timetable information. Check your telephone directory for details of where to obtain information about services and a copy of the timetable. In larger cities there's more than one bus station serving the different companies and routes. In Wellington the main stations are at Waterloo Quay and Courtenay Place. In Auckland, buses use the Downtown and Midtown terminals (although Midtown is only a series of lay-bys rather than a proper terminal). The buses themselves are usually driver-operated and you buy your ticket from the driver as you enter the bus. Some buses accept the exact fare only.

Bus Fares: fares for town bus services are calculated on a zonal basis and depend on how many zones you travel through. In Auckland, a journey within the central zone costs 40¢ and a journey to the furthest zone $7. In Wellington, the shortest journey costs $1 and the longest $2.70 (mainly because the distances aren't so great). Most areas offer daily and weekly passes, which work out much cheaper if you plan to do a lot of travelling by bus. The cheapest pass in Auckland costs $8, while in Wellington a daytripper pass costs $6.50. In both cases you cannot begin your journey until 9am Monday to Friday, although there are no restrictions at weekends. In Christchurch an 'All Day Bus Pass' giving unlimited travel costs $5 per person or $10 for a family of four.

Trams: trams operate in several cities in New Zealand including Wellington (although called trolley buses), where they operate on several routes in the inner city and central suburbs. The cost is the same as for buses and the daytripper pass issued for buses can also be used on trams. Wellington also has a cable car operating between Lambton Quay and the Botanic Gardens in Kelburn. This is a popular tourist attraction, but is also used daily by commuters as it's an easy way to travel up one of Wellington's steepest hills. Trams operate on a city centre loop in Christchurch, stopping at nine points along the way, and mostly attract tourists but are handy for commuters and shoppers in the city centre. You can buy a one hour, half day or full day ticket from the conductor on board (the service operates between 9am and 6pm).

COACHES

New Zealand has a comprehensive and reliable long-distance coach service, which is the main way of travelling long distances for those who don't have a car or who cannot afford or don't want to fly. Three companies have carved up most of the trunk services between them. InterCity Coachlines is a subsidiary of NZ Rail operating countrywide and serving over a thousand destinations. Consequently the service is much more comprehensive and useful than its parent company's rail service. Newmans is their main competitor in the North Island and Mount Cook operate in the South Island. There are also around a dozen smaller companies such as Pioneer Coachlines and Murphy Turley Buses, who operate their own services but mainly provide services on a sub-contract basis for InterCity.

Reservations: it's usually possible to just turn up and travel by coach except at busy times such as summer and public holiday periods. However, if you know when you want to travel it makes sense to book as it costs no extra when booking direct. The direct reservations telephone numbers are: InterCity Coachlines (Auckland (09) 357

8400) or Christchurch (03) 379 9020), Mount Cook (0800 800737) and Newmans (0800 733500). You can also book at InterCity Travel Centres in the main towns or with a travel agent (when you're charged a $3 booking fee). Reservations can be made up to six months in advance.

Fares: coaches are the cheapest way of travelling long distance in New Zealand. For example, the standard one way adult fare from Auckland to Wellington is $96 (around ten hours), Rotorua to Wellington $75 (eight hours) and Picton to Christchurch $55 (6 hours 15 minutes). Special offers are available when travelling at off-peak times. If you're travelling from the North to the South Island or vice versa, it's worth noting that the Interislander ferry fare isn't included in the price and you need to pay separately for the North and South Island legs of your trip (although you can book them together and services are timed to connect). Each of the main coach lines offers its own travel pass allowing unlimited travel for a set period. InterCity Coachlines offer them on a zonal basis or allow you to combine any two passes into a 'combo' pass. If you want to combine coach and train travel, then a travelpass comes into its own (see page 147).

Timetables: you can obtain a copy of coach timetables from InterCity Travel centres (for InterCity Coachlines), which are found in every city and large town, Visitor Information Network (VIN) centres or by calling the numbers given above (under reservations). Coach timetables, like all public transport in New Zealand, use the am/pm time system rather than the 24-hour clock. When booking take note of exactly where your service operates from, which will depend on the coach company and isn't necessarily the same location from where local city buses depart. In Wellington, Newmans' services operate from the Interislander ferry terminal while InterCity services operate from near the railway station. In Auckland, InterCity services depart from Hobson Street whereas Newmans operate from Quay Street.

Coach services, even of competing companies, are well co-ordinated so that they connect, not only with other coach services, but also with other modes of transport. So, for example, if you take the train from Auckland to Wellington, the Interislander ferry across the Cook Strait and then a coach to Christchurch, it's possible to plan a route which connects smoothly allowing just enough time to get from one terminus to another. Unlike the train, there are several coach services a day on the main routes such as Auckland-Wellington.

Children under four travel free if they don't occupy a seat and there are reduced fares for children aged between 5 and 15. A reduced fee is also charged for under fives if they take a seat, which is probably worth paying on a long journey. You can take one large and one medium size suitcase per person on coach services, although exceeding this allowance costs no more assuming that there's room. Bicycles can be carried for a flat fee of $10 per journey, regardless of the length of the trip (you must remove the pedals and cover the chain with newspaper).

Modern coaches such as Volvo and MAN are used and provide facilities such as washrooms, reclining seats and air conditioning. On routes that are popular with tourists the driver usually provides a commentary on sights and places of interest. On services operating in more remote areas, you may find that half the coach is given over to freight and parcels. Snacks and drinks aren't available on board coaches but they stop regularly for refreshments, although drivers tend to choose the more expensive places (so it pays to take your own snacks with you). Smoking isn't permitted on coach services.

Backpackers' Buses: an economical way of travelling for young people are backpacker's buses which operate throughout New Zealand (similar to those in Australia). Backpacker's buses are operated by a number of companies, of which New Zealand Experience is the most well known. Services operate on a pass basis whereby once you have bought a ticket you can switch between buses and stop off along the route, whether for a few hours or a few days. Sporting and adventure activities are also sometimes offered along the way, such as white-water rafting or kayaking. These services tend to be cheap and cheerful and aimed at those aged between 18 and 35. A ticket between Auckland and Wellington for travel over two days costs $65 and is the cheapest way of travelling between these two cities. The Auckland-Wellington overnight train service costs around the same (after a student or YHA discount), but of course you cannot stop off along the way and you won't be able to watch the scenery pass by (unless you have excellent night vision).

FERRIES

As a country consisting mainly of two large islands, New Zealand is highly reliant on ferry services between the two. The Interislander ferry service is highly efficient and employs two roll-on roll-off ferries most of the year, the Arahura and the Aratika, which carry passengers, vehicles and rail wagons. They cross the Cook Strait, the stretch of water separating the North and South Island, sailing from Wellington in the North Island to Picton in the South Island in around three hours. The actual ferry journey is 96km/60mi although the Straits are only 20km/12mi wide at their narrowest point. A new ferry, the Aratere, is scheduled to replace the Aratika over the next year. The Arahanga, a freight vessel, also operates across the Straits.

Timetables: the number of daily sailings varies between summer and winter. In summer (December to April) there are five daily sailings (but only four on Sundays and Mondays), but in winter the service is usually reduced to two or three crossings per day as one of the vessels is taken out of service for maintenance. Summer timetables vary only slightly from year to year: ships leave Wellington at 1.30am, 9.30am, 2.30pm, 5.30pm and 10.30pm and Picton at 5.30am, 10.30am, 1.30pm, 6.30pm and 9.30pm.

Bookings: it isn't essential to book ahead for the Interislander ferry except at busy times, such as the beginning of school holidays, although it's cheaper as discounted tickets can only be purchased in advance. If you turn up without a ticket you must pay the full fare, even if you travel off-peak. Reservations can be made at any Tranz Rail appointed travel agent or by calling freephone (0800) 802802. The standard single fare is $44 for adults and $160 for a vehicle up to 6.6m in length. Discounts range from between 15 and 60 per cent depending on the time of travel and the availability of discounted tickets.

Ferry Terminals: the Interislander ferry departs from the dedicated Inter-island Terminal in Wellington and the Inter-island Terminal in Picton, both of which are well signposted. There are terminal buildings at both terminals where tickets can be purchased and where foot passengers can check in their luggage for the journey rather than carry it on board. There are also car parks and car hire facilities and if you have a hire car or are staying on the other island for a short time only, it's cheaper to leave your car on one island and hire another on the next island. A free bus service (the Interislander Shuttle Bus) runs between Wellington railway station and the Inter-island terminal, leaving platform nine 35 minutes before ferry sailings. A return bus departs from the Inter-island terminal and arrives at the railway station in time to catch the evening Northerner train to Auckland. At Picton, shuttle buses operate from the Inter-island terminal to the station and return to meet the arrival and departure of trains, which run directly to Christchurch.

The latest check-in time is 30 minutes prior to departure for foot passengers and one hour for those with vehicles. Foot passengers may take only two pieces of luggage weighing a maximum of 30kg and no more than 200 linear centimetres in size (a combination of the height, width and breadth). There are extra charges for excess luggage, bicycles, canoes and wind-surfers, unless they can be dismantled. Prominent notices at the terminals also state that 'Excess Charges Are Involved for Lawnmowers', so it pays to think twice before taking your lawnmower on holiday with you. Pets travel free in vehicles, but otherwise a charge is made for use of on-board kennels as they cannot be taken on deck (if you're travelling during school holidays you may wish a similar facility was available for children!).

Interislander ferries are well equipped, which is just as well given the length of the crossing, and include a cinema, telephones, several bars, children's nursery and play areas, Visitor Information Network (VIN) centres and a number of eating places including fast food outlets. There are also fruit machines, something of a novelty in a country where gambling is so tightly controlled. For a supplement you can also use the club class lounge which provides free drinks and snacks, newspapers and an oasis of peace away from the bustle of the ship (children under 18 aren't permitted!).

Other Services: in addition to the Interislander there are several smaller ferry services linking up the islands, particularly in Auckland's Hauraki Gulf (e.g. operated by Fuller's – for a copy of their timetable and details of fares ☎ (09) 367 9111). As few of these islands have a large population, ferries mainly attract tourists.

The Lynx: during the summer months (December to April), Tranz Rail also operate a futuristic high speed ferry between Wellington and Picton. There are three crossings each day for foot passengers and cars, taking 1 hour 45 minutes. The standard single fare is $59 for adults and $190 for cars, although it's possible to obtain discounted tickets at off-peak times and by booking in advance. Foot passengers don't usually require a reservation, but if you want to take a car at busy periods (December to February and public holidays) it's advisable to make one. You can make a Lynx reservation at any travel agent or by calling Tranz Rail direct on freephone (0800) 802802. British travellers in New Zealand may feel strangely at home when travelling on the Lynx, as the vessel shuttles to the other side of the world in the New Zealand winter and spends its time ferrying holidaymakers across the English Channel. An additional fast ferry service, which will operate year round, is expected to start operation within the next few years.

TAXIS

Taxis are plentiful in most cities and towns in New Zealand. They are usually ordinary saloon cars (or minibuses) painted in distinctive colours, which vary depending on the town or city. You can pick one up at a taxi rank or order one by telephone. Taxis cannot be hailed in the street and will pick you up only if they are already stopping to let the last passenger out (but you had better be quick!). All taxi fares are metered and rates work out at around 40¢ to 50¢ per minute or $20 to $25 per hour. You pay the amount showing on the meter only and aren't expected to tip (Americans please note!). An extra charge is made for telephone bookings, items of luggage, and when travelling during the evening and at weekends, when taxis are most in demand due to the curtailment of bus services.

AIRLINE SERVICES

Air travel is a popular form of domestic travel in New Zealand, but it certainly isn't cheap. Domestic air fares are on a par with European scheduled services (i.e. expensive) and nothing like as good value for money as US services. In spite of this, New Zealanders travel by air as frequently as possible (or as frequently as they can afford) as it's by far the fastest way to cross the country.

Airlines: New Zealand is served by some 25 international airlines, most of which fly to Auckland or Christchurch. New Zealand's main domestic airline (and also its international airline) is Air New Zealand, previously state owned but now privatised, which is regularly acclaimed as one of the world's best airlines. It has a comprehensive route network operating over 3,000 individual flights throughout the country each week. It's domestic services are sold under the name of 'ANZ National' (major domestic routes) or 'ANZ Link' flights (minor domestic routes).

Air New Zealand's only significant competitor is Ansett·New Zealand, a subsidiary of the Australian airline of the same name. Ansett New Zealand operates quiet BAe146 whisper jets and competes with Air New Zealand on a comprehensive network, although flights linking Auckland, Wellington and Christchurch are its mainstay. Mount Cook Airlines also operate domestic services, although it's a partner airline to Air New Zealand (operating services on their behalf) rather than a real competitor. A number of other competitors have started up or been proposed over the years, including the aptly named Kiwi Air (or inappropriately named considering the kiwi is a flightless bird!), although most have fallen by the wayside. Many domestic services provide in-flight bar facilities, which is a relatively new innovation in New Zealand where the sale of alcohol is strictly licensed. Smoking isn't permitted on the domestic services of any airline. Surprisingly, however, the health-conscious New Zealanders haven't banned that other risk to the well-being of air travellers – airline food!

Fares: Air New Zealand's services were notoriously expensive until Ansett arrived on the scene a few years ago, which prompted more competitive pricing (wonderful thing, competition). However, standard fares are still high and it's necessary to shop around and compare prices to obtain the best deal. Of the two airlines, Ansett is most likely to have 'special offers' and cut-price deals. The cheapest fares are to be had by booking at least seven days ahead. Sample fares are Auckland-Wellington (1 hour flight), $265, Auckland-Christchurch (1 hour 20 minutes) $355 and Rotorua-Christchurch (the longest domestic service at 2 hours 10 minutes) $320. These are full-fare one way prices and are the most you should pay.

Airpasses: a New Zealand Airpass provides a set number of domestic flights on Air New Zealand for a fixed price. Better terms are offered to those who buy an Airpass in conjunction with an international ticket purchased outside New Zealand than to New Zealand customers. Ansett is much more innovative when it comes to airpasses. The New Zealand Airpass (same name, different airline, not valid on Air New Zealand services and vice versa) offers between three and eight flights for a fixed cost. The Scenic Standby Airpass provides unlimited travel for either 10 or 30 days on a standby basis (it's a bargain if you have time to hang around). The Student/Backpacker's Budget Airpass offers a discount by selling you a number of 'points' which you then redeem as part or full cost for flights of your choice. If you're visiting New Zealand and also travelling to Australia you can buy an Ansett G'Day Airpass, which is valid in both countries and for flights between them

Other Services: a Skyferry service operates between Wellington and Picton. This short flight is the fastest and cheapest air route between the two islands although at $59 is more than twice the cost of the cheapest ferry ticket. There are also a number of mini-airlines serving minor destinations and often using aircraft with as few as four seats. Great Barrier Airlines (GBA) operate a service connecting Great Barrier Island (a paradise-like island, likened to Fiji or Tahiti) in the Hauraki Gulf off Auckland with Auckland, Tauranga, Whangarei, Pauanui, Whitianga, Thamas, Coromandel and Matarangi. For details ☎ freephone (0800) 275912.

Airports: New Zealand's main international airport is Auckland, which is connected by direct flights to most main cities in Asia, several cities in the USA and Europe (particularly London), plus several Polynesian destinations. The airports at Wellington and Christchurch also dub themselves 'international', but offer a much smaller number of international flights, mainly to Australia, although Christchurch has recently spent a small fortune on new terminal facilities and is now connected to Singapore several times a week by Singapore International Airlines. There are also airports at Alexandra, Blenheim, Dunedin, Gisborne, Hamilton, Hastings, Hokitika, Invercargill, Kaitaia, Kerikeri, Te Anau, Mount Cook, Napier, Nelson, New Plymouth, Oamuru, Palmerston, North Queenstown, Rotorua, Taupo, Tauranga, Timaru, Twizel, Wanganui, Westport, Whakatane and Whangerei. These airports service mainly domestic flights and private aviation, and their facilities range from a modest but modern terminal building to a motley collection of huts.

Auckland International airport is 23km/14mi south of the city at Mangere. There are three separate terminals, one for ANZ international flights and foreign airlines, and separate mini-terminals for ANZ and Ansett New Zealand's domestic services. There's no public bus service, but a privately operated Johnston's Airbus shuttle is provided to the city centre (between 6.10am and 8.50pm) taking 35 minutes and costing $10 single or $16 return. The airport operates an information hotline (☎ freephone (0800) 101048).

Wellington International Airport is 8km/5mi south of the city at Rongotai. It provides a small number of international flights, but is also the country's domestic air hub as many flights from all points north and south stop at Wellington to allow passengers to change planes. It has also been designated a 'low noise' airport and may be used only by the quietest planes, which, even so, aren't permitted to arrive or depart at night. Wellington's airport is also notoriously windy and renowned among pilots as a difficult place to land or take off. As with Auckland, there are three terminals serving international, Air New Zealand domestic and Ansett domestic flights (maybe these two airlines don't get on?). The airport shuttle bus, again privately operated by Tranzit Coachlines, costs $5 and takes 20 minutes to central Wellington. Christchurch International Airport is 11km/7mi north of the city centre and is easily reached by bus for a fare of $2.70 (half price at off-peak times). For information ☎ (03) 358 5029.

A departure tax of $20 (which is likely to be increased to $32 in 1999) is levied on passengers on departing international flights, which should be paid before you pass through immigration. At Auckland International Airport it can be paid at the Bank of New Zealand offices on the ground and first floors.

HOLIDAY & VISITORS PASSES

The most comprehensive travel pass available for travel within New Zealand is the 'Travelpass' (a name which must have taken some New Zealand marketing wizz years to dream up!). The travelpass offers unlimited travel for an inclusive price to some 1,100 destinations within the country. The 3-in-1 travelpass gives unlimited travel on Tranz Rail's eight long-distance passenger rail services, InterCity Coachlines and the Interislander ferries. It represents good value if you're doing a lot of travelling. The 4-in-1 travelpass allows you to take one Ansett New Zealand flight during the validity of the pass and buy up to three extra flight sectors at a discount price. It isn't quite as good value and unless you know that you definitely want to take four flights it's better to buy a 3-in-1 travelpass and travel overland.

The travelpass can be purchased through most travel agents, both world-wide and in New Zealand, and at most Tranz Rail/Tranz Scenic or InterCity Coachlines Travel Centres. Travelpass holders must book each individual journey in advance, which can be done at travel centres or by calling freephone (0800) 686862 for coach journeys or (0800) 802802 for Tranz Rail and Interislander journeys. If you have a 4-in-1 travelpass, you can book your flight sectors only by calling or visiting the InterCity or Tranz Rail/Tranz Scenic Travel Centres in Auckland, Wellington Christchurch or Queenstown. You cannot book with Ansett New Zealand direct. Once you've made your booking for rail or coach services, you don't need a ticket and just turn up and present your receipt to the conductor or driver.

Prices for a 3-in-1 travelpass are (child prices in brackets): five days travel over ten days $350 ($234), eight days travel over three weeks $470 ($313), 15 days travel over five weeks $590 ($393) and 22 days travel over eight weeks $690 ($460). The cost of a 4 in 1 travelpass is (child prices in brackets): five days travel over ten days $580 ($389), eight days travel over three weeks $700 ($468), 15 days travel over five weeks $820 ($548) and 22 days travel over eight weeks $920 ($615). Additional flight sectors are $230 ($155).

Other passes for coach travel only include the Explorer Coach Pass which gives unlimited travel on Newmans (North Island) and Mount Cook (South Island) services. At $378 (adult) and $189 (child) for seven days it's only worthwhile if you're travelling extensively in both islands. A periodic special offer also provides purchasers of this pass with a free (one way) flight on the Wellington-Picton Skyferry. It can be purchased from travel agents in most countries world-wide. A much better bargain when travelling by coach in the North Island is a Newmans' stopover pass, which costs just $95 for seven days unlimited travel. The only condition is that you must travel in either a northerly (Wellington-Auckland) or southerly (Auckland-Wellington) direction and cannot backtrack, although you can stop off as many times as you like en route. The pass can be purchased from any Newmans appointed agent. If you're travelling from Auckland to Northland and the Bay of Islands, a Northliner pass is useful (for reservations ☎ (09) 307 5873).

11.

MOTORING

In the absence of a comprehensive rail system, the road network is the mainstay of both public and private transport in New Zealand, covering 92,306km (around 57,000 miles) of which around 60 per cent are sealed (tarmac). The country has no national motorway (freeway) network and those that exist are short sections only, e.g. in and around cities such as Auckland and Wellington (although more are planned). Most New Zealand roads have just one lane in each direction, but they are invariably well surfaced and maintained, even when they pass through areas with difficult terrain (which is frequently). All New Zealand roads are entirely free and there are no toll roads.

New Zealand has one of the highest rates of vehicle ownership rates in the world, with over 2.55 million registered vehicles (or 538 for each 1,000 people) and over 14,000 new registrations a month. The main reason for this devotion to the motor vehicle is that driving is simply the most convenient way of getting around the country where many places aren't accessible by public transport or services are infrequent. A car is highly recommended if you live in a rural area, where you'll find getting around difficult without one. Even in Auckland and Wellington people make use of their cars a great deal as traffic congestion and parking aren't yet bad enough (in this fairly sparsely populated country) to make driving a headache. However, traffic density is increasing, along with the resultant pollution, which is just starting to become an issue in this environmentally-minded nation. Motoring is more expensive than taking the coach or the train, but much cheaper than flying, particularly over long distances. The New Zealand Automobile Association estimates that a small car (with an engine under 1.3 litres) costs 54.6¢ a kilometre to run, while a larger car (with an engine in the 2.0 litre range) costs 77.91¢ a kilometre, including all running expenses, petrol and servicing.

The travel brochures portray motoring in New Zealand as an idyllic pursuit, where the roads are uncrowded and the passing scenery breathtaking. To some extent this is true and in rural areas, particularly outside the tourist season, it's possible to drive for miles without seeing another motorist (or having to crawl behind a caravan). However, this disguises the fact that New Zealand is **one of the most dangerous countries for motorists in the world**. The country has one of the highest rates of road accidents (and deaths) per head of population anywhere in the world (even more surprising given the width of the roads) and it's reckoned that only Portugal and South America are more dangerous places. Your chances of being involved in a road accident in New Zealand are twice that in the UK (which has some of the safest roads in the world) and the USA, and substantially higher than in France, Italy and Spain, none of which are noted for their safe driving. Much has been done to make motoring safer in the last decade and a recent survey found that the accident rate in New Zealand was falling faster than in any other country. But, be warned, it's still very high and taking to the open road in New Zealand can be a dangerous business!

CAR IMPORTATION

The long sea crossing from most countries means that's is usually cheaper to buy a car on arrival in New Zealand rather than import one. However, if you have a collector's car or a vehicle to which you're attached (or you're making the comparatively short trip across the Tasman from Australia), you may wish to import your own car. If you're coming to New Zealand for the first time to take up residence, you're permitted to import at least one car, motorcycle or other motor vehicle free of duty and taxes. You may even be allowed to import more than one vehicle tax and duty-free if you can show you have good cause, e.g. you have a collection of vehicles or there are several drivers in your family. The conditions are as follows:

- You must never have lived in New Zealand previously (short stays as a non-resident are excluded).

- You must have owned and used the vehicle personally for at least one year before leaving for New Zealand. A purchase invoice or registration document is required as proof.

- You must be importing the vehicle for your own personal use and not with the intention of giving it away or selling it (nor may it be used in a business).

- You must intend to keep and use the vehicle for at least two years. If you sell it or give it away during this period you're required to pay tax on its full value.

If you're unable to comply with these conditions you must pay customs duty and Goods and Services Tax (GST) on a car when importing it into New Zealand. This is calculated according to its local market and not its value in your home country. The Collector of Customs publish a booklet entitled *Private Motor Vehicle Imports* which explains how tax is calculated and how to calculate your tax liability (or you can ask the customs to assess the tax due). In any case, it's advisable to find out the cost of tax and duty in advance, which will prevent any unexpected tax demands after your vehicle has arrived on New Zealand soil. You can contact the Collector of Customs at the following offices: PO Box 29, Auckland (☎ (09) 377 3520), PO Box 2098, Christchurch (☎ (03) 371 5000) or PO Box 2218, Wellington (☎ (04) 473 6099).

Left-Hand Drive Cars: New Zealanders drive on the left as in Australia, Japan and the UK, so vehicles used there need to be right hand drive. Consequently there's a restriction on importing and registering left-hand drive cars, such as vehicles from the USA. If you wish to import a left-hand drive car you should first make enquiries with the Ministry of Transport (PO Box 3175, Wellington). Left-hand drive cars aren't usually permitted for ordinary daily use and usually only collectors' cars or vehicles which are left-hand drive for practical purposes (e.g. plant or agricultural machinery) are permitted.

Steam Cleaning: in line with New Zealand's strict policy of trying to exclude plant and animal pests, all vehicles imported into New Zealand must be thoroughly steam cleaned before they are admitted. This can be done before the vehicle is shipped to New Zealand and most shippers will do it, but you should ensure that they obtain a 'Certificate of Steam Cleaning' for New Zealand customs. All vehicles are inspected on arrival and any which haven't been steam cleaned or weren't adequately cleaned must be cleaned after arrival, for which owners must pay at least $60. Vehicles arriving from Australia don't need to be steam cleaned unless they're found to be dirty on arrival.

Shipping: as there are no regular ferry services to New Zealand, all vehicles need to be shipped on cargo vessels. Most international shipping companies can arrange this for you. It takes at least five weeks to ship a vehicle from Europe and three weeks from the west coast of the USA, although it can take much longer when loading, unloading and customs clearance are included.

CAR REGISTRATION & ROAD TAX

Registering a brand new or imported car attracts an initial registration fee of $180. This entitles you to a Vehicle Registration Certificate (VRC) and a pair of licence plates which must be displayed at the front and rear of your vehicle. All motor vehicles are also subject to an annual registration fee which is collected by the Land Transport Safety Authority. This is essentially a road tax, although it's known as a registration fee in that it entitles your car to be registered and display the relevant licence plates for the coming year. The fee for cars and small trucks is $206.13 and for small motorcycles it's $74.50. GST is levied on the registration fee. You can pay your registration in person at most postal shops or by post, for which you need the re-registration application forms that are sent to owners automatically around a month before your registration expires.

CAR INSPECTIONS

All vehicles to be used on public roads in New Zealand are subject to an official inspection test after which (assuming they pass) they are awarded a Vehicle Inspection Certificate (VIC), more commonly known as a Warrant of Fitness (WOF), an old term still in widespread use. All vehicles require a new WOF every six months unless they were first used after 1st December 1985, in which case they require a WOF every year until they are three years old and every six months thereafter. As an incentive to support local industry, cars assembled in New Zealand are granted a WOF valid for one year at a time up until they are six years old and every six months thereafter.

WOF's are issued at official government testing stations or approved garages, which abound (most small garages can issue WOFs). Many garages offer a WOF service while you wait. A WOF inspection costs $20 for a car and checks are only made for basic roadworthiness covering such things as brakes, lights and tyres, similar to vehicle inspections carried out in most US states. It isn't as stringent as either the British MOT or German TUV inspections. As well as a VIC, you'll receive a WOF sticker which must be displayed behind the windscreen of the vehicle (the penalty for failing to display a WOF is $150).

BUYING A CAR

There have never been any indigenous New Zealand cars and therefore when it comes to buying a car New Zealanders must choose a foreign make. Although cars aren't actually manufactured in New Zealand, Toyota, Nissan, Honda and Mitsubishi all have plants there where motor vehicles are assembled from imported parts. The plants were initially built as a way around stiff taxes on imported vehicles, although these have now been reduced considerably and are due to be abolished completely by 2002. Therefore it's likely that these assembly plants will close in the not too distant future, making New Zealand entirely reliant on imports for motor vehicles. One of the largest assemblers, Ford-Mazda, has already closed its New Zealand assembly plant and now imports all its vehicles from Japan and the USA.

Since the government's policy of restricting imported cars was abandoned, the New Zealand car market has been dominated by Japanese vehicles. This isn't surprising given New Zealand's proximity to Japan and the fact that Japanese cars are well made, reliable, offer good value and several models are assembled in New Zealand. Japanese car dealerships (particularly Honda, Nissan and Toyota) are found in every town and offer every kind of vehicle including family saloons, station wagons (estate cars), luxury executive cars and sports models. It's possible to buy most European makes such as BMW, Peugeot and Volkswagen and others in New Zealand, although these are regarded as more up-market makes, and so most family cars tend to be of Japanese origin. The main non-Japanese makes on the market are Ford, which are variants of American (rather than European) models, and Holden, which are made in Australia by General Motors (and sold in Europe as Opels and in the UK as Vauxhalls). Lovers of classic cars will be delighted to see many old British-made cars such as Minis and Morris Minors still in daily use in New Zealand. These date back to the days when 'patriotic' local car buyers bought mainly British cars and kept them for 'ever' due to the high cost of new vehicles.

New Cars

New cars used to be astronomically expensive in New Zealand. However, the reduction in import taxes in recent years has brought prices.down to a more reasonable level and in recent months on-the-road prices of some models have fallen by almost 10 per cent. In general, cars are still more expensive than the UK and other European countries, and substantially more expensive than the USA, even for identical models. However, further tax reductions are expected in the future and in the last couple of years fierce discounting by Japanese manufacturers has seen prices fall so that many more people can now afford a new car, which was previously something of a luxury.

You should shop around when buying a new car in New Zealand and be prepared to haggle over the price. Although cars are officially sold at list price, there's usually a discount to be had somewhere, whether by inflating the allowance paid for your part exchange vehicle or a cash discount. Ensure that the price you're quoted includes GST (12.5 per cent) and registration, which can add around $400 to the price of a new car. The new car market is covered by a magazine entitled *New Zealand Cars* which reports motor industry news, previews new models, runs road tests and provides an update on prices. New cars prices start at around $20,000 for a small Japanese car and $30,000 for a small European family car, up to around $60,000 for a quality European car such as an Audi, BMW or Saab.

Used Cars

Until recently used cars used to command high prices in New Zealand, although the reduction of prices in the new car market in recent years has had a knock-on effect in reducing used prices (and also accelerating depreciation). The easiest way to buy a used car is from a used car dealer, although it's advisable to ask a colleague or neighbour if they can recommend one. When buying a car from a dealer you should check that he's a Licensed Motor Vehicle Dealer (look for the LMVD logo). Anyone who sells or exchanges more than six vehicles within a 12 month period must be licensed, although small dealers often lack LMVD membership and pose as private sellers (which is illegal). An alternative is to check the local newspapers or the weekly *Auto Trader* magazine, which lists hundreds of cars for sale (most accompanied by a photograph), both privately and from dealers. Used car dealers and private sellers also advertise cars for sale on the internet (www.autonet.co.nz). In some towns there are weekend car markets where private sellers offer their cars for sale, such as the Saturday morning market (starting around 7am) on the Khyber Pass Road in Auckland.

Important Precautions: as when buying a used car anywhere, it requires a great deal of caution and both the vehicle and seller should be carefully scrutinised:

- Ensure that the seller owns a vehicle or is entitled to sell it. In a private sale, ask to see the vehicle registration certificate together with some other proof of the seller's address. If the addresses match, this gives you some indication that the seller is probably who he says he is.

- Inspect the bodywork carefully for damage as a lot of cars in New Zealand have been involved in accidents. A car with a few minor cosmetic knocks is preferable to one that looks immaculate but which has been repaired following a major accident.

- Try to confirm that the odometer (km) reading is correct as odometer rigging is common. Service records from a main dealership and repair invoices showing the km reading are a good way of proving this.

If you know little or nothing about cars it's wise to arrange an inspection by a competent engineer. The New Zealand Automobile Association (AA) provides this service to members. The Ministry of Justice maintains an Autocheck register which lists vehicles which are subject to a hire purchase or leasing arrangement or have been pledged as security. Always check the Autocheck register before buying a used car. This doesn't, however, guarantee that a vehicle hasn't been stolen or suffered accident damage, or that the kilometre reading is correct.

Warranties and Guarantees: used car dealers offer warranties and guarantees. All car sellers (including private sellers) are legally obliged to sell cars in a roadworthy condition. If you buy a car and find that it isn't roadworthy, a threat to report the seller to the police may receive you a refund (always assuming that you can find him!). If you have a complaint about a new or used car purchased from a dealer, you can take it up with the Motor Vehicle Disputes Tribunal. If the tribunal finds that your complaint is justified they can order the dealer to take the car back and refund your money. Around 66 per cent of cases dealt with in this way result in a successful outcome for buyers, but it applies only to cars costing up to $30,000. The Institute of Motor Vehicle Dealers (IMVD) also has a fidelity fund which compensates buyers when a dealer cannot pay, e.g. when he's gone bust.

Imported Used Cars: a particular area of concern for buyers of used cars in New Zealand is that of imported used cars, i.e. vehicles that have been used in another country and then exported to New Zealand, as opposed to used cars which were bought new in New Zealand. There have been problems in recent years with cars which have been stolen, usually in the UK, and shipped to New Zealand and resold. This mainly applies to prestige and executive cars. If you're offered a used vehicle such as a Mercedes or BMW at a temptingly low price, you should check its history particularly carefully. A popular bar-room tale in New Zealand (probably untrue) tells of the Pom (Briton) who emigrated and bought back his BMW which had been stolen in London six months previously!

A problem can also occur with used cars imported from Japan, which are imported legally by dealers and sold at low prices (used cars are worth little in Japan), often with low mileage (kilometres). However, several dealers have been convicted for winding back the odometers of cars on their sea journey from Japan, thereby defrauding buyers. Even with genuine used cars imported from Japan, there's often concern that the wear and tear on the engine is greater than the kilometre reading may suggest (Japanese cars spend most of their life crawling in traffic jams). On the other hand, several dealers have been caught winding the odometers of imported used cars *forward*, in order to reduce their value and cut the import taxes payable (thus defrauding customs). In summary it's fair to say that buying a used car in New Zealand is something of a mine-field, although it's no different from most other countries in this respect.

SELLING A CAR

Before selling a car in New Zealand, you must obtain a new vehicle inspection certificate (VRC) or warrant of fitness from a local garage, unless your current WOF was issued in the previous month. When you find a buyer, simply give him the VRC which he will need to register the car in his name. Registration can be done by post or in person at a postal shop. The same applies when buying a car, except when buying from a dealer who will do it for you. Other points to note when selling a car are:

● Inform your insurance company.

● When selling a car privately, insist on payment in cash or with a banker's draft (cashier's cheque), which is standard practice in New Zealand. If you accept a personal cheque, make sure that it clears before you part with the vehicle.

● The best places to advertise a car for sale are in local newspapers or the *Auto Trader* magazine. Some people also put a 'for sale' notice in their car window with a phone number and park it in a prominent place or sell it at a car market.

DRIVING LICENCE

The minimum age for driving in New Zealand is 15, although there are proposals to increase it to 17 in the future as the 15 age limit dates back to the days when the school leaving age was 15 and children were often required to drive vehicles on farms. However, young New Zealanders are only entitled to a provisional licence at age 15 and they aren't entitled to a full licence until they are 18. Even then, drivers under the age of 20 are subject to additional licence restrictions including a lower blood alcohol limit (30mg of alcohol per 100ml of blood which in practice means they cannot drink and drive legally) and no driving after sunset.

If you already have a driving licence it can be used in New Zealand for up to one year, assuming it's written in English. If it isn't it must be accompanied by an international driving permit which you can obtain from a motoring organisation in your home country. After one year your foreign driving licence must be exchanged for a New Zealand licence. You must take a short written test on the road rules and driving theory, and undergo an interview with a traffic policeman, after which, assuming you're successful, a New Zealand licence is granted. If you don't currently hold a driving licence, you must take a practical driving test. Licences are issued in paper form and last for life, although a credit card style licence incorporating a photograph is planned and will need to be renewed every ten years. You aren't required to carry your driving licence or car papers with you when driving in New Zealand, although given the frequency of spot checks it's advisable.

Before taking to the road in New Zealand you should familiarise yourself with the official guide to driving rules and regulations known as the *Road Code*, which is available from bookshops and is New Zealand's best selling book. It's also available on CD-ROM which includes the contents of the book, the road code test, written and oral practice tests, first aid information and demonstrations on how to manoeuvre a vehicle.

CAR INSURANCE

In most countries motorists are required to have minimum third party insurance so that, for example, if they injure or even kill another road user their insurance company pays compensation. This isn't legally required in New Zealand due to the country's innovative Accident Compensation Scheme, whereby anyone who suffers a personal accident or injury is compensated directly by the government. This system works reasonably well, although it isn't free as everyone (not just those who cause the accidents) pays for it through their taxes. One knock-on effect of this system is that it isn't possible to sue anyone who causes an accident or injury for compensation.

The scheme doesn't, however, compensate drivers for damage to their cars and it's therefore advisable to have at least third party insurance for your car. Most people with cars worth more than a nominal amount take out fully comprehensive motor insurance. The cost of motor insurance varies depending on the make and type of car, the driver and where you live (Aucklanders pay up to 30 per cent more than country dwellers), with the average fully comprehensive insurance premium around $650 per year.

GENERAL ROAD RULES

First time visitors may be forgiven for thinking that there are no road rules in New Zealand. However, there are, and some of the main ones are as follows:

● Among the many strange habits of New Zealanders is that of driving on the left-hand side of the road, as in Australia, Japan and the UK (and many other countries). You may find this a bit strange if you come from a country which drives on the right, however, it saves a lot of confusion if you do likewise. It's helpful to have a reminder (e.g. 'think left!') on your car's dashboard (many rental cars have a fluorescent sticker stating 'DRIVE ON THE LEFT' on the dashboard). Take extra care when pulling out of junctions, one-way streets and at roundabouts. Remember to look first to the *right* when crossing the road on foot. If you're unused to driving on the left, you should be prepared for some disorientation or even terror, although most people have few problems adjusting to it.

● At crossroads and junctions where no right of way is assigned, traffic coming from the right has priority (as on the continent of Europe). At major junctions, right of way is indicated by a triangular 'GIVE WAY' (yield) sign or an octagonal red 'STOP' sign. There are also usually road markings. When faced with a stop sign you must stop completely (all four wheels must come to rest) before pulling out onto a major road, even if you can see that no traffic is approaching. At a give way sign, you aren't required to stop, but must give priority to traffic already on the major road. You must also give way to traffic on your right when entering a freeway or dual carriageway from a slip road.

- On roundabouts (traffic circles), vehicles on the roundabout (coming from your right) have priority and not those entering it. Traffic flows clockwise round roundabouts and not anti-clockwise, as in countries where traffic drives on the right. Some roundabouts have a filter lane which is reserved for traffic turning left. You should stay in the lane in which you entered the roundabout, follow the lane markings to leave and signal as you approach the exit you wish to take. There are many roundabouts in New Zealand, which although they are a bit of a free-for-all, speed up traffic considerably and are usually preferable to traffic lights, particularly outside rush hours (although some busy roundabouts also have traffic lights).

- The use of seatbelts is compulsory for all front and rear seat passengers when they are fitted and children must be properly restrained by an approved child restraint or adult seatbelt if fitted to a vehicle. In the absence of an approved restraint or seatbelt, they must travel in the back of a car. A child must *never* travel in the front seat without using a child restraint or seatbelt, even when the back seat is full. Seatbelts or restraints must be approved (to the requisite New Zealand standard) and be appropriate for the age and weight of a child. Babies up to six months of age must be carried in an infant seat and children aged up to four must be carried in a child seat. Older children may use either a child seat or an adult seatbelt.

- It's estimated that seatbelts would prevent around 75 per cent of deaths and 90 per cent of injuries suffered by those involved in accidents not wearing seat belts. In addition to the risk of death or injury, you can receive a fine for ignoring the seatbelt laws. Note that it's the driver's responsibility to ensure that children are properly fastened. If you're exempt from using a seatbelt for medical reasons, a safety belt exemption certificate is required from your doctor.

- Be particularly wary of cyclists, moped riders and motorcyclists. It isn't always easy to see them, particularly when they are hidden by the blind spots of a car or when cyclists are riding at night without lights. **When overtaking, ALWAYS give them a wide . . . WIDE berth.** If you knock them off their bikes, you may have a difficult time convincing the police that it wasn't your fault; far better to avoid them (and the police).

- If you needed spectacles or contact lenses to pass your sight test, you must always wear them when driving. It's advisable to carry a spare pair of glasses or contact lenses in your car.

- White or yellow lane and road markings are painted on the road surface in towns and cities, e.g. arrows to indicate the direction traffic must go in a particular lane. You should stay in the centre of the lane in which you're driving and, where there are no lane markings, keep to the left side of the road. White lines mark the separation of traffic lanes. A solid single line or two solid lines means no overtaking in either direction. A solid line to the left of the centre line, i.e. on your side of the road, means that overtaking is prohibited in your direction. You may overtake only when there's a single broken line in the middle of the road or double lines with a broken line on your side of the road.

- Headlights must be used when driving between sunset and sunrise or at any time when there's insufficient daylight to be able to see a person wearing dark clothing at a distance of 100 metres (so keep an eye out for people in dark clothing). It's illegal to drive on side (parking) lights and headlights must usually be dipped (low beam) when driving in built-up areas where there's street lighting. Headlamps must also be dipped within 200 metres of an approaching vehicle, immediately an oncoming vehicle has dipped its headlights and when travelling within 200 metres behind another vehicle.

- Headlight flashing has a different meaning in different countries. In some countries it means 'after you', while in others it means 'get out of my way'. It can even mean 'I'm driving a new car and haven't worked out what all the switches are for yet'. **In New Zealand headlamp flashing has only one legal use – to warn another vehicle of your presence,** although most people use it to give priority to another vehicle, e.g. when someone is waiting to exit from a junction. Note that it's illegal to warn other vehicles that they are approaching a speed trap or police road block by flashing your lights (although many drivers do it). Hazard warning lights (all indicators operating simultaneously) are used to warn other drivers of an obstruction, e.g. an accident or a traffic jam on a highway.

- The sequence of New Zealand traffic lights is green, amber, red and back to green. Amber means stop at the stop line and you may proceed only if the amber light appears after you have crossed the stop line or when stopping may cause an accident. A green filter light may be shown in addition to the full lamp signals, which means you may go in the direction shown by the arrow, irrespective of other lights showing. Cameras may be installed at busy traffic lights to detect motorists driving through red lights (a favourite pastime of many New Zealand motorists).

- Always approach pedestrian crossings with caution and don't park or overtake another vehicle on the approach to a crossing. At some crossings a flashing amber light follows the red light, to warn you to give way to pedestrians before proceeding. **Note that pedestrians have the legal right of way once they have stepped onto a crossing without traffic lights and you must STOP. Motorists who don't stop are liable to heavy penalties.** Where a road crosses a public footpath, e.g. when entering or emerging from a property or car park bordering a road, motorists *must* give way to pedestrians.

- Tail-gating (driving too close to the vehicle in front) is commonplace in New Zealand and most other countries, where few drivers have any idea of safe stopping distances (including thinking distance, i.e. the time it takes a driver to react). In good conditions you should leave a gap equal to three seconds between your vehicle and the one in front in order to be able to stop in an emergency. Note that the three-second rule applies to cars with good brakes and tyres, on dry roads, in good visibility and with an *alert driver*. If you're half asleep and driving an old banger on a wet or icy road, you had better not exceed 20kph (12mph), otherwise you'll never stop in an emergency! As a safety precaution, try to leave a large gap between you and the vehicle in front. This isn't just to allow you more time to stop, should the vehicles in front decide to get together, but also to give the 'tail-gater' behind you more time to stop. The closer the car behind you, the further you should be from the vehicle in front.

- Watch out for permanent and temporary pedestrianised streets (which are closed to traffic during certain periods indicated by a sign) in city centres. Note that bicycles may not be ridden in pedestrianised streets or even wheeled-through in some cases.

- Keep a look out for livestock on roads in country areas where fields are often unfenced and livestock are free to graze at will. Many motorists are injured following collisions with livestock, particularly at night.

- Snow chains may be used on snow-covered roads, but should be removed as soon as the road is clear.

TRAFFIC POLICE

The policing of road traffic and drivers in New Zealand comes under the auspices of the Traffic Safety Service (TSS), which is a joint authority between the police and the Ministry of Transport. TSS officers drive black and white cars to distinguish them from police vehicles and like most police officers aren't armed. Officers deploy a range of radar and laser apparatus to detect speeding motorists, and carry out frequent roadside checks and mount random roadblocks (stopping all motorists or filtering out 'suspicious looking' ones), checking documents and vehicles and administering breathtests. Officers cannot impose on the spot fines other than for minor violations (such as illegal parking or not displaying a valid WOF) and traffic offenders are usually issued with a traffic infringement notice and summoned to appear at a district court. In a recent controversial step, court bailiffs have attended spot checks looking for people with outstanding fines, including those imposed for offences that have nothing to do with motoring offences. Anyone with an unpaid fine or outstanding court order is liable to be arrested.

NEW ZEALAND ROADS

Roads in New Zealand are divided into three main categories: motorways, state highways and secondary roads. Motorways are found only in the major cities where they provide a direct route from the suburbs into the centre. They consist of two or more lanes in each direction and are known by names rather than numbers. For example, in Auckland the northern, southern and north-western motorways radiate out from the city centre in their respective directions and the Wellington Urban Motorway runs from the city centre northwards. Special rules apply on motorways which may not be used by pedestrians, cyclists, animals or small-capacity motorcycles. You may only stop in an emergency, when you must use the nearside verge or hard shoulder. Motorways are identified by signs with white lettering on a green background and junctions are numbered (a new system has been proposed which will number junctions according to their distance in kilometres from the start of the motorway, rather than their numerical order). For example, junction ten would be 10km/6mi from the start of the motorway.

State highways are major trunk roads with usually just one lane in each direction on which you can expect to average around 55 to 65kmh when travelling cross-country. They are marked in red on maps and identified by a shield symbol, both on road signs and on maps. There are eight major state highways in New Zealand:

Highway No.	Route
1	Awanui–Auckland–Wellington–Picton–Christchurch–Invercargill
2	Auckland–Tauranga–Gisborne–Napier–Wellington
3	Hamilton–New Plymouth–Palmerston North
4	Te Kuiti–Wanganui
5	Putaruru–Napier
6	Blenheim–Invercargill (via the Southern Alps)
7	Greymouth–Waipara (near Christchurch)
8	Timaru–Milton (inland route)

Secondary routes are marked in yellow on most maps and by a shield symbol on maps and road signs. They are identified by a two digit number and in most cases the first digit of the number indicates that the road starts or finishes (as the case may be) on the state highway with the same number. All other roads are unclassified and unnumbered and indicated by white lines on most maps, but have no special identification or road signs. They are usually of reasonable quality and sealed unless they are specifically marked on a map or signposted as 'unsealed' or 'not tar sealed' which means that they are gravel or compacted earth. They are passable by standard two wheel drive cars in good weather and four-wheel-drive vehicles at any time.

New Zealand's roads rarely have special facilities such as service areas or rest stops, although they are well served by petrol stations, cafes, restaurants and motels (most state highways pass through towns rather than bypassing them) where you can stop for fuel, food, accommodation or breakdown services. The only exception to this is remote parts of the country, mainly in the South Island, where you should use a road map to plan overnight stays, refuelling and rest stops.

Parking is never easy in city centres, but unlike many other countries it's at least possible. Rush hour in the cities is between 7.30 and 9am and 4.30 and 6.30pm, when it takes a little longer to make a journey, although outside cities there's no such thing as a rush hour. Roads are naturally busier during holiday periods, particularly between December and February. The beginning of summer school holidays (the end of the first week in December) and the week before Christmas are the only times when it's advisable to think twice before making a long journey by road, as everyone else will be doing the same thing.

Most roads are passable all year round except in the more inhospitable areas of the South Island, when some roads, particularly state highway 6 through the Southern Alps, are made impassable by snow falls and icy conditions. In the winter you should check to make sure that you can reach your destination before setting out. On some roads there are automatic warning signs to warn you of a road closure further along the highway. Don't be tempted to ignore them, as each year many people are stranded and a number lose their lives by doing this. In the North Island, several main roads are subject to flooding during heavy rain, particularly where they pass through the volcanic plateaux.

NEW ZEALAND DRIVERS

In normal circumstances New Zealanders are friendly and polite. However, all this changes the minute they get behind the wheel of their cars, when they become uncharacteristically aggressive, intolerant and discourteous. The average New Zealander's attitude is to reach his destination as fast as possible with little regard for whoever he may maim or kill in the process. There are, on average, around 15 road deaths every week in New Zealand, together with 20,000 convictions annually for careless or dangerous driving. Being a foreigner doesn't exempt you from this carnage, although the Land Transport Safety Authority estimates that less than 3 per cent of fatal accidents are caused by foreign drivers.

The three greatest threats to road safety are drink driving, excessive speed (see page 165) and dangerous overtaking. Another problem is lane changing and pulling in or out without looking or without leaving sufficient room. This is a significant problem in New Zealand where there are few multi-lane roads and many drivers have no lane discipline. Young men tend to be the worse offenders, although even young women and mature drivers compete in New Zealand's 'drink the pub dry' and 'get there first at all costs' road race. Road rage is the latest trend to emerge in New Zealand and there have been several cases of motorists who, after having been hit by a car, have remonstrated with the offending driver only to be hit again – this time in the face!

It's advisable never to drink and drive in New Zealand (and never to accept a ride with anyone who has been drinking), as apart from the effect on your driving you'll need extra reaction time to cope with other drivers who have been drinking. It pays to regard the speed limits as an absolute maximum and if necessary drive slower, particularly in towns. Finally, avoid overtaking except where there's enough clear road ahead to land a jumbo jet! All this shouldn't put you off driving in New Zealand as you'll pass through some breathtaking scenery (best admired by stopping the car), even on the most routine trips to the office or the shops. Best of all, roads are relatively uncrowded outside cities, so your chances of meeting many kamikaze drivers are slim.

MOTORCYCLES

Motorcycling is popular in New Zealand, both as a means of transport and a leisure pursuit. It can, however, be a dangerous undertaking partly because drivers of other vehicles have little regard for motorcyclists (usually they don't even notice them) and because many motorcyclists take advantage of New Zealand's wide open roads to reach some incredible speeds. Crash helmets must be worn and riders must display dipped headlamps at all times. It also pays to wear bright, fluorescent or reflective clothing but, even then, don't expect car drivers to see you. In recent years motorcycle accidents have been reduced due to helmets, better bikes and protective riding gear, better training and defensive riding by bikers. In general, laws that apply to cars also apply to motorcycles.

It's possible to buy (or rent) a wide range of bikes in New Zealand ranging from lovingly preserved British classics to the latest German and Japanese superbikes. A motorcycle can be imported duty-free on the same terms as a car (see page 150).

ACCIDENTS

New Zealanders aren't generally perturbed by road accidents and many people delight in recounting the details of their latest scrape over dinner or in the pub. If you're unfortunate enough to be involved in a car accident in New Zealand (perhaps that should be *when* you're involved in your first accident), the procedure is as follows:

1. Stop immediately. Switch on your hazard warning lights. In bad visibility, at night, or in a blind spot, try to warn oncoming traffic of the danger by sending someone ahead to flag down oncoming cars.

2. In the case of minor accidents try to move your car off the road immediately. Many serious accidents are caused by other drivers speeding down an empty road and running into vehicles that have had a minor bump.

3. If anyone is injured call an ambulance and/or the fire service immediately by dialling 111. If there isn't a public phone just call at the nearest house.

4. Don't move an injured person unless it's absolutely necessary to save him or her from further injury and don't leave him alone except to call an ambulance. Cover them with a blanket or coat to keep them warm.

5. If there are no injuries and damage to vehicles or property isn't serious, it's unnecessary to call the police to the accident scene. Contacting the police may result in someone being fined or prosecuted for a driving offence. If another driver has obviously been drinking or appears incapable of driving, call the police. Note that you must never leave the scene of an accident, however minor, as this is a serious offence.

6. If either you or the other driver(s) involved decide to call the police, don't move your vehicle or allow other vehicles to be moved. If it's necessary to move vehicles to unblock the road, mark their positions with chalk. Alternatively take photographs of the accident scene or make a drawing showing the position of all vehicles involved before moving them.

7. Check whether there are any witnesses to the accident and take their names and addresses, particularly noting those who support your version of what happened. Write down the registration numbers of all vehicles involved and their drivers' names, addresses and insurance details. If asked, give any other drivers involved your name, address and insurance details. Bear in mind, however, that motorists aren't legally required to have insurance, so don't be too surprised if the other driver doesn't have any!

8. If you have caused material damage, you must inform the owner of the damaged property as soon as possible. If you cannot reach him, contact the nearest police station (this also applies to damage caused to stationary vehicles, e.g. when parking).

9. If you're detained by the police, ask someone you're travelling with to contact anyone necessary as soon as you realise you're going to be detained. Don't sign a statement unless you're certain you understand and agree with every word.

10. In the case of an accident involving two or more vehicles, it's normal practice for drivers to complete a standard accident report form provided by most insurance companies. Each driver completes the standard form which is then countersigned

by the other and a copy exchanged. It isn't necessary for each driver's versions of the event to agree.

11. Your insurance company must be notified of an accident as soon as possible.

Claims for personal injury where the other driver is wholly or partly at fault can be directed to the government's Accident Compensation Corporation (ACC). If your claim is complex you may need a lawyer to help with this. You must, at the very least, have the licence number of the other vehicle if you're to succeed with a claim.

DRIVING & DRINKING

It's estimated that a large proportion of road accidents in New Zealand are due to drunken driving (and also a fair number due to drink-walking), which is acknowledged as one of the country's most pressing social problems. It's still quite socially acceptable in New Zealand to drive after a 'few drinks' and the limited licensing hours for hotels (pubs) often encourage people to travel in search of a drink when their local pub is closed on a Sunday or in 'dry' areas. Drunken driving is endemic at all levels, from older drivers who consider they're experienced enough to drive a car after drinking, to bravado young drivers who may even encourage their mates to drive when drunk. Drunk drivers in New Zealand are often very drunk indeed. One driver who ended up in court on a drink driving charge was reported to have 1,863mcg of alcohol per litre of breath when breathalysed – over four times the legal limit of 400mcg (a medical expert at his trial reckoned he should have been 'brain dead' after consuming so much alcohol!).

In recent years the government has made great efforts to reduce drinking and driving through public education campaigns and stricter laws. These have had some effect although drunken driving remains a serious problem. The alcohol limit for motorists in New Zealand is 80mg per 100ml of blood (0.08 per cent), similar to the UK but higher than many European countries. For motorists under 20 years the limit is 30mg or effectively zero. The maximum penalty for drunken driving is a six month loss of your licence, a $1,500 fine and up to six months in prison. Your car can also be confiscated, although this is usually applied only to repeat offenders. Each year over 30,000 New Zealanders are convicted of drunken driving, although few are jailed.

Police and TSS officers can breathalyse drivers at any time in New Zealand without a reason and drivers involved in accidents, however minor, are routinely breathalysed. Random breath tests are common and roadblocks can be set up or moved at a few moments notice. All motorists stopped are tested and a reading above 400mcg of alcohol per litre of breath leads to a blood test, after which if you're still over the limit you're charged with drunken driving. The latest threat on New Zealand's roads is driving under the influence of drugs. Although there are no official figures, a significant number of drivers are believed to be under the influence of illegal drugs (mainly cannabis) when driving and the government plans to introduce roadside drug testing when a reliable test becomes available.

CAR THEFT

Usually when you leave your property unattended in New Zealand you can expect it to be in the same place when you return. This, however, doesn't always apply to cars (plus motorcycles and bicycles for that matter), as New Zealand has a surprisingly high incidence of car theft considering the fairly low crime rate in general. It's rare for a stolen car to disappear completely in New Zealand as there's no easy way for a thief to take a car abroad and most are unlikely to pay the Inter-island ferry fare to spirit your car to the other island. Therefore if your car is stolen you're highly likely to get it back. The bad news, however, is that many cars are stolen by joy-riders or petty criminals, so when you do get it back it may be damaged or completely wrecked. There's a huge variation in the incidence of car crime between city and country areas, and while Auckland is the car crime capital of New Zealand, in most country areas car theft is rare and even a theft from a car may make headline news.

To reduce the chance of theft, don't take unnecessary risks and always lock your car, engage your steering lock and completely close all windows (but don't leave pets in an unventilated car). Never leave you keys in the ignition, even when filling up at a petrol station or when parking in your driveway. Put any valuables (including clothes) in the boot or out of sight and don't leave your vehicle registration papers in the car or any form of identification. If possible, avoid parking in commuter (e.g. at railway stations) and long-term car parks (e.g. at airports or shopping centres), which are favourite hunting grounds for car thieves. When parking overnight or when it's dark, always park in a well-lit area, which helps deter car thieves.

If you drive a new or valuable car it's wise to have it fitted with an alarm, an engine immobiliser (preferably of the rolling code variety with a transponder arming key) or other anti-theft device, and to use a visible deterrent such as a steering or gear change lock. This is especially important if you own a car that's desirable to car thieves. Car theft has spawned a huge car security business in the (losing) battle to prevent or deter car thieves. These include a multitude of car alarms, engine immobilisers, steering and gear stick locks, personal wheel clamps, window etching with a car's registration number, locking wheel nuts and petrol caps, and removable/coded stereo systems (a favourite target of thieves). Although a good security system won't stop someone from breaking into your car (which usually takes a professional a matter of seconds) or prevent it being stolen, it will make it more difficult and may prompt a thief to look for an easier target. If you plan to buy an expensive stereo system, buy one with a removable unit or control panel/fascia (which you can pop in a pocket), but *never* forget to remove it, even when stopping for a few minutes. If your car is stolen, report it to the police and your insurance company as soon as possible. Don't, however, expect the police to find it or even take much interest in your loss.

PETROL

There are no less than six kinds of motor fuel sold in New Zealand. Petrol (or gasoline) is available in unleaded grades of 91 and 96 octane, super and regular. Most new and recent cars run only on unleaded fuel as they are equipped with catalytic converters. However, super and regular are still available at most petrol stations for older cars and should never be used in cars equipped with a catalytic converter as they will destroy the catalytic converter. Fortunately the fuel nozzles and filler caps on 'cat' equipped cars are smaller than those for leaded, so a mistake is unlikely (they are also usually coloured green). The cost of unleaded 91 fuel is around $1 per litre, with unleaded 96 (intended for high performance cars) and leaded costing a little more. In recent years, supermarkets have opened petrol stations selling fuel at discount prices, which has created something of a price war in some areas.

Diesel fuel is also available at most petrol stations at around 55¢ per litre, which means that running a diesel vehicle can work out much cheaper, as they also usually offer more kilometres per litre. New Zealand doesn't have a great number of diesel powered cars and it's mainly used in commercial vehicles, although many campervans are diesel powered. Another kind of fuel available is Liquid Petroleum Gas (LPG) or Compressed Natural Gas (CNG), which can be used only in specially converted cars. Liquid gas is cheaper than petrol and provides slightly better fuel consumption, although it's currently used only in the North Island and it's possible that its use may diminish over the next few years as petrol is now cheaper.

There are plenty of petrol stations in towns and cities, but they can be few and far between in rural areas, particularly in the South Island. It's advisable to plan your fuel stops on long trips using a reliable map – when you see a 'last fuel for 70 miles' sign it may well be true and not just a cynical marketing ploy! Also note that many petrol stations close at 6pm and are closed on Saturday afternoons and all day Sundays, although now it's at least possible to buy petrol in New Zealand on Sunday (a fairly recent development).

SPEED LIMITS

The speed limits in New Zealand couldn't be simpler: 50kph (31mph) in built-up areas and 100kph (62mph) in rural areas, except where (rarely) a different limit is posted. The rural limit is reduced to 90kph (55mph) for buses and heavy lorries, and to 80kph (50mph) for school buses and vehicles towing trailers. Although speed limits are low compared with many other countries, excessive speed is a major factor in New Zealand's road accident toll and the authorities are taking increasing steps to reduce and control vehicle speeds. Speed traps are commonplace and employ a variety of methods to detect speeders including radar and laser. One device that the road safety authorities have taken to enthusiastically in their bid to persuade (or force) motorists to slow down is the speed camera, which measures the speed of passing vehicles and takes a photograph of the licence plate of those that are speeding. These devices exist, of course, in other countries, but they aren't usually employed with the fervour they are in New Zealand where they raise $75 million for the government annually ('spotting the speed camera' has become a national pastime).

When speed cameras were first introduced they were placed in clearly marked, fixed locations. However, their effects on traffic speeds soon diminished once everyone knew where they were. Visible, mobile cameras were introduced which again had an effect for a short time only. More recently, however, the TSS has taken to hiding them, often quite cleverly, behind buildings, signs and even in bushes. One speed camera on highway 23 was reported to have caught the same driver doing at least 150kph six times in one day! Even so, New Zealanders aren't about to be beaten by 'big brother' and it isn't uncommon for a friendly local to put up a handwritten 'Speed Camera Ahead' sign by the side of the road. The motorist's latest weapon against speed cameras is an aerosol spray called 'Flash Back' (available by mail order for the modest sum of $125) which is supposed to make your licence plate reflective so that it cannot be photographed.

GARAGES

When buying a car in New Zealand, you would be wise to take into account local service facilities. Ford, Holden, Honda, Mazda and Toyota dealers abound in every large town, although outside these makes dealers may be few and far between. It's difficult to find garages that can repair many European cars (which are often considered specialist or luxury cars) and the nearest dealer may be located a long way from your home or workplace. If you drive a rare car, it's advisable to carry a basic selection of spare parts, as service stations in New Zealand may not stock them and you may need to wait several days (or even weeks) for them to arrive from Auckland or even abroad. Local mechanics, however, have a reputation for being able to improvise a repair on virtually any vehicle given a few nuts and bolts and a couple of pieces of wire!

Garages in New Zealand usually charge an hourly rate for their work, which varies considerably between main dealers and small country garages. Some franchised dealers operate a 'menu pricing' system, charging a fixed fee for a particular job no matter how long it takes. However, it's generally much cheaper to have your car serviced at a local country garage than at a main dealer, although they may lack expertise in such areas as automatic transmissions and ABS braking systems. If you have an accident and you car needs body repairs, it's usually best (and cheaper) to take it to a specialist body shop, of which there are many in New Zealand (a reflection of the high accident rate).

Note that when a car is under warranty, it must usually be serviced regularly by an approved dealer in order not to invalidate the warranty. However, if you need urgent assistance, particularly with an exotic foreign car, you're more likely to receive sympathetic help from a small local garage than a large dealer. Garages in New Zealand generally open from 8am to 5pm Monday to Friday and may also open on Saturday mornings, but are closed on Saturday afternoons and all day Sundays. In most areas there's a 24-hour breakdown service, although it's expensive and it's cheaper to join the AA (see page 168).

Service stations in New Zealand don't usually provide a free 'loan car' while yours is being serviced or repaired, although some garages are agents for local hire services which are cheaper than the national companies. Some garages will collect your car from your home or office and deliver it after a service, or alternatively will drop you off at a bus station or in a local town and pick you up when your car is ready for collection.

ROAD MAPS

A variety of motoring maps are available in New Zealand including the *AA New Zealand Road Atlas*, which is the best-selling general map. If you want a more comprehensive guide, one of the best maps available is the *Explore New Zealand Motoring Guide* which shows motorways, state and secondary highways and unsealed roads, town maps with one way streets, railway lines and stations, airports, public toilets and hospitals. It also provides historic information on individual towns and cities, geological features, national and forest parks, campervan and camping sites, hot springs and skiing areas. Good maps are also produced by the major oil companies (obtainable from petrol stations) and many publishers. Free maps of New Zealand are also available from Visitor Information Network (VIN) centres, libraries and car rental companies. Local town maps are available from tourist offices.

CAR RENTAL

A variety of companies in New Zealand rent cars by the day or week, including the ubiquitous multinational names such as Avis, Hertz and Budget and a wide variety of local firms. The multinationals offer the newest cars but are more expensive than local firms which usually offer cheaper, older cars. One big advantage of renting from a national firm is that you can pick up a car in one town and drop it off in another, whereas local firms usually insist that a car is returned to the same place. Note that many car rental firms don't allow you to take a car from the North to the South Island (or vice versa) on the ferry and those that do impose a stiff surcharge. This, together with the cost of the ferry, means it's usually cheaper to drop a rental car off at the ferry terminal (where major rental companies have offices), travel as a foot passenger, and rent another car on the other island.

Typical car brands and daily rental costs (including GST) from a multinational are Ford Festiva 1.3 $70, Toyota Corolla 1.6 $80, Ford Falcon 4.0 Station Wagon $95 and Toyota Previa $110. You can rent a car for substantially less from local rental companies, although it will be far from new with perhaps a couple of hundred thousand kilometres on the clock. Extras which can be ordered with a rental car include mobile phones, roof/ski racks, child seats (compulsory in New Zealand) and snow chains (recommended when venturing into an Alpine area during winter).

The above rates (from multinationals for brand new vehicles) include basic third party insurance and unlimited kilometres, but exclude fuel or personal accident insurance. There's an extra charge for damage excess waiver (DEW) of around $8.50 per day, which removes any liability for damage caused to a rented vehicle. If you don't have DEW (called collision damage waiver/CDW in many other countries) you must leave a cash or credit card deposit of $500 or more. It's important to note that no matter how comprehensive the insurance cover, you're unlikely to be covered for damage caused by driving off tarmac roads (i.e. unsealed roads), even if your vehicle is of the four-wheel-drive type. Some companies forbid their cars to be driven on unsealed roads.

The minimum age for renting a car in New Zealand is usually 21 and a full licence must have been held for at least 12 months. Some rental companies levy a supplement for larger vehicles when the driver is aged under 25. Popular car rental companies include Maui, which has offices in Auckland and Christchurch (freephone 0800 651080) and Budget Rent-a-Car with offices in various locations (freephone 0800 181181). Dial-a-Wreck (Auckland, ☎ (09) 358 0188) have bargain-priced (i.e. well-worn) cars for rent from around $25 per day excluding insurance.

MOTORING ORGANISATIONS

The Automobile Association (AA, PO Box 5, Auckland, ☎ (09) 377 4660) is the main motoring organisation in New Zealand. It's similar to the British organisation of the same name (it even uses the same logo of black 'AA' letters on a yellow background), but shouldn't be confused with Alcoholics Anonymous! The AA provides technical and legal advice, route planning, traffic information and a variety of maps and books on motoring, together with an emergency breakdown service. Visitors who are members of most major foreign motoring organisations can use all AA services *except* the breakdown service. Membership of the basic breakdown service costs $50 in return for which the AA will send a mechanic to repair your car at the roadside or, if this proves impossible, get it to the nearest garage. Extra services, such as a 'get you home' service, hire car and hotel accommodation can be provided for an extra fee. The AA publishes a magazine called *Directions* which is useful for keeping up with the latest motoring news. Several other organisations in New Zealand provide motoring breakdown cover, although most won't send a mechanic when you breakdown. Instead you must arrange your own repairs and the service then pays the bill up to a maximum amount.

PARKING

Parking is rarely a problem in New Zealand and there's usually plenty of space to go round. Street parking can, however, be difficult in city centres during the day, although there are off-street (including multi-storey) car parks. Many hotels and public buildings have underground car parks that are open to the general public. Car parks can be recognised by the internationally recognised 'P' symbol and several cities publish a *Guide to Parking* which you can pick up at local VIN offices. Parking is usually either pay-and-display, where you buy a ticket and display it behind the windscreen of your car, or a 'pay on exit' system. Most public car parks have extra-wide, easy-access spaces for disabled drivers offering free or reduced cost parking. You need a concession ticket to use them which is obtainable from New Zealand CCS Inc., PO Box 6450, Auckland. Applications must be supported by a certificate of disability from a doctor.

No Parking Zones: restricted on-road parking zones are indicated by yellow lines painted at the roadside. A nearby sign will explain whether parking is banned at all times or within certain hours only, and whether a time limit applies. Where parking is restricted rather than being prohibited at all times, restrictions usually operate between 8am and 6pm Monday to Friday. Restrictions don't apply on Sundays but are usually in force on Saturdays, e.g. from 8am to 1pm. In areas where there's late night shopping or night-time entertainment (e.g. restaurants or theatres), parking limitations often apply until 9pm. If so, expect them to be enforced with the same vigour as they are during the day. Where parking is permitted, you should park only on the left-hand side of the road facing the direction of the traffic flow.

Meters: most city and town centres have meter zones. The charge, together with the time you may stay, varies according to the location, but is usually around 50¢ per half hour (a nearby sign will explain the charges). Meters take 20¢, 50¢ and $1 coins. Some cities (such as Wellington) are experimenting with free weekend parking in an attempt to entice shoppers back to city centres and away from out-of-town shopping centres. Check carefully, however, as schemes are always changing.

Parking offenders receive fines ranging from between $10 and $40 depending on the severity of the offence (overstaying on a meter is a minor infringement, whereas parking on yellow lines is more serious).

PEDESTRIAN ROAD RULES

Given the state of New Zealand driving the best advice for pedestrians is to stay off the road completely. However, as this obviously isn't practical, you should take every care when crossing the road in New Zealand. Pedestrian crossings in towns are indicated by white stripes and yellow flashing beacons. Once on the crossing drivers should stop, but it's advisable to make sure they have before venturing into the road. There are also crossings controlled by traffic lights. Take extra care when with children, many of whom are killed or injured by speeding, drunk or dangerous drivers each year. Never let them play on a road, however quiet. Bear in mind that young children are unable to judge traffic speeds accurately and should usually be escorted to and from school. Take particular care in country areas where there are no footpaths. Wear bright coloured clothing and carry a torch (flashlight) at night. It's best to step off the road when you hear or see a vehicle approaching, even though you have a perfect right to walk on a road without a footpath.

Take care when using pedestrianised streets, some of which allow access to vehicles at certain times or may be shared by delivery vehicles and buses (cyclists also use pedestrianised streets, although it's illegal). When using footpaths keep an eye open for skateboarders and rollerbladers (as well as cyclists). Many city authorities have banned skateboarding on footpaths and roads, although it remains a hazard even though offenders face a fine of $500.

ROAD SIGNS

Road signs in New Zealand can be extremely variable. In most cities and towns you'll find extensive road signs to all destinations and local facilities, such as schools, swimming pools and car parks. However, outside towns, signposting can be vague and you'll frequently not find any (or many) signs at junctions. The main reason for this is that there's often only one major road between cities and towns. For example, if you leave the Interislander ferry at Picton heading for Christchurch and keep to the major road at every junction, the only place you can end up is Christchurch! If you're stuck for directions, simply stop and ask. Most locals will be pleased to help you and, unlike some countries, it's usually quite safe to stop anywhere at any time of the day or night.

On short stretches of motorway, signs usually indicate the street to which an exit leads, rather than a town or suburb. For example, when heading north into Auckland on the southern motorway and wishing to travel to the suburb of Newmarket, you're advised to take the exit marked Broadway, the main road that passes through Newmarket. Therefore check the name of the street before setting out. Some roads are promoted as tourist attractions (indicated by blue and white signs), for example the Pacific Coast Highway, which runs from Auckland to Hastings.

Roadside information signs in New Zealand traditionally contained written instructions, for example 'SHARP BEND' or 'MAJOR ROAD AHEAD', and there are still many of these signs around (which may puzzle visitors from America who must wonder how a bend can be sharp). However, international pictorial signs are becoming commonplace, although in some cases they are still accompanied by written explanations, e.g. No entry signs consist of a red circle with a white bar accompanied by the words 'No Entry'. An inverted red triangle on a white background means give way or yield and is marked 'Give Way' just to remind you (not that most New Zealand motorists take too much notice of it!). One sign that's peculiar to New Zealand is the 'LSZ' sign, consisting of black lettering on a white border surrounded by a red circle. This means Limited Speed Zone and is found where a major road runs through a town or village (often so small that you don't notice it, which is why the sign is there to remind you). The sign generally means slow down, take care and look out for pedestrians and animals. Instructions are also sometimes marked on the road, but in the reverse order so that motorists can read the message in the correct sequence, e.g. 'Give' followed by 'Way' a little further down the road means that you're approaching a junction where you must yield right of way.

12.

HEALTH

The quality of healthcare in New Zealand is excellent and comparable with other developed countries. Most illnesses and chronic conditions are treated in New Zealand hospitals with the exception of a few highly specialist areas (such as certain transplants), when it may be necessary to travel abroad. The standard of public health is generally high although there are some differences between racial groups, with Maoris in particular suffering from ill health more often than those of European origin. New Zealanders tend to suffer more from alcohol-related diseases than Europeans, but less from smoking-related diseases. A disturbing trend in recent years is that diseases associated with poverty, such as rickets and TB in children, are on the increase after being virtually wiped out. The infant mortality rate is around nine deaths per 1,000 live births (relatively high compared with other OECD countries) and life expectancy some 77 years.

New Zealand provides free or subsidised healthcare to all its citizens, permanent residents and certain visitors. This is comparable to the system in European countries such as France or Germany, where the state covers the bulk of the cost of medical treatment, but expects patients to make a contribution. Free care isn't as comprehensive as the British National Health Service, which aims to provide free care to almost everyone, including emergency treatment for visitors. On the other hand, it's nothing like that in the USA where every last pill, potion and sticking plaster must be paid for.

The Ministry of Health is responsible for funding and providing state healthcare in New Zealand, which it delegates to Regional Health Authorities (RHAs) whose job is to meet the government's health objectives by spending their budgets in the most cost-effective way. This system has been in existence since 1993 and introduced the commercial market into the public healthcare sector. RHAs use their funding to 'buy' healthcare services from various 'suppliers' including family doctors, hospitals, nursing homes and other health organisations. This arrangement has seen most hospitals reformed as Crown Health Enterprises (CHEs or 'cheeses' in local slang), which are effectively in competition with each other to provide the best standard of healthcare at the lowest cost.

The state healthcare system has come under huge pressure in recent years due to an increasing demand for services amid severe financial constraints, as politicians have sought to reduce the spiralling health budget in order to fund tax cuts. A number of hospitals have been closed and waiting lists for non-emergency treatment, once unknown in New Zealand, have soared to almost 100,000. There has also been disruption to healthcare as successive governments have experimented with various measures aimed at providing a better service for less money (a formidable task), including an attempt to introduce market forces into the public healthcare sector. The resulting hospital closures and cuts in services have prompted a public backlash and mass demonstrations in the country's cities. The government's response to this politically embarrassing situation has been to promise $1.5 billion over the next few years to provide additional free health services and establish a 'waiting list fund' to cut hospital admission times.

Although you won't be denied medical attention in New Zealand (assuming you don't mind waiting), alternative treatments are also popular. A recent survey by *Consumer* magazine claimed that half of all New Zealanders have tried alternative therapies, usually for conditions for which they had been seeing a 'traditional' doctor. The most popular alternative therapies are chiropractic, herbal medicine, homeopathy and osteopathy. New Zealand doctors are generally sympathetic to these therapies and occasionally refer patients to alternative practitioners.

EMERGENCIES

In a medical emergency in New Zealand simply dial 111 and ask for an 'Ambulance', which will be despatched to take you to the nearest hospital. The ambulance service is free and is provided by different organisations depending on the region (e.g. Wellington Free Ambulance in the capital). In most regions, the ambulance service has paramedic teams and also use helicopter ambulances. In remote areas, specially trained search-and-rescue teams are available and usually include a doctor who can administer treatment and perform minor operations on the spot.

If you're physically able, you can make your own way to the accident or emergency department of your nearest hospital. When you move to a new area it's wise to acquaint yourself with where your nearest emergency hospital is situated, as a number have closed or merged their accident and emergency departments in recent years or operate them only part-time. Therefore, while there will always be an accident and emergency facility in your area, not every hospital is equipped to handle emergencies. If your condition isn't serious enough to warrant a hospital visit you should consult your family doctor. In towns and cities there are 'after-hours clinics' where you can see a doctor concerning minor ailments when your doctor's surgery is closed.

A private company called Accident Info Services operates a telephone information service and advises callers on how to access New Zealand's health system. It can advise you on local doctors and hospitals and arrange for a doctor to visit you at home, and is particularly useful when medical attention other than immediate hospital attention is necessary. You can contact Accident Info Services on 0900 54411 (the first minute is free and additional minutes costs $2.99).

SOCIAL SECURITY HEALTH BENEFITS

New Zealand doesn't deduct social security health contributions from salaries and the cost of providing public health services is largely met from general taxation. All citizens and permanent residents are automatically entitled to state healthcare and it isn't necessary to establish a contributions record. The basic principle of state healthcare in New Zealand is that hospital in-patient treatment is provided free, whereas the cost of out-patient and non-hospital treatment (e.g. consultations with a family doctor and prescribed medicines) must be paid for by patients (although services are subsidised). Those on low incomes can apply for a Community Services Card (CSC) which entitles them to a discount on healthcare costs (☎ freephone (0800) 805494 for information). There's no automatic reduction in charges for special groups, although free doctor's services are provided for children aged five and under. Pensioners aren't automatically entitled to reduced-cost services unless they have a low income. Note that dental treatment and optical services are largely outside the scope of the state health scheme.

For information about public health services in New Zealand contact the Ministry of Health, PO Box 5013, Wellington (☎ (04) 496 2277).

Accident Compensation Scheme

Medical treatment and on-going healthcare necessary as the result of an accident isn't covered by the state healthcare scheme, but by the Accident Compensation Scheme run by the Accident Compensation Corporation (ACC). The ACC scheme (see page 189) is funded by a levy on employers' payrolls and the salaries of employees and the self-employed. Benefits paid by the ACC are more comprehensive than the basic state health scheme and include all treatment, including surgery, hospital care, specialists, doctor's fees and medicines, irrespective of where or how the accident occurred and who was to blame. It also pays long-term financial benefits if you're unable to work as a result of an accident. The advantages of this scheme, which is unique, are that you don't need to buy private accident insurance or sue a guilty party for compensation (in fact the law forbids you to do this). The main disadvantage is that the benefits aren't usually as generous as they would be with private insurance or what you could receive as a result of taking legal action against someone who causes an accident.

PRIVATE HEALTH CARE

Private health practitioners operate both hand-in-hand with the public health service and independently of it. In addition to specialist appointments and hospital treatment, people commonly use private health treatment to obtain second opinions, private health checks or screening, and for complementary medicine (which isn't usually available under the public health service). If you need to see a GP or specialist privately, you (or your insurance company) must pay the full fee, which is usually left to the doctor's discretion. Most patients who receive private health treatment in New Zealand have private health insurance (see page 193), usually in order to circumvent the public health waiting lists for non-emergency specialist appointments and hospital treatment. Private patients are free to choose their own specialist and hospital, and are usually accommodated in a single hotel-style room with a radio, telephone, colour TV, en suite bathroom and room service.

Make sure that a doctor or medical practitioner is qualified to provide the treatment you require and when choosing a private specialist or clinic you should be extremely cautious and only go to someone who's highly recommended. It's sometimes advisable to obtain a second opinion, particularly if you're diagnosed as having a serious illness or require a major operation (but don't expect your doctor or specialist to approve). Although not common in New Zealand, unnecessary operations aren't unknown.

Note that the quality of private treatment isn't any better than that provided by the public health service and you shouldn't assume that because a doctor (or any other medical practitioner) is in private practice, he's more competent than his public health counterpart. In fact you'll often see the same specialist or be treated by the same surgeon under the public health service and privately.

DOCTORS

New Zealand has a community-based system of healthcare, where your first point of contact for any medical problem is your family doctor or general practitioner (GP), who treats minor conditions and refers more serious cases to specialists or hospitals.

It's advisable to find and register with a doctor as soon as you arrive in a new area, although it isn't compulsory to do so and you can just turn up at any doctor's surgery and will usually receive prompt attention. You're allowed to choose any doctor you wish, though it's obviously more convenient to use one near your home. Telephone directories contain a list of local doctors in the preface.

Most doctors' surgeries are well equipped and often take the form of health centres or group practises where several doctors practise together and specialise in different areas, such as obstetrics or paediatrics. Many also have their own nurses whom you can consult for minor problems and treatments, which is cheaper than seeing a doctor. New Zealand nurses are highly trained and qualified, and are authorised to prescribe certain drugs and administer treatments (such as intravenous injections) which aren't permitted in many other countries. Under the state healthcare scheme, a flat rate is charged for each visit to a doctor, whether you're consulting him about a pimple or a possible cancer. The basic consultation fee is $35 for adults and $16 for children over five (or $10 for a visit to a nurse), plus the cost of any medicines prescribed. There's no charge for a prescription as such (just the cost of the drugs), but a repeat prescription costs $6 to $10. Under a new scheme, children aged five and under are entitled to free doctor's visits and prescriptions. If you hold a 'Community Services Card' (see page 177) a doctor's visit costs $20.

Surgery hours are usually 8.30am to 5.30pm Monday to Friday, although it's necessary to make an appointment and a doctor may not always be available (e.g. he could be out on a house call). Some family doctors provide a service outside surgery hours and make house calls, although this is rare; in cities calls outside surgery hours are directed to an after-hours clinic. If you don't know where your nearest after-hours clinic is located, call your doctor's regular number and your call will be diverted (or a recorded message will tell you where the clinic is).

DRUGS & MEDICINES

Drugs and medicines are sold in pharmacies, know in New Zealand by the British name 'chemist', which may be part of another business. They sell prescription drugs and medicines, non-prescription medicines, plus other products such as cosmetics and toiletries, but don't usually carry such an extensive range of goods as an American drugstore. Normal opening hours are 9am to 5.30pm Monday to Friday (occasionally later on Thursdays or Fridays) and sometimes on Saturday mornings. In most areas there's a duty chemist that's open longer hours or an emergency contact number is provided for those needing drugs in an emergency (details are posted in chemists).

The cost of prescribed drugs is subsidised by the government drug agency, Pharmac, and should cost no more than $15 per item or less if you have a community services card (CSC). After you have paid for 20 prescription items in a year, you're entitled to apply for a Pharmaceutical Subsidy Card (PSC), irrespective of your income, which entitles you to receive further prescriptions for as little as $2 each for the rest of the year (or free if you have a CSC). Pharmac periodically adds and removes drugs from its subsidised list, e.g. several new AIDS-inhibiting drugs such as Ritonavir have recently become added to the list, while a number of acne treatments have been removed. If you're obtaining a prescription item from a chemist you'll pay the same price everywhere. However, the cost of non-prescription items can vary considerably and non-drug items such as toiletries are considerably cheaper at supermarkets.

Most pharmacists provide general advice regarding the best medicines for particular conditions and some are specially trained to provide individual consultations and advice to customers under the 'Comprehensive Pharmaceutical Care Service'. Many patients use this system as a cheaper alternative to visiting a doctor, with the result that some pharmacists have begun charging $30 to $50 for consultations, plus the cost of the drugs! It's still possible, however, to find pharmacists who dispense free specialist advice and in the case of minor ailments this can save you a great deal of money compared with the cost of a visit to a doctor, as they will also tell you which drugs can be purchased over the counter for less than the $15 prescription fee.

HOSPITALS & CLINICS

Members of the public can use hospitals directly only in the case of accidents and emergencies. In all other cases your first point of contact is your family doctor who will refer you to an appropriate hospital as necessary. The main criticism of the healthcare reforms in recent years has been the increase in hospital waiting lists, which are long and growing longer. There have been many horror stories of patients requiring urgent hospital treatment having to wait ten hours or more for a bed (not that this makes New Zealand any worse than many other countries). However, once you get a bed in a public hospital the standard of medical and nursing care is as good as you're likely to find anywhere.

Under the current system, regional health authorities must 'buy' the services you require (e.g. an operation) from the most cost effective source, which will usually be your local hospital. However, if you're willing to travel to another (or any) hospital you should inform your doctor, as he may be able to book you into another hospital where the waiting lists are shorter. It can be difficult to identify hospitals in New Zealand since the 1993 changes to the state healthcare system, when they became known by various euphemisms such as 'healthcare centres', 'mental care units' (mental hospitals) or 'elder care units' (geriatric hospitals).

New Zealand hospitals provide free in-patient healthcare which includes medical and nursing care, drugs and accommodation. The government experimented with a $50 per day 'hotel charge' in hospitals between 1991 and 1993, but this was dropped due to public opposition (although it's possible that some form of hospital usage charge could be re-introduced in future). Out-patient treatment in accident and emergency departments isn't free and is paid for in the same way as visits to a family doctor (CSC holders pay reduced fees). If you make use of the accident and emergency service frequently, i.e. more than five times a year, you can obtain a Hospital Service Card (HSC) entitling you to free treatment for the remainder of the year.

In addition to public hospitals there are also many private hospitals in New Zealand, which allow the wealthy and those with medical insurance to avoid the waiting lists in the public sector. Many private hospitals are owned by the medical insurance companies (as public hospitals don't accept private patients) and accommodation may be more luxurious than in public hospitals, although the standard of medical care is the same and they're often staffed by the same doctors. Some private hospitals receive government subsidies and there are a number of projects where the public and private sectors co-operate to provide specialist services such as coronary care. Some charities also provide health services such as community clinics which are partially funded by the government. Some private hospitals and clinics specialise in non-essential cosmetic surgery.

The New Zealand Ministry of Health helpfully publishes hospital death rate statistics to help you choose a hospital, although this won't do you much good if you're rushed to the nearest hospital in an emergency.

CHILDBIRTH

The first port of call for pregnant women in New Zealand is their family doctor, who can undertake preliminary tests and checks and refer you for antenatal and (subsequently) post natal care, either within the practise itself or at a nearby clinic. It's usual for a birth to take place in a local hospital, although it's possible to have a baby at home attended by a midwife. This is more usual in rural areas, where the nearest hospital may be a considerable distance away.

Abortion is legal in New Zealand, under strict terms and conditions, which include when continuing with a pregnancy would pose a threat to the physical or mental well-being of the mother, or when a child is likely to be born seriously handicapped. Two specially approved doctors or counsellors must authorise an abortion.

CHILDREN'S HEALTH

Family doctors provide a health service for children and where necessary refer them to consultants and specialists at an appropriate hospital. New Zealand's leading children's hospital (with a similar status there to London's famous Great Ormond Street Children's Hospital) is Auckland's Starship Children's Hospital, which recently caused an outcry among doctors and dieticians for allowing McDonalds to open a fast food outlet in the foyer (although it went down well with the kids)!

New Zealand has a tradition of promoting access to the great outdoors for children and there are 'health camps' throughout the country for children aged 12 or under with special needs who attend for up to six weeks. Children are referred to the camps by doctors, social workers and teachers, and undertake a programme of remedial education, health education, sports and games, in addition to learning life skills. Camps also have psychologists who counsel children regarding behavioural problems. Health Camps are largely financed by special 'health postage stamps' issued by NZ Post in the spring, from which a donation is made to help fund camps. Health authorities also operate various health education and development programmes for children, including a recent screening programme for Auckland teenagers to try to minimise the risks of future heart disease.

DENTISTS

There are excellent dentists throughout New Zealand: indeed New Zealanders travelling abroad often search high and low in cities such as London or New York for a New Zealand dentist. If you wish, you may be able to find a British or American dentist in Auckland or Wellington, although they all inflict the same sort of torture regardless of nationality! Most dentists in New Zealand are in private practise as the public health scheme doesn't extend to dentistry, except in the case of children. Children at primary schools see a school dental nurse and many primary schools have a dental surgery on the premises. Children are entitled to see a school dentist every 12 months, although a backlog has been developing for several years resulting in most children seeing a dentist only once every 18 months (they don't seem to mind!). All children up to the age of 16 (18 if still at school) are entitled to free treatment by the dentist of their choice, assuming he participates in the 'free dental scheme' (many dentists have withdrawn from the scheme due to the inadequate fees paid by the Ministry of Health).

To find a dentist, ask for recommendations from neighbours, colleagues and friends, or consult your local telephone directory. It's advisable to shop around as charges can vary considerably, particularly for extensive repair work. However, most dentists, unless they target wealthy patients, charge fees that are affordable to the average person (although it can still be an expensive business). It's wise to obtain a quotation before having any 'expensive' treatment – many dentists have 'menu pricing', although this should be regarded only as a guide. Typical dental fees include $65 for an examination and scaling and $70 for a small filling, while a set of dentures (including extractions and fitting) is likely to set you back at least $1,000.

It's possible to take out special insurance against dental costs and cover for dental treatment may also be included in general medical insurance policies, which can be purchased from medical insurance companies and from dentists. The cost varies according to the state of your teeth and whether all or part expenses are covered. Most people find that it's cheaper not to have dental insurance, but to put a little money aside for dental costs and pay bills from their own pocket.

OPTICIANS

Opticians in New Zealand are known as optometrists and have surgeries (more often shops) in all towns and cities where they provide eye tests and sell lenses, frames and contact lenses. Optometry is an entirely private business in New Zealand and outside the scope of the public health system. You can save money by shopping around and buying spectacles and contact lenses somewhere other than the fancy optometrists found in modern shopping centres. A basic pair of spectacles with lenses costs around $200. If you think that you have a medical problem affecting your eyes (such as glaucoma), you should ask your family doctor to refer you to a specialist at a hospital, in which case treatment will be provided free.

COUNSELLING & SOCIAL SERVICES

Counselling and assistance for health and social problems is available under the public health system, and from many local community groups and volunteer organisations, ranging from national associations to small local groups (including self-help groups). Local authorities provide social workers to advise and support those requiring help within their community. If you need to find help locally, you can contact your local council, local voluntary services or a Citizens Advice Bureau for advice. A list of 24-hour emergency services (including many counselling services) is included in telephone directories, plus community help and welfare services, and help for young people.

Many colleges and educational establishments provide a counselling service for students, and general hospitals usually have a psychiatrist on call 24 hours a day. Problems for which help is available are numerous and include drug rehabilitation; alcoholism (e.g. Alcoholics Anonymous); gambling; dieting (e.g. Weight Watchers); smoking; attempted suicide and psychiatric problems; homosexual related problems; youth problems; battered children and women; marriage and relationship counselling; and rape. A number of voluntary organisations and local authorities run refuges for battered wives (and their children) or maltreated children, whose conditions have become intolerable (some provide 24-hour emergency phone numbers). If you or a member of your family are the victims of a violent crime, the police will put you in touch with a local victim support scheme. New Zealand has an extensive network of Disability Resource Centres providing help and advice to disabled people.

SEXUALLY-TRANSMITTED DISEASES

Like most countries, New Zealand has its share of sexually-transmitted diseases, including the deadly Acquired Immune Deficiency Syndrome (AIDS). Fortunately New Zealand has one of the lowest incidences of Aids in the developed world and only 30 people a year are found to have the disease, down from a peak of 79 in 1989. Aids is transmitted by sexual contact, needle sharing among drug addicts, and less commonly, through transfused blood or its components. All blood used in transfusions in New Zealand is screened for HIV (human immunodeficiency virus), the virus which usually leads to Aids.

The furore over Aids has died down in the past few years, which many fear may cause those most at risk to be lulled into a false sense of security (many teenagers still practise unsafe sex). The explosion of Aids predicted by 'experts' in many countries hasn't materialised, particularly among the heterosexual population, although the number of heterosexual cases is increasing. **Aids is always fatal and to date there's no cure.** The best protection against Aids is for men to wear a condom, although they aren't foolproof (against Aids or pregnancy) and the only real protection is celibacy. In an attempt to combat AIDS, the use of condoms has been widely encouraged through a comprehensive (if obscure) advertising campaign, although it has taken a long time to get the message across about safe sex. Condom machines can be found in various public places (there's an on-going debate about whether they should be installed in secondary schools) and purchased from chemists and other outlets (but they aren't cheap).

Family doctors in New Zealand can provide basic information about Aids prevention and can refer those with particular problems and worries to specialists. Gay and other organisations are also active in providing help and advice. Some positive news for sufferers is that several Aids-inhibiting drugs have been placed on the subsidised drugs list in recent years at a cost of millions of dollars a year.

SMOKING

New Zealand has become one of the leading countries in the battle against smoking, which has resulted in a significantly lower death rate from lung disease and other smoking-related diseases than, for example, in most European countries. Cigarettes have become increasingly expensive due to sharp tax rises in the last few years. The government spends around $20 million a year on anti-smoking programmes, although this represents only a fraction of the amount raised in tobacco taxes. In future cigarette packets will contain no less than six dire warnings about the perils of smoking (including one in Maori). The most recent anti-smoking law has seen a ban on the sale of cigarettes in 10-packs, which was thought to be a handy, affordable size for teenage smokers, particularly those of school age. Those under 16 are prohibited from purchasing tobacco products and the age limit may soon be increased to 18. The penalty for selling tobacco to those under age is $2,000 and a $40 fine is planned for teenagers caught buying tobacco under age.

Smoking is officially banned in most public places and you cannot smoke in most public buildings or on buses, coaches, trains and aircraft. Most workplaces have banned smoking altogether, although the more tolerant have a small smoking area, and the majority of restaurants are entirely non-smoking (if they aren't they must have a non-smoking area). Quite apart from the anti-smoking legislation, smoking is considered socially unacceptable in New Zealand. You would be extremely unwise to smoke in a non-smoking area and even when indulging in the evil weed perfectly legally you may attract angry glances, remarks, or even requests to stub it out if your smoke is causing annoyance to others. In the latest development in the battle against smoking, the government is considering claiming damages for public health costs (as a result of smoking) from tobacco companies, as has already happened in the USA.

HELP FOR THE HANDICAPPED

Official government statistics show that around 20 per cent of New Zealanders have some kind of 'handicap', varying from a serious physical disability to a minor visual impairment (curiously the rate is higher in the South Island than the North Island). All public offices and businesses are required to make special provision for handicapped people (e.g. special access ramps, facilities for the hard of hearing, etc.) although provision of these services is patchy as a lot of older buildings cannot be modified. Most buses cannot accommodate those with mobility problems, although a small number of taxis can. There are several organisations that provide help to the handicapped in New Zealand, which includes practical help, financial assistance and advice (including advice on state benefits). The main organisation is the New Zealand Disability Resource Centre (☎ (06) 356 2311), which has centres throughout the country. Invalidity benefit is payable to those unable to work due to a physical or mental disability, and provides a weekly payment equivalent to around half the average wage. Those who are handicapped as a result of an accident receive payments from the Accident Compensation Corporation (see page 189).

BIRTHS & DEATHS

Births in New Zealand must be registered within seven days at your local registry office for births, marriages and deaths. They will provide you with a copy of the entry in the register otherwise known as a birth certificate (necessary for official purposes such as claiming benefits and school registration). Deaths should be registered at the same office as births (also within seven days) with a copy of the death certificate provided by the hospital or doctor attending the death. This is usually carried out by the undertaker. As anywhere, dying is a major expense in New Zealand where an average funeral and burial costs around $1,500 and possibly much more with 'extras' such as cars and flowers. The cost of shipping a body to another country for burial is considerable and is to be avoided if at all possible. Most medical insurance policies provide cover for funeral expenses (with the size of benefits linked to the cost of the policy). It's also possible to take out a funeral plan to cover these expenses. For those without insurance or private means, a government funeral grant of up to $1,000 is available, which depends on the means and assets of the deceased and his next of kin (it's generally available only to those who already receive social security benefits).

MEDICAL TREATMENT ABROAD

If you're entitled to social security health benefits in New Zealand you can take advantage of reciprocal healthcare arrangements in other countries with which New Zealand has a reciprocal agreement. This includes Australia and the UK (but not the USA), where you're entitled to the same public health benefits as citizens and residents simply by producing your New Zealand passport or migration documents. In Australia you receive free hospital treatment and subsidised prescriptions through the Medicare system, while in the UK you receive most medical treatment free, paying only prescription and subsidised dental charges.

If you're a visitor and a resident of a country with a reciprocal health agreement with New Zealand (including Australia and the UK) you can take advantage of public healthcare services in New Zealand. These entitle you to free hospital in-patient treatment and free medicines while in hospital. When visiting a doctor you'll be charged at the same rate as New Zealanders for consultations and will also be able to purchase subsidised prescriptions. To claim these benefits simply show your passport to the doctor or pharmacist. There's no entitlement to subsidised dentistry (except for children) or optical services and you aren't entitled to free treatment for conditions which existed before you entered New Zealand (if you knew or could reasonably have been expected to have known about them). It's important to note that citizens of countries without a reciprocal health agreement with New Zealand aren't entitled to free hospital treatment or subsidised doctor's consultations or prescriptions, and must pay the full cost of all treatment (which is substantially higher than the subsidised rate). Therefore it's essential to have private medical insurance when visiting New Zealand.

13.

INSURANCE

New Zealand has an innovative approach to insurance which is quite different from that in, for example, the USA and most western European countries. As in those countries there are state schemes which pay health, sickness and unemployment benefits. Unlike most other countries, however, the New Zealand system isn't largely insurance based and individuals aren't required to make contributions in order to benefit (although as the substantial costs are funded by general taxation, they cannot be said to be free). New Zealand has taken the concept of state insurance a step further and provides universal accident insurance to all citizens, residents and visitors. If you have an accident at work or on the roads you'll be compensated by the government-operated Accident Compensation Corporation (ACC), regardless of who was to blame or whether you have paid any contributions.

New Zealand's ACC operates what's essentially a mandatory accident insurance system, financed both through taxes and (unlike most other state benefits) by a levy on earnings. However, entitlement to benefits isn't based on contributions as it would be with a commercial insurance scheme. The aim of this scheme was originally to provide New Zealanders with superior accident insurance at low cost by taking the commercialism out of insurance. For many years the scheme worked well and was renowned for its generous compensation payments, although in recent years spending cutbacks have forced a reduction in benefits (accident victims are now compensated through weekly payments of limited duration rather than huge lump sums, as used to be the case) and the scheme has come in for much criticism. The fact remains, however, that New Zealand provides its citizens with various kinds of 'free' insurance, a situation unthinkable in many other countries.

One spin-off of New Zealand's approach to insurance, and one that would have grossly overpaid personal injury lawyers in the USA gasping in horror, is that suing the party who caused an accident isn't usually possible under New Zealand law. You must simply accept the payment awarded by the ACC, which although it means that you're unlikely to receive a multi-million dollar payout (as you may in the USA), ensures that a lot of money isn't wasted on long, drawn out court cases.

It should be noted, however, that the situation regarding insurance in New Zealand doesn't mean that you don't need to take out private insurance. The state schemes don't, by any means, cover every eventuality and neither are the benefits necessarily generous, making private insurance provision advisable, if not essential.

INSURANCE COMPANIES

There are numerous insurance companies from which to choose in New Zealand, providing either a range of insurance services or specialising in certain fields only. You can buy insurance from many sources including traditional insurance companies selling through their own salesmen or independent brokers, direct insurance companies (selling direct to the public), banks and other financial institutions, and motoring organisations. An increasingly common trend in New Zealand is for banks to offer property, life and even motor insurance to their customers, which they do on an agency basis, i.e. they don't compare prices from various companies to find you the cheapest policy. Their premiums, however, are usually competitive. The major insurance companies have offices or agents (brokers) throughout the country, most of whom will provide a free analysis of your family or business insurance needs.

Brokers: if you choose a broker, you should use one who's independent and sells policies from a wide range of insurance companies. Some brokers or agents are tied to a particular insurance company and sell policies only from that company (which includes most banks). An independent broker should research the whole market and take into account your individual requirements, why you're investing (if applicable), the various companies' financial performance, what you can afford and the kind of policy that's best for you. He mustn't offer you a policy because it pays him the highest commission, which incidentally you should ask him about (particularly regarding life insurance).

Direct Insurance: in recent years direct marketing and direct response insurance companies (bypassing brokers) have resulted in huge savings for consumers, particularly for car, building and home contents' insurance. Direct marketing companies give quotations over the phone and often you aren't even required to complete a proposal form. Compare premiums from a number of direct sales insurance companies with the best deals from brokers before choosing a policy.

Shop Around: when buying insurance, you should shop 'til you drop and then shop around some more! Premiums vary considerably (e.g. by 100 to 200 per cent), although you must ensure that you're comparing similar policies and that important benefits haven't been omitted. Bear in mind that the cheapest policy isn't necessarily the best, particularly regarding the prompt payment of claims. Many analysts believe that it's better to pay for independent insurance advice rather than accept 'free' advice, which may be more expensive in the long run. You should obtain a number of quotations for each insurance need and shouldn't assume that your existing insurance company is the best choice for a new insurance requirement. Buy only the insurance that you *want* and *need* and ensure that you can afford the payments (and that your cover is protected if you're sick or unemployed).

INSURANCE CONTRACTS

Read all insurance contracts carefully before signing them. If you don't understand everything, ask a friend or colleague to 'translate' it or obtain professional advice. Policies often contain traps and legal loopholes in the small print. If a policy has pages of legal jargon and gobbledegook in *very* small print, you have a right to be suspicious, particularly as it's common practice nowadays to be as brief as possible and write clearly and concisely in language which doesn't require a doctorate in law. Note that an insurance certificate or schedule won't list all the conditions and exclusions, which are listed only in the full policy document. Many of the new telephone direct-selling companies handle all quotations, enquiries and claims by phone on a paper-less basis, so you may never see a form or document explaining your policy. This saves companies money which they allegedly pass onto policyholders in the form of lower premiums. Take care how you answer questions in an insurance proposal form, as even if you mistakenly provide false information, an insurance company can refuse to pay out when you make a claim.

Most insurance policies run for a calendar year from the date on which you take out a policy. All insurance policy premiums should be paid punctually as late payment can affect your benefits or a claim, although if this is so, it should be noted in your policy. Before signing an insurance policy, you should shop around and take a day or two to think it over (never sign on the spot as you may regret it later). With some insurance contracts, you may have a 'cooling off' period during which you can cancel a policy without penalty.

Claims: although insurance companies are keen to take your money, many aren't nearly so happy to settle claims. Like insurance companies everywhere, some insurance companies will do almost anything to avoid paying out in the event of a claim and will use any available loophole. Fraud is estimated to cost the insurance industry $millions a year (particularly motor insurance fraud) and staff may be trained to automatically assume that claims are fraudulent. If you wish to make a claim, you must usually inform your insurance company in writing by registered letter within a number of days of the incident (possibly within 24 hours in the case of theft). **Failure to do so will render your claim void!** Don't send original bills or documents regarding a claim to your insurance company unless it's absolutely essential (if necessary you can send a certified copy). Keep a copy of all bills, documents and correspondence, and send letters by recorded or registered mail so that your insurance company cannot deny receipt.

Don't bank a cheque received in settlement of a claim if you think it's insufficient, as you may be deemed to have accepted it as full and final settlement. It's also inadvisable to accept the first offer, as many insurance companies try to get away with making a low settlement (if an insurer pays what you have claimed without a quibble, you probably claimed too little!). When dealing with insurance companies, perseverance often pays. Insurers are increasingly refusing to pay up on the flimsiest of pretexts, as they know that many people won't pursue their cases, even when they have a valid claim. Don't give up on a claim if you have a good case, but persist until you have exhausted every avenue.

SOCIAL SECURITY

New Zealand has a comprehensive social security system that provides a wide range of benefits to cover sickness and invalidity, unemployment and old age. Around one in four New Zealanders receives some sort of social security payment. As in many other countries, the social security system has suffered a funding crisis in recent years and (in real terms) benefits are being reduced, even though they are officially increased each year (benefits are reviewed annually, with increases taking effect in January). The government spends over $10 billion annually on social security benefits, most of which aren't based on contributions or previous earnings, but on a flat rate set by the government. On average this provides claimants receiving benefits with around 40 to 50 per cent of the average annual weekly wage, which is barely adequate to live on.

The government has introduced a number of schemes over recent years to try to ensure that benefits are paid only to those in genuine need and, even then, only so long as they need them. An increasing number of benefits are paid only after means-testing (an appraisal of an applicant's savings and other financial circumstances). In other cases claimants are regularly called to account and expected to prove that they still genuinely need a benefit and cannot manage without it or go back to work.

Despite an increasingly tough stance on paying out government (or rather taxpayers') money, the authorities still positively encourage people to claim benefits to which they may be entitled on a 'we may turn you down but you're welcome to try' basis. Applications for benefits should be made to the Income Support Service or, in some cases, the Inland Revenue Department, the addresses of which can be found in your local telephone directory.

Eligibility: New Zealand nationals, permanent residents and foreign workers temporarily employed in New Zealand are automatically covered by social security, without the need to make social security contributions. They must, however, make contributions to the ACC (see below), although these aren't social security contributions as such. As the ACC isn't a social security scheme, continuing to pay into the social security scheme in your home country (which you're usually entitled to do) doesn't exempt you from paying the ACC levy on your earnings. Visitors are also covered by the ACC scheme without the need to make contributions. If you should suffer an accident and make a claim on the scheme it will cover your medical and associated expenses in New Zealand, but it won't cover repatriation or medical expenses arising abroad in connection with an accident or loss of earnings abroad.

Social security benefits in New Zealand are paid only after a minimum period of residence, for example, unemployment benefit is available only after you have lived in New Zealand for 12 months and national superannuation (state pension) usually requires a 12-year residency period. However, New Zealand has reciprocal agreements with certain countries (including Australia, the Netherlands and the UK) under which those migrating from these countries can apply for New Zealand social security benefits as soon as they arrive to take up permanent residence. It's important to note that a reciprocal agreement only entitles you to apply for benefits and whether or not the benefit is paid depends on other eligibility criteria such as your income and other means. Under a recent change in the immigration rules, prospective immigrants are excluded if they don't have sufficient resources to support themselves for at least 12 months without claiming state benefits. For further information contact the Manager, International Affairs, New Zealand Income Support Service, PO Box 27-178, Wellington (☎ (04) 385 0102).

Contributions: although New Zealand doesn't require employees to make social security contributions, you must contribute to the ACC scheme (see page 189). These deductions, known as the 'earner's levy', are fixed annually and are deducted from your salary by your employer. The levy is used to pay compensation for accidents which occur outside the workplace. Your employer also makes a contribution to the scheme, known as the 'employer's levy', which is used to provide compensation for accidents in the workplace. It's illegal (punishable by a $5,000 fine) for an employer to try to recover the employer's levy from employees, either by a direct deduction or any kind of informal agreement.

ACC contributions (which are changed periodically) for employees are $1.20 for each $100 of gross income and $2.35 for each $100 of payroll for employers. Your employer automatically registers you for the ACC levy when you start work in New Zealand and deducts contributions from your salary. The self-employed must also pay the levy and should obtain advice from their local Inland Revenue Department (IRD) office.

Benefits: social security benefits are paid at a flat rate, irrespective of your previous income. This isn't to say that everyone can actually receive benefits as other eligibility tests may be used to determine whether you're entitled to benefits. Social security benefits in New Zealand are taxable (assuming you earn enough to pay tax) and (if applicable) the Department of Social Welfare deducts tax due before paying benefits. If you receive a benefit for the first time and aren't registered for tax, you should contact your local IRD office who will issue an IRD number which the Department of Social Welfare needs in order to deduct tax before paying your benefits. Those who receive no income other than benefits receive a 'G' tax code and those who have other income receive an 'SEC' tax code.

Health Benefits: your entitlement to health benefits in New Zealand doesn't depend on you having established a contributions record. If you're either a New Zealand citizen or a permanent resident you're automatically entitled to health services which include free hospital in-patient treatment together with subsidised doctor's consultations and prescriptions. If you're a visitor or temporary migrant but a national of a country with which New Zealand has a reciprocal agreement (such as Australia and the UK) you can also receive these benefits. Otherwise you must pay the full cost of all healthcare.

Sickness & Maternity Benefits: sickness benefit is payable to those who are unable to work due to illness on a temporary basis, as opposed to invalid benefit which is a permanent or semi-permanent benefit. In social security terms pregnancy also counts as a 'sickness' in that expectant mothers can apply for sickness benefit when they're unable to work, both during and after a pregnancy. There's a campaign to enable pregnant women to receive 12 weeks' maternity pay, which is currently unpaid. Sickness benefit is payable at four rates: single aged 16 to 17, single aged 18 to 24, single aged 25 and over, and a married couple's rate which is slightly less than twice the single person's rate. The benefit isn't increased if you have dependent children.

Accidental Injury Benefits: the Accident Compensation Corporation (ACC) scheme is the cornerstone of New Zealand's innovative state insurance scheme. If you have an accident at work or anywhere else in New Zealand (including when motoring), all expenses and appropriate compensation is paid by the ACC scheme. This avoids the need to take out personal injury insurance (although you can if you wish) or having to sue the other party, assuming someone else was to blame.

Expenses covered by the ACC are comprehensive and include hospital and doctor's bills (if they aren't already free under the state healthcare system), loss of earnings, loss of future earnings, physiotherapy, home nursing care, expenses involved with rehabilitation or future disability, and an allowance if you're unable to work. Payments made under the ACC scheme used to be extremely generous and consisted of lump sum payments on a fixed scale. However, this resulted in large amounts of money being paid both to people with severe injuries and those with relatively minor injuries.

A recent change in the scheme resulted in a general tightening of the ACC budget and cases are now settled on merit. While medical expenses are still paid in full, claimants tend to be paid compensation (or an allowance if they're unable to work) by means of a weekly allowance rather than a lump sum. The scheme aims to provide claimants with 80 per cent of their previous salary, although this is likely to be reduced to 65 per cent in future. The ACC no longer operates on the basis of providing lifetime support and those who have been disabled by an accident are expected to undergo rehabilitation. If a disabled person is considered capable of doing some other kind of work but chooses not to do so, he can have his allowance reduced or stopped, or can be transferred to another (less lucrative) state benefit. However, it's still much more generous than most other countries, most of which don't pay out a penny to accident victims, certainly not without a long legal struggle.

If you wish, you can take out personal injury insurance, which is likely to pay considerably higher compensation in the case of an accident and may also compensate you for damage to property (which the ACC doesn't). So don't expect the government to pay for a new car if you smash up your old one! For further information contact the Accident Compensation Corporation, PO Box 242, Wellington.

Family Assistance: family assistance is a social security benefit available to those with children. Whether or not you're entitled to it and at what rate it's paid depends on your family's income and the number of children you have. A family with one child whose total annual income doesn't exceed $30,001 qualifies for family assistance and if you're in the happy (or unhappy?) position of having six children you can earn up to $58,501 and still receive family assistance. Family assistance is paid at a rate of $47 per week for your first child and $32 for all other children ($40 if they are aged 13 or over). The threshold limits and amounts payable are increased annually.

To apply for family assistance contact your local IRD office, which will require proof of your income (e.g. a pay slip), the ages of your children (their birth certificates) and your bank account details. Depending on your other income and benefits, you may receive your family assistance as either a direct payment into your bank account or as a credit against income tax deducted from your salary (known as an 'independent family tax credit').

Unemployment Benefit: some 170,000 people are registered as unemployed in New Zealand. Both New Zealand citizens and permanent residents are entitled to apply for unemployment benefit (or 'dole') and no history of contributions or tax deductions is required to make a claim. However, newcomers must wait 12 months before they can apply for unemployment benefit and claimants who resign from their jobs or are dismissed must wait 13 weeks before they can receive benefits. The benefit is paid at a flat rate regardless of your previous income, although there are variations according to age and family status. Single people age 18 to 24 receive the lowest rate and those aged 25 or more receive a slightly higher rate. Single parents and married couples with children receive more by way of a family support supplement. Married couples without children receive slightly less than twice the single person's rate. Unemployment benefit is payable at a modest, subsistence rate (around $150 per person, per week) although it doesn't exclude you from receiving other state benefits.

The unemployment benefit system in New Zealand is being reviewed and under a new system the various agencies involved in working with the unemployed, primarily the Income Support Service and the Employment Service, will have their services combined into one agency. These have been dubbed 'one-stop shops' and will provide job vacancy information, training opportunities and benefits. A much tougher approach than in the past is being taken and claimants are required to register with the New Zealand Employment Service (NZES) and make a 'job seeker commitment' requiring them to positively look for work. Claimants are also required to have regular meetings with Income Support Services to determine what they are doing to find work (and to ensure that they aren't working while claiming benefits!). Those who fail to do this can have their benefit reduced by 20 per cent for each refusal and even if they later comply, their benefit isn't restored until after a period of several weeks. The government has also introduced a policy which aims to ensure that no one is out of work (and receiving benefit) for more than six months at a time and there are plans to employ claimants on community projects in return for a $10 per hour payment instead of receiving dole.

Domestic Purposes Benefit (DPB): domestic purposes benefit is mainly intended for single parents with dependant children who don't receive maintenance or support from a partner, although it's also sometimes paid to eligible widows and widowers and those caring for sick or disabled relatives at home. It's only payable to New Zealand citizens or permanent residents, although under a reciprocal agreement those moving from Australia and the UK can apply for the benefit immediately. DPB is payable only to those on low incomes and is reduced by between 30¢ or 70¢ per $1 for those earning above certain threshold limits (reviewed annually).

Widow's Benefit: widows benefit is payable to widows and widowers. It's a means tested benefit payable only to those of limited means. A higher rate is payable to those with dependent children.

Invalid's Benefit: invalid's benefit is payable to invalids and the disabled who are unable to work or who have had to give up work on a permanent basis. Invalid's benefit is granted following a medical examination and based on the opinion of the examining doctor. As in other countries there has been concern that many people receiving this kind of benefit aren't incapable of work. The eligibility criteria have therefore been tightened and the cases of claimants who receive this benefit are periodically re-examined to ensure that they still qualify.

Funeral Grant: a funeral grant of up to $1,000 is payable to those who suffer a death in the family. It is, however, a means tested benefit payable only to those with limited resources and the assets of the deceased person are also taken into account when assessing whether it's payable.

National Superannuation: New Zealand provides an old age retirement pension known as national superannuation or 'super' for short. It's funded from general taxation rather than individual contributions and anybody who has worked in New Zealand for 12 years is entitled to it. If you come to New Zealand from a country with a reciprocal agreement (including Australia and the UK) you can claim national superannuation without a minimum period of residence, providing you would have been entitled to a state pension in your home country. This is paid at the New Zealand rate, even if this is higher than in your home country (the New Zealand government generously makes up the difference). If you move to New Zealand while already receiving a state pension, you can usually receive it there instead of national superannuation. Note, however, that in the case of British pensioners, it's frozen at the rate you received when you left the UK permanently and isn't increased annually as it is for UK residents.

National superannuation is paid at a rate of $208 per week and is intended to provide a basic standard of living only. In a recent survey the Retirement Commission found that most pensioners would require a weekly income of an average of at least $370 per week in order to maintain the standard of living that they enjoyed before retirement.

There are plans to abolish the national superannuation scheme and replace it with a system of private pensions, under which all employees would be required to join a company superannuation scheme or take out a private pension. Employees would be able to contribute as much as they liked (or could afford) to this scheme and the government would guarantee that they would receive at least a basic minimum pension on retirement (payments would also be protected if a private pension company failed). However, a referendum on introducing such a scheme was held in 1997 and was rejected by an overwhelming 90 per cent of the 2 million people who voted.

Nevertheless, the cost of funding pensions from tax revenue is so costly (and unsustainable without tax increases) that plans for compulsory private pensions will inevitably surface again. For further information about national superannuation contact the Government Superannuation Fund, PO Box 3310, Wellington (☎ (04) 496 1400).

PRIVATE PENSIONS

Private pensions are common in New Zealand as national superannuation (see above) provides only enough income to maintain a basic standard of living. Many companies provide contributory pension schemes for their employees and if your employer doesn't you would be well advised to consider taking out a private pension. These are available from a variety of insurance companies and are also offered by many banks (shop around). Most private pensions are based on a savings scheme which accumulates a lump sum that, on retirement, is used to purchase an annuity providing a regular income. In a recent survey the retirement commission found that men would need a lump sum of $119,000 and women $139,000 in order to purchase an annuity that would increase their state pension to the average level of income. Tax relief on private pension contributions was abolished in 1987.

If you don't intend to remain in New Zealand indefinitely, you should ensure that you can take your private pension with you when you leave. Note that generally you cannot 'export' a private pension from New Zealand to another country unless you have been paying contributions for at least two years.

HEALTH INSURANCE

Everyone who's either resident in New Zealand or a visitor from a country with which New Zealand has a reciprocal agreement, is covered by the national insurance scheme which provides for either free or reduced cost medical treatment. However, while treatment under the state health scheme is considered perfectly adequate, many people also have private health insurance. The main purpose of this is to pay the cost of doctor's consultations, prescriptions and dentistry (which aren't covered by the state healthcare system), and also to pay for treatment in private hospitals, thus circumventing public hospital waiting lists. Private health insurance schemes also provide other benefits such as cover for loss of earnings due to illness. Around 40 per cent of New Zealanders have some form of private health insurance, which can be purchased from a variety of insurance companies of which the largest is Southern Cross Medical Care Society, Private Bag 99934, Newmarket, Auckland (☎ (09) 377 5509).

The cost varies depending on exactly what's covered, with an average policy covering 80 per cent of medical bills for a family of four costing around $1,500 a year. Private health insurance costs have skyrocketed in recent years (e.g. Southern Cross have increased their premiums by around 20 per cent in the last year alone) as more people make claims to avoid waiting for treatment at public hospitals, and they are likely to continue increasing at a rate well above inflation. Huge increases for the elderly has led many to cancel their policies.

Checklist

- When comparing the level of cover provided by different health insurance schemes, the following points should be considered:
- Does the scheme have a wide range of premium levels and are discounts or special rates available for families or children?
- Is private hospital cover available and are private rooms available at local hospitals? What are the costs? Is there a limit on the time you can spend in hospital?
- Is dental cover included? What exactly does it include? Can it be extended to include extra treatment? Dental insurance usually contains numerous limitations and doesn't cover cosmetic treatment.
- Are there restrictions regarding hospitalisation, either in New Zealand or abroad?
- What is the qualification period for special benefits or services?
- What level of cover is provided outside New Zealand and what are the limitations?
- What is the cover regarding pregnancy, hospital births and associated costs? What is the position if conception occurred before joining the insurance scheme?
- Are drugs and medicines included?
- Are convalescent homes or spa treatments covered when prescribed by a doctor?
- What are the restrictions on complementary medicine, e.g. chiropractic, osteopathy, naturopathy, massage and acupuncture? Are they covered? Must a referral be made by a doctor?
- Is life insurance or a disability pension included, possibly as an option?
- Are possible extra costs likely, and if so, what for?
- Are spectacles or contact lenses covered, and if so, how much can be claimed and how frequently?
- Is the provision and repair of artificial limbs and other essential health aids covered?

If you're planning to change your health insurance company, you should ensure that no important benefits are lost. If you change your health insurance company, it's advisable to inform your old health insurance company if you have any outstanding bills for which they are liable.

DENTAL INSURANCE

With the exception of school children (see page 179), dental treatment isn't provided free under the state healthcare system. It's unusual to have full dental insurance in New Zealand as the cost is prohibitive, although some health insurance companies include basic dental care such as checkups, X-rays and cleaning in their standard premium, and may offer more comprehensive dental cover as an optional extra. Some international health policies include basic dental care and most offer optional (or additional) dental cover, although there are many restrictions and cosmetic treatment is excluded. Where applicable, the amount payable by a health insurance policy for a particular item of treatment is usually fixed and depends on your level of dental insurance. A detailed schedule of refunds is available from insurance companies.

HOUSEHOLD INSURANCE

As when living anywhere, it's important to ensure that your home and it's contents are fully insured in New Zealand. Premiums are modest in most areas, particularly for home contents insurance (a reflection of the country's modest crime rate). However, your insurance company will probably claw back the savings on buildings insurance, as damage caused by severe weather (particularly flooding) isn't uncommon in certain parts of the country and subsidence can also be a problem in some areas.

When insuring your home (rather than its contents) you're offered a choice between fully comprehensive insurance (known as 'accident damage insurance'), which covers all risks, and 'defined risk insurance', which covers specified risks only. Defined risk insurance is the cheaper option, particularly in an area subject to subsidence or flooding, where these risks would be expensive to insure against and can be excluded from a policy (although you should ask yourself why you want to live there in the first place!). You're also offered a choice between a policy that pays out at replacement value or indemnity value. Under a replacement value policy, a destroyed home is replaced with a new building of similar quality, while an indemnity value policy simply pays out the market value of your home. As the market value of your home is usually less than the cost of rebuilding, an indemnity value policy is cheaper, although it should cover the purchase of a property of similar age and quality. In all cases the value of the land on which your home is built is excluded.

Home contents insurance is usually separate from buildings insurance, although most people have buildings and contents insurance with the same company. It covers all home contents up to a predetermined figure against risks such as theft, fire or accidental damage. If you have particularly valuable possessions you should take out extra cover, when items must usually be itemised and photographs and documentation (e.g. a valuation) provided. When claiming for contents, you should produce the original bills if possible (always keep bills for expensive items) and bear in mind that replacing imported items may be much more expensive than what they cost originally. Note that contents' policies usually contain security clauses and if you don't adhere to them a claim won't be considered. Most policies don't cover possessions (such as cameras and music apparatus) when they are used outside your home, although you can usually pay an extra premium to cover this.

Earthquake Insurance: New Zealand is within an earthquake zone and minor (usually unnoticeable) tremors occur almost monthly, although records show that serious earthquakes occur, on average, only once every 210 years. As the consequences of a major earthquake would be astronomical and no insurance company could possibly cover them, the New Zealand government assumes the responsibility of providing earthquake insurance. The Earthquake Commission operates an insurance scheme which is funded through a small levy on all property insurance policies. In the event that an earthquake devastates your property the Earthquake Commission will pay you compensation up to a maximum of $100,000 for a property and $20,000 for contents. If your property is insured for less, you'll receive no more than the sum insured. This scheme ensures that, in the event of an earthquake, most property owners are compensated, even if the government goes bust as a result! Because $100,000 is unlikely to be sufficient to rebuild anything other than a modest home, most insurance companies offer top-up insurance to cover the difference between the $100,000 paid by the government and the value of your home, which is a must for owners of valuable properties.

HOLIDAY & TRAVEL INSURANCE

Travel insurance is recommended for all who don't wish to risk having their holiday or travel spoilt by financial problems, or to arrive home broke. As you're no doubt aware, anything can and often does go wrong with a holiday, sometimes before you even reach the airport or port (particularly when you don't have insurance). In addition, New Zealand has some of the world's most dangerous roads, is a haven for dangerous (and downright suicidal) sports and is in an earthquake zone. If you don't fall victim to bungee jumping or a crazed New Zealand motorist, there's always the possibility of falling into the boiling mud (it has happened to hapless hikers on a number of occasions)!

Travel insurance is available from many sources including travel agents, insurance agents, motoring organisations, transport companies and directly from insurance companies. Package holiday companies also offer insurance policies (some are compulsory), although most don't provide adequate cover. Before taking out travel insurance, carefully consider the level of cover you require and compare policies. Most policies include cover for loss of deposit or holiday cancellation, missed flights, departure delay at both the start and end of a holiday (a common occurrence), delayed baggage, personal effects and lost baggage, medical expenses and accidents (including repatriation home if necessary), personal money, personal liability, legal expenses or a tour operator going bust.

Medical expenses are an important aspect of travel insurance and you shouldn't rely on reciprocal health arrangements, assuming you're entitled to them (Americans, among others, aren't). It also isn't advisable to depend on travel insurance provided by charge and credit card companies, household policies or private medical insurance, none of which usually provide adequate cover (although you should take advantage of what they offer). The minimum medical insurance recommended by experts when travelling to New Zealand is $2 million. If applicable, check whether pregnancy related claims are covered and whether there are age restrictions for those aged over 65 or 70 (pregnancy restrictions don't usually apply to pensioners).

Check any exclusion clauses in contracts by obtaining a copy of the full policy document (all relevant information won't be included in the insurance leaflet). Skiing and other winter sports aren't usually covered unless you take out a policy specifically for this purpose, which are widely available but expensive. Risky activities such as bungee jumping and parachuting are never covered in standard travel insurance and it's often difficult to cover them at any price. When participating in a dangerous sport check what (if any) insurance cover the organisers provide, as many include (or will sell you) dangerous sports insurance, although it may only cover you for third party liability (e.g. if you sky-dive through someone's roof) and may not cover personal injury. However, you may be covered under New Zealand's ACC scheme (see page 189) if you have an accident, but the pay out may be inadequate if your injuries are serious and it won't pay for repatriation and medical expenses or loss of income abroad.

Although travel insurance companies gladly take your money, they aren't so keen to pay claims and you may need to persevere before they pay up. Be persistent and make a claim irrespective of any small print, as this may be unreasonable and therefore invalid in law. Insurance companies usually require you to report a loss (or any incident for which you intend to make a claim) to the local police (or carriers) within 24 hours and obtain a written report. Failure to do this may mean that a claim won't be considered. If you're travelling on holiday take out insurance before you arrive. Bear in mind that it's difficult or impossible to sue for compensation for personal injuries in New Zealand, although if you have taken out insurance in another country you may have a slightly better chance of obtaining compensation.

MOTOR BREAKDOWN INSURANCE

It's important to bear in mind that motor breakdown insurance isn't included in most New Zealand motor insurance policies. When you buy a new or used car from a dealer you'll usually receive an insurance-based warranty package as part of the deal, which covers the costs of a breakdown (e.g. garage fees and towing) and the cost of repairing most major components of a vehicle. However, these warranties are riddled with loopholes and even if you get past the exclusions and excesses, you'll probably find that the payout is minimal. The cheapest way to insure against breakdowns is to join the New Zealand Automobile Association (see page 168) who will attend to minor repairs on the spot or arrange for a vehicle to be taken to a garage.

LIFE INSURANCE

Although there are worse things in life than death (like spending an evening with a life insurance salesman), your dependants may rate your death *without* life insurance high on their list. You can take out a life insurance policy with dozens of companies in New Zealand, although it's important to shop around before doing so. Be extremely wary of insurance sales people (whose credibility is on a par with used car salesmen, real estate agents and politicians), some of whom use dubious soft and hard-sell methods to hook customers. You have no guarantee of receiving good or independent advice or indeed any advice at all.

Most companies offer a variety of life insurance policies, e.g. term, whole life and endowment (a bit like life insurance, except that it pays out even if you don't die). It's usually necessary to take out an endowment policy if you have an interest-only mortgage, which can be used to repay the capital at the end of the mortgage. Note that although it's often referred to as life *insurance*, life policies are usually for life *assurance*. Assurance is a policy which covers an eventuality which is certain to occur (for example, like it or not, you must die one day). Thus a life assurance policy is valid until you die. An insurance policy covers a risk which *may* happen, but isn't a certainty, for example, accident insurance (unless you're exceptionally accident prone).

Commissions and Charges: one disadvantage with all life insurance policies is the large commissions paid to salesmen, which may be equivalent to a year's premiums, so it pays to shop around and ask salesmen or brokers about their rates of commission. Added to commissions are expenses including management and administration fees. When buying life insurance, you're usually better off dealing with an independent insurance adviser or broker who does business with a number of insurance companies. Most banks are unable to give independent advice on life policies and many are tied to a particular insurance company. Try to ensure that you have a cooling-off period, during which you can cancel a policy without incurring a penalty.

Health: whether you need to undergo a medical examination depends on the insurance company, your age, state of health and the amount of insurance required. You must complete a medical questionnaire and depending on your age and health record, your GP may be required to provide a medical report. If you have no family doctor or previous medical history, you may be required to have a medical examination. Many policies don't pay out when death is the result of certain illnesses, e.g. an aids-related illness. If you're a clean living, non-smoking, teetotaller, you may be able to obtain cheaper life insurance than an alcoholic, sensation-seeking, chain-smoker (although you'll probably die early of boredom!).

Some companies provide free life insurance as an employment benefit (although it may be accident life insurance only) and a private pension scheme may provide a death-in-service benefit. A life insurance policy can be used as security for a bank loan and can be limited to cover the period of the loan. Performance tables are published regularly in financial magazines showing the best-performing unit trusts, pension funds and other long-term investments. You would be wise to consult them and other independent sources of information before taking out a policy from which you expect either a lump sum on maturity or a regular income, as choosing the wrong investment can be *very* costly.

Finally, it's advisable to leave a copy of all insurance policies with your will (see page 216) and with your lawyer. If you don't have a lawyer, keep a copy in a safe deposit box. A life insurance policy must usually be sent to the insurance company upon the death of the insured, with a copy of the death certificate.

14.

FINANCE

Although lagging behind Australia, most European Union countries and the USA, New Zealand is a relatively wealthy country with a Gross Domestic Products (GDP) per head of around US$18,500 in 1997. A period of recession between 1987 and 1992 saw the economy contract, but it has since grown by an average of around 4 per cent over the last few years, with an inflation rate in 1997 of some 2 per cent (just within the Reserve Bank of New Zealand's target range of 0.2 to 2 per cent). New Zealand has fewer extremes of wealth and poverty than many other developed countries, with a large middle class and comparatively few poor people (although there's poverty in New Zealand) and incredibly wealthy people are rare enough for them to be 'famous' (or notorious). New Zealanders are generally restrained when discussing money, much the same as the British, although the '80s saw the creation of a 'yuppy' class who did well in business and the professions and didn't mind flaunting their wealth.

The New Zealand banking and financial sector is modern and efficient. For example, it's possible to clear cheques virtually instantaneously in New Zealand – something which isn't even possible in the UK or USA (although this a deliberate policy on the part of banks in these countries). Wide use is made of electronic banking, rather than shuffling pieces of paper around the country, and New Zealanders have taken enthusiastically to the cashless economy – the use of credit, debit and electronic-funds-transfer-at-point-of-sale (EFTPOS) is widespread. This isn't because New Zealanders are enthusiastic about credit, but simply that it's so convenient. The banking sector is dominated by a relatively small number of large institutions, although competition for your business is healthy. When you arrive to take up residence in New Zealand it's advisable to have a bank account established with funds on deposit, plus some New Zealand currency for immediate use. Credit and EFTPOS cards are widely used in New Zealand and cheques are becoming much less popular, therefore you may find that your spending activities are restricted if you don't have some 'plastic' to flex.

If you're planning to invest in property or a business in New Zealand financed with funds from abroad, it's important to consider both the present and possible future exchange rates (don't be too optimistic). On the other hand, if you earn your income in New Zealand dollars, this may affect your commitments abroad, particularly if the New Zealand dollar weakens. If you plan to live and work in New Zealand you should ensure that your income is (and will remain) sufficient to live on, bearing in mind the cost of living. Anyone receiving a pension from abroad should be particularly careful in this regard, as you'll be at the mercy of not only exchange rates, but the fact that your pension is calculated according to the cost of living in your home country, which may be inadequate to support you in New Zealand.

NEW ZEALAND CURRENCY

The New Zealand unit of currency is the New Zealand dollar, affectionately know as the 'Kiwi Dollar' or just the 'Kiwi' (New Zealanders having given up the old British-style pounds, shillings and pence in 1967). It isn't one of the world's strongest currencies but has a reputation for stability, although it fell to a 12-year low against the $US in 1998 which was driven up in value by the crisis in world financial markets. You cannot spend foreign currency in New Zealand, although there are a few duty-free and tourist shops that will accept both Australian and US dollars (at an unfavourable exchange rate).

The New Zealand dollar is divided into 100 cents (¢). Banknotes are issued in denominations of 100, 50, 20, 10 and 5 dollars, and coins are minted in 1 and 2 dollars, 50, 20, 10 and 5 cents. Americans should note that there's no one dollar bill. The smallest coin in circulation is 5¢, colloquially known as the 'pest', which may be withdrawn in the future thus making the 10¢ coin the smallest unit of currency. Prior to 1992, Her Majesty Queen Elizabeth II appeared on all New Zealand banknotes, but she was 'retired' (despite protests from many people) in 1992 and now appears only on the $20 note. Famous New Zealanders have been installed on all other notes with Lord Rutherford on the $100, Apirana Ngata (a Maori statesman) on the $50, Kate Sheppard (a suffragette) on the $10 and Sir Edmund Hillary (one of the first men to climb Mount Everest) on the $5 note.

Note that the 20¢ and 10¢ coins are difficult to distinguish from Australian coins of the same value and Australian coins occasionally turn up in your change in New Zealand (you can either put your loss down to experience or experience a smug satisfaction as you pop them into a parking meter!). The New Zealand dollar is usually identified by the international $ sign and is rarely prefixed by NZ, except in some banking documents involving currency exchange and in international trade (in this book $ equals NZ$ unless otherwise noted). The cent is identified by the symbol ¢, although occasionally you'll see them expressed as a decimal, e.g. $0.75, or values in dollars expressed as cents, e.g. 115¢, neither of which are officially correct.

It's advisable to obtain some New Zealand currency before your arrival in the country. However, because international bureaux de change don't usually handle coins, the smallest unit of currency you'll be able to obtain outside New Zealand is $5. Ask for a selection of $5, $10 and $20 notes which are the most useful. Many shops, taxi drivers and small businesses are reluctant to accept $50 and $100 notes, although legally they cannot reject any notes or coins (if you proffer a $100 note they're likely to have no change). These notes also attract most scrutiny as they are more likely to be the target of forgers, although counterfeit currency isn't a serious problem in New Zealand.

FOREIGN CURRENCY

Exchange controls operated in New Zealand between 1938 and 1984, but have since been abolished and there are now no restrictions on the import or export of funds. A New Zealand resident is permitted to open a bank account in any country and to export unlimited funds from New Zealand. It's also possible to transmit funds to New Zealand without being hindered by bureaucratic procedures.

When transferring or sending money to (or from) New Zealand you should be aware of the alternatives. One way to do this is to send either a personal cheque or a bank draft (cashier's cheque), which should both be sent by registered mail. Money shouldn't be treated as having been paid until the cheque or draft has cleared the system, which can usually be effected within seven days of receipt. Note, however, that a bank draft shouldn't be treated as cash, as you cannot be sure payment has been made until it has cleared. A quicker and safer method of transferring money is to make a direct transfer or a telex or electronic transfer between banks. A direct transfer involves a process similar to sending a cheque or bank draft and usually takes at least seven days (but can take much longer). A telex or electronic transfer can be completed within a few hours. However, bear in mind that banks in New Zealand close for the day before they open in Europe or the USA, and therefore it will be at least the next day before funds are available in New Zealand. The transfer process is usually faster and less likely to come unstuck when it's between branches of the same or affiliated banks (in any case delays are more likely to be overseas than in New Zealand). The Commonwealth Bank of Australia, which has branches in Europe and the USA, can transfer funds almost instantaneously to its branches in New Zealand, although its branch network there (around 130) isn't the most extensive.

The cost of transfers vary considerably, not only commission and exchange rates, but also transfer charges (shop around and compare rates). Usually the faster the transfer, the more it will cost. Transfer fees also vary depending on the amount being transferred and there are usually minimum and maximum fees. For example, Midland Bank in the UK charge from £4 to process a cheque for £50 or under, and up to £30 for a cheque worth the equivalent of £10,000 (most banks in the UK charge in the region of £10 to £45 for electronic transfers). If you routinely transfer money between currencies you should investigate Fidelity Money Funds, which operate free of conversion charges and at wholesale rates of exchange. In emergencies, money can be sent via American Express offices by Amex card holders.

When you have money transferred to a bank in New Zealand, ensure that you give the name, account number, branch number and the bank sort code. Bear in mind that the names of some New Zealand banks (and towns) are strikingly similar, so double check your instructions. If you plan to send a large amount of money to New Zealand or abroad for a business transaction such as buying property, you should ensure you receive the commercial rate of exchange rather than the tourist rate. Check charges and rates in advance and agree them with your bank (you may be able to negotiate a lower charge or a better exchange rate). If you send a cheque or bank draft to New Zealand, it should be crossed so that it can be paid only into an account with exactly the same name as shown on the cheque.

Most banks in major cities have *bureaux de change* and there are banks and *bureaux de change* with extended opening hours at both Auckland and Wellington international airports, plus other airports when international flights arrive (which may be just a few times a week). At *bureaux de change* you can buy and sell foreign currencies, buy and cash traveller's cheques, cash personal cheques, and obtain a cash advance on credit and charge cards.

There are private *bureaux de change* in the major cities and tourist resorts with longer business hours than banks, particularly at weekends, e.g. they open on Saturdays from 9.30am to 12.30pm when banks are closed, and there are 24-hour, automatic, money-changing machines in some major cities (e.g. Quay Street, Auckland). Most *bureaux de change* offer competitive exchange rates, low or no commission (but always check) and are easier to deal with than banks. If you're changing a lot of money you may be able to negotiate a better exchange rate. Note, however, that the best exchange rate is usually provided by banks. The New Zealand dollar exchange rate against most major international currencies is displayed in banks and listed in daily newspapers.

Traveller's Cheques: if you're visiting New Zealand, it's safer to carry traveller's cheques than cash. Traveller's cheques in all major currencies including US dollars and £sterling are easily exchanged in New Zealand, but aren't usually accepted by businesses, except perhaps in some luxury hotels, restaurants and shops, which usually offer a poor exchange rate. You can buy traveller's cheques from any New Zealand bank where they charge a commission fee on the value with a minimum fee of $8. Shop around as fees can vary, particularly on larger amounts. Some banks exchange traveller's cheques free of commission, although their charges are usually built into the (inferior) exchange rate, so always compare the net amount you'll receive. Keep a separate record of cheque numbers and note where and when they were cashed. American Express provides a free, three-hour replacement service for lost or stolen traveller's cheques at any of their offices world-wide, providing you know the serial numbers of the lost cheques. Without the serial numbers replacement can take three days or longer. Most companies provide freephone telephone numbers for reporting lost or stolen traveller's cheques in New Zealand including American Express (☎ freephone (0800) 801122).

Note that there isn't a lot of difference in the cost between buying New Zealand currency using cash, buying traveller's cheques or using a credit card to obtain cash. However, many people simply take cash when travelling overseas, which is asking for trouble, particularly if you have no way of obtaining more cash locally, e.g. with traveller's cheques or a credit card. **One thing to bear in mind when travelling anywhere, is <u>never</u> to rely on only one source of funds!**

BANKS

There are officially just two kinds of financial institution in New Zealand: registered banks and what are euphemistically known as 'other financial institutions'. The main exception is the Reserve Bank of New Zealand, which doesn't fit into either of these categories and is the country's central bank and occupies a role similar to the Bank of England or the Federal Reserve Bank in the USA. It performs a range of functions including managing the money supply, supervising commercial banks, implementing the government's financial policy, controlling the exchange rate, providing a banking service to the government and acting as a registrar for government stocks.

Savings banks in New Zealand were traditionally mutual organisations owned by their members or investors which concentrated on accepting personal savings and granting mortgages for residential property. In this respect they were much like building societies in the UK and savings and loan organisations in the USA. However, deregulation in the financial sector during the '80s allowed commercial banks to enter this market. With their greater financial clout and marketing expertise they have managed to largely take it over, and as a result many savings banks have either converted to commercial or registered banks or been taken over by them.

Changes in the banking system over the last few years have meant that most individuals and businesses in New Zealand carry out all their banking, including savings, loans, mortgages and day-to-day transactions with one of the registered commercial banks. Banks operating in this sector include the Australia New Zealand Bank (ANZ), the Bank of New Zealand, the National Australia Bank (NZ), the Westpac Banking Corporation, the National Bank of New Zealand, Postbank and Trustbank. As you may have noticed from the names, Australian banks have been highly active in the New Zealand market, a situation which hasn't gone unnoticed among patriotic New Zealanders. The New Zealand banking operations of Australian banks are completely separate operations and therefore customers of, for example,

Australian Westpac cannot access their Australian accounts at Westpac in New Zealand (or vice versa). The National Bank of New Zealand is associated with Lloyds Bank in the UK, although, again, they are completely independent operations. It's estimated that only some 12 per cent of the New Zealand banking market is operated by indigenous banks.

In addition to locally registered banks, you'll also find many international banks in New Zealand, which are mainly located in the financial district of Wellington and don't have extensive branch networks around the country. Other financial institutions that aren't registered banks include merchant banks and leasing companies which mainly serve the business sector. They aren't authorised to accept deposits from the public and in any case registered banks offer a more comprehensive range of services to the public and the business community. Finance companies aren't registered banks, but provide consumer credit such as loans and hire purchase (or time purchase as it's also known in New Zealand).

All New Zealand banks are efficient and highly automated. You'll usually find that staff are friendly and informal, and in most banks work behind low counters or desks rather than armoured glass. This isn't to say that banks in New Zealand aren't robbed (they most certainly are), but the transition towards cashless banking has done much to reduce the amount of cash shuffled across bank counters (or used in shops and other businesses).

Opening Hours: normal banking hours are from 8.30 or 9am until 4.30pm, Monday to Friday, although banks may stay open for half an hour later on one evening a week (which is the exception rather than the rule). Banks don't open at weekends and are also closed on all public holidays, although *bureaux de change* open longer at weekends.

Opening An Account: you can open a New Zealand bank account from outside the country or after your arrival, although given the widespread use of cashless transactions in New Zealand, it's advisable to open an account before you arrive. To open an account from abroad you need to find the nearest office of a New Zealand bank, e.g. by looking in the telephone directory or asking your bank for assistance. You probably won't find a great deal of choice, but there are branches of New Zealand banks in most major cities in Europe, North America and Asia. You don't usually need to visit a branch in person as an account can be opened by telephone or post. It's also possible to open an account with a zero balance so that funds don't need to be transferred until nearer your planned arrival date.

To open a bank account in New Zealand simply choose any of the registered banks. As there's little to differentiate them, most people choose a bank branch that's most convenient for them. All you'll need to open an account is to have a permanent address and show some form of identification. If you think that you may apply for an overdraft, loan or mortgage in New Zealand at some time, it's advisable to obtain a reference from your overseas bank manager to the effect that your account has been maintained in good order.

Cheque Accounts: the normal account for day-to-day transactions in New Zealand is a current or cheque account. You'll receive a cheque book within a week of opening your account, which is worth having even though they are becoming less widely used in New Zealand (where most people pay bills in shops with debit cards and pay their regular household bills by direct debit from a bank account). There are no cheque guarantee cards in New Zealand and therefore if someone accepts a cheque they need to take it on trust that it won't bounce, which is why you may be asked to produce a driving licence or credit card as proof of identity when paying by cheque. Not surprisingly, many shops and businesses are reluctant to take personal cheques (there may be a notice to this effect in shops).

The design of cheques is basically the same as that in most other countries; you enter the name of the payee, the date, the amount in words and figures, and sign it. All cheques should be crossed, although crossed cheques are a fairly recent innovation in New Zealand. A crossed cheque can only be paid into a bank account in the name of the payee and cannot be cashed at a bank. The use of a cheque incurs cheque duty (a kind of stamp duty) of 5¢, which is automatically included in bank charges when you write a cheque and needn't be paid separately (although it makes it difficult to reconcile cheques you have written with the amounts that appear on your bank statement).

Cheque clearing in New Zealand is highly efficient and a cheque paid into your account is usually credited the next day (occasionally the same day if it's at the same branch or bank). A cheque drawn on your account and given to someone else may also be debited from your account on the same or next day and there isn't a delay of between three and ten days as in some other countries. That said, when paying a cheque into your account, it's as well to wait a few days to spend the money just in case the drawer didn't have enough money to cover the cheque (in which case the cheque will be returned to you by mail, which may take a couple of days). On the other hand, you should assume that a cheque drawn on your account is debited from it on the same day.

Account statements are usually provided monthly, although you can ask to have them sent weekly. It's also possible to obtain details of your most recent transactions, request a mini-statement or make a balance enquiry at an automated teller machine (ATM), commonly referred to as cash dispensers. Although you can withdraw cash from your account at any branch of your own bank by writing a cheque, it's much easier to use an EFTPOS card in a cash machine (it's also possible to pay cash or cheques into your account at some machines).

Savings Accounts: you can open a savings (or deposit) account with any registered or savings bank. Over the last few years registered banks have become more competitive in this sector and have largely taken over the functions of the savings banks in this respect. Most financial institutions offer a range of savings and deposit accounts with interest rates varying depending on the amount deposited, the period for which the money must be left on deposit, and the notice which must be given before you can withdraw it. This kind of account is also known as a term deposit. You can open a term deposit account ranging from four weeks to five years, with a correspondingly higher rate of interest the longer the term. The rate of interest may fluctuate according to the bank rate, be fixed for the entire term, or escalate (where the rate of interest paid rises annually irrespective of general interest rates).

General Information: the following points are applicable to most New Zealand banks:

● All regular bills such as electricity, gas, telephone, mortgage or rent, etc., can be paid automatically by direct debit from your bank account. The creditor, or your bank, will provide the necessary form which you complete and return to them. You're protected against loss as a result of error or fraud in the system.

- To stop a cheque contact your bank. If your cheque book or EFTPOS card(s) are lost or stolen contact your bank immediately.

- Safety deposit boxes are provided at most branches and are an expensive way of keeping your valuables secure. The average rental for a small box is typically $200 per year plus a $10 (per visit) access fee.

- Registered banks offer a range of investments in addition to regular savings accounts, including stocks and shares, bonds and securities. Although you can also obtain these from a stockbroker, banks offer competitive transaction fees, particularly for smaller transactions. You don't need to use your own bank and may be able to find a cheaper stock and share service elsewhere.

- Most registered banks offer a range of other services which don't strictly fall within the province of banking, such as insurance, life assurance and pensions. Charges and premiums are usually competitive compared with similar products available from other sources such as insurance brokers. However, it's still important to shop around as some banks sell only their own products or those from certain companies, rather than choosing the best deal from the whole range available.

CASH & DEBIT CARDS

When opening a bank account you should request an 'electronic funds transfer at point of sale' (EFTPOS) card, also known as a debit card, which can be used to pay for goods and services, with the balance being debited from your account, usually on the same day. The use of EFTPOS cards is widespread in New Zealand, much more so than in many European countries, and most hotels, garages, restaurants and even small shops accept them. Your EFTPOS card can also be used to withdraw cash from cash (ATM) machines throughout the country and abroad, for which you need a PIN number (which is usually sent automatically separately from the card itself). Guard your EFTPOS card and PIN number carefully and if the card is lost or stolen inform your bank immediately so that it can be cancelled. It's common practice in New Zealand for people to give their EFTPOS card and PIN to other people (e.g. partners, children or friends) to enable them to withdraw money on their behalf. This practice is discouraged by banks and if a card is misused they will hold you personally responsible for any debits charged to the card, whether you authorised them or not. If your card is lost or stolen, you won't be responsible for any more than a token amount (and even then it isn't usually charged) providing you have used your card properly and informed your bank as soon as you discovered it was missing.

Usually you aren't charged a fee when using an EFTPOS card in a shop or other outlet, although (unlike in most other countries) it's perfectly legal for shops to charge a fee to cover their costs. Most don't and those that do must display a notice advising you of the fees, which is usually 50¢ or $1. When using an EFTPOS card to withdraw cash from a cash dispenser, you aren't usually charged a fee if the cash dispenser belongs to your own bank. Many banks have mutual arrangements with other banks whereby their EFTPOS cards can be used in other banks cash dispensers, although where this is possible you may be charged a fee of up to $2 (therefore only use another bank's cash dispenser in an emergency).

CREDIT & CHARGE CARDS

New Zealanders aren't enthusiastic users of credit and charge cards, preferring instead to use EFTPOS or debit cards, where payments are immediately debited from their account. However, credit and charge cards are issued by most banks and are acceptable almost anywhere and can also be used to withdraw cash from cash dispensers or over the counter at banks (on which you're charged interest from the day of the withdrawal). To use cash dispenser machines you require a PIN number. Most international credit and charge cards are widely accepted in New Zealand including Visa, Mastercard, Diner's Club and American Express, plus the local Bankcard, which is also widely accepted in Australia. Most businesses in New Zealand accept all major credit cards, so you're unlikely to be stuck if you possess only one card.

Some large store groups in New Zealand issue their own charge cards, to which you can charge purchases made in their stores, branches and associated shops. However, you should note that they usually charge a high rate of interest, which is significantly higher than the main credit cards.

If you lose your credit or charge card, you must report it to the issuer immediately by phone. The law protects you from liability for any losses when a card is lost or stolen unless a card has been misused with your consent (e.g. by a friend), in which case you would be liable. Credit card fraud is a big problem in New Zealand.

LOANS & OVERDRAFTS

To apply for a loan or overdraft you must have both a permanent address in New Zealand and a regular income. The amount of a loan or overdraft, the interest rate, and the period of repayment depends on your financial status, which a bank appraises using a credit scoring system. You can expect them to be quite cautious (or even to refuse facilities altogether) unless you have been resident in one place for at least three years. Some banks offer a 'buffer' overdraft (e.g. $100 or $200) automatically to new customers, which is intended to cover you against minor overspending and isn't intended as a permanent overdraft facility (they may charge high fees for this privilege).

It pays to shop around for a loan, as interest rates vary considerably depending on the bank, the amount and the period of the loan. Don't neglect banks other than your own, as it isn't always necessary to have an account with a bank to obtain a loan. Ask your friends and colleagues for their advice. If you have collateral, e.g. New Zealand property (or you can get someone to stand as a guarantor for a loan), you'll be eligible for a secured loan at a lower interest rate. It's also possible to take out payment protection insurance which covers your payments in the event of illness or death, and may entitle you to a lower interest rate. To compare the interest rate on different loans, check the annual percentage rate (APR). Borrowing from finance companies, such as those advertised in newspapers and magazines, is usually more expensive than borrowing from banks.

A popular form of loan in New Zealand is a so-called 'revolving loan', where you make a repayment each month which is fixed depending on your income. You can then borrow up to a set multiple of the monthly payment, e.g. if you can repay $200 per month the lender may allow you to borrow up to 20 ($4,000) or 30 times ($6,000) this amount. The advantage of such a scheme is that you have access to loan finance whenever you need it and don't need to borrow the entire amount all at once. As you make repayments the money you have repaid again becomes available for you to borrow up to your limit. The disadvantage is that the loan is never ending and if you keep spending you'll need to keep repaying – theoretically for ever!

MORTGAGES

Mortgages (home loans) are available from all New Zealand banks, finance houses and some foreign banks. Generally there's little difference between the interest rates charged, although there are a myriad of different mortgage plans with various terms, conditions and fees, so it's worth shopping around for the best deal. By and large, New Zealand financial institutions are accommodating when it comes to granting mortgages and put a great deal of effort into gaining your business. Some banks don't even require you to attend an interview at their local branch and offer mortgages by phone or via the internet. All you need do is telephone a freephone number (or send an e-mail) providing details of the property you wish to purchase and your personal details, and you'll receive an 'in principal' decision virtually on the spot. One of the main telephone mortgage companies is Freedom (the absolute last word that ought to be associated with a mortgage), a subsidiary of National Mutual. Telephone mortgage companies are highly competitive (although they offer a 'no frills' service) and are particularly suitable if you know exactly what kind of mortgage you require. If you don't, then you would be advised to visit your local bank where staff will explain the different types of mortgages on offer (however, they all cost the same in the end – a lot!).

There are no fixed lending criteria in New Zealand, although you're granted a mortgage where the repayments equal no more than 30 per cent of your net income (which is combined for a couple). It's sensible, however, to take a mortgage on which the repayments constitute no more than 20 to 25 per cent of your income. The most you can usually borrow is 80 per cent of the value of a property, although some lenders will advance up to 90 per cent providing that they make their own valuation and that you take out mortgage guarantee insurance which guarantees that they get their money back if you default on your repayments. You pay for the privilege of providing them with this reassurance. Mortgages can be obtained for any period up to 25 years although the trend nowadays is for people to take 20 or even 15-year mortgages. The reason for this is to give New Zealanders sufficient time to redeem their first mortgage and then take out and repay a second mortgage in order to pay for their children's education or a holiday home, before they retire. Although the repayments on a shorter mortgage are higher, you'll pay much less interest in the long term.

Types of Mortgages

The two main kinds of mortgage offered are table mortgages, where you make equal repayments of capital and interest throughout the period of the loan (and which are equivalent to repayment mortgages in other countries) and interest-only mortgages. With an interest-only mortgage you pay only the interest on the sum borrowed and are required to repay the original capital sum at the end of the term. Most lenders require you to take out an insurance policy to repay this advance and in this way it's similar to an endowment mortgage offered in some other countries. Some lenders allow you to take such a mortgage without insurance, which makes the repayments temptingly low, but unless you become fabulously wealthy (or win Lotto) during the period of the mortgage, you may need to sell your home at the end of the term in order to repay the capital. A final kind of mortgage that's sometimes found is the 'straight line' mortgage, where you repay capital and interest throughout the loan and repayments reduce over the years as the amount of capital owed reduces.

The interest rate on a New Zealand mortgage is either floating, so that it varies with interest rates generally, or fixed for the period of the loan, the repayment period being adjusted accordingly. A recent trend is for lenders to offer mortgages that are fixed (usually at a 'bargain' rate) for a period such as one, three or five years, and then revert to a floating rate. These offer a temptingly cheap chance to step on to the property-owning ladder, providing you budget for the fact that your repayments are likely to increase after the fixed rate period expires depending on how interest rates move in the meantime. A New Zealand mortgage usually provides a high degree of flexibility. Many lenders allow you to convert from one type of mortgage to another, increase or decrease your payments, take a payment 'holiday' for a few months, or repay part of the capital early (thus reducing your repayments or the term of the mortgage). It's even possible to transfer your mortgage to another property. In fact, providing you keep making repayments you're likely to find your lender accommodating.

As you work your way through the mortgage maze, you should bear in mind that banks and financial institutions in New Zealand are experts at dressing up mortgages in a user-friendly way and creating a variety of seemingly too-good-to-be-true packages. At the end of the day your mortgage can only be, however, either a table, straight line or interest-only mortgage, with either a fixed or floating rate – no matter what fancy marketing name may be applied to it. Make sure that you compare the interest rate and calculate how much you're going to have to repay at the end of the day.

Should you need to, it's usually quite easy to remortgage your property and gain access to some of the equity capital that you have (hopefully) built up in it. It's also possible to have a mortgage linked to a revolving loan facility, where (as you repay the mortgage) the difference between the capital borrowed and the value of your property can be advanced for other uses such as home improvements, car purchase or a holiday. This is a cheap way of borrowing as the mortgage interest rate is usually much lower than, for example, a car loan. Many New Zealanders use either of these methods to finance the purchase of a holiday home (bach or crib), which due to their often rather flimsy construction, don't qualify for a full mortgage.

Once a loan has been agreed in principle, a lender will provide you with a conditional offer of a loan outlining the terms. You need to provide proof of your income and all outgoings such as other mortgage payments, rent, and other loans or regular commitments. Proof of income includes three month's pay slips for employees and if you're self-employed you require an audited copy of your trading accounts for the past three years. If you decide to accept the offer you'll usually need to pay a deposit (likely to be at least $500) to your mortgage lender. If the sale doesn't go ahead for any reason the deposit should be refundable, although many lenders charge a 'discontinued application fee' which is deducted from the deposit, so it isn't advisable to accept a mortgage offer unless you're certain you want to go ahead with a property purchase.

There are various fees associated with mortgages. All lenders charge an application fee for setting up a loan, usually 1 per cent of the loan amount (you won't be charged all of this if your application is rejected). There's usually a minimum fee and there may also be a maximum. It isn't usually necessary to have a survey unless you're borrowing more than 80 per cent of the value of a property, although when necessary you must pay the fee. It's customary in New Zealand for a property to be held as security for a loan taken out on it, i.e. the lender takes a first charge on the property. The Land Transfer Registration Fee is an additional $150.

If you fail to maintain your mortgage repayments, your property can be repossessed and sold at auction, although this rarely happens in New Zealand as most lenders are willing to arrange lower repayments when borrowers get into financial difficulties. It's advisable to contact your lender immediately if you have repayment problems rather than wait until an even more sizeable debt builds up. You may be offered the chance to transfer to another type of mortgage or may be able to remortgage entirely and gain access to some of the equity in your property.

Foreign Currency Mortgages: it isn't unusual in New Zealand for property buyers to take out a foreign currency mortgage, i.e. in a currency other than New Zealand dollars. In the '80s many 'canny' individuals took out mortgages in European currencies and some people take out mortgages in Japanese yen, often directly with Japanese banks who are more than happy to 'buy up' pieces of New Zealand. The Japanese interest rate is consistently much lower than the New Zealand rate (in 1998 yen mortgages were available at 3 per cent) and coupled with the fact that the New Zealand dollar has strengthened over the last few years this has offered property buyers the opportunity to save tens of thousands of dollars. This trend started with yuppy types in the '80s who initially made a killing, although changing market conditions meant that by the time the mass market caught on it had become a much less attractive proposition, certainly as far as mortgages in European currencies were concerned, and many homeowners with less financial acumen got their fingers burnt or even went bankrupt.

You should be extremely wary about taking out a foreign currency mortgage, as interest rate gains can be wiped out overnight by currency swings and devaluations. When choosing between a New Zealand dollar loan and a foreign currency loan, be sure to take into account all costs, fees, interest rates and possible currency fluctuations. Note that if you have a foreign currency mortgage, you must usually pay commission charges each time you transfer money into a foreign currency to meet your mortgage repayments, although some lenders offer to do this free of charge. Don't, however, allow this to cloud your judgement: a foreign currency mortgage can be an opportunity for the shrewd speculator to save a small fortune, but it can also be a risky business.

GOODS & SERVICES TAX

A Goods and Services Tax (GST) is levied in New Zealand, which is essentially the same as value added tax levied in all European Union countries, but it isn't a sales tax as in the USA. GST is levied at a single rate of 12.5 per cent on most goods and services with the exception of residential property, long-term property rentals and the provision of financial services. It's also levied on the sale or rental of business property (including farms and building land), although it's possible for registered traders to reclaim tax paid. When you import goods into New Zealand, GST is assessed on their value (and probably also customs duty as well), unless they are exempt or imported under a tax-free arrangement. Immigrants can import their personal possessions free of duty and tax providing they have been owned and used prior to their arrival. This also applies to used cars (see page 150).

All businesses with a turnover of $30,000 or more within a 12 month period must register for GST with the IRD and levy GST on all goods and services supplied (unless they are exempt). Similarly, businesses can reclaim GST paid on goods and services used in their business. A GST return must usually be filed every two months, although in some cases it can be done monthly, and businesses with a turnover of less than $250,000 a year can choose to file a return every six months. A penalty of 10 per cent of the tax due is levied if a return isn't filed by the due date, plus a cumulative penalty of 2 per cent per month.

INCOME TAX

Generally speaking, income tax in New Zealand is below average for that of a developed country. Over the last decade most people have seen their income tax reduced and the government is committed to reducing it even further. Much of this has, however, been achieved by vicious cuts in public spending which have been almost as unpopular as tax rises. There has also been a switch from direct to indirect taxes in recent years, with wage earners seeing less of their income deducted in tax and the burden falling more heavily on consumers. Most New Zealanders are resigned to paying taxes (tax evasion isn't a national sport as it is in some countries) and in any case the country has a system of pay-as-you-earn (PAYE) that ensures that tax is deducted at source from employee's salaries. The tax system in New Zealand isn't particularly complicated and the only contact most people have with the taxman is when they complete their annual tax return using information taken from pay slips. The system is designed so that most people can prepare and file their own tax returns, although if your tax situation is complicated you may need to seek advice from an accountant.

Liability

Your country of domicile determines whether you're liable to pay New Zealand income tax. New Zealand residents are taxed on their world-wide income, while non-residents are subject to income tax only on income derived from New Zealand. To determine 'domicile' the tax authorities apply what's known as the 'permanent place of abode test', although this is arbitrary and isn't enshrined in New Zealand tax law. Usually anyone who's present in New Zealand for more than 183 days in a 12 month period is considered resident there and liable to pay taxes. You don't need to be a permanent resident to be liable and the existence of financial and social ties (including bank accounts and club memberships) may be taken as evidence of a permanent place of abode. Income that's subject to tax in New Zealand includes all salary and wages, profits or gains from a business, commissions, rents, royalties, trust distributions, interest and dividends.

Double Taxation: New Zealand has double taxation treaties with several countries which are designed to ensure that income that has been taxed in one treaty country isn't taxed again in another treaty country. A treaty establishes a tax credit or exemption on certain kinds of income, either in the taxpayer's country of residence or the country where the income is earned. Where applicable, a double tax treaty prevails over local law. Countries with which New Zealand has a double tax treaty include Austria, Belgium, Canada, China, Denmark, Fiji, Finland, France, Germany, India, Indonesia, Ireland, Italy, Japan, Korea, Malaysia, the Netherlands, Norway, the Philippines, Singapore, Sweden, Switzerland, the UK and the USA.

You can usually be considered fully exempt from New Zealand taxes only if you aren't present in New Zealand for 325 days in a 12 month period. However, if you maintain a home in the country you cannot be considered non-resident no matter how brief your stay. If you decide to leave New Zealand, you should inform your local IRD office. Note that the 325-day time limit doesn't start until the IRD have confirmed that you have ceased to become a resident.

Income Tax Return & Tax Bill

When you start work in New Zealand you should register with your local Inland Revenue Department (IRD) office, who will issue you with an IRD or tax file number, which must be quoted on all tax documents and enquiries. Everyone who earns an income in New Zealand must file an income tax return annually with the Commissioner of the Inland Revenue Department. The return, known as an IR5, is sent to you automatically each year. The New Zealand tax year runs from 1st April to 31st March each year and wage and salary earners must file their returns by 7th June. The IRD then issues a tax assessment (i.e. a tax bill) showing the amount of income tax payable. Employees whose income tax is deducted at source by their employer under PAYE, and who don't have any other income, shouldn't have any more income tax to pay.

Tax Rates and Allowances

It has become common practice in recent years for the rate of income tax to be adjusted annually in the July budget. There are three tax rates in New Zealand: standard, lower and higher. Income tax rates range from 15 per cent on income up to $9,500 rising to 33 per cent on income in excess of $38,000. The standard rate for income in the intermediate band is 19.5 per cent.

Before you're liable for income tax you can deduct certain allowances (known as rebates) from your gross salary, which serve to reduce your tax bill. Those on low incomes are entitled to a low earner rebate, which in effect reduces their tax rate to 15 per cent on all income up to $9,500, assuming their income doesn't exceed that amount. Other key rebates include a child taxpayer rebate ($156), a transitional tax allowance (a further rebate for low earners of $728), a housekeeper rebate ($310) and a charitable donations rebate ($500). Expenses associated with employment (such as clothing or travel to work) cannot usually be claimed as a tax allowance in New Zealand. However, the self-employed can claim all legitimate business expenses as a tax allowance. Interest on a mortgage cannot be claimed as a tax allowance, as is the case in some other countries.

Bank Interest: interest on bank and other savings accounts is paid after deduction of Resident Withholding Tax (RWT) at a rate equivalent to the standard rate of income tax (19.5 per cent). If, however, you don't provide your tax file number to a bank when opening an account, it's taxed at the higher rate (33 per cent). This means that taxpayers who pay only the standard rate of income tax have no further tax liability on their investment income at the end of the tax year. Those who pay tax at the higher rate are subject to additional tax on investment income.

Businesses and Self-Employment

Income tax for the self-employed and small businesses is broadly similar to wage and salary earners. You're sent a tax return (form IR3) at the end of your financial year, which you must complete and return by the seventh day of the fourth month following the end of your financial year. If your financial year is the same as the tax year (April to March), your tax return must be filed by 7th July each year. You can apply to have a financial year which differs from the tax year, but the same rules applies for filing your tax return. The self-employed are required to pay an estimated proportion of their tax on a monthly basis, which is estimated according to their last year's return. When your tax return is submitted, the IRD reconciles the tax due with the sum already paid and issues a tax assessment for any tax payable or a refund if you have paid more (through your monthly instalments) than you're were liable to pay.

PROPERTY TAXES

Property taxes (rates) are levied by local authorities and are based on the capital value of properties. Bills are sent out at the beginning of the financial year and are payable by whoever occupies the property, whether it's the owner or a tenant. If you occupy a property for just part of a year, then only a proportion of the tax is payable. The annual bill for an average family house is between $1,000 and $2,000 (Auckland's average is $1,142). It isn't uncommon for residents, either individually or collectively, to appeal against their property taxes and try to obtain a reduction. Property taxes pay for local services such as street cleaning, lighting, and subsidies paid to local public transport companies. They usually include rubbish collection, although an extra charge is levied in some areas, and water (although in a few areas water is billed separately).

MISCELLANEOUS TAXES

There are no local income taxes, wealth tax or estate taxes (inheritance taxes) in New Zealand and there's also no capital gains tax (the current government has also pledged that it won't introduce one). However, income tax may be levied on income derived from any undertaking or scheme entered into or devised for the purpose of making a profit. For example, income from the sale of real estate or personal property and land if the principal purpose of purchasing it was to resell it or if your business is dealing in property. In addition, gains resulting from certain investments, such as debentures and some preference shares, options and leases, may be taxable irrespective of whether the true nature of the gain is capital or income.

Gift duty is imposed at fixed rates on dutiable gifts, which include gifts of property in New Zealand or elsewhere if the donor was domiciled in New Zealand at the time of the gift. Certain gifts aren't dutiable including those made to charities, gifts for the maintenance or education of your immediate family, and gifts of up to $2,000 per year to an individual if they are made as part of the donor's normal expenditure (e.g. birthday and Christmas presents). The rates of gift duty range from 5 per cent on amounts over $27,500 up to 25 per cent on amounts in excess of $72,000.

Fringe Benefits Tax (FBT) is payable on the value of most fringe benefits paid to employees in New Zealand. These include company cars (24 per cent of the cost is taxable); subsidised or low-interest loans or mortgages; subsidised transportation; contributions to a sickness, accident or death benefit fund; and the value of free, subsidised or discounted goods and services. FBT is imposed at a rate of 49 per cent on the value of the fringe benefit, which allows for a charge for GST based on the value of the benefit. It's calculated and paid by employers rather than employees.

It's important to note that income such as interest, rents, dividends and royalties are taxable within the province of income tax in New Zealand, rather than separately as is the case in some other countries.

WILLS

It's an unfortunate fact of life, but you're unable to take your worldly goods with you when you take your final bow (even if you have plans to return in a later life). Once you've accepted that you're mortal (the one statistic you can confidently rely on is that 100 per cent of all human beings eventually die), it's advisable to make a will leaving your estate to someone or something you love, rather than leaving it to the government or leaving a mess which everyone will fight over (unless that's your intention). The good thing about dying in New Zealand (at least for your beneficiaries) is that there's no inheritance tax or death duties. Many people in New Zealand die intestate, i.e. without making a will, in which case their property is subject to New Zealand's intestacy laws, which, in general, divides your estate equally between your spouse and children. If you die in New Zealand without making a will and aren't domiciled there, the intestacy laws of your home country will apply to the disposal of your estate.

As a general rule, New Zealand law fully entitles you to make a will according to the law of any country and in any language, providing it's made according to the laws of that country. If you're a foreign national and don't want your estate to be subject to New Zealand law, you may be eligible to state in your will that it's to be interpreted under the law of another country. To avoid being subject to New Zealand inheritance laws, you must establish your country of domicile in another country. If you don't specify in your will that the law of another country applies to your estate, then New Zealand law will apply. A legal foreign will made in an overseas country dealing with overseas assets is valid in New Zealand and will be accepted for probate there. However, you should have an New Zealand will to deal with your New Zealand assets.

It isn't a legal requirement in New Zealand to use a lawyer to prepare your will, although the relatively small fee (e.g. $150) may save difficulties later. If you want to make your own will you can simply write your instructions and sign them, which is known as a holographic will and doesn't need to be witnessed. If your circumstances change dramatically, for example you get married, you must make a new will, as under New Zealand law marriage automatically annuls an existing will. Both husband and wife should make separate 'mirror' wills. Similarly, if you separate or are divorced, you should consider making a new will, although divorce doesn't automatically annul a will. A new bequest or a change can be made to an existing will through a document called a 'codicil', without writing another will. You should check your will every few years to make sure it still fulfils your wishes and circumstances (your assets may also increase dramatically in value). A will can be revoked simply by tearing it up.

You'll also need someone to act as the executor of your estate, which can be particularly costly for modest estates. Your bank, building society, solicitor, or other professional will usually act as the executor, although this should be avoided if at all possible, as fees can be very high. If you appoint a professional as executor of your estate, check the fees in advance (and whether they could increase in future). **It's best to make your beneficiaries the executors, who can then instruct a solicitor after your death if they need legal assistance.**

Keep a copy of your will in a safe place (e.g. a bank) and another copy with your solicitor or the executor of your estate. It's useful to leave an updated list of your assets with your will to assist the executor in distributing your estate. You should keep information regarding bank accounts and insurance policies with your will(s), but don't forget to tell someone where they are!

COST OF LIVING

It's useful to try to estimate how far your dollars will stretch and how much money you'll have left (if any) after paying your bills. The inflation rate in New Zealand is low at around 2 per cent in 1997 and the government is committed to maintaining it at this rate (or less). New Zealanders have enjoyed a growing economy and a healthy dollar in the last few years, although the Asian crisis and plummeting world stock markets in late 1998 caused the New Zealand dollar to lose value and increased the price of imports. Prices of many imported goods have fallen in real terms in recent years, particularly cars and electrical appliances. Income tax has also been reduced in recent years, although some of it has been clawed back through the imposition of GST. In general, New Zealanders enjoy a high standard of living, although salaries are lower than in Australia, North America and many European countries.

It's difficult to estimate an average cost of living in New Zealand as it depends on your location as well as your style of living. If you live in Auckland with a view over the harbour, drive a BMW and dine in expensive restaurants, then your cost of living will be much higher than if you live in a rural part of the South Island, drive a small locally assembled car and can happily live on roast lamb. You can live most economically by buying New Zealand produce when possible and avoiding expensive imported goods, which aren't only more expensive because of the distance they have to travel, but are often overpriced simply because they are considered fashionable.

Examples of typical salaries, housing costs and the price of many everyday items can be obtained from Statistics New Zealand (internet: www.stats.govt.nz), the statistical office of the New Zealand government.

15.

LEISURE

When it comes to leisure, New Zealand is a country where full advantage is taken of the natural environment and the great outdoors. New Zealanders and most tourists spend a great deal of time touring or trekking (hiking) round the country or simply sitting back and admiring it over a few drinks. New Zealand is one of the most beautiful and scenic countries in the world with a surprisingly varied landscape. Whether your idea of leisure involves the beach, mountains, forests or the strange thermal areas where forces deep in the centre of the earth make their presence felt, you'll never be short of something to see and do. New Zealanders take their leisure time seriously and city (many of which are rural towns by European and North American standards) dwellers cannot wait for the weekend to come round so that they can take off to their cabin in the country.

In comparison with many other countries, New Zealand doesn't offer a great variety of organised leisure activities, particularly cultural events. However, the situation has improved in recent years and many cities now boast impressive theatres and arts festivals. Nevertheless, if you're a lover of the arts you'll need to travel to the major cities to indulge your leisure interests and even then the choice of activities won't be as great as in many other countries. Rural New Zealand has little to offer in the way of culture and even Australians, a race not generally known for their cultural awareness, make jokes about the backwardness of small-town New Zealand. The New Zealander's description of themselves as a nation of 'rugby, racing and beer' isn't wholly accurate but there's rarely smoke without fire!

One of the compensations of this reliance on outdoor activities is that there's much to be enjoyed that's inexpensive or even free. The American and European trend for massive Disneyland-style theme parks, where it's possible for a family of four to spend a week's wages in one day, is unlikely to overwhelm New Zealand, although Auckland does have a modest amusement park (situated at the rather intriguingly named Rainbow's End).

Information about local events and entertainment is available from tourist offices or Visitor Information Network (VIN) centres and is also published in local newspapers and magazines. In the main cities there are magazines and newspapers devoted to entertainment, and free weekly or monthly programmes are published by tourist organisations in all major cities and tourist centres. Many city newspapers also publish weekly magazines or supplements containing a detailed programme of local events and entertainment.

The main aim of this chapter, and indeed the purpose of the whole book, is to provide information that isn't found in general guide books. General information about New Zealand is available in numerous excellent guide books including *Baedeker's New Zealand*, the *Blue Guide New Zealand*, *Fodor's New Zealand*, *Let's Go New Zealand*, *Lonely Planet New Zealand* and the *Rough Guide New Zealand* (see **Appendix B** for a comprehensive list). There are also a number of guides to the main cities.

TOURIST OFFICES

All cities, towns and popular tourist spots in New Zealand have a tourist office, usually known as Visitor Information Network (VIN) centre, of which there are over 80 in New Zealand (there are eight in Auckland alone). VIN centres are co-ordinated by the New Zealand Tourism Board (NZTB) but are usually independently owned, although a few (such as Christchurch) are run by the local authority. Tourist offices or VIN centres are usually located in a prominent position, for example in the city hall or another public building. Note that railway stations in New Zealand don't usually have tourist offices, although you'll find them at airports. Look for the internationally recognised (green) 'i' symbol. Opening hours vary considerably and during the winter months (April to October) even main city offices open only limited hours, such as 10am to 4pm, and in small towns and resorts offices they are usually closed completely (except in winter sports resorts).

Tourist offices provide a wealth of information about local attractions, restaurants, accommodation, sporting events and facilities, package holidays, tours, public transport, car rental and much more. Offices can provide information on a wide range of leisure activities and sports, so you should mention any special interests when making enquiries. They can also book your accommodation, although unless you plan to arrive late or don't have time to look around, it's often better to find accommodation on the spot. If you book through the tourist office you'll pay the full rate and probably also a booking fee, while if you book direct you won't only save the booking fee but may also be able to negotiate a lower rate.

Tourist offices use the latest technology and VIN centres can access the NZ Host National Tourism database at the touch of a button and call up and print information. An increasing number of tourist offices in New Zealand are also equipped to deal with enquiries by e-mail (e.g. visitor@auckland.tourism. co.nz. for the Auckland tourist office). You can also obtain information from Tourist Information FM radio, which broadcasts in many areas indicated by blue signs at the roadside (tune to 88.2FM). Most cities and regions publish free entertainment magazines and newspapers containing maps and a plethora of information about local attractions and events (distributed by tourist offices, hotels, transport companies and information bureaux).

New Zealand is promoted overseas by the excellent New Zealand Tourism Board (NZTB), which is a mine of information and has offices in many countries including Austria, Belgium, Canada, Denmark, Finland, Germany, Ireland, Italy, Japan, Luxembourg, the Netherlands, Norway, Portugal, Spain, Sweden, Switzerland, the UK and the USA. Among the many publications available from the NZTB is a *Holiday Planner* which is useful reading for anyone travelling to New Zealand for the first time and the first step to the wealth of other literature available from (or via) the NZTB. The *Holiday Planner* provides an information service where you can simply indicate on a card what your interests are (e.g. hotel chains, package tours, car rental or particular cities) and your name and address is sent to the relevant organisations. The NTZB also has an internet site (www.nztb.govt.nz), while other useful sites include www.nz-travel.com and www.travelenvoy.com.

HOTELS

In New Zealand the term hotel can be rather confusing for the newcomer. As in Australia, a public house or a bar is usually called a hotel, when in fact it doesn't provide accommodation. Or rather, it may keep a bedroom or two 'for rent' to satisfy a quaint old law that says hotels must offer accommodation, but you aren't expected to ask to stay there! However, you'll be pleased to hear that New Zealand has a plethora of 'proper' hotels with accommodation ranging from the most humble to the most luxurious. Standards and service are usually high and an increasing number of hotel staff having completed the nationally-recognised 'Kiwi Host' customer service workshop. Most guide books contain a selection of hotels and other kinds of accommodation.

Luxury Hotels: top hotels in New Zealand are comparable with those in any other country, both in terms of facilities and room rates, and can be found in all major cities and resort areas. Many leading international names have hotels in New Zealand including Stamford Plaza, Hyatt, Southern Pacific, Sheraton, Carlton and Parkroyal. There are also privately-owned luxury hotels. You should expect to pay between $200 and $1,000 per night for a double room in a luxury hotel.

Sporting Lodges: sporting lodges are rural country house hotels and are a unique feature of the luxury hotel business in New Zealand. They are invariably set in superb locations in the mountains, by lakes or the sea. Each lodge is individually styled and many are noted for their excellent cuisine. Lodges usually offer fishing (e.g. brown or rainbow trout in a nearby river or lake, or marlin at sea) and golf (New Zealand has over 400 courses), hence the name 'sporting'. Many also offer sports facilities such as diving, snorkelling, water-skiing, sailing, riding, trekking, rafting, jet-boating or skiing. Rates for sporting lodges are usually higher than city centre hotels, ranging from between $400 and $1,200 per night for a double room, although tariffs include meals. The New Zealand Lodge Association publishes a catalogue containing details of lodges (e-mail: nzla@xtra.co.nz).

Mid-Range Hotels: for those unable to afford the indulgence of a sporting lodge, there are plenty of mid-range hotels, both in cities and resort areas. These may not be in such prime locations but they usually have good facilities including a bar and restaurant (usually open to non-residents), and possibly a swimming pool and health club. The main chains include Best Western, Flag Inns, Golden Chain, Manor Motor Inns, Quality Hotels and Pacifica. Room rates in a mid-range hotel are usually between $80 to $250 per night for a double room.

Motels: motels are found throughout New Zealand, even in quite remote areas, and although they're rarely located in prime positions they are usually easily accessible on or near main roads. In cities they are normally located in the suburbs, but normally offer good access to public transport. One unique feature of a New Zealand motel is that most (although there are a few exceptions) accommodation is more like an apartment than a hotel room, with one or two bedrooms, a living area, kitchenette and a full-sized bathroom. Because they are so well equipped, New Zealanders frequently use motels as holiday bases and not just for the odd one or two night stay. Some motels have restaurants, bars and swimming pools on site, although they aren't generally as well served as hotels. A refreshing change is that chain motels (which can be as soulless as in other countries) in New Zealand are often family run and while of a consistent standard, also offer genuine, friendly personal service.

Another feature of motels is that they frequently operate 'all in' pricing, which means that you pay a fixed room rate no matter how many people occupy it. You're unlikely to find more than $5 or $10 difference between the rate for a single room and a double or family room, and therefore they are an economical place for families to stay. The main motel chains in New Zealand are Best Western, Flag, Golden Chain and Budget. Expect to pay $50 to $100 per night for a motel room or suite.

Prices: all hotel prices are quoted inclusive of taxes (GST at 12.5 per cent) and in line with New Zealand's no-tipping policy you won't be charged extra for service. Many hotels in popular resorts have slightly higher room rates during the summer and a minimum stay of three nights, although outside the high season hotels often offer a discount for stays of three nights or longer. Many offer low season discounts, particularly during the winter and early spring months, which may include three nights for the price of two or two nights for the price of one at weekends. Note that many motels don't charge extra in the summer. Hotel prices in New Zealand don't usually include meals, unless otherwise stated, although they frequently have 'special offer' rates which include meals (but you won't be obliged to pay for meals if you require only a room). In smaller hotels and motels without a restaurant, you may be offered breakfast, which is often served in your room so that you can enjoy breakfast in bed.

Facilities: although facilities vary considerably with the price and category of accommodation, you can usually expect en suite facilities (bath or shower) in a New Zealand hotel. Hotel and motel rooms are usually equipped with a telephone, radio or TV, including satellite TV in top hotels and some motels, plus tea and coffee-making facilities and a small fridge (even in modestly priced hotels) complete with a complimentary bottle of milk (a peculiar New Zealand tradition). The better hotels provide room service and a mini-bar, which is always expensive. Power points are usually provided and there's often a razor socket in the bathroom (you'll need an adapter to use any appliance without a New Zealand style plug). Most hotels (except those in city centres) have private parking and where they don't there's usually on-street parking or a secure off-road car park nearby.

In general, New Zealand hotels don't cater well for business travellers, as few business people make a lot of overnight business trips. Business centres with secretarial staff and translation services are usually confined to a few luxury hotels in Auckland. However, most hotels have photocopy, telex and fax facilities for their guests' use. Some hotels have swimming pools and health and sports facilities such as gymnasiums, and most top class hotels have a restaurant, coffee shop and bar, although you can often obtain a better and cheaper meal at a local restaurant.

Booking: it isn't usually necessary to book far ahead in New Zealand, except in summer or on public holiday weekends, and during international trade fairs, conventions and festivals in the major cities. In any case, if your chosen hotel or motel isn't available there's usually somewhere similar nearby. The only exception to this is if you're venturing to the more remote southern tip of the South Island, where it's advisable to book as accommodation is more scarce. You won't usually be shown a room unless you ask and it's usually safe to accept a room without inspecting it. Certainly in the case of a large hotel or a motel, your room will have the same facilities as a similarly priced establishment in Miami or Manchester and may even be decorated in the same 'international' style.

If you're staying in a chain hotel or motel, the receptionist will call ahead and book your next night's accommodation, assuming of course that there's a member in the area where you wish to stay (if not, they may be willing to recommend a hotel in a rival chain). Alternatively there's usually a free courtesy phone in the reception area where you can make your own bookings. If you book ahead within a chain you're usually asked to pay a referral deposit, typically $30. If you change your mind later and wish to cancel, you're expected to notify the hotel by 4pm if you don't want to lose your deposit. Checkout time is usually noon at the latest and if you stay any later you may be charged for an extra day. If you're staying in a small hotel or guest house and wish to leave early in the morning, it's advisable to pay your bill the evening before and tell the proprietor when you plan to leave, otherwise you may find your hosts are still in bed!

BED & BREAKFAST

New Zealand has a long tradition of providing bed and breakfast accommodation, usually known as guest houses, which in rural areas are often on working farms. The cost is similar to the cheaper hotels, although guest houses offer a more individual service. The price of a guest house bed usually includes a hearty breakfast, which isn't normally the case in a hotel, therefore the price is actually more reasonable than it looks. Expect to pay around $50 to $90 per night for a room. Not all guest house rooms have en suite facilities, although they will be available nearby and the owners usually allow guests access to most of the facilities of their home, therefore in many ways a guest house is often better served than a hotel. In modest guest houses you may find facilities rather well worn or homely to say the least, but if you need anything such as extra blankets or pillows, you only need to mention it to your host and it will appear as if by magic.

You can find guest houses through local tourist offices and VIN centres, from the Federation of Bed and Breakfast Hotels (don't take the term 'hotels' too literally), 52 Armagh Street, Christchurch (☎ (03) 366 9796) and from books such as *The New Zealand Bed and Breakfast Book* (Moonshine Press).

HOMESTAYS

It's also possible to stay in private homes in New Zealand as a 'personal guest' of a family. If you're travelling by public transport your hosts will usually pick you up from the nearest town or village. The difference between this kind of accommodation and a guest house is that you're treated as a member of the family and invited to join them at mealtimes and in other activities around the house (like doing the housework or having a bath!). Homestay hosts don't usually accept more than one group of guests at a time and most offer homestays as a way of meeting people, rather than simply making money. As many homestays are on farms, you may be able to try your hand at sheep-shearing or roam the wide open spaces on a tractor or horse, while your children help raise new-born lambs. The duration of a stay can be anything from one night to three weeks or more, with the cost between $120 to $400 per night for two people, including all meals (homestays shouldn't be considered as a cheap form of accommodation).

Various organisations arrange homestays including New Zealand Farm Holidays Ltd., PO Box 256, Silverdale, Auckland (☎ (09) 426 5430) and Rural Holidays New Zealand Ltd., PO Box 2155, Christchurch (☎ (03) 366 1919, e-mail: ruralhol@xtra.co.nz).

HOSTELS

There's a variety of inexpensive accommodation in New Zealand including youth and other hostels. These include both privately owned hostels and hostels owned by the Youth Hostel Association of New Zealand (YHANZ). It's necessary to be a member of YHANZ or the International Youth Hostels Federation (IYHF) to use YHA hostels. You can join on a night-by-night basis when you arrive at a hostel, although it's cheaper to take out annual membership, either abroad or in New Zealand. The YHANZ (PO Box 436, Christchurch, ☎ (03) 379 9970) publish *The NZ Hostelling Handbook*, containing hostel addresses, plus *The Good Bed Guide*, a condensed (free) version of the handbook.

There are no age restrictions at New Zealand hostels. Hostels fill up early in summer, so you should book in advance if possible, although some hostels don't accept reservations and restrict stays to a maximum of three or four nights. Linen is sometimes provided and where it isn't it can be hired. Hostels vary considerably in size from around 10 to 300 beds, with larger hostels usually having dormitories, although rooms for one to four people are available in many hostels. A dormitory bed costs around $16 per person, per night and a double/twin room in the region of $20 per person.

Hostel hosts are an excellent source of information about the surrounding area and will gladly pass on tips about places to see and things to do (or even temporary employment opportunities). They will also usually book your next night's hostel accommodation.

CAMPING

Camping and, to a lesser extent, caravanning are extremely popular in New Zealand with both New Zealanders and tourists, who flock to the country each year to enjoy holidays in the open air. Campsites vary considerably from small wilderness sites with fairly basic facilities (or even no facilities) to luxury establishments with a wide range of amenities. Rates range from around $10 per night (usually from noon to noon) at a basic site up to $50 or more at a four-star site for a family of four, a car, and a caravan site or camping space. Some sites charge extra for the use of showers, sports facilities (such as tennis courts) and amenities such as ironing or the use of a freezer. Most sites have different rates for high and low seasons.

Permission is required to park or camp on private property or anywhere outside official campsites. Whether or not it's legal to camp in the countryside depends on the attitude of the local authority (VIN centres can advise you). In rural areas, camping by the roadside is a popular practice, although elsewhere the availability of campsites makes rough camping less popular than in some other countries. Note that areas where there are no campsites may be remote, with even facilities such as clean drinking water difficult to find, and therefore rough camping may be discouraged, particularly if the area is so remote as to make rescue difficult (e.g. in case of a medical emergency). Camping isn't usually permitted alongside walking trails (for which New Zealand is famous), although huts are available in most areas with bunk beds, cooking facilities, toilets and possibly showers, for a fee of from $8 per night.

The Camp and Cabin Association of New Zealand (CCANZ) produces a directory describing the facilities at around 240 member sites, including sites with cabins to rent. It's available directly from CCANZ (PO Box 394, Paraparaumu, ☎ (04) 298 3283) or from bookshops, camping, caravanning and motoring organisations in New Zealand. The CCANZ also provide caravan and travel insurance, travel services, rallies, holidays, reservations and a range of other benefits for members.

MOTOR CARAVANS

Motor caravans, known variously as campervans or motorhomes in New Zealand, are much more popular than touring caravans (which are towed behind a car). They vary from luxuriously appointed American-style, Winnebago-type vehicles which can accommodate six people in luxury, to conversions of small Japanese vans with room for just two (accommodated very intimately!). Many smaller vehicles have the advantage of being four-wheel-drive, making out of the way places accessible.

You can rent a motor caravan by the day or week from a variety of companies in New Zealand from around $90 per day for the cheapest two berth vehicle up to around $230 per day for the largest. These rates are for reasonably new vehicles and include basic third party insurance, although there's an extra charge for damage excess waiver (DEW) of around $14 per day, which removes the liability for damage caused to a rented vehicle. If you don't have DEW you must leave a credit card deposit of $800 or more. It's important to note that no matter how comprehensive your insurance cover, you're unlikely to be covered for damage caused by driving on dirt roads (known locally as unsealed roads), even if your rented motor caravan is of the four-wheel-drive type. Rates exclude fuel and personal accident insurance, but include unlimited kilometres. Note that a diesel-powered vehicle is much cheaper to run than one that uses petrol, as they not only offer greater economy but diesel is little over half the price of petrol in New Zealand.

You can book a motor caravan from many companies including Maui, which has offices in Auckland and Christchurch (☎ freephone (0800) 651080), and Budget Campervans (part of Budget Rent-a-Car) which has offices in various locations (☎ freephone (0800) 758822). Dial-a-Wreck in Auckland (☎ (09) 358 0188) offer bargain-priced (i.e. well-worn) campervans from around $40 per day excluding insurance.

SELF-CATERING

New Zealand offers an abundance of self-catering accommodation and a wide choice including mobile homes, cabins, serviced motels, tourist flats and condominiums. The most luxurious dwellings have private swimming pools, tennis courts and acres of private grounds, although you may need to take out a second mortgage to pay the bill! Standards vary considerably, from basic, no-frills cabins to luxury flats with every modern convenience.

Cabins: one particular feature of self-catering accommodation in New Zealand is the cabin, which is usually basic containing only beds and essential furniture, but a step up from a tent. You must provide your own bedding or sleeping bag. In addition to dedicated cabin sites, cabins are also available at many camping and caravanning sites from between $25 to $55 per night. The Camp and Cabin Association of New Zealand (PO Box 394, Paraparaumu, ☎ (04) 298 3283) publishes a directory containing details of around 240 member sites.

Tourist Flats: a tourist flat is the New Zealand term for a holiday apartment. Unlike cabins they are usually located in purpose-built buildings and can vary from fairly basic one-room studios to two or three bedroom apartments. They usually contain bedding and linen and a well equipped kitchen, and better quality flats are fully serviced and contain washing machines, dishwashers and TVs (they also provide the use of swimming pools and sporting facilities). A tourist flat typically costs between $40 to $70 per night, depending on the facilities.

Condominiums: an increasingly popular trend in New Zealand is American-style condominiums, which are essentially the same as tourist flats but more luxurious. They are sometimes found in the grounds of luxury hotels and sporting lodges, and boast every modern facility including swimming pools, spas, tennis courts and extensive gardens. The cost ranges from $700 to $2,000 per week, per unit.

It isn't usually necessary to book far in advance for self-catering accommodation, as there's a wide choice and there isn't much of a peak holiday season in New Zealand. If you wish to stay in a particular unit for a particular week during the summer, then you should certainly book, although if you're fairly flexible then you need book only a week or two in advance or you can simply turn up and find somewhere on the spot (if your preferred accommodation isn't available there's usually somewhere similar nearby).

Various organisations publish guides to self-catering accommodation and an excellent *Where to Stay Guide* is also published by the New Zealand Tourism Board listing the different accommodation options in New Zealand. It's available free from NZTB offices, although a charge is made if you want the guide posted to you. Other good guides includes Jasons *Holiday and Leisure Accommodation* and *Motels and Motor Lodges* (the New Zealand equivalents of Michelin guides).

MUSEUMS, ART GALLERIES, ETC.

Most exhibits in New Zealand museums and galleries are from recent history, although you can enjoy ancient treasures and old masters at art galleries in some cities. However, there's definitely a preference for more contemporary works and many of the exhibits are by present day Maori and Pakeha (a local term for white, European settlers) artists. The standard of museums and art galleries is generally high (many have living or interactive displays) and even in small towns you're likely to find a local museum where you can learn something of the local history and culture. Admission is usually free except for collections housed in historic buildings, where a small charge is made. The New Zealand Historic Places Trust maintains 45 properties around the country where displays are maintained.

Among the most famous museums and galleries in New Zealand are the Auckland City Art Gallery, the National Art Gallery in Wellington (which exhibits both New Zealand and European paintings, drawings, prints and sculptures), the Dowse Art Gallery in Lower Hutt, Wellington (contemporary art) and the Robert McDougall Art Gallery in Christchurch, which is one of the few galleries to exhibit European masters. For information contact the Art Galleries and Museums Association of New Zealand, 40 Kings Crescent, Lower Hutt.

It's also possible to visit many businesses in New Zealand, particularly those connected with the food and drink industry including vineyards, distilleries, breweries, mineral water springs, farms and dairies. Technology enthusiasts may prefer to visit a hydroelectric power plant or a mine.

THEATRE, OPERA & BALLET

New Zealand has seven professional theatre companies resident in one or other of the main cities and a number of repertory theatre groups throughout the country, even in smaller towns. Among New Zealand's best known playwrights are Bruce Mason, Joe Musaphia, Greg McGee and Roger Hall, whose play 'Middle Aged Spread' was a major success in London's West End. The New Zealand Opera Company dates back to 1954 and the National Opera was established in 1979. New Zealand Opera is more famous outside the country than within, although opera singer Dame Kiri te Kanawa is revered in New Zealand (mainly because she's a New Zealander who has made it on the world stage, rather than because of the average New Zealander's interest in opera). The New Zealand Ballet was founded in 1953 and the National School of Ballet (now part of the New Zealand School of Dance) was established in 1968. Like its counterparts in opera, the New Zealand Ballet has an excellent repertoire of 19th century and more modern works, and performs regularly in New Zealand and abroad.

MUSIC

New Zealand's Symphony Orchestra regularly tours the country and undertakes overseas tours, particularly to Australia and Japan. Most major cities also have their own symphony and concert orchestras. Prominent New Zealand musicians include concert organist Gillian Weir and pianists Michael Houston and Maurice Till. New Zealand is also noted for its metropolitan brass bands (a local tradition), which frequently take part in international competitions and have been world champions on several occasions.

There are few well-known home-grown rock and pop bands, Crowded House being one of the few to attain international fame, and most groups leave for Europe as soon as they achieve some success. Internationally known rock and pop stars do, however, tour New Zealand on a regular basis, mainly in November and December, with tickets for top acts costing at least $50. There are rock, folk and jazz clubs in most cities, although these tend to be quieter and less cosmopolitan than those found in Europe and North America.

CINEMA

New Zealand produces a number of home-grown feature films which are popular with local cinema-goers and some, such as Roger Donaldson's *Sleeping Dogs*, have even received international recognition. Cinema-lovers needn't be concerned, however, as most of the world's big movies are released in New Zealand sooner or later (sometimes before Europe). There are cinemas in all cities and most towns of any size, including multi-screen centres in the major cities. Tickets cost an average of around $9 and there are usually special offers for afternoon and Monday evening performances, when you can see the latest releases for around $5.

Films are graded by censors according to a unique classification system: G rated films are for general viewing and are the same as the U (universal or unrestricted) rating in other countries. GY films are similar but recommended for those aged 13 or over and GA films are for those aged 18 and over. The above are recommendations, unlike R18 and R16 films, which are legally restricted to those of the appropriate age and above. RP rated films, such as RP13 or RP16 may be seen by those of the age indicated, but only when they are accompanied by an adult aged 18 or over. The censors frequently add a descriptive tag to their rating, such as 'violent content' or 'explicit sexual content', which gives additional guidance and makes it easier for parents to decide which films their children shouldn't see (or conversely, which films teenagers will do anything to try to see!).

SOCIAL CLUBS

There are many social clubs and organisations in New Zealand catering for both foreigners and locals. These include Anglo-New Zealand Clubs, Business Clubs, International Men's and Women's Clubs and Rotary Clubs. Expatriates from many countries have their own clubs in major cities, a list of which is often maintained by embassies and consulates in New Zealand. The Country Women's Institutes of New Zealand and the Women's Division Federation Farmers (WDFF) play an important part in the social life of women in rural areas, where there are few formal social facilities. All towns have a YWCA and YMCA, many of which organise extensive programmes. In keeping with the country's sporting heritage, there are sports clubs in almost every town, the most common of which are rugby, soccer, cricket, hockey and netball.

Many local clubs organise activities and pastimes such as chess, bridge, art, music, sports activities, outings, and theatre and cinema trips. Joining a local club is one of the best ways to meet people and make new friends or to integrate into your local community or New Zealand society in general. Ask your local library for information.

EVENING CLASSES

Evening classes are provided by various organisations in all cities and large towns in New Zealand. In addition to formal adult and further education, evening classes offer courses and lectures in everything from astrology to zoology. The range and variety of subjects offered is endless and includes foreign languages, handicrafts, hobbies and sports, and business-related courses. Among the most popular classes are cookery (proof that New Zealanders *are* interested in food, contrary to what many people believe) and motor and home maintenance. New Zealanders have a long tradition of do-it-yourself dating back to the days of the early settlers and few people would dream of paying somebody to fix their home or car if they could do it themselves (an old New Zealand saying is 'you can fix it fine with binder twine' – the string used to bind bales of hay!). If you live in a remote area you may find it difficult to find a local tradesman to do odd jobs on your home, therefore classes have a practical as well as a leisure purpose.

NIGHT-LIFE

New Zealand night-life varies considerably depending on the town or region and in small towns you may be fortunate to find a bar with music. New Zealand pubs are traditionally serious drinking places and shun any trends towards making them more attractive with live music. In cities you'll find a wide range of attractions including jazz clubs, discos, music clubs, karaoke bars, trendy bars, night-clubs and music halls. Although some are fast-paced by New Zealand standards, you're unlikely to find a night-spot that's as dynamic as the top establishments in New York, London or Paris. All such establishments restrict entry to those over 20, which in part accounts for the more mature (i.e. conservative) atmosphere. The most popular clubs change continually and are listed in newspapers and entertainment magazines. Although there are a few places in Auckland which keep going until the small hours, you'll find that most close early by international standards (many a New Zealand night-club is closed by 1am, simply because all the revellers have gone home!).

GAMBLING

Gambling is a national passion in New Zealand, where it's strictly controlled by the state to such an extent that gambling in some other countries seems completely unfettered in comparison. Slot machines and electronic amusement arcade gambling games have been legal only since 1987 and even now may be played only in strictly licensed premises. The national lottery (Lotto) is the most widespread form of gambling in New Zealand where over two-thirds of the population buys a ticket every week (the minimum stake is $3). Tickets can be purchased at designated shops including most dairies (corner shops) and postal shops, and the draw is shown live on prime-time TV on Saturday evenings. Instant-win scratch cards can also be bought from the same outlets. Some of the proceeds of Lotto are donated to charity, including charities which help compulsive gamblers!

After Lotto, gambling on horse racing is the next most popular activity, with over 500 regular horse race meetings throughout the country each year (an average of ten a week). New Zealanders are even more passionate about horse racing (including harness racing or trotting and flat racing) than Australians and the size of bets are often huge. Bets can be placed at betting offices licensed by the Totalisator Agency Board (TAB), which also accepts bets on Australian races.

Those looking for a more genteel outlet for their gambling passions may like to try their hand at bingo, known locally as housie. Most pubs and clubs have a housie night at least once a week (some every night), where for around $8 you can buy a card entitling you to play some 40 games. Casinos have been legalised within the last few years and include the Sky City casino in Auckland with 97 gaming tables, a Keno lounge and over 1,000 slot machines. Sky City has recently become one of New Zealand's most famous landmarks with the completion of the 1,000ft Sky City Tower topped by a revolving restaurant. Opening hours are 11am to 3am daily and continuously from 11am Thursday until 3am Monday morning. All advertising for casinos in New Zealand is accompanied by a gambling 'health warning' and the number of an organisation which helps compulsive gamblers (☎ freephone (0800) 888711).

BARS & PUBS

As a nation for whom drinking is a national obsession, New Zealand has a vast choice of drinking establishments. Every town of any size has at least one hotel or pub and in many town and city suburbs there's one on every corner. However, despite (or perhaps because of) the popularity of drinking, New Zealand has some of the world's most bizarre licensing laws. The traditional New Zealand drinking place is the local hotel, which is roughly equivalent to a pub in Britain or a bar elsewhere. Despite being called hotels, they rarely offer accommodation. At its most basic the New Zealand hotel can be very rudimentary indeed, with plastic chairs, fluorescent lighting and no music, although the larger establishments offer a choice between public and lounge bars (a lounge bar is more attractively furnished but up to 50 per cent more expensive). Some country places have beer gardens.

New Zealand hotels are public houses in the true sense of the word, in that usually all-comers are served. Women drinking in a public bar may attract a few stares in remote places, but are unlikely to meet with disapproval. In country areas you may initially feel that you're intruding upon the locals' private territory, but you'll usually be warmly welcomed and engaged in conversation. Indeed, you should make an attempt to talk to the regulars as it may be considered rude not to do so. Most traditional hotels don't serve food and those that do have a rather limited menu. All hotels have a so-called bottle sales counter where you can buy alcohol to take away, which is a consequence of the licensing laws that allow shops and supermarkets to sell wine, but not beer or spirits (although this may change in the next few years).

Bars are generally more up-market establishments and are usually found in cities and large towns, where you can choose from French-influenced bars, cafe-bars, brasseries, wine bars and pavement cafes. These places offer none of the traditional New Zealand atmosphere, but as in other countries they are fashionable places to see and be seen. Drinks are invariably more expensive than a hotel, although establishments may also serve food.

Licensing Hours: until 1967 hotels could only serve alcohol until 6pm and although licensing hours have been liberalised in recent years, the 5 to 6pm 'swill' is still often the busiest time for drinking. The same liberalisation has also resulted in a confusing array of licensing hours applying to different premises in different places. In theory drinking establishments can apply for a 24-hour licence allowing them to open all day and night except on Sundays, when they must close by 3am. In practice, most hotels and bars are open daily from 11am to 10pm and until 10.30pm on Friday and Saturday. Even places with a 24-hour licence may be closed by 1am, simply due to a lack of demand for late night drinking. Establishments that don't serve food aren't usually allowed to sell alcohol on Sundays, although Sunday drinking is permitted in night-clubs, private clubs and places of entertainment, in addition to restaurants.

A few areas of Auckland, Wellington and Christchurch have even stricter than usual local licensing authorities and don't licence any establishments to serve alcohol and are therefore effectively 'dry' (there's still a strong temperance movement in New Zealand). The main effect of this, however, is to encourage drink-driving, as drinkers are forced to travel a few miles down the road to quench their thirst. The legal age for drinking in public establishments in New Zealand is 20 unless a drinker is accompanied by an adult relative, when it's reduced to 18. There's presently talk of reducing the drinking age to 18, but it may take some time to come to fruition. On the spot fines for under-age drinking are also planned, together with identity cards for young people old enough to drink.

Beer: the most popular drink in New Zealand is beer, which is usually sold in draught form and is similar in taste and strength to British bitter. There are two main breweries in the country, Lion and Dominion Breweries (who together also own the vast majority of drinking establishments), which produce a range of beers and lagers.

There are also a number of independent breweries and micro (tiny) breweries producing their own draught and bottled brands. Imported and locally brewed versions of foreign beers are available in larger hotels and trendier establishments. Beer is sold in a wide variety of measures which may vary depending on the city or region. Beer glasses are designed to hold metric quantities, although it can also be ordered in the old imperial quantities, e.g. asking for a pint or half pint will get you around 500ml to 600ml or 250ml to 300ml respectively. The most common measures are 360ml or 280ml (ask for a three-sixty or two-eighty) and you can also buy beer by the jug containing one or two litres. In remote areas, particularly in the South Island, beer may be ordered in (for example) a 7oz or 12oz glass, but is served in a metric glass with around the same capacity. Perhaps it's better just to ask for a small or large beer.

Wine: New Zealand wine production has boomed in recent years and there are now some 150 large commercial vineyards and over 15,000 tonnes of grapes a year are harvested annually in the main wine producing area of Gisborne. Most vineyards are open to the public and usually offer free tastings to encourage visitors to buy a few cases. New Zealand wine has gained a first class international reputation for quality in the last decade or so and has even earned the accolade of being described by one English wine expert as smelling like 'cat's pee on a gooseberry bush' (also the name of a local wine), which apparently is a compliment when applied to sauvignon! The best New Zealand wines are white (experts say the country's climate is unsuited to red wine grapes), of which sauvignon, chablis and chardonnay are considered the best. You'll rarely find a bad New Zealand wine, although the poorer brands tend to be inflicted on the home market rather than be sent overseas to taint the reputation of New Zealand exports! Foreign wines are also available in New Zealand, although they are significantly more expensive due to steep taxes, including those which make the short journey from Australia. You can buy wine by the glass in hotels, although as they are invariably dominated by beer-swilling men, most offer a poor selection.

Spirits: spirits are available in most hotels although the choice is usually limited. Imported Scotch whisky is expensive but locally produced gin is good value at around $14 per bottle. Kiwi fruit liqueur makes a change from the usual coffee and fruit liqueurs found in other countries.

RESTAURANTS

New Zealand doesn't rank among the great gastronomic countries of the world as far as restaurant food is concerned, although the choice and quality has improved in recent years. However, the majority of restaurants still follow the meat-and-two-veg concept and if you like lamb you'll be spoilt for choice in your average New Zealand high street restaurant. Most towns also have a fish and chip shop where the quality is invariably excellent. Lovers of sponge and custard puddings and ice cream (New Zealand ice cream is excellent) will also be perfectly happy with the fare on offer at their local dining establishments. This isn't to say that ethnic cuisine isn't available in New Zealand and most towns have at least one Chinese restaurant (although the food is of the westernised Chinese variety rather than authentic Chinese cuisine) and you can also find French, Italian, Thai, Mexican, Japanese and Indian food in the main cities. The advantages of eating out in New Zealand include generous portions, friendly service and surprisingly low prices – four people can enjoy an excellent (if unadventurous) meal for $50 excluding drinks.

If you're an enthusiastic epicure you'll need to head for the main cities in order to indulge your palette, where you'll find excellent restaurants comparable with the best London or Paris has to offer. Auckland's Parnell district has a good choice of top restaurants with prices that are much lower than those in similar establishments abroad. However, outside the major cities there's a relative dearth of gastronomic excellence with the notable exception of fish and seafood restaurants, where fresh seafood is prepared and cooked imaginatively often with a strong Maori influence.

Bring-Your-Own (BYO) Restaurants: BYO restaurants date back to the days when liquor licences were hard to come by and restaurants without a licence allowed customers to bring their own wine or other drinks. In return for a small corkage fee, which is limited by law and shouldn't be more than around 50¢, the waiter uncorks and serves you with your own wine. Although licences are easier to come by nowadays, many restaurants choose not to become licensed as it allows customers greater freedom to choose their own drinks at the price they want to pay (or can afford). Some licensed restaurants also allow customers to bring their own drinks, although the policy on this is patchy and you should make discreet enquiries in advance, particularly if you're inviting guests to dinner. One drawback is that non-BYO restaurants can fix their own corkage fee and you may find yourself paying as much for 'uncorking' as you paid for your bottle of supermarket plonk!

Opening Hours: restaurant opening hours reflect licensing hours and as a result many restaurants don't open on Sundays (therefore it's wise to check if you plan to eat in a particular place). Alternatively some restaurants that open on Sundays close on Mondays. Reservations aren't usually necessary in New Zealand, but are recommended in the more fashionable places, particularly on Fridays and Saturdays.

Tipping: as in other areas of New Zealand life, a no-tipping policy applies in all restaurants (if only other countries would follow suit!). You won't be expected to tip and indeed should you try to it may be greeted with surprise and even embarrassment by your waiter. Neither is there any service charge. The menu price is the price you pay and no extra charges will be added to your bill and you won't be expected to add anything.

Vegetarianism: New Zealanders have an unsympathetic attitude towards vegetarians, who are thin on the ground. Not eating meat is almost considered unpatriotic in a country which earns millions of dollars from meat exports and where the number of sheep make lamb one of the cheapest and most frequently served dishes. There are a few vegetarian restaurants in the major cities, although if you eat fish there are many excellent seafood restaurants.

Smoking: smoking in a restaurant (or indeed anywhere in public) is much less socially acceptable than in many other countries. All restaurants have a non-smoking area and many have banned it altogether.

Dress: apart from a few pretentious places in Auckland, Wellington and Christchurch that insist on a jacket and tie, most restaurants don't impose dress restrictions. Most New Zealanders don't dress up to eat out and smart casual dress is usually adequate even for the best of restaurants. BYO restaurants are normally more casual than non-BYO establishments.

At Home: although New Zealanders eat much the same meals as people in most other western countries, they may have a different emphasis. The traditional cooked 'English' breakfast of bacon and eggs is still eaten in some homes, although many families have adopted the modern fashion for cereal and fruit juices. Cooked lunches are less popular nowadays, with many people opting for a quick snack instead. In most homes high tea or tea, eaten between 4 and 7pm, is the main meal of the day rather than dinner. One great 'British' tradition that lives on in New Zealand is that of Sunday lunch, usually consisting of roast lamb and two or three vegetables, which all the family eat together.

LIBRARIES

Almost every town in New Zealand has a local library. Many New Zealanders are avid readers and the relatively high cost of books (there are few New Zealand publishers and most books are imported from Australia, the UK or the USA) makes the library a popular place to stock up on reading material. Library opening hours and the range of books stocked vary considerably depending on the size of the town. The larger libraries offer a range of services including newspapers and periodicals, archives, book reservation services and photocopying. To join your local library you simply need to provide proof of your address, such as a utility bill or bank statement.

16.

SPORTS

New Zealand has the ideal climate and terrain for a wide range of sports, including world class skiing and surfing, both of which it's possible to undertake on the same day (although why anyone would want to is another matter). Most New Zealanders are passionate about sport which serves as a symbol of national pride and New Zealand sportsmen and women are world renowned in a number of sports, notably rugby and sailing. The New Zealand government recently confirmed the country's sport and health-conscious image by appointing a 'Sports, Leisure and Fitness' minister and making the provision of access to sport for all official government policy. A recent survey found that over 50 per cent of the adult population belong to a sports or health club, although the New Zealander's love of exercise hasn't had much impact on the rate of heart disease, which kills up to 8,000 people a year. The doctrine that sport is very much for 'the people' is illustrated by the fact that the majority of sports in New Zealand are played at amateur level with little paid, professional sport. The main exception is rugby which is primarily a professional game at the top level and one of the few sports where professional athletes in New Zealand can earn telephone-number salaries, such as are common in other countries.

While team sports are popular, there's also a large following for many solo sports, particularly those where competitors can pit their wits against the natural elements, such as climbing, rafting and surfing. Despite the dominance of traditional sports such as rugby, New Zealand is by no means old-fashioned in the field of sporting endeavour and many of the latest 'daredevil' sports are practiced in New Zealand including bungee jumping (some, such as jet-boating, are claimed to be a New Zealand invention).

RUGBY

Rugby is New Zealand's national sport and in the past even the prime minister has become embroiled in the selection of the national rugby (union) team, the All Blacks. While many New Zealanders are interested in playing and watching rugby, many more are supporters simply because the success of the national team brings New Zealand such fame and prestige around the world. Interest in rugby in New Zealand fell in the '70s and '80s when the national team maintained links with apartheid South Africa, but following the demise of apartheid its popularity and match attendances have soared. Top players such as Cullen, Lomu and Mehrtens are as revered in New Zealand as top soccer players are in other countries and they have the opportunity to earn more through rugby than almost any other profession.

The rugby season traditionally lasts from May until September, during which clubs play both rugby union and rugby league at all levels including international, regional, representative, city and local. While primarily a men's game, New Zealand also has a small but enthusiastically supported women's rugby movement. New Zealand teams play in a huge variety of league and cup competitions, with the top divisions in both codes (the Super 12 and Super League) including teams from outside New Zealand. The South African national team, the Springboks (or 'Boks') are the All Blacks' traditional arch enemy and the Tri-Nations tournament (consisting of New Zealand, South Africa and the Australian 'Wallabies' team) is regarded as one of the country's major sporting events. Although rugby largely transcends racial groups, there's also a national Maori side at league level. Tickets to top rugby matches usually cost from $10 to $30.

Anyone with a keen interest in rugby will find they are warmly welcomed by local clubs and even those with absolutely no interest will find that they are unable to escape the country's passion for their national sport. Success for the All Blacks results in almost non-stop coverage of the sport and much merriment and rejoicing, while failure may result in all mention of rugby being unofficially purged from the media as if the sport had been 'disinvented' overnight. Expatriates report that an air of misery descends on the country following an All Blacks defeat, with sulking and moodiness lasting for several days (the country must have been particularly downcast in 1998 after an unprecedented five defeats in a row, three by Australia!).

Despite the game's supposedly gentlemanly image, rugby can be a dangerous business in New Zealand. Post-match violence and drunkenness (as is sometimes associated with soccer in other countries) occurs occasionally and being a rugby referee isn't without its risks, with the rate of attacks on referees during and after matches increasing amid demands for greater protection and strike threats from referees.

SOCCER

Football is played in New Zealand where it's usually known as soccer (or footie), to differentiate it from rugby football which most New Zealanders consider 'proper' football. In New Zealand the popularity of soccer lags way behind rugby and its cause hasn't been helped by some schools actually banning it in the past in the fear that pupils would be tempted away from the 'superior' game. Interest in soccer boomed some years ago when the New Zealand national team, the All Whites, qualified for the world cup. However, in recent times, the New Zealand team has been notably unsuccessful, particularly against the Australian national team, a country not noted for its prowess at soccer. A new Irish director of coaching has recently been appointed with the aim of taking New Zealand to the world cup finals (one day).

National, northern, central and southern soccer leagues operate in New Zealand, where soccer is played both in summer and winter, although the 'official' soccer season runs from May to September. New Zealand soccer 'stars' are nonentities compared with the cult status of top rugby players and the game is light years away from the standard seen in top European leagues such as the Italian Serie A or the English Premiership. Local clubs occasionally sign foreign players and the signing of a British player from a second or third division side makes headline news in New Zealand. Interest is, however, growing at the amateur level and there are local leagues in most areas. There are plans for a combined New Zealand team to play in the Australian soccer league, which it's hoped will increase the competitiveness and general standard of soccer in New Zealand.

CRICKET

Cricket is a national passion in New Zealand, as it is in many other countries that derive their national heritage from Britain. There's wide support for the national team and it's popular among participants and spectators at all levels. International one-day series matches between New Zealand and England attract crowds of 25,000 at Christchurch's floodlit Lancaster Park Stadium. Top cricket players are held in as high a regard as top rugby stars, although support for cricket has declined in recent years and most young people have a preference for rugby. The cricket season runs from November to April and tickets to major international matches cost around $20. There's also a small but significant women's cricket movement in New Zealand and the national team's matches are followed keenly.

TREKKING

Trekking (or tramping as it's also known) is New Zealand's name for hiking, which is an institution enjoyed by New Zealanders of all ages, from toddlers to pensioners. Trekking comprises anything from a leisurely afternoon walk to an endurance-testing, near-military route march lasting several days or weeks. The advantage of trekking is that you can make it as easy or as demanding as you wish, and there are plenty of places to trek, even close to the major cities. A vast amount of New Zealand is divided into parks (e.g. national, forest and maritime parks) and there's always somewhere new to explore, which in the more remote areas include many breathtaking spots that are only accessible on foot.

Despite its allusion to wilderness ways, trekking is highly organised in New Zealand and the whole country is criss-crossed with numerous tracks, some of which are internationally famous and attract hikers from around the world. The more popular tracks are well signposted (look for 'W' signs) and maintained and often radiate from the city suburbs. The more demanding tracks may not be signposted but are marked on trekking maps. Some of the longer tracks are legendary including the South Island's Routeburn (usually a three to four day trek through rain forests, mountains and alpine passes), Milford (four days), Kepler (three to four days), Greenstone (two to three days), Hollyford (five to six days), Abel Tasman (three to four days), Heaphy (four to five days) and the North Island's Whirinaki Track (three to four days). Some tracks, such as the Abel Tasman, can be walked year round, while others such as the Routeburn are at higher altitudes and may be impassable in winter. October to April is unofficially regarded as the trekking season and some of the most popular routes can be quite congested in January and February.

Although many trekkers (or should they be called trekkies?) take to the tracks independently, it's possible to take a trekking package holiday, which is ideal for the slightly less adventurous. Companies specialising in trekking holidays provide an experienced guide and accommodation in luxury lodges, mountain huts or tent camps, with hot showers and meals. The cost of guided treks range from $500 to $950 for a five-day trek (one such operator is Routeburn Walk Ltd., PO Box 568, Queenstown, ☎ (03) 442 8200, internet: http://nz.com/SouthIs/Routeburn). If you don't wish to take a full package tour, you can hire an experienced local guide to show you a route and provide commentary on the flora and fauna.

When trekking independently you need to carry your own food and equipment (take plenty of warm clothing even in summer). Accommodation can be found in Department of Conservation huts situated along tracks, which may be free or require a modest fee (e.g. between $5 and $15 per night) when bunks, cooking facilities and clean water are provided. Accommodation is basic and is provided on a first-come, first-served basis. Some independent trekkers prefer to take tents which can usually be pitched near huts, but cannot usually be pitched alongside tracks in order to protect the unique character of treks. Note that you must pre-book to walk the Milford track, even when walking independently. There are numerous trekking guides available in New

Zealand, including Lonely Planet's *Tramping in New Zealand*, the definitive book on the subject.

General Information

The following notes may help you survive a stroll in the mountains:

- If you're going to take up hiking seriously, then a good pair of walking shoes or boots is mandatory (available from sports and trekking shops). Always wear proper walking shoes or boots where the terrain is rough. Unfortunately walking boots are usually uncomfortable or hurt your feet after a few hours (if they don't hurt, it isn't doing you any good). Wearing two pairs of socks can help prevent blisters. Break in a new pair of boots on some *gentle* hikes before setting out on a marathon hike around the country.

- Don't over-exert yourself, particularly at high altitudes where the air is thinner. Mountain sickness usually occurs only above 4,000 metres, but can also happen at lower altitudes. A few words of warning for those who aren't particularly fit: **take it easy and set a slow pace.** It's easy to over-exert yourself and underestimate the duration or degree of difficulty of a hike. Start slowly and build up to those weekend marathons. If the most exercise you usually get is walking to the pub and crawling back, don't forget to take along a life-support 'machine' (a crate of beer?). If you're unfit, you can use chair-lifts and cable-cars to get to high altitudes in some areas.

- **Don't attempt a major hike alone as it's too dangerous.** Notify someone about your route, destination and estimated time of return. Check the conditions along your route and the times of any public transport connections (set out early to avoid missing the last bus). Take into account the time required for both ascents and descents. If you're unable to return by the time expected, let somebody know. If you realise that you're unable to reach your destination, for example due to tiredness or bad weather, turn back in good time or take a shorter route. If you get caught in a heavy storm, descend as quickly as possible or seek protection, e.g. in a hut.

- Check the weather forecast, usually obtainable from the local tourist office. Generally the higher the altitude, the more unpredictable the weather.

- Hiking, even in lowland areas, can be dangerous, so don't take any unnecessary risks. There are enough natural hazards including bad weather, rockfalls, avalanches, rough terrain, snow and ice, and wet grass, without adding to them.

- Don't walk on closed tracks at any time (they are signposted). This is particularly important in the spring when there may be a danger of avalanches or rockfalls or tracks may be closed due to forestry work. If you're in doubt about a particular route, ask in advance at the local tourist office.

- Wear loose fitting clothes and not, for example, tight jeans, which can become uncomfortable when you get warmed up. Shorts (short trousers to Americans!) are excellent in hot weather. Lightweight cotton trousers are comfortable unless it's cold. You can wear your shorts underneath your trousers and remove your trousers when you have warmed up.

- Take a warm pullover, gloves (in winter) and a raincoat or cape. Mountain weather can change suddenly and even in summer it's sometimes cold at high altitudes. A first-aid kit (for cuts and grazes), compass, identification, maps, small torch and a pocket knife may also come in handy. A pair of binoculars are useful for spotting wildlife (or hikers having fun in the bushes). Take a rucksack to carry all your survival rations. A 35 to 40 litre capacity rucksack is best for day trips or a 65 litre capacity for longer hikes.

- Take sun protection, for example a hat, sunglasses and sun and barrier cream, as you'll burn more easily at high altitudes due to the thinner air (the ozone layer is thin in New Zealand and the sun can be very strong). Use a total sunblock cream on your lips, nose and eyelids, and take a scarf or handkerchief to protect your neck from the sun. You may also need to protect yourself against ticks and mosquitoes in some areas.

- Take a water bottle to prevent dehydration. This is also much appreciated when you discover that the restaurant or hotel that was just around the corner is still miles away because you took the wrong turning.

- Don't take young children on difficult hikes unless you enjoy carrying them. Impress upon children the importance of not wandering off on their own. If you lose anyone, particularly children, seek help as soon as possible and before nightfall. It's advisable to equip children with a loud whistle and some warm clothing, in case they get lost.

- Hikers are asked to observe the following general rules:
  - take care not to damage trees, flowers and bushes;
  - leave animals in peace (dogs mustn't be allowed to disturb farm animals);
  - be careful with fire and never start a fire in a forbidden area;
  - watch where you walk and keep to the paths;
  - don't litter the countryside;
  - think of others;
  - close all gates after use.

FISHING

Fishing, whether in the sea, rivers, streams or lakes, is the most popular participation sport in New Zealand and one of the few which doesn't involve a great deal of exertion. Salmon and trout (weighing up to 5kg) are plentiful in the country's lake and rivers and are the most popular freshwater catches. There are two species of salmon in New Zealand: landlocked quinnats (which spawn near the sources of the country's main rivers) which can weigh up to 11kg and sea-run quinnats (which emerge from the sea to spawn in river estuaries) that rarely exceed 1kg. The fishing season varies depending on the area and the catch and usually starts around the 1st October and finishes sometime between the 30th April and the 30th June.

Fishing tackle can be imported into New Zealand without restriction (and can be purchased in the USA via the internet at huge savings over local prices), although it's advisable not to import fishing flies as they must be fumigated before passing through customs (at your expense), which can be frustrating bearing in mind their relatively small value. All anglers require a fishing licence which can be purchased from tackle and sports shops, although Maoris claim they have the right (enshrined in the Treaty of Waitangi) to fish without a licence and this has occasionally been upheld by the courts. The cost of a fishing licence is $11 per day, $22 per week, $37 per month or $55 for a whole season. The country is officially divided into 26 fishing regions, where it's supervised by conservation officers or countryside rangers. It's possible to hire a local guide (ask for a quotation first) to find the best local fishing spots. The New Zealand Professional Fishing Guides Association, PO Box 16, Motu, Gisborne (☎ (06) 863 5822) can also provide information and assistance.

New Zealand's clear coastal waters are ideal for sea fishing; deep-sea fishing is also popular, although it's naturally more expensive as it requires the purchase or hire of a boat and special equipment (for information contact the Game Fishing Charter Association, PO Box 263, Paihia). The best location for deep sea fishing is the north-east of the North Island, while other good spots include the Bay of Islands around Russel, Mercury Bay, Tutukaka near Whangari, Tauranga and Whakatane. Some keen fishermen even venture as far as the Chatham Islands, 850km/528mi east of New Zealand. Boats and tackle can be hired throughout New Zealand and no licence is needed for game or deep sea fishing. Popular catches include mako; thresher and hammerhead shark; blue, black and striped marlin; kingfish; and tuna (which is also the Maori word for eel).

BOATING & WATERSPORTS

New Zealand is a mecca for boating and water-sports, the most popular of which are outlined below:

Jet-boating: New Zealand invented jet-boating and it's enjoyed by people of all ages. A jet-boat (or jet-ski) is a propeller-less, LPG-powered, craft which can reach up to 70kph (43mph) an hour, turn through 360 degrees within its own length and plane over just a few inches of water. Jet-boating is usually done in coastal waters and on lakes, although they can also negotiate shallow river gorges that are inaccessible to most other craft. The most popular areas for jet-boating pleasure rides are Waimakariri near Christchurch, the Buller and Makaroa regions, the Rangitaiki River gorges, and the Wanganui and Waikato River below the Huka Falls. Jet-boats can be hired in many beach resorts and on some inland lakes. There are restrictions on the use of jet-boats in most resorts. **However, unless you're an experienced rider, it's advisable to steer well clear of jet-boats which are deadly in the wrong hands (both to riders and anyone who comes into contact with them).**

Kayaking: kayaking is broadly similar to canoeing and is a popular New Zealand water-sport, particularly among the less well-off water-sports' enthusiasts. Kayaking is enjoyed in coastal waters and on lakes and rivers, and can range from a sedate paddle along a lakeside to negotiating the torrents of a raging river gorge. Kayaks and safety equipment (a helmet should always be worn) can be bought or hired in most popular kayaking areas.

Rafting: rafting is a slightly more challenging alternative to kayaking, entailing the navigation of often hostile white-water in a large inflatable raft accommodating four to eight people. The most popular (and safe) way to raft is to take part in an organised trip which includes a qualified guide and tuition. Trips usually last from two to five days and all food and camping equipment is included. Rafting is also a popular winter sport, when a wetsuit is considered essential.

Rowing: New Zealanders are enthusiastic rowers and there are plenty of lakes and rivers on which to practice this sport in all its guises, including both leisure and competitive rowing. The country also fields a team in dragon boat racing, which is particularly popular in Southeast Asia.

Scuba Diving & Snorkelling: New Zealand is a mecca for scuba divers and snorkellers, and the country's waters are full of exotic fish and plant life. Popular diving spots include the Poor Knights Islands near Whangerei (where the waters are particularly clear), the South Island fjords (famous for their unusual red and black coral) and the kelp forests off Stewart Island (and their huge paua shell fish). The main diving season is from February to June, although in the warmer, more sheltered waters off the Bay of Islands near Auckland it's possible to dive all year. The former Greenpeace flagship 'Rainbow Warrior' (sunk by French secret service agents in an operation against anti-nuclear protestors) has been scuttled in this area to provide a haven for sea life.

Along the coast there are numerous dive stores offering tuition, equipment rental, the filling of air bottles, and information on dive locations and organised trips. Divers need a PADI (Professional Association of Diving Instructors) certificate, tuition for which is offered in most diving areas in New Zealand. Always learn with a qualified and reputable outfit and avoid 'cowboy' operators. Further information can be obtained from the NZ Underwater Association, PO Box 875, Auckland.

Swimming: most New Zealanders are taught to swim at an early age and it's a popular leisure and competitive sport. Despite the country's abundance of sea, rivers and lakes, it isn't necessary to head for the great outdoors if you're a keen swimmer. Most towns have at least one public indoor swimming pool, some of which are equipped with waterchutes, wave machines and a range of other facilities such as saunas and gymnasia. In several places in New Zealand it's possible to swim with dolphins, which apart from the thrill is claimed to have valuable therapeutic powers. 'Dolphin swimming' is possible (subject to the dolphins being able to fit you into their schedule) in the Bay of Islands, Whakatane and Kaikoura in the South Island.

On surfing beaches, swimmers must stay within the swimming area defined by flags, which may be hoisted from around 6am until 6 or 7pm in summer. They are placed to indicate the safest swimming area in the prevailing conditions and also indicate the area under closest scrutiny by lifesavers. **Due to the dangers, swimmers are urged by lifesaving associations never to swim outside patrolled areas (most beach drownings are on unpatrolled beaches).** If you get into trouble while swimming off a beach manned with lifesavers, you should raise one arm in the air which will alert the lifesavers. Take care not to venture too far out as it isn't uncommon for swimmers to be swept out to sea. Note that there's a danger of stinging jellyfish and sharks in some waters, although your chances of encountering either of these on patrolled beaches are rare.

Surfing: New Zealanders don't quite share the passion for surfing that their Australian neighbours have, although it's a popular pursuit. Many coastal areas have a SLSC or surf lifesaving club for children and adults where surfing, swimming and surf rescue combine as both a sport, leisure pursuit and a public service (i.e. lifesavers on beaches and at swimming pools). Wind surfing and river surfing are also popular in New Zealand. Information can be obtained from the NZ Surfriders Association, PO Box 737, New Plymouth.

Yachting: yachting is one of New Zealand's favourite sports (the country boasts the world's highest per capital boat ownership) and Auckland has even gone so far as to dub itself the 'City of Sails' (like Wellington it has a reputation for being windy). New Zealand secured an impressive and unexpected victory in the 1995 America's Cup and will be defending the title in the Hauraki Gulf in 1999/2000. However, the country's pride soon turned to embarrassment when the trophy was damaged by a Maori activist in a hammer attack, although it has been repaired. Yacht harbours are found throughout the country, the most popular of which include the Bay of Islands, Hauraki Gulf and the Marlborough Sounds. The more adventurous yachtsmen venture to the Pacific islands, which with their idyllic climate and unspoilt beauty make ideal yachting territory (providing you discount nuclear testing by the French, which has understandably made France unpopular with New Zealanders).

Yachting isn't necessarily a pursuit only for the wealthy (unless you yearn to own an ocean-going yacht) as there are numerous opportunities to rent a vessel and spend some time on the ocean wave or pottering around the coastline. A variety of vessels are available for 'bare-boating', where a hire company provides the yacht and sailing equipment and you provide the crew and provisions. For less intrepid sailors, it's possible to hire a professionally crewed yacht, where the crew also wait on you. All instructors and operators of organised water-sports in New Zealand must comply with Ministry of Transport safety codes, but it's advisable to check that they do before booking. There are yacht clubs in most areas, details of which can be obtained from the New Zealand Yachting Federation, PO Box 4173, Auckland.

SKIING

Few people associate New Zealand with snow, but the first commercial ski slopes opened in 1947 and the country is internationally recognised as a top skiing destination. The New Zealand ski season extends throughout the European and North American summer, beginning in June and ending in November, and professional skiers and ski bums from the northern hemisphere often ski and train in New Zealand during the northern hemisphere's summer.

There are twelve commercial skiing areas in both the North and the South Islands, all of which can be reached by road. All skiing areas have ski lifts, ski schools, equipment rental facilities, and a choice of accommodation from guest houses to good quality hotels. Most skiing areas don't have accommodation virtually on-piste, as is common in Europe, and a short journey is usually necessary to reach the slopes. Helicopter and glacier skiing is also possible in several places. A number of package tour operators offer skiing package holidays. If you're travelling independently, lift passes cost from $30 to $55 per day; the rental of skis, boots and poles from $15 to $30 per day; and lessons from $25 for a half-day group class. Nordic (cross-country) skiing is also possible in New Zealand, where there's one nordic skiing area and twelve club fields (open to the public) with more basic facilities.

An unusual feature of New Zealand skiing is that a range of facilities not usually associated with skiing are also offered in (or near) ski resorts including jet-boating, rafting, canoeing, trekking and bungee-jumping. These are often available in the valleys which are usually free of snow.

North Island: Whakapapa and Turoa are the North Island's main skiing areas, situated on Mount Ruapehu (an active volcano) around four hours by road from Auckland. They attract over 400,000 visitors a year and the high altitude (2,800 metres) means that skiing is possible well into November.

South Island: one of the most popular ski resorts in the South Island is Mount Hutt, which is around one hour by road from Christchurch. Its location and advanced snow-making system means that it's often the first resort to open and the last to close. It's popular with all-round sports fans as its proximity to Christchurch makes it possible to surf in the morning and ski in the afternoon. Other resorts include Wanaka, located in New Zealand's Alpine zone five hours from Christchurch. It features slopes suitable for both beginners and experts, plus facilities for hell-skiing and snowboarding. Wanaka is the only ski resort in New Zealand where it's possible to find accommodation on the mountain. The powder snow and demanding terrain has made the area popular with snowboarders in the last few years. Queenstown has the best all-round facilities of all the country's resorts in addition to two world class ski areas, the Remarkables and Coronet Peak, both of which are within 30 minutes drive from the town. Queenstown boasts over 100 restaurants, night-clubs, cafes and bars, several big hotels and good shopping. It's also possible to enjoy trout fishing or go wine tasting in the nearby vineyards.

Skiers Highway Code

As ski slopes become more crowded, the possibility of colliding with a fellow skier has increased dramatically. Happily, the result of most clashes is just a few bruises and dented pride, nevertheless the danger of serious injury is ever present. You cannot always protect yourself from the lunatic fringe. e.g. the crazy novice who skis way beyond his limits and the equally loony 'expert' who skis at reckless speeds with a total disregard for others. The following guidelines from the International Ski Federation's (FIS) Code of Conduct for skiers may, however, help you avoid an accident:

- **Respect for others:** a skier must behave in such a way that he neither endangers nor prejudices others.

- **Control of speed and skiing:** a skier must adapt his speed and way of skiing to his own personal ability, and to the prevailing conditions of terrain and weather.

- **Control of direction:** a skier coming from above, whose dominant position allows him a choice of paths, must take a direction which assures the safety of the skier below.

- **Overtaking:** a skier should always leave a wide enough margin for the overtaken skier to make his turn. (As when motoring, the most dangerous skiing manoeuvre is overtaking.)

- **Crossing the piste:** a skier entering or crossing a piste must look up and down to make sure that he can do so without danger to himself or to others. The same applies after stopping.

- **Stopping on the piste:** unless absolutely necessary, a skier must avoid making a stop on the piste, particularly in narrow passages or where visibility is restricted. If a skier falls, he must clear the piste as soon as possible.

- **Climbing:** a climbing skier must keep to the side of the piste and in bad visibility, keep off the piste altogether. The same goes for a skier descending on foot.

There's no foolproof way to avoid an accident (apart from avoiding skiing altogether). Obey the FIS code and make sure that you're well insured for both accidents and private liability.

CYCLING

Cycle touring is a popular sport and pastime in New Zealand, although it's some way behind countries such as France. While it's true that much of the terrain is mountainous or hilly, roads are generally well surfaced and largely traffic free (which is just as well given New Zealand's high accident rate). However, the hilly terrain is a boon for mountain biking, which is also popular. Mountain bikes may not be ridden in New Zealand's national parks, although its growing popularity has led the authorities to reconsider and it may be permitted in some parks in the future. Helmets must be worn at all times when cycling in New Zealand.

It's hardly worth taking your own cycle to New Zealand as a wide range of new and used cycles are available at reasonable prices. It's also possible to hire touring cycles, mountain bikes and even tandems in many places. Organised cycling package holidays are popular and in some areas (such as Mount Ruapehu on the Otago Peninsula) there are shuttle bus services which take you to the top of the mountains or extinct volcanoes, thus allowing you to experience the pleasure of the downhill descent without the pain of the uphill journey. One contradiction to New Zealand's otherwise cyclist-friendly culture is that cycles cannot be taken on buses or trains. Long-distance coaches accept bikes, but usually only if you remove the pedals and wrap the chain with newspaper or similar. Note also that despite New Zealand's relatively low crime rate, the theft of cycles is high and care should be taken to secure your bike when it isn't in use, particularly when it's an expensive model.

GOLF

New Zealand is a relatively new player in the golf world, although several of its courses have obtained international recognition. There are, in fact, over 400 golf courses in the country of which around 70 have opened in·the last ten years (it's said that nowhere in New Zealand is more than 50km/31mi from a course). Courses are relatively uncrowded which makes them increasingly popular with Japanese golfers who, coming from such a densely populated land, are unaccustomed to the choice and space of New Zealand's golf courses. An added attraction for most golfers (certainly those of more modest means) is the relatively liberal attitude of most golf clubs, which, with the exception of a few top clubs don't have long waiting lists or high membership fees. The vast majority of clubs also welcome non-members, with a round costing anything from $5 to $40. The bigger clubs have resident professionals, clubs, pull carts (known as trundlers) and motorised buggies for hire, while smaller clubs offer few facilities – you may even be expected to leave your green fees in an honesty box.

The New Zealand Tourism Board can provide a wealth of information about golf in New Zealand or you can contact the NZ Golf Association, PO Box 27-012, Wellington.

CLIMBING & MOUNTAINEERING

New Zealand is home to some of the highest peaks in the southern hemisphere, offering challenges for even the most experienced mountaineers. Most mountaineers head for the Southern Alps and it's usual to hire a guide or take advice from a local alpine club, of which there are several. Rock climbing, a slightly less demanding form of mountaineering, is also popular in New Zealand. In the North Island, popular climbing areas include the Mount Eden Quarry near Auckland, Whanganui Bay and Motuoapa near Lake Taupo. The Wharepape rock climbing field near Te Awamutu offers over 40 different rock climbs suitable for both advanced climbers and beginners. In the South Island, Port Hills near Christchurch and Castle Hill are popular climbing spots. Tuition and equipment (for sale and hire) is available in climbing areas.

Note that a number of climbers are killed annually in New Zealand, many of whom are inexperienced and reckless, and others owe their survival to rescuers who risk their own lives to rescue them. **It's extremely foolish, not to mention highly dangerous, to venture into the hills without an experienced guide, proper preparation, excellent physical condition, sufficient training, and the appropriate equipment and supplies.**

Useful addresses for mountaineers and climbers include the Federated Mountain Clubs of New Zealand Inc., PO Box 1604, Wellington, the New Zealand Alpine Club, PO Box 41-038, Eastbourne, Wellington and the NZ Mountain Guides Association Inc., PO Box 22-590, Christchurch.

ADVENTURE SPORTS

Although New Zealand may have a rather staid reputation (undeservedly) in certain areas, this certainly isn't true when it comes to adventure sports. The New Zealanders' passion for potentially dangerous sports, which often involve throwing yourself from great heights or challenging the forces of nature, is virtually unparalleled. Sporting daredevils certainly need never be short of challenges in New Zealand, where ever more risky adventure sports are continually being invented by the thrill-seeking (or should it be suicidal) New Zealanders.

Bungee Jumping: bungee (or bungy) jumping (throwing yourself off a bridge or other high elevation while attached to an elasticated rope) is available at a number of locations throughout the country and New Zealanders claim to be responsible for commercialising the 'sport' by offering daring individuals the chance to pay per jump. The home of Bungee jumping is Queenstown, where you can jump from the Kawarau River Bridge (43m) or the Skippers Bridge (71m). If those aren't high enough you can try jumping from the 102m Pipeline or from a helicopter (whatever height you fancy, but preferably not when coming in to land!).

Caving & Cave Rafting: caving is a popular sport and there are numerous clubs. However, New Zealanders have also invented cave rafting, a pursuit whereby intrepid cavers sail through underground cave systems on large inner tubes. Cave rafting is available at Waitomo (North Island) and Wesport and Greymouth (South Island).

Flightseeing: when New Zealanders aren't scrambling over their country's terrain or wading through its water, they enjoy nothing more than taking to the air and admiring it from afar, a pursuit which has been dubbed flightseeing. You can take a trip (or learn to fly) in a skiplane or floatplane, a helicopter, a vintage aircraft or even a hot air balloon (which is popular in Auckland, Christchurch, Hamilton and Rotorua).

Glacier Walking: a walk along a glacier is one way to appreciate one of the most incredible feats of nature. The Fox, Franz Josef and Tasman Glaciers in the Southern Alps are all open to walkers, although it's advisable to join a guided tour if you aren't an experienced mountaineer.

Parachuting & Sky-Diving: both solo and tandem parachuting and sky-diving are available in New Zealand, where there are centres near Auckland, Greymouth, Mount Hutt, Napier, Nelson, Queenstown and Taup.

Parapenting: parapenting is a combination of hang-gliding and parachuting. It's available in Queenstown and Wanaka, where it's also possible to try tandem parapenting (parapenting attached to an instructor) if you don't have the time or inclination to undergo training.

Rap Jumping: rap jumping is another New Zealand invention and much like abseiling, which is common in most countries, except that it involves descending a cliff face head first rather than feet first. The Bay of Islands, Wanaka and Queenstown are popular rap jumping areas, where instructors are available to initiate newcomers into the sport.

OTHER SPORTS

The following are a selection of other popular sports in New Zealand:

Baseball: baseball has been popular for many years in New Zealand, where it's mostly played at the amateur, non-competitive level.

Basketball: basketball is growing in popularity in New Zealand, where it's played enthusiastically in schools. There's also a national basketball league, the season commencing in April and finishing around October. The national basketball team is named the Tall Blacks, a tongue-in-cheek pun on the name of the national rugby team.

Bowls: bowls is a sport enjoyed mainly, but not exclusively, by older people in New Zealand. There are outdoor bowling greens in most towns and also indoor bowling greens in some areas which can be used year-round. Bowling clubs often serve tea and cucumber sandwiches in the British tradition, which tells you something about the kind of members they tend to attract.

Hockey: hockey is played to a high standard in New Zealand by both men and women, although it loses out to more popular sports in the media. There are both club and national teams, and the New Zealand women's team has been particularly successful in recent years.

Horse Riding: New Zealand has a world-wide reputation for breeding high quality bloodstock and horses still have a working role on many country farms where they remain the best way of crossing the often rough terrain. Although competitive riding is common in New Zealand, the most popular form of riding is horse trekking, which involves spending anything from a day to a week or more trekking across the country's farmland, forests, hills and beaches. Stables are found in all areas where it's possible to hire a horse and tack (or stable your own horse) and join an organised trip. A hard hat must be worn at all times when riding. New Zealand produced a number of world class horsemen and achieved notable success in international competitions (although the nearest most New Zealander's ever get to a horse is betting on them).

Marching: marching is a traditional New Zealand female sport which dates back to the 1930s and is still popular today. It's taken seriously and participants are divided into four grades: adults (16+), junior (12 to 16 years), midget (7 to 12 years) and introductory.

Netball: although most New Zealand sports have a predominantly masculine image (not surprising given the dominance of rugby and adventure sports), women participate in most sporting activities and also have their own women-only sports. One of the most popular women's sports in New Zealand is (English) netball, which is generally taken much more seriously here than in the 'mother' country. New Zealand netball is known for its precision and strict adherence to the rules and traditions, which makes it much more than just a casual pastime. The national netball team (the Silver Ferns) has enjoyed considerable success in international competition.

Shooting: despite its conservation-minded image, shooting has a large following in New Zealand, where there are few inhibitions about bagging the local wildlife. Sika stags are hunted in the North Island and red stags in both the North and South Islands, while in the more mountainous areas hunters take pot-shots at wily tahr and chamois. Most shooters hire a local guide to lead them to their prey, which is highly advisable due to the difficult terrain and unpredictable weather in the main hunting areas. On a more modest level, ducks, swans, pheasant, quail and geese are the main game birds in New Zealand. The only drawback for the keen hunter (or advantage for the quarry) is that a short season is enforced, commencing on the first weekend in May and extending for a maximum of eight weeks. A permit is required to own a gun in New Zealand. Further information can be obtained from The Firearms Advisory Officer, Police National Headquarters, PO Box 3017, Wellington (☎ (04) 474 9422).

Tennis: tennis is played throughout New Zealand and is particularly popular in the more fashionable suburbs of Auckland and Wellington. Most places are never far from public courts or a private club. If you wish to join a private club you should find it neither particularly expensive or conservative, although most have strict dress codes.

Triathlon: triathlon events (a gruelling combination of swimming, running and cycling, all of which are carried out consecutively on the same day), are as popular in New Zealand as they are in Australia. Many New Zealanders participate in triathlon events simply as a way of keeping (super) fit, although there are also many highly regarded competitive triathlons for athletes of all abilities and both sexes.

17.

SHOPPING

New Zealand isn't noted for offering a very interesting or exciting shopping experience – only some ten years ago a famous fashion designer is claimed to have said (no doubt with a little exaggeration) that shopping in New Zealand was 'not much of an improvement over shopping in the Communist bloc countries'! This dates back to the days when many New Zealanders were almost self-sufficient and shopped only for the basic necessities which they couldn't grow or make themselves (they still have a strong preference for making or growing things themselves wherever possible, particularly in the country). Fortunately, the situation has improved considerably in recent years, with an influx of international chain stores and designer shops in towns and cities. As in most other western countries, many modern shopping centres have been built outside towns in recent years, which has resulted in shops moving out of towns leaving them run-down and neglected. Naturally you won't find the same choice of shops or merchandise on offer in New Zealand that you'll in the USA, the UK or even Australia, because the market is so much smaller than those countries. However, a shopping trip in New Zealand is now a much more rewarding experience than was previously the case.

Although New Zealand shoppers complain endlessly about increasing prices, they now receive a better deal than they did in the past. The removal or reduction of punitive taxes on imported goods (such as electrical equipment) has made many goods better value for money, even if they have risen in price in dollar terms, and increased competition has also helped reduce prices. Competition has additionally forced retailers to take more care in the quality of goods and services they offer and how they present their wares, which in the past was at best uninspired and at worst poor. People from the UK will recognise several names on the New Zealand high street, although it's important to note that they don't usually sell the same goods as their British equivalents. For example, Woolworth is a major supermarket chain and Boots is purely a chemist, so you shouldn't expect to buy music and household wares there as you can in the UK. Australians will also find many of their favourite stores in New Zealand, many of which are operated on a franchise basis.

Credit cards (e.g. Visa and Mastercard) are widely accepted in shops in New Zealand, even in out of the way places. Cheques are also accepted, although shops are reluctant to accept them as there are no cheque guarantee cards in New Zealand. When paying by cheque you should have some form of identification – many shops ask for a credit card for this purpose, although this makes the practice of carrying a cheque book around rather pointless. Debit or EFTPOS cards are the preferred method of payment in most shops (New Zealanders can even pay court fines with a debit card in many areas). The Mondex system, a kind of debit card where a card is 'charged' with a sum of money which is subsequently deducted by shops, has recently been introduced in New Zealand, although it's by no means in widespread use.

Goods and services tax (GST, 12.5 per cent) is levied on almost everything you buy in New Zealand. You can assume that tax is included in the price unless there's an indication to the contrary. Usually tax-exclusive prices are displayed only in outlets which attract mainly traders, e.g. a hardware store which serves local farmers.

SHOPPING HOURS

The standard shopping hours in New Zealand are 8.30 or 9am until 5pm Mondays to Fridays and 8.30 or 9am to noon on Saturday. Shops don't usually stay open on Saturday afternoons, therefore Saturday afternoon family shopping expeditions aren't possible (much to the relief of thousands of husbands and children), although shops in tourist spots may stay open on Saturday afternoons in summer. Most shops have late night opening one day a week (usually Thursday or Friday) when they stay open until 8.30pm or 9pm. A limited amount of Sunday shopping is permitted in New Zealand, but as some shops stay closed while others open, planning a Sunday shopping trip can be an uncertain business. As in other countries, supermarkets tend to buck the trend and in cities many stay open late every day. You'll also find that the traditional New Zealand dairy (New Zealand's ubiquitous 'corner' shops) operates an open-all-hours policy, remaining open from when the proprietor gets up until he's too tired to continue (usually until 9pm or 10pm in the evening). All shops are closed on Christmas Day, Good Friday and Easter Sunday.

LOCAL SHOPS & SERVICES

Despite the proliferation of out-of-town shopping centres, there are still plenty of small local shops in most towns and city suburbs in New Zealand, although fewer than in the past. Shops tend to follow the British pattern with a grocer (general provisions), butcher, baker, greengrocer (fruit and vegetables) and a chemist (pharmacy). Most suburban shopping streets have a Pacific Island shop selling housewares, toys and assorted other household essentials and bric-a-brac. A curiosity left over from New Zealand's British heritage, although becoming less common, is that fresh milk is delivered to homes each morning in many areas. In smart suburbs in major cities many shops that used to sell everyday goods (such as food) have been taken over by outlets selling gifts, stationery, arts and crafts, and Maori and Polynesian artefacts and reproductions. Although interesting for visitors these are of little use to residents who often need to visit shopping centres and supermarkets for the essentials. This is particularly true in many shopping arcades in Auckland and Wellington.

The dairy is a great New Zealand tradition and proves a boon to those living in the city or country. A New Zealand dairy isn't just a dairy, in fact, in most cases it isn't a dairy at all (although they were once dairies, there appear to be few New Zealanders who can remember when they made butter and cheese). The more accurate description for a dairy nowadays is a corner shop, convenience store or mini-market. The dairy was once the mainstay of New Zealand shopping where everyone did just about all their daily shopping, although nowadays (with the proliferation of supermarkets) most tend to be patronised only for odds and ends that have been forgotten from the supermarket shop or in emergencies. However, the traditional dairy soldiers on and provides a useful local service, although some are suffering from declining trade and look rather neglected. Dairies are, however, the one place where you can be sure of buying basic essentials on Sundays when everything else is closed.

Dairies sell a 'little bit of everything', particularly tinned and packet foods, and in some you can also buy fresh fruit, vegetables and meat, perhaps locally produced. There's usually a display of lollies (confectionery), a variety of soft drinks (but generally no alcohol) and an impressive range of ice cream, which is of excellent quality and consumed enthusiastically in New Zealand. A dairy is also often the best place to buy snacks at any time of the day and they usually offer a choice of sandwiches and pies, although they may be limited to meat (lamb mince) or bacon and egg. In country areas you may also find a range of hardware and clothing (though you shouldn't expect much choice). Dairies are noted for their personal service (they are usually owner-operated) and if there's anything you particularly want the friendly proprietor will usually obtain it for you. Prices in dairies are usually higher than in supermarkets, although they have the advantage of being focal points for the local community and an excellent source of help, information, advice and local gossip.

In common with other countries, petrol (gas) stations in New Zealand carry a selection of basic grocery items and are particularly handy in the evenings and on Saturday afternoons and Sundays when other shops are closed.

SUPERMARKETS

Most people do their food shopping at supermarkets, many of which are located out of town, so you may need a car to get there (a few supermarkets in cities offer free shuttle buses for car-less customers). Woolworth has recently introduced an internet service (www.shoppingmall.co.nz) in Auckland where orders can be placed by computer and delivered to your home (there are plans to extend this system to all main towns and cities). There's a huge variety of supermarkets in New Zealand and it's advisable to do some local research when moving into a new area. Some supermarkets, such as Pak 'N' Save, Foodtown and New World, operate on a pile-em-high and sell-em-cheap basis, where you'll find warehouse-style decor (i.e. none), little choice, budget brands and minimal service, but rock-bottom prices.

If you want attractive surroundings, a wide choice of household brands, separate bakery and delicatessen counters, attentive service, and a pack-and-take-to-your-car service you'll find that several supermarkets offer this, but their prices are correspondingly higher. The better quality supermarkets offer some popular brands from the USA and Europe, although due to shipping costs they can be expensive and there's usually a local New Zealand equivalent that's just as good. Note that supermarkets sell wine, but don't sell any other alcohol, which you must buy from hotel (pubs) bottle shops, although this is expected to change in the near future.

FOOD

One of the pleasures of New Zealand is the wide range and value of fresh food that's available. However, shopping for many foods, particularly fruit and vegetables tends to be seasonal, as most shops sell only what's in season and available from local farmers. Unlike in Europe and North America, you cannot usually buy most produce out of season (e.g. strawberries in mid-winter) as they would need to be imported and the cost would be prohibitively high (they may be available but will be expensive). The authorities are also careful about the foreign produce they allow into the country as a protection against importing pests and diseases. However, New Zealand is a major food producer and exporter (particularly in meat, dairy produce and fruit), and although the choice may not be as great as in some other countries, quality is excellent and prices competitive.

Meat: meat is usually good value in New Zealand, as it's one of the country's major industries, and most families can afford to dish up a hearty meat dish at every meal. There are over 70 million sheep in New Zealand and the country exports around $1,500 million of lamb annually. Not surprisingly, lamb is good value and all joints are inexpensive and readily available, plus a range of lamb products such as pies, burgers, sausages (known as snarlers) and paté. Hogget is one year old lamb, i.e. it actually is a lamb and not mutton optimistically sold as lamb, as in many other countries. If you have the freezer space you may wish to consider buying a whole lamb (bought either whole or jointed as preferred), which with prices starting from as low as $25 represents excellent value. Poultry, pork and beef are also common, but less popular than lamb, although New Zealanders do like their steak which is of top quality (it's often served garnished with oysters in a dish known as 'carpet bagger'). You can buy meat from a supermarket or a local butcher, where it may be fresher and locally produced – the grazing lamb you passed on your way to work in the morning may well be riding home in your car boot in the evening, but this time in joint form! Venison is also an increasingly popular meat in New Zealand and is available from many butchers and supermarkets (it has also become a major export in recent years).

Dairy Products: dairy products are plentiful and cheap in New Zealand, so much so that hotels and motels often leave a free bottle of milk in every room. They are one of the country's major exports and New Zealand even exports to the Caribbean countries. However, although the quality of dairy produce is excellent, the choice often isn't, and many dairies offer a choice of cheddar, cheddar or cheddar. It's possible to buy New Zealand versions of soft cheeses such as Brie and Camembert and even imported cheeses, although you must usually buy them from a delicatessen rather than a dairy or supermarket. If you eat a lot of cheese you may find a trip to a cheese factory (mostly found in the South Island) worthwhile, many of which open their doors to the public and sell huge portions of cheese at factory prices.

Fruit and Vegetables: New Zealand greengrocers (and supermarket fruit and vegetable sections) offer a relatively wide choice of fruit and vegetables, which is midway between what you would find in Western Europe and a street market in the Pacific islands. Among the commonplace Gala apples, pears, strawberries, tomatoes and potatoes, you'll find a variety of exotic fruits and vegetables. Pumpkin and asparagus are popular accompaniments to a main meal, particularly in areas with large Maori communities. Unusual produce include the feijoa (a lemon-like fruit with a much sweeter flavour), tamarillos (with a subtle, slightly tart flavour), kumara (a sweet potato and a staple of the Maori diet), boysenberries, kiwano and the ubiquitous kiwi fruit. In many areas of New Zealand you'll find roadside stalls selling freshly picked fruit and vegetables, and you can also pick your own produce. Stalls often operate on the honour system and when they are unattended you leave the money for what you take in a box. They are a good way to buy kiwi fruit (the small, furry fruit which New Zealand exports around the world) in season, which can be bought for just a few cents each when the crop has been larger than expected.

Seafood: a wide range of seafood is available in New Zealand, appealing to all tastes. If you want 'international' species such as cod and haddock, you can find them, but there's also a huge variety of local fish available. More exotic seafood includes green-lipped mussels, pacific oysters, smoked eel, pipis, paua, toheroas (local clams) and shark (sometimes known as lemon fish). Note that New Zealand whitebait isn't the same fish as in other countries and is a tiny, thread-like, transparent fish with a subtle flavour. Generally seafood isn't such good value as meat, as much of New Zealand's catch goes for export and the country's fish wholesalers must buy fish from South America to satisfy local demand. It's illegal to deal in trout commercially so, if you enjoy trout you'll usually need to catch it yourself. This isn't difficult as the country's rivers, lakes and streams are teeming with both rainbow and European trout. The same applies to oysters, which are frequently found in New Zealand's clear waters, but which you aren't permitted to harvest at whim.

Bakery and Confectionery: New Zealand bakers and supermarkets sell a fairly predictable range of bread and confectionery. You can buy the white and brown loaves (sliced or unsliced) together with a variety of rolls in different shapes and sizes and pink iced buns which are a national tradition. As anywhere, shop bread varies between delicious and tasteless, and it's usually a matter of shopping around until you find a baker you like. In some of the more adventurous bakeries and supermarkets you can also find French-style baguettes, croissants and even Italian-style ciabatta bread. The New Zealand 'national dessert' is Pavlova (or 'pav'), named after the famous Russian ballerina and introduced from Australia where it was invented. It consists of meringue, cream and fruit (usually kiwi fruit) and is available in all shapes and sizes both baked in-store or 'factory' made.

Those from the UK and USA should note that all foodstuffs in New Zealand shops are sold in metric quantities, although it's still common for older people to ask for half a pound of butter or two pounds of potatoes. This is a foreign language to the ears of young shop assistants, who have never heard of imperial weights and measures. A price guide for the most popular foods is published by Statistics New Zealand (internet: stats.govt.nz) and available from New Zealand missions.

MARKETS

Most towns have markets on one or two days a week and in major cities there may be a market (or a number) on most days of the week. Markets are cheap, colourful and interesting, and are often a good place for shrewd shoppers to pick up bargains, although you need to be careful what you buy. Items commonly for sale in markets include fruit and vegetables, meat, fish, general food, clothes, arts and crafts, household goods, jewellery and books. Food markets are often the best place to buy fresh food. In areas with a large Maori community there are Polynesian markets selling ethnic foodstuffs, seafood and textiles. Arts and craft markets are also common in major cities and resort towns, where artisans can often be seen at work, although prices may be substantially higher than at local shops.

Flea markets are popular in the major cities and sell second-hand goods including clothes, books, records, antiques and miscellaneous bric-a-brac. In some places you may find that what are advertised as markets are actually indoor mini-shopping centres, where the area is divided into small shop units operated on a permanent basis. Note that haggling isn't usually done in New Zealand markets where prices are as displayed. Check with your local council or tourist office for information about local markets.

DEPARTMENT & CHAIN STORES

New Zealand has a variety of department and chain stores with branches in most major towns and cities. For the uninitiated, a department store is a large store, usually with several floors, which sells almost everything and may also include a food hall. In a large department store, each floor may be dedicated to a particular kind of goods, such as ladies' or men's fashions or furniture and furnishings. Chain stores are simply stores with a number of branches, usually in different towns and cities.

One of the major New Zealand department stores is Farmers (nothing to do with farming), which sells almost anything and offers medium quality goods at modest prices. K-Mart is also a cheap-and-cheerful, sell-anything store. DIC and DECA are chain stores with a wide variety of products and a good selection of household goods and electrical appliances. Smith and Caughey is a famous Auckland department store, while Wellington has Kirkcaldies. Most department stores experienced tough trading conditions during the early '90s leading to the closure of several branches, including the Farmers flagship store in Auckland. However, New Zealand's retailers are fighting back and in recent years have adopted some of the latest display and marketing techniques used in the UK and USA (Farmers have opened a number of so-called 'new generation' stores to emphasise their new approach).

ALCOHOL

New Zealand has some of the world's most bizarre licensing laws which date back to Britain's oppressive licensing laws during the First World War, when the workers were kept as far away from alcohol as possible lest their performance in the munitions factories was affected (or they blew up the factory!). New Zealand's laws have been reformed at a much slower pace even than in Britain, although further changes are planned over the next few years (plans for liberalisation seem to slip back further every time there's an outbreak of drunken behaviour at a cricket or rugby match). All in all, buying a bottle of your favourite tipple can prove rather frustrating in New Zealand, where you cannot buy alcohol anywhere on Sundays and may even have difficulty finding somewhere to get a drink.

Hotels (pubs) usually have a bottle sales counter or a separate bottle store (liquor store or off-licence) on the premises. A visit to a New Zealand bottle store will probably prove disappointing for newcomers with their limited opening hours, relatively poor selection and high prices. Bottle shops usually have a good choice of beer, but the selection of wines and spirits are usually limited and prices high (the price of wine is significantly cheaper in supermarkets). Supermarkets have entered the alcohol market in recent years, but are currently permitted to sell only wine (of which they stock a wide variety at competitive prices), although if changes in the law go through they will soon be permitted to sell beer and possibly even spirits. They are easily the cheapest place to buy wine unless you buy direct from vineyards (known as a wineries). New Zealand's wineries are allowed to sell their produce direct to the public and have become a good source of inexpensive (depending on where you go) wine in bulk. Dairies and grocery shops can also obtain a licence to sell wine.

The majority of New Zealand wine is white and of the sauvignon blanc variety, although chardonnay is becoming increasingly popular. You can also choose from a wide selection of Australian wines. Wine is sold in 75cl bottles, wine boxes and also small barrels (casks) of varying capacities. Imported wines (other than from Australia) are also available, but aren't popular as they are simply too expensive for most people. Beer is sold in cans of 440ml usually in trays of 24 known as a 'two dozen lot' (Kiwis have a way with words). You can also buy a flagon containing 2.25 litres, which is sometimes still known as a 'half g' (half gallon) as it's equivalent to four pints. New Zealanders are generally not great spirit drinkers partly because they aren't as readily available and are expensive. However, if you miss your favourite tipple most major brands are available including whisky (e.g. American, Canadian and Scotch) and local gin, which is relatively good value for money.

TOBACCO

New Zealanders aren't generally heavy smokers, which is just as well as it's fast becoming socially unacceptable (see page 181) and has been banned in public buildings and some restaurants. As in most other countries the cost of tobacco is becoming ever more expensive. The government grabs over 80 per cent of the cost of a packet of cigarettes in duty, ostensibly to encourage people to give it up and promote good health. Both international and local brands are available with the cost starting at around $5.50 for a packet of 20, although a recent test declared that New Zealand brands contained twice as much nicotine as American and Canadian brands. Rolling tobacco is much less expensive (presumably the government believes it's less damaging to your health), costing around $8 for 50g.

FASHION

New Zealanders aren't noted for their fashion consciousness, although a wide range of clothing (both locally made and imported) is available. As in any country, prices vary considerably depending on the quality and where you shop. The cheapest clothing is available from chain stores, such as K-Mart or Farmers, where you'll find uninspiring design but plenty of choice. Mid-range shoppers may favour department stores, which stock better quality clothes at higher prices. Katies is a leading chain of women's clothing stores which has done much to make women's clothing more competitive (like many New Zealand retailers, it originated in Australia).

Factory outlet shops are a growing influence in the fashion industry and include Dressmart in Auckland, which offers good value and unparalleled choice. Main cities such as Auckland and Wellington have a increasing number of trendy boutiques and designer stores, where you'll find designer clothes (e.g. Barbour, Driza-Bone and Timberland) from leading American, Australian and European designers with correspondingly high prices. There are also several up-and-coming local designers in New Zealand including Chrissie Potter and Amanda Nicolle. Unless you're a fashion victim or move in the trendiest circles, it isn't usually worthwhile buying expensive designer clothing in New Zealand, where people don't usually go in for label snobbery. Casual clothing is acceptable for most situations and, as in many of the English shires, country or farm clothing is fashionable even among those who never go near a farm let alone work on one.

Despite the ready availability of wool, woollen garments can be expensive, although anything in sheepskin is a bargain (which is good news if it ever comes back into fashion). Hand-knitted garments are popular. Cotton based clothes are the cheapest and most popular in New Zealand as they are cool in summer and warm in winter, particularly when worn in layers. Canterbury is famous for its rugby shirts which can be worn for all occasions (providing they are all black!). Swanndri is a famous brand of woollen shirts and jackets that have become something of a classic and which are affectionately known as 'Swanni's' in New Zealand. Shoes tend to be expensive although the country manufactures over one million pairs a year.

FURNITURE & FURNISHINGS

The average New Zealand home is furnished much as it would be in Europe or North America. The staple items of living room furniture are the three-piece suite (usually called a lounge suite), together with a dining table plus four or six chairs. All kinds of furniture are available, from antique or reproduction to modern, at prices ranging from bargain-priced flat-pack or second-hand furniture up to high quality top of the price range handmade and designer items. Most properties in New Zealand have large fitted wardrobes in the American style, which are often large walk-in rooms fitted with shelves and rails, thus rendering bedroom furniture other than a bed and a dressing table unnecessary. Fitted kitchens are also standard in new properties and basic appliances (cooker, hob and refrigerator, and possibly also a washing machine and dishwasher) are included in the price.

HOUSEHOLD GOODS

New Zealand used to have a notorious reputation for the high cost of domestic appliances as a result of swingeing import taxes designed to protect local industries. In the '80s, however, the government decided to allow imports on more favourable terms and as a result New Zealanders have been able to replace their ageing '50s and '60s home appliances with modern equipment at more reasonable prices. A huge choice of home appliances are available in New Zealand these days and smaller appliances such as vacuum cleaners, grills, toasters and electric irons aren't expensive and are usually of good quality. It pays to shop around, as quality, reliability and prices vary considerably (the more expensive imported brands are usually the most reliable). Before buying household appliances, whether large or small, it may pay you to check the test reports in consumer magazines.

It's isn't usually worthwhile shipping bulky domestic appliances to New Zealand such as a refrigerator, washing machine or dishwasher, which apart from the shipping expense may not meet local safety regulations or fit into a New Zealand kitchen. However, if you own good quality small household appliances it's worth bringing them to New Zealand, as all that's usually required is a change of plug. If you're coming from a country with a 110/115V electricity supply (e.g. the USA) you'll need a lot of expensive transformers (see page 89). Don't bring a TV to New Zealand (other than from Australia) as it won't work.

SECONDHAND BARGAINS

There's a lively second-hand market in New Zealand for almost everything, from antiques to motor cars, computers to photographic equipment. You name it and somebody will be selling it second-hand. With such a large second-hand market there are often bargains to be found, particularly if you're quick off the mark. Many towns have a local second-hand or junk store and charity shops (e.g. Salvation Army) selling new and second-hand articles for charity (where most of your money goes to help those in need). In some places (e.g. Wellington) you can even buy goods which have been rescued from the city dump and which are displayed in a special warehouse at the site!

If you're looking for a particular item, such as a camera, boat or motorcycle, you may be better off looking through the small ads. in specialist magazines, rather than in more general newspapers or magazines. The classified ads. in local newspapers are also a good source of bargains, particularly for items such as furniture and large household appliances. Shopping centre and newsagent bulletin boards and company notice boards may also prove fruitful. Another place to pick up a bargain is at an auction, although it helps to have specialist knowledge about what you're buying (you'll probably be competing with experts). Auctions are held in New Zealand throughout the year for everything from antiques and paintings to motorcars and property.

There are antique shops and centres in most towns, and antique street markets and fairs are common in the major cities (where you can pick up interesting early New Zealand artefacts – but you must get there early to beat the dealers to the best buys). For information about local markets, inquire at your local tourist or information office. Car boot (trunk) and yard sales, where people sell off their surplus belongings at bargain prices, are gaining popularity in New Zealand. Sales may be advertised in local newspapers and signposted on local roads (they are usually held at weekends).

NEWSPAPERS, MAGAZINES & BOOKS

New Zealand doesn't offer a particularly wide choice of daily newspapers, a situation that has been exacerbated by the closure of a number of long-established newspapers in recent years. There are no national newspapers in New Zealand, where newspapers are regional and based on the major cities and aren't distributed throughout the country. As a result, most New Zealand newspapers tend to have a fairly provincial feel about them, although they do contain national and international news. The major newspapers include the *New Zealand Herald* (Auckland), the *Dominion Times* (Wellington), the *Waikato Times* (Hamilton), the *Christchurch Press* and the *Otago Press* (Dunedin). Most daily newspapers are published from Monday to Saturday and separate titles are published on Sunday, for example, the *Sunday Star* in Auckland. Other popular publications include the weekly *National Business Review*, New Zealand's main business magazine, and *The Truth*, a weekly shock-horror type tabloid.

Politically most newspapers take an even-handed approach as they are mainly independently owned. The content of most newspapers, which are usually broadsheets, is pretty standard and includes news, business, sports and TV programmes, while the Thursday, Friday and Saturday editions are the best for advertisements such as situations vacant (jobs), property and cars. Friday editions of most newspapers include a substantial 'what's on' entertainment section. Newspapers are sold by newsagents and from street stands (where you leave the money in an honesty box) and vending machines, where depositing your money opens the door giving you access to the newspapers inside. You can also have your newspaper delivered to your home. A daily newspaper costs around 60¢.

Expatriates will be pleased to hear that you can buy Australian, American and British newspapers (e.g. the *Observer* and *Sunday Times*) in major cities a day or two after their publication date. There are also eight Chinese newspapers in New Zealand serving the local Chinese community of almost 90,000. Free local newspapers are distributed to homes in most cities and are useful for finding local services, jobs, property and cars for sale.

A wide range of magazines is available for sale in New Zealand catering for all tastes including sport, hobby, home and business. However, due to the relatively small population many are imported from abroad, particularly from Australia and the USA, and only some 70 titles are home grown, of which the *New Zealand Women's Weekly* has the largest circulation.

Most bookshops in New Zealand stock a good selection of books, including a wide choice of titles published in Australia, the UK and the USA. However, due to the relatively small print runs of New Zealand publishers and the cost of shipping books from other countries, they are relatively expensive (Americans will be horrified). Note that it's possible to buy books at reasonable prices via the internet from a number of internet 'bookshops', the largest of which is the American company Amazon (www.amazon.com). Second-hand bookshops thrive in the major towns, many of which allow you to trade in your old books in part exchange for others, and public libraries also offer a good selection.

DUTY-FREE & SHOPPING ABROAD

Apart from their immediate personal effects, those entering New Zealand aged over 17 (whether as visitors or residents) are permitted to import a limited amount of goods duty-free. These include 200 cigarettes or 250g tobacco or 50 cigars (or a mixture of all three so long as they don't weigh more than 250g); one 1,125ml bottle of spirits or liqueur; up to 4.5 litres of wine (six 75cl bottles); and other goods up to a value of $700. When leaving New Zealand you may purchase duty-free goods at duty-free shops in central Auckland, Wellington or Christchurch and at airports. If you buy duty-free goods from a city duty-free shop, they are delivered free to the airport in time for your departure and it isn't possible to take them with you. If you prefer, you can have your purchases shipped to an address abroad, which duty-free shops are happy to arrange. Buying goods duty-free saves you at least the 12.5 per cent goods and services tax on your purchases, although if you're travelling via the Far East or the USA, you may be able to obtain a better deal there, depending on what you wish to buy.

Many New Zealanders take advantage of trips to locations such as Hong Kong and Singapore to buy luxury items such as cameras, watches, jewellery, small electronic goods and computer software, which are substantially cheaper in these places than in New Zealand. The savings are, however, limited by the high cost of air travel, even to the nearest far eastern city. Considerable savings can also be made by buying goods via the internet, and although you'll need to pay duty and GST on imports (check in advance), substantial savings can still be made on many goods particularly CDs, books and sporting goods (e.g. fishing equipment) purchased in the USA. Note that when buying expensive goods overseas, you should insure them in transit for their full value.

RECEIPTS & GUARANTEES

When shopping you should always insist on a receipt and keep it until you have left the store or have reached home. This isn't just in case you need to return or exchange goods, which may be impossible without the receipt, but also to verify that you have paid if an automatic alarm goes off as you're leaving the shop or any other questions arise. You should check receipts immediately on paying (particularly in supermarkets), as if you're overcharged it's often impossible to obtain redress later. You need your receipt to return an item for repair or replacement (usually to the place of purchase) during the warranty period. It's advisable to keep receipts and records of all major purchases made while you're resident in New Zealand, particularly if your stay is for a limited period only. This may save you both time and money when you finally leave the country and are required to declare your belongings in your new country of residence.

If you buy something which is faulty, damaged or doesn't work or measure up to the manufacturer's or vendor's claims, you can return it and obtain a replacement or your money back. Note that extended warranties or money-back guarantees don't affect your statutory rights as a purchaser, although the legal status of a warranty may be unclear. Some stores offer an exchange of goods or a money-back guarantee for any reason, which isn't required by law, although this guarantee is usually for a limited period only and goods must be returned unused and as new. Some stores attempt to restrict your rights to a cash refund or to exchange goods when an item is faulty or unfit for use, which is illegal.

In New Zealand you have the right to a refund if you buy a faulty product (with the exception of goods purchased at auction). Signs such as 'no refunds given', 'no responsibility for loss or damage', 'goods left for repair at your own risk' and 'all care but no responsibility taken' are meaningless and unlawful. All goods must be of 'merchantable' (reasonable) quality and fit for the purpose for which they were sold, and it's illegal for sellers to include a clause in the conditions of sale that exempts them from liability for defects, product faults and lack of care. Most traders will back down once you show that you know the law and are determined to obtain your legal rights.

Consumer protection laws are monitored and enforced in New Zealand by the Ministry of Consumer Affairs (PO Box 1473, Wellington, ☎ (04) 474 2750), which has local offices throughout the country. You can also obtain advice and assistance from a local citizens' advice bureau.

18.

ODDS & ENDS

This chapter contains miscellaneous information. Although all topics aren't of vital importance, most are of general interest to anyone planning to live or work in New Zealand, including everything you ever wanted to know (but were afraid to ask) about subjects as diverse as tipping, toilets and the Treaty of Waitingi.

NEW ZEALAND CITIZENSHIP

After three years' residence in New Zealand you can apply for New Zealand citizenship, which carries the right to vote in New Zealand elections and hold a New Zealand passport, making it no longer necessary to apply for a returning resident's visa (see page 54) when leaving the country. Children born of New Zealand residents automatically become New Zealand citizens and can hold dual nationality where permitted under the law of their parents' countries of birth or nationality. Foreign nationals who marry New Zealanders can apply for citizenship immediately they take up residence in New Zealand and those who live with a New Zealand partner in a genuine de facto relationship can apply for citizenship after two years. Enquiries regarding citizenship should be made to the Department of Internal Affairs, PO Box 805, Wellington.

CLIMATE

New Zealand has an oceanic, temperate climatic and overall is relatively mild without huge seasonal differences. Being an island nation, New Zealand's climate tends to be dominated by its ocean setting, although it experiences a variety of climatic patterns due to its mountainous terrain. Climatic conditions vary considerably and include sub-tropical, sub-Antarctic, semi-arid (mainly in the Northland region), super-humid, frost-free, and sub-Alpine with permanent snow and ice in the mountainous areas. The eastern regions experience a drier climate than the west, with the wettest in the south-west, west of the Southern Alps. Being in the southern hemisphere, the seasons in New Zealand are the opposite of those in the northern latitudes, i.e. summer (December to February), autumn (March to May), winter (June to August) and Spring (September to November). Extremes of unseasonal weather outside the usual seasons are rare, although there are exceptions.

The North Island tends to be warmer and drier than the South Island, although the highest mountain peaks often have snow all year round. It has an average rainfall of around 130cm and prevailing westerly winds. Temperatures in Auckland average 23°C in summer and 14°C in winter, while in Wellington they range from 26°C in summer to as low as 2°C in winter. Wellington is renowned for its extremely windy weather, which can also make the sea crossing between the two islands rough. The differences in weather and temperature in the South Island are more pronounced and the Southern Alps have noticeable 'wet' and 'dry' sides. Snow is a permanent feature on the highest peaks. On the east side of the Southern Alps rainfall can be as low as 30cm (droughts are fairly common) and temperatures a lot warmer than on the west side. Christchurch averages temperatures of around 22°C in summer and 12°C in winter, while Dunedin averages 19°C in summer and 10°C in winter.

Average temperatures, rainfall levels and sunshine hours for the main towns and cities are shown below. Bear in mind that the temperatures are averages and it can be much warmer or colder on individual days:

Town/City	Average Temp °C Summer	Average Temp °C Winter	Annual Rain (mm) Year	Sunshine Hours/Year
North Island:				
Bay of Islands	25	15	1648	2020
Auckland	23	14	1268	2140
Rotorua	23	12	1511	1940
Napier	24	13	780	2270
Wellington	20	11	1271	2020
South Island:				
Nelson	22	12	999	2410
Christchurch	22	12	658	1990
Queenstown	22	8	849	1940
Dunedin	19	10	772	1700
Invercargill	18	9	1042	1630

CRIME

New Zealand is a safe country by international standards and you can safely walk almost anywhere at any time of the day or night in most parts of the country. However, it's important to take the usual safety precautions as you would in any country. The only real no-go areas are certain parts of Auckland, where residents of the more affluent parts of the city dare not venture. The North Shore area of Auckland has recently experimented with New York-style 'zero tolerance' policing. In reality, although strangers wandering into high-crime areas are at risk of being mugged, knifed or even murdered, the risk is much, much lower than, for example, in most US cities. A worrying trend, however, is that an increasing number of violent attacks and rapes are racially-inspired, particularly against Asians and Pacific Islanders. However, it should be noted that, overall, race relations in New Zealand are excellent and the envy of many other countries.

New Zealand has a reputation as a low-crime country, although both serious crime (such as murder) and petty crime (such as housebreaking) have risen considerably in the last few decades. There's a huge difference between crime levels in the major cities and in rural areas, where it's still common to find communities where people never lock their homes or their cars when leaving them unoccupied, a practice which used to be common throughout New Zealand. However, this practice is inadvisable in urban areas where good door and window locks and an alarm system are considered essential. Car theft (see page 164) is also a problem in cities and it's advisable to have an immobiliser and alarm system fitted to your car (although little notice may be taken of it when it's triggered).

Beware of pickpockets and bag-snatchers in cities and keep a close eye on your belongings in shops and when using public transport, particularly trains and the Interislander ferry. If your luggage is stolen on public transport you should make a claim to the relevant authority as they may make an ex-gratia payment for lost, stolen or damaged baggage. Most New Zealanders are law-abiding and their 'criminal' activities amount to little more than speeding, pulling a 'sickie' (i.e. taking a 'sick' day off work to go to the beach), or exaggerating a road or workplace accident in order to secure a more generous payout from the ACC. However, insurance companies recently reported that genuine insurance claims were believed to be inflated by $50 million annually by otherwise law-abiding citizens. White collar fraud and corruption has also become a more serious problem in recent years and a number of respected companies have been rocked by financial scandals, which were previously unknown in New Zealand.

Gangs: gangs are a problem in New Zealand, particularly in the poor inner-city areas of Auckland and Wellington, although there's gang activity to some extent in most large towns. As their main activities tend to be inter-gang warfare, most people rarely come into contact with them, except when they organise 'conventions' in public places or at major rock concerts or sporting events. The best advice is to follow the New Zealander's example and never consider buying or renting a home in an area known for gang activity and stay well away from events or areas where gangs are likely to congregate. Gang 'meets' are usually well publicised and characterised by a much larger than usual police presence.

Prisons: tougher sentencing in recent years has created something of a prison crisis in New Zealand, where the prison population is expected to rise from 5,000 to 5,500 in the next few years, a substantial rise for such a small country. Three new prisons are due to be completed by 2002 and the authorities are experimenting with more liberal punishments, such as home detention and electronic tagging, although in trials these methods were found to be more expensive than committing offenders to prison.

Drugs: New Zealand has been described as having the perfect climate for the cultivation of cannabis and plantations are tucked away in all parts of the country, particularly in Northland which is dubbed New Zealand's 'Cannabis Capital'. Police regularly trace and destroy plantations, but many more are believed to remain undiscovered and this doesn't allow for plants that are grown literally on the window sills and balconies of homes throughout the country.

Recreational smoking of cannabis or marijuana (electric puha as it's known in some places) is commonplace, although it's illegal and its possession is punishable by a $1,000 fine and/or 12 months' imprisonment. As in many other countries, there's a sizeable campaign to legalise cannabis, headed by the National Organisation For The Reform of Marijuana Laws (NORML). While most people feel this is unlikely to happen, plans to punish possession by on-the-spot fines, similar to parking tickets, have been seriously proposed in recent years. The police tend to concentrate on tracing and prosecuting growers (using helicopter patrols in rural areas) and dealers, rather than casual users and rarely raid homes in search of small quantities. However, vehicles driven by 'likely looking' drug users (those with glazed eyes and flowers in their hair?) that are stopped for traffic offences are also likely to be searched for drugs.

Ecstasy is a popular alternative to cannabis, particularly among teenagers, and hard drug use such as heroin and cocaine is increasing. However, the problem is much less marked than in the USA or Western Europe, as New Zealand maintains relatively effective border controls aimed at keeping 'nasties' (including illicit fruit and vegetables) out of the country. New Zealand's official 'Just Say No' anti-drugs campaign is often criticised for its lack of impact.

ECONOMY & TRADE

New Zealand is a prosperous country with a successful economy and a gross domestic product (GDP) in 1997 of some US$70 billion (the GDP per head is around US$18,500). Approximately 60 per cent of GDP derives from services, one-third from manufacturing and 10 per cent from agriculture. The national economy is, however, highly reliant on farming, particularly the export of wool, meat, and dairy products. Any slump in world prices of these commodities badly affects the economy. The economy is also highly dependent on far eastern markets and a worsening of the economic crisis which befell the region in 1997-98 would leave the economy vulnerable (it was 'technically' in recession in late 1998).

Agriculture: modern methods and machinery are used extensively on New Zealand farms where productivity is among the highest in the world. The land is ideally suited for dairy farming and raising sheep and cattle, as winter housing for livestock is unnecessary and grass grows almost year round in the north of the country. The main cereal crops includes wheat (around 180,000 tonnes per year), maize, (185,000 tonnes), barley (400,000 tonnes), and oats (60,000 tonnes). Other important crops include kiwi fruit, apples, pears, tobacco, potatoes and peas. The livestock population of New Zealand includes around 55 million sheep (over 15 for each man, woman and child in New Zealand), some 8 million cattle, over 1 million goats and 450,000 pigs. New Zealand ranks second only to Australia in wool production, with an annual clip of around 300,000 tonnes.

Forestry: timber production is an important industry in New Zealand which produces some 14 million cubic metres annually. Over half (85 per cent of which is pine) is used for lumber and around 40 per cent for pulp. Most native forests were cut down by the early European settlers in the late 1800s and an extensive reforestation programme in recent decades has seen the planting of imported varieties of fast-growing trees such as Douglas fir instead of native New Zealand trees such as rimu and miro, most of which are slow-growing. A plantation of a North American species of pine in the Kaingaroa State Forest, said to be the largest planted forest in the world, is commercially exploited by a consortium of government and private industry.

Fishing: fishing is a small but important industry in New Zealand, where the annual catch is some 600,000 tonnes, much of which is exported. The most common freshwater and marine species are blue grenadier, orange roughy, mackerel, barracuda, blue whiting, crayfish, lobster, and squid.

Mining: in the '70s, New Zealand mineral output increased substantially as new deposits of oil and natural gas were exploited. Annual output is around 2.1 million tonnes of coal, 9.3 million barrels of oil and 3.5 billion cubic metres of natural gas. Other minerals produced in large quantities include gold, silver, limestone, iron ore, bentonite, silica sand and pumice.

Manufacturing: in 1992, around a quarter of a million people were employed in manufacturing (mostly in Auckland), although this has declined in recent years to a little over 200,000. The principal products include paper and paper products, chemicals, metal goods, machinery, clothing, timber, electrical machinery, refined petroleum, printed materials and motor vehicles. The motor industry is in decline as quotas on imported vehicles have been removed and motor manufacturing (or more correctly assembly) may end completely in the next few years, which will have a knock-on effect in component industries. Manufacturing is modern and automated, although New Zealand has insufficient workers and raw materials to support much heavy industry.

Energy: in keeping with its environmentally-friendly image, around 75 per cent of New Zealand's electricity is produced by hydroelectric power and most of the rest from coal and oil-fired plants. In addition, underground steam is used to produce substantial amounts of electricity in the North Island. Major hydroelectric facilities are located on the Waikato River in the North Island and on the Clutha and Waitaki rivers in the South Island. New Zealand has an electricity generating capacity of around 7.4m kilowatts, with an annual output of around 27 billion kilowatt-hours (figures which are merely academic to the residents of Auckland who suffered a catastrophic power blackout lasting several months in early 1998!).

Foreign Trade: the value of exports from New Zealand total around US$8 billion annually. The UK, the USA, Japan and Australia are among the country's major trading partners. New Zealand is the largest exporter of dairy products in the world (dairy products are exported chilled to many regions, including the Middle East and the Caribbean) and is second only to Australia in the export of wool. Other important exports include kiwi fruit, fish, lamb, mutton and beef. Imports total US$7.5 billion annually and primarily include manufactured goods, heavy machinery, petroleum, chemicals, iron, steel, plastic materials and textiles. New Zealand import tariffs are generally low (many having been reduced or abolished in recent years) and around half of all manufactured goods are imported free of duty.

GEOGRAPHY

New Zealand lies in the South Pacific Ocean south-east of Australia and comprises two main islands, imaginatively named the North and South Islands (the Victorian British had a way with words), plus numerous smaller islands (of which Stewart and Chatham islands are the most important). Associated with New Zealand are Ross Dependency (in Antarctica), Niue, Tokelau and the Cook Islands (in the Pacific Ocean). The capital of the country is Wellington, although Auckland is the largest city. Contrary to popular belief (and much to the relief of most New Zealanders) New Zealand isn't just off the coast of Australia, but 2,000km (some 1,250mi) away across the Tasman Sea. New Zealand covers an area of 270,534 sq. km (104,461 sq. mi).

New Zealand is a mountainous country, some 60 per cent of which is between around 200m and 1,070m (656 to 3,510ft) above sea level, including over 220 mountains above 2,000m/6,561ft. The principal mountain ranges in the North Island extend along the eastern side, where the north central region has three active volcanic peaks: Mount Ruapehu (2,797m/9,176ft), the highest point on the island, Mount Ngauruhoe (2,291m/7,516ft) and Tongariro (1,968m/6,456ft). Mount Taranaki (2,518m/8,261ft), a solitary extinct volcanic cone, is situated near the western extremity of the island. The North Island has numerous rivers, most of which rise in the eastern and central mountains, including the Waikato River (435km/270mi), the longest river in New Zealand. It flows north out of Lake Taupo (606 sq. km/233 sq. mi), the largest lake in New Zealand (where mineral springs are also found), into the

Tasman Sea in the west. The North Island has an irregular coastline, particularly on its northern extremity, the Auckland Peninsula, where it's just 10km/6mi wide.

The South Island has a more regular coastline than the North Island and in the south-west is characterised by deep fjords. The chief mountain range of the South Island is the Southern Alps, a massive range extending from the south-west to the north-east for almost the entire length of the island (17 peaks in the range are over 3,000m/9,842ft high). Mount Cook (3,754m/12,316ft) is the highest point in New Zealand and rises from the centre of the range, which also contains a number of glaciers. Most of the rivers of the South Island, including the Clutha River (338km/210mi long), the longest river on the island, rise in the Southern Alps. The largest lake is Lake Te Anau (342 sq. km/132 sq. mi) in the southern part of the Southern Alps. The Canterbury plains in the east and the Southland plains in the extreme south are the only extensive flat areas on the South Island.

The islands of New Zealand emerged in the Tertiary period and contain a complete series of marine sedimentary rocks, some of which date from the early Paleozoic era. Much of the topography of New Zealand has resulted from warping and block faulting, although volcanic action also played a part in the formation of the islands, particularly in the North Island, where it continues to this day. Geysers and mineral hot springs occur in the volcanic area, particularly around Rotorua. Earthquakes and tremors are fairly frequent throughout New Zealand, although most are too minor to be noticed.

Land is New Zealand's most important natural resource and the country's soil and vegetation is ideal for arable, beef, dairy and sheep farming, all of which are vital to the economy. Forestry is also important as are mineral deposits such as coal, gold, pearlite, sand, gravel, limestone, bentonite, clay, dolomite and magnesite. There are vast natural gas fields on the North Island and off its south-west coast, and deposits of uranium and thorium are also believed to be present on the islands.

Much New Zealand plant life is unique and of the 2,000 indigenous species, some 1,500 are found only here, including the golden kowhai and the scarlet pohutukawa. The North Island is home to predominantly subtropical vegetation, including mangrove swamps in the north. The forest, or so-called bush, of the North Island is mainly evergreen with a dense undergrowth of mosses and fern. Evergreen trees include the kauri (the traditional wood used for house building in New Zealand), rimu, kahikatea and totara, all of which are excellent timber trees. The only extensive area of native grassland in the North Island is the central volcanic plain. The eastern part of the South Island is, for the most part, grassland up to an elevation of around 1,500m, while most forests are situated in the west (consisting mainly of native beech and alpine vegetation at high altitudes).

With the exception of two species of bat, New Zealand has no indigenous mammals. The first white settlers (who arrived early in the 19th century) found a kind of dog and a black rat, both of which had been introduced by the Maoris around 500 years earlier and are now almost extinct. The only wild mammals at present are descended from deer, rabbits, goats, pigs, weasels, ferrets, and opossums, all of which were imported by the early settlers. No snakes and few unusual species of insects inhabit New Zealand (unlike Australia which is infested with them), although it does boast the tuatara, a lizard-like reptile with a third eye believed to be a distinct relative of the dinosaurs. New Zealand has a large population of wild birds, including 23 native species which include the songbirds bellbird and tui, and flightless species such as the kiwi (from which New Zealanders take their colloquial name), kakapo, takahe and weka. The survival of flightless birds is attributed to the absence of predatory animals (with the exception of domestic cats). The sparrow, blackbird, thrush, skylark, magpie and myna are among the common imported species.

New Zealand's rivers and lakes contain a variety of native edible fish, including whitebait, eel, lamprey and freshwater crustaceans, particularly crayfish. Trout and salmon have been imported and are found in waters throughout the country. The surrounding ocean waters are the habitat of snapper, flounder, blue cod, hapuku, tarakihi, swordfish, flying fish, shark, and whales, in addition to a variety of shellfish including oysters, mussels and toheroas.

HISTORY

Although experts disagree on the original inhabitants of New Zealand, the earliest known settlers (recognised as bringing a degree of civilisation to the islands) are acknowledged as being the Maoris, who arrived from Tahiti, Samoa and the Cook Islands around 1350 (although Maori legend claims the islands were discovered in 925). The Dutch navigator Abel Janszoon Tasman was the first European to reach New Zealand in 1642. The British explorer Captain James Cook visited the islands in 1769 and took possession of them for Great Britain, but almost 75 years elapsed before the British government recognised his claim to the islands on behalf of the British Crown.

The Treaty of Waitangi: the Treaty of Waitangi is popularly regarded as the founding document on New Zealand. It was written in English under instructions from the British government by Captain William Hobson and later translated into Maori by the Rev. Henry Williams. It was originally signed by local tribes at Waitangi in the Bay of Islands on the 6th February 1840 and was then circulated throughout New Zealand to gain further signatures. The treaty set out an agreement between the British crown and the Maori people, and essentially ceded control of the territory that's now New Zealand to the British Crown in exchange for certain rights and guarantees of freedom for the Maori people. The treaty established New Zealand as a British Colony and still has a significant role in the government of the country. Waitangi Day is also New Zealand's most important public holiday.

The principle of 'partnership' between the British Crown and the Maori people is the underlying tenet of the treaty, rather than the specific words used. However, differences between the meaning of the English and Maori versions of the treaty have been increasingly debated in recent years and have given rise to several disputes, usually involving Maori claims to rights or land under the Maori translation of the treaty, which aren't apparently enshrined in the English version of the treaty. A tribunal was set up in 1975 with the authority to investigate and make recommendations on claims by Maoris regarding breaches of the treaty by the British crown. In 1995 land grievance claims were settled in accordance with the principles of the treaty by returning land owned by the descendants of European settlers to the Maoris, thus demonstrating the enduring power and validity of the treaty. A landmark settlement was reached between the government and the Tainui people (a Maori tribe) with respect to land confiscated during the 19th century. Legislation in New Zealand is occasionally subject to the principles of the treaty of Waitangi.

From 1840 until 1947 New Zealand was a British Colony. National sovereignty was granted by the British parliament in 1947, although New Zealand still retains constitutional ties with Britain and is a member of the British Commonwealth. HM Queen Elizabeth II, the Queen of England, is Head of State of New Zealand and also holds the title Queen of New Zealand. The Queen grants honours (such as knighthoods) to New Zealanders, similar to those bestowed in the United Kingdom.

GOVERNMENT

New Zealand is a parliamentary democracy modelled on the British system. It is, however, unicameral, that is with one legislative body only, the House of Representatives, and no upper house as is the case in many other democracies (it was abolished in 1951 and is unlikely to be reinstated). The House of Representatives or parliament consists of Members of Parliament (MPs) who sit in the Parliament Building situated in Wellington. The House of Representatives is widely regarded by most New Zealanders as the country's largest source of hot air, easily outperforming any of New Zealand's impressive geothermal geysers (not that it's any different from most others in this respect).

The executive branch of the government consists of the Prime Minister and his (or her – New Zealand had a female Prime Minister, Jenny Shipley, for the first time in 1997) cabinet. New Zealand has a Governor-General (G-G), who's appointed by the British Crown, although it's largely an honorary position and he rarely participates in government and usually intervenes only in constitutional matters. The Governor-General is appointed by the sovereign every five years on the recommendation of the government of the day and his most important (ceremonial) role is to dissolve the outgoing parliament and invite the leaders of the parties elected to power to form a new government.

Voting System: New Zealand recently changed to a system of proportional representation (PR), rather than the first-past-the-post (FPP) system previously used. The kind of PR used in New Zealand is known as Mixed Member Proportional (MMP) system, which is designed to ensure that each political party's share of seats in parliament corresponds to its share of the vote. Voters have two votes: one known as a party vote is cast for the party of their choice and the other for their preferred candidate. Parties are allocated seats in proportion to the votes they receive and then candidates are allocated to those seats according to the votes they polled individually. The House of Representatives consists of 120 MPs, 60 of whom represent general electorates and 55 who are allocated pro rata from party lists. The final five seats are reserved for Maori electorates. Some politicians have recently proposed that the number of MPs be reduced to save money (a sensible idea which would no doubt prove popular in many countries!).

New Zealand's new system of MMP, while generally being recognised as an improvement over FPP, has caused something of an upheaval in the political system, and has allowed smaller parties to obtain a presence in parliament for the first time. Not surprisingly, it has also created a situation where it's impossible for a single party to obtain an overall majority and thus two or more parties are forced to co-operate in a coalition to form a government. Some politicians have argued for a return to FPP, although this is unlikely to happen.

Political Parties: politics in New Zealand has traditionally been dominated by two parties, the National Party, which favours right-wing social policies and a market-orientated approach to the economy, and the Labour Party. The Labour Party traditionally favoured left of centre policies including comprehensive social welfare spending, but during the '80s 'converted' to what were previously thought to be National Party policies, including economic reform and financial market deregulation. Other parties which currently have a voice include New Zealand First (a National Party splinter group with which the current government has been forced to co-operate), ACT and the Alliance Party, a coalition of left wing parties. Most elections attract a string of independents and minority parties, together with what can best be described as 'loony' parties (such as Legalise Cannabis and Natural Law). Under MMP no party can obtain a seat in parliament unless it obtains at least 5 per cent of the total vote.

Voting & Elections: all New Zealand nationals can vote in parliamentary elections and enrolment is compulsory for all those eligible to vote, although voting isn't. Parliamentary elections are held every three years, although the government of the day can call an early election if they wish (which they rarely do, preferring instead to allow each parliament to run its course). Although many New Zealanders are apathetic about politics on a daily basis, they are usually keen to exercise their right to vote and the turnout in elections are some of the highest for any democracy and rarely less than 80 per cent of the electorate. Additionally, the New Zealand government doesn't hesitate to call referenda on subjects considered of great importance to the country. Recent referenda have included proportional representation (which was accepted by a small majority) and changes to the national superannuation system (which was rejected by a small percentage). However, critics claim that referenda often lead to the acceptance or rejection of proposed legislation simply because the electorate (in general) fails to fully comprehend the issues at stake (which is no doubt true in most countries).

Legislative Process: new laws in New Zealand begin life as a bill which is introduced to parliament. Bills undergo first and second readings before being passed to a select committee for discussion and consideration of submissions from interested parties. The select committee must report back to parliament within six months. A bill is then debated and the House of Representatives considers it on a clause-by-clause basis. After it receives its third reading it's passed to the Governor-General (G-G) for assent and then becomes law. In theory the G-G can reject laws using reserve power, particularly if he feels that the government is acting unconstitutionally. However, in practice he's bound by the constitution and by convention to follow the advice of the government and give his assent to bills. Under the Constitution Act 1986, the British parliament is unable to make laws affecting New Zealand, although some British laws (the Imperial Acts, such as the Magna Carta and Habeas Corpus) are enshrined in New Zealand law.

Judiciary: New Zealand has a fiercely independent judiciary which, as with many other aspects of law and government, is modelled on the British system with some antipodean modifications. Judges are nominated from the ranks of the legal profession (barristers or solicitors with a minimum seven years' service) and appointed by the G-G (not by the government or by election). Judges must automatically retire on reaching the age of 68, although they may be re-appointed for up to two years. The Judicial Committee of the Privy Council is New Zealand's highest legal authority. The highest court is the Court of Appeal, which exercises appellate jurisdiction only, and decisions made by the court are final unless leave is granted to appeal to the Privy Council. The principal trial courts are the high court, staffed by the chief justice and 32 high court judges, and the district courts. Justices of the peace may, in some cases, try minor criminal cases. Special courts and tribunals determine matters relating to labour disputes, workers' compensation, land rights and family law.

All registered electors between the ages of 20 and 65 may be summoned to serve on a jury, although those in certain occupations, such as police officers, or those with criminal convictions which resulted in more than three years' imprisonment are excluded. Anyone called for jury service may apply to be excused on religious grounds or when service would cause unnecessary hardship.

Local Government: New Zealand is divided into 14 local government regions, an arrangement which was instituted in 1989. These regions include Auckland, Bay of Plenty, Hawke's Bay, Northland, Taranaki, Gisborne, Waikato, Manawatu, Wanganui, and Wellington in the North Island; and Canterbury, Otago, Nelson-Marlborough, Southland, and West Coast in the South Island. These 14 regions are subdivided into 20 cities and 59 districts, with elections held every three years.

LEGAL & GENERAL ADVICE

As in other developed countries, fees charged by solicitors and barristers are sky-high and legal fees for even a simple case (such as a divorce or breach of contract) can soon run into tens of thousands of dollars. Junior lawyers charge at least $125 per hour and advice from a senior lawyer is likely to cost at least $175 an hour. Most New Zealand lawyers are qualified both as solicitors and barristers, i.e. they can work as advocates in court and don't need to appoint a separate barrister to perform this task. New Zealand has a system of legal aid which provides assistance to those who cannot afford to pay a solicitor, although the budget is tight and changes are continually being made to the system in order to streamline it and make it more cost effective. Those requiring legal aid for civil cases may find it difficult to obtain free legal assistance.

The legal services board also provides a 'duty solicitor' scheme which provides free and immediate legal aid to anyone who's arrested by the police. If you're arrested you're entitled to a consultation with a solicitor and to have him present during an interview. In most towns and cities, usually in the poorer areas, there are community and neighbourhood law centres financed by public funds and other means (such as fund-raising). They provide free legal advice and representation to those unable to afford it, within the limits of their resources. Most towns have a Citizens' Advice Bureau (head office, 48 Aro Street, Wellington, ☎ (04) 384 8287) where you can obtain free advice on a wide range of matters.

MARRIAGE & DIVORCE

Like many countries, New Zealand has declining marriage and rising divorce rates, with the average length of a marriage around 15 years (longer than in most other western countries). Around 20,000 marriages were performed in 1997, a decline of 1.5 per cent over the previous year. An increasing number of New Zealanders are choosing to marry later in life or to remain single. New Zealand also has many single mothers, many of whom are in this position by choice and happily juggle career and family. While more women are choosing to wait to have families until later in life (the average childbearing age has risen from 25.5 to 28 in the last three years), New

Zealand also has one of the world's highest rates of unmarried teenage pregnancies. An increasing number of New Zealanders choose a simple civil ceremony rather than a church service, mainly due to the informality it provides and the much reduced cost. It's possible to marry anywhere in New Zealand, not just in a church or at a register office, assuming that you can find a clergyman or registrar willing to perform the ceremony (a Dunedin couple recently married in the city's municipal swimming pool!).

New Zealand recognises de facto relationships in which unmarried couples live together as man and wife and have many of the rights and responsibilities of married couples, although they don't currently have the same rights of inheritance or property (this is due to change under new proposals). In future de facto couples will be entitled to an equal share of the family home and other 'chattels', regardless of who owns them. However, the new law will apply only to de facto relationships of three years or longer and won't apply to homosexual relationships. Note that under the present law, if you want your de facto partner to inherit some or all of your property upon your death, you must state this in your will otherwise your estate will automatically be bequeathed to your blood relatives.

MILITARY SERVICE

There's no conscription (draft) in New Zealand, where all members of the armed forces are volunteers. The minimum age for enlistment has recently been raised to 17 in line with United Nations guidelines on the enlistment of minors. The New Zealand Army, Royal New Zealand Air Force (RNZAF) and Royal New Zealand Navy (RNZN) are separate services under the control of the Ministry of Defence. The army numbers around 4,800 regular personnel, the navy around 2,300 and the air force around 3,700. In addition there's a part-time reserve force called the Territorial Army (or 'Terries'), which trains in the evenings and at weekends and can be called up to assist the regular forces in an emergency. Members of the armed forces can expect to be posted to a new base every two to three years, a practice which may be changed as it's believed to be largely responsible for the high number of service personal who resign after their initial term. In a bid to make military life more attractive, the navy has recently (among other steps) introduced a trendy new logo and a new maternity uniform to allow pregnant women to continue military service throughout their pregnancy.

New Zealand spends around 1 per cent of its GDP on defence. Budget cuts of 30 per cent since 1989 have recently been reversed by an almost $750 million package to provide new equipment such as armoured personnel carriers and transport aircraft and recruit another 500 personnel. The size of New Zealand's military forces reflects the small size of the country and there has been discussion about whether the navy (whose strength could be reduced to just two major warships within the next few years) and some other elements of the armed forces are viable on such a small scale, and whether they should be merged with the Australian armed services. For its part, Australia periodically takes its smaller neighbour to task for spending what it considers to be too little on defence. Australia spends around 2 per cent of its GDP on defending not only Australia, but also the surrounding region.

New Zealand is a member of a number of defence treaties including the Five Power Defence Agreement with Malaysia, Singapore, Australia and Britain, and the

ANZUS alliance with Australia and the United States. New Zealand contributed forces to the western alliance during the Gulf War and contributes to peacekeeping duties around the world. However, the country operates a strict anti-nuclear defence policy and doesn't allow visits by foreign military forces carrying nuclear weapons, e.g. warships, which has caused friction between New Zealand and the USA.

PETS

New Zealanders are enthusiastic animal lovers and many people keep dogs and cats. However, cats have received a 'bad press' in recent years as they are believed to be responsible for the decimation of much of New Zealand's wildlife. Cats aren't indigenous to New Zealand and flightless birds such as the kiwi had few natural predators until the first European settlers landed their pets on the country's shores. If you plan to take a pet to New Zealand, it's important to check the latest regulations. Given the distance (unless you're travelling from Australia) it's advisable to entrust the transportation of pets to a specialist shipping company, e.g. Par Air Services (☎ 01206-330332) or Airpets Oceanic (☎ 01753-685571) in the UK.

New Zealand has strict regulations regarding the importation of animals in order to prevent animal diseases entering the country, and pets and other animals cannot be imported without prior authorisation from customs. You require a health certificate from a veterinary surgeon in your home country and your pet will need to undergo a period of quarantine after its arrival in New Zealand. There are limited exemptions for pets imported from Australia, Hawaii, Sweden, Norway and the UK. The cost of transporting a cat or small dog from Europe or the USA, including all necessary paperwork, is likely to be at least $600, with quarantine accommodation costing from around $25 per day.

For further information contact a New Zealand diplomatic mission or the Collector of Customs at one of the following offices: PO Box 29, Auckland (☎ (09) 377 3520), PO Box 2098, Christchurch (☎ (03) 371 5000) or PO Box 2218, Wellington (☎ (04) 473 6099).

POLICE

New Zealand has a single national police force, controlled by a commissioner appointed by the Minister of Police, which is divided into six operational regions each headed by an assistant commissioner. In 1997, over 500,000 crimes were reported in New Zealand, of which less than half were solved by the police (although this is much better than police forces in many other countries). Police officers can be identified by their dark blue (almost black) uniforms and peaked chequered-band caps. Ordinary rank and file members of the police force are known as 'constables' (in the British fashion) rather than officers.

The police force has undergone something of a manpower crisis in recent years as several Australian state forces have 'poached' New Zealand police officers. The fact that policing is similar in both countries and police exams are standardised has contributed to the problem, although the main attraction for officers is that they can earn 10 to 20 per cent more in Australia. New Zealand police officers are generally approachable, although some people consider them tyrannical. Police morale is low as a consequence of poor pay and insufficient resources. Police officers are forbidden to strike, although several hundred recently took part in a silent protest march (against poor pay and conditions) in Wellington during their off-duty hours.

New Zealand police officers don't usually carry firearms, although they do carry handcuffs, batons and controversial pepper sprays. When firearms are necessary (usually only when confronting armed criminals) members of the Armed Offenders Squad (AOS) are called in to deal with the incident. AOS members serve only part-time and many have more mundane duties between armed call outs. The police force doesn't routinely deal with motorists in New Zealand, which is the responsibility of the Traffic Safety Service that patrols highways, sets speed traps (their favourite pastime) and handles motoring offences.

POPULATION

The population of New Zealand in mid-1998 was an estimated around 3.8 million (it's difficult to keep track, as at any given time half the population is overseas, mostly in Australia) and is forecast reach around 5 million by 2025. New Zealand is a sparsely populated country, with only some 12 inhabitants per square kilometre or around 31 per square mile (there are actually more New Zealanders per square kilometre in London!). Around three-quarters of the population lives in the North Island, 85 per cent of whom reside in urban areas (half in cities). The population of New Zealand's major cities are roughly as follows: Auckland 850,000, Wellington 350,000, Hamilton 165,000, Dunedin 115,000, Napier/Hastings area 105,000 and Palmerston North 95,000.

New Zealand is less ethnically diverse than most other developed nations, even when compared with Australia. Approximately 85 per cent of New Zealanders are of European (mainly British) descent, known as *pakehas* by Maori (meaning 'white man' and not a derogatory term). The majority of the remaining inhabitants are Maori and other Polynesian Islanders. At the last census there were around 320,000 Maoris, 45,000 West Samoans, 24,000 Cook Islanders, 9,000 Niue Islanders and 7,500 Tonga Islanders. Around 1 per cent of the population is of Chinese extract and just under 1 per cent of Indian origin. In recent years the population balance has been slowly changing in favour of non-Europeans. Two factors are responsible for this: firstly, the Maori and Polynesian population have an increasing birth rate and a decreasing death rate compared with those of European descent (which have remained static), as standards of health and welfare in these communities have improved, and secondly, the proportion of new immigrants of British descent is falling in favour of immigrants from other regions, particularly Asia.

RELIGION

New Zealand has a tradition of religious tolerance and every resident has total freedom of religion without hindrance by the state or community. New Zealand is a secular society and has no official state religion, although the majority of people are Christians with the main denominations being Anglican (25 per cent), Presbyterian (18 per cent) and Roman Catholic (16 per cent). Methodist and other Protestant denominations are also represented and there are also sizeable numbers of Jews, Hindus, and Confucians. Most Maoris are members of the Ratana and Ringatu Christian sects. Only some 15 per cent of New Zealanders regularly attend religious services and the number is declining, even among those who claim to be followers of a particular religion.

SOCIAL CUSTOMS

All countries have their own particular (and peculiar) social customs and New Zealand is no exception. As a country substantially populated by people of British ancestry, it's inevitable that many New Zealand social customs are modelled on British customs with local influences that have become more pronounced over the years. In general, New Zealanders tend to think that the British and their social customs are prudish or even snobbish. On the other hand, they tend to think that Australians and Americans are crass, although they share their pioneering spirit, common in all countries with a strong European heritage. The average New Zealander tries to strike a balance between these two extremes while also doing things differently, just to prove that they really are different from their neighbours and ancestors. It's also important to note that although New Zealand's Maori community is a minority in terms of numbers, its cultural influence extends across racial barriers. The following are a few New Zealand social customs:

- New Zealanders tend to prefer first name terms except when it clearly isn't appropriate (for example when addressing your prospective boss during an interview). When in doubt take your cue from your host or colleagues. It's usual for people at work to call each other by their first names, even when they are much higher or lower in the pecking order, and those who work together often also socialise together. It's common for friends to shorten names or use nicknames.

- It's considered perfectly acceptable to drop in on friends and acquaintances uninvited (and they will almost certainly do the same to you). You can also expect your neighbours to drop in uninvited, which is usually out of genuine friendliness rather than nosiness (or a desire to pass judgement on your interior decor). Indeed, if your new neighbours don't pop round it's considered polite to call on them and introduce yourself.

- Direct questions about, for example, your likes and dislikes or your family, shouldn't be considered as rudeness, as it usually indicates genuine interest and friendship (in addition to which New Zealanders prefer not to 'beat about the bush').

- Don't be surprised to receive invitations to social gatherings, such as parties or barbecues, from people you hardly know. This is particularly common when moving into a new area or starting a new job. It's done out of genuine warmth rather than any sense of duty and should be accepted in the spirit in which it's intended. Indeed, it would be considered rude to turn down such an invitation out of hand. It's usual to 'bring a bottle' if you're invited to a party or to a BYO (Bring Your Own) restaurant, i.e. a restaurant which doesn't have a licence to sell alcohol.

- Casual dress is normal in most situations, e.g. shorts are often worn to work in the summer, and jeans are acceptable in most restaurants and night-clubs. New Zealanders rarely wear formal dress such as evening dresses and dinner jackets. If you're invited to an event where formal attire is required, it will be clearly stated on the invitation.

● New Zealanders generally respect other people's customs, cultures, tastes, traditions and orientations, whether social, political or sexual. In fact, they usually have a particular regard for independent thinkers and those who dare to be different. This dates back to the pioneering days and even today tolerance towards other ideas and cultures, providing they don't involve physical or emotional harm, is enshrined in New Zealand law. Nevertheless, if you have any bizarre tastes and customs it's wise to keep them under wraps until you have ascertained whether or not your colleagues or acquaintance share them. Some New Zealanders, particularly older people, can be prudish and may even consider it a virtue.

TIME DIFFERENCE

New Zealand lies within a single time zone. Summer daylight saving time, an advance of one hour, is observed between the first Sunday in October and the third Sunday of the following March. New Zealand hasn't taken to the 24-hour clock system and times in most timetables are shown under the 12-hour clock 'am' and 'pm' system. Therefore times are either marked 'am' or 'pm', or printed in light type to indicate before noon and heavy type to indicate after noon. If in doubt it's advisable to ask, which is preferable to arriving 12 hours late (or early) for your flight or bus!

Bear in mind that there's a substantial time difference between New Zealand and Europe (and to a lesser extent the USA) and therefore it's advisable to check the local time abroad before making international telephone calls. It's difficult to find any time when it's convenient to call Western Europe, for example, if you call mid-morning you may well find that your European friends or relations are more interested in going to bed than chatting with you. The time difference between Wellington at noon in January and some major international cities is shown below:

SYDNEY	LONDON	CAPE TOWN	TOKYO	LOS ANGELES	NEW YORK
10AM	MIDNIGHT	2AM	9AM	4PM	7PM

(the previous day)

TIPPING

Tipping isn't a general custom in New Zealand (Americans please note!), although you may wish to leave a tip when you've had exceptional service or have received good value for money. New Zealanders almost never tip and, in fact, some people regard it as patronising or even insulting. Neither is it customary to round up amounts (e.g. taxi fares) to the nearest dollar or so, although most people won't complain if you do. Service charges aren't added to the bills in hotels and restaurants and you won't be expected to add your own.

TOILETS

Public toilets in New Zealand are generally clean, and are commonly found in parks, council and tourist offices, shopping centres, department stores, and bus and railway stations. The most sanitary (sometimes even quite luxurious) toilets are found in hotels, restaurants, public and private offices, stores, museums, galleries, airports, car parks, petrol stations and near popular beaches. Hotel (as in drinking places) and bar toilets vary from no-go areas to spotless. New Zealanders don't use the terms powder room, restroom or bathroom as Americans do, and the toilet is more likely to be referred to as the 'loo', which is considered quite a polite term, or the 'dunny'. Public toilets are usually free (when they aren't you may be required to pay a few cents to gain access to a cubicle) and don't normally have an attendant.

Some toilets have nappy (diaper) changing facilities and facilities for nursing mothers and an increasing number also have special facilities for the disabled. Toilets are usually marked with the familiar male and female symbols, whereas disabled toilets are generally used by both sexes and indicated by the international wheelchair sign. Toilets for the disabled may be locked to keep out 'unauthorised' users, in which case there will be a notice nearby explaining where the key can be obtained.

19.

THE KIWIS

Who are the New Zealanders? What are they like? Let us take a candid and totally prejudiced look at the New Zealand people (Kiwis), tongue firmly in cheek, and hope they forgive my flippancy or that they don't read this bit (which is why it's hidden away at the back of the book). The typical Kiwi is friendly, generous, outspoken, hard working, honest, inquisitive, patriotic, adventurous, bold, chauvinistic, modest, lethargic, down to earth, optimistic, relaxed, parochial, a compulsive gambler, self-reliant, practical, sartorially challenged, emotionless, hospitable, polite, decent, a beer drinker, open, conservative, prudish, garrulous, a suicidal driver, old-fashioned, casual, understated, cosmopolitan, a conservationist, good-humoured, a conformist, classless, a rugby and cricket fan, self-deprecating, generous, sincere, naíve, nationalistic, a carnivore, open, insular, a philistine, competitive, proud, an habitual traveller, informal, sociable, idealistic and a foreigner.

You may have noticed that the above list contains 'a few' contradictions (as does life in New Zealand), which is hardly surprising as there's no such thing as a typical Kiwi and few people conform to the popular stereotype (whatever that is). People from the North and South Islands are also supposed to have different characters, although foreigners will hardly notice the difference. New Zealand is a multicultural country (though not nearly as much as Australia) and a nation of foreigners – even the Polynesians, the country's oldest inhabitants, came from somewhere else – many of whom have little in common. However, despite its racial mix New Zealand isn't a universal melting pot and different ethnic groups such as Maoris, Chinese, British and assorted other Europeans, often live separate lives with their own customs, neighbourhoods, shops, clubs, restaurants, newspapers and sports.

New Zealanders pride themselves on their lack of class-consciousness and don't have the same caste distinctions and pretensions common in the 'mother' country (England) and consider the British to be snobbish (although descended from the British, the Kiwis have been trying to live it down for over a last century). However, New Zealand isn't exactly a classless society and status is as important there as it is anywhere else, although it's usually based on education or money rather than birthright. New Zealand generally has no class or 'old school tie' barriers to success and almost anyone, however humble his origins, can fight his way to the top of the heap (although colour barriers aren't always so easy to overcome). Kiwis don't much like Asians or any 'exotic' foreigners, although you'll generally be accepted providing you can blend into the background (green aliens will have no problems). Economic necessity (particularly after Britain joined the European common market in 1974) has led to closer ties with Asia and the Pacific countries and increased immigration from Asia (much to the horror of New Zealand's xenophobes).

Ties between New Zealand and Britain remain strong, although they have loosened somewhat in recent years and there's even talk of changing the New Zealand flag (a silver fern on a black background has been suggested – which would certainly be different) and even becoming a republic, although there isn't much of a republican movement in New Zealand (unlike, for example, Australia). Despite that fact that most Kiwis are of British stock, few have close connections with Britain nowadays and many have no attachment to the Union Jack (which is incorporated in their flag). However, there remain many similarities between Kiwis and the British, and New Zealand still copies many of the old country's habits (and new ideas) and in some ways Kiwis are considered to be more British than the British. The country even shares Britain's obsession with the weather, which is a popular topic of conversation.

Not surprisingly, all New Zealand's bad weather comes from Australia, which usually consists of torrential rain in the South Island and howling gales in the North Island.

Most rancour is reserved for the Aussies, who spend much of their time making jokes about Kiwis (e.g. 'The Kiwis have found a new use for sheep – wool' and 'What do you call a Kiwi in a suit? The defendant.'). New Zealanders feel culturally threatened by 'loud-mouthed' Aussies (in the same way that Canadians do by Americans) and New Zealand is often referred to disparagingly as the eighth state of Australia (tens of thousands of Kiwis live in Australia and Sydney has a larger population of Kiwis than most New Zealand towns). Kiwis have much in common with their closest neighbours (who thankfully aren't *too* close) and they have even been known to marry them. Although they don't much like comparisons being made, Kiwis are actually quite similar to Aussies (but much quieter) with whom they share their colourful language (with local idioms and Maori words thrown in for good measure), drinking habits, tucker, sports, sheep, lack of culture and isolation from the real world (among other things).

Most immigrants get on well with their Polynesian cousins (they officially stopped fighting one another in the 19th century), who sensibly mostly live in the warmer North Island (only one in 16 lives in the South Island). The main cause of (mild) friction is the competition for top dog between the inhabitants of the country's two major cities, Auckland (New Zealand's largest city and the world's largest Polynesian city) and Wellington (the nation's capital). The Maoris arrived in 'the land of the long white cloud' (*Aotearoa*) by canoe around 925 AD from other Pacific islands (they are superb sailors and have been called the 'Vikings of the South Seas'). The white man (*pakeha*) didn't arrive in any great numbers until the 19th century, although it didn't take him long to assert (usurp) his 'authority' and rob the Maoris of their land, which was done 'legally' with the infamous Treaty of Waitingi (which cleverly has never been ratified, otherwise the Maoris would own a lot more land than they do at present).

In recent years there has been an upsurge in Maori cultural awareness and *Maoritanga* (the Maori way of life) is now taught in schools along with the Maori language. This has inevitably resulted in the question of land ownership and fishing rights (perhaps influenced by the Aboriginals' example in Australia) being raised by Maori activists and has led to a number of clashes in recent years. Although many Maoris are second-class citizens, their plight is much better than that of Australia's Aboriginals. Despite their differences of opinion, intermarriage between Maoris and whites is common and there are fewer and fewer full-bloodied Maoris left in New Zealand (it's estimated that 1 in 12 New Zealanders are half Maori and many more are part Maori). This may have something to do with the traditional Maori greeting (*hongi*) which consists of pressing noses together with the eyes closed and making a low 'mm-mm' sound (maybe it's a secret mating ritual?).

Kiwis are passionate about sport and when not debating the price of lamb they are discussing the latest rugby or cricket results. The All Blacks rugby team is internationally acclaimed and star players are Gods and feted in the same way as soccer stars in other countries. The All Blacks perform their famous *haka* war dance before matches to intimidate their opponents (although having Jonah Lomu on your side is enough to scare anyone), but it didn't seem to be working too well in 1998 when they lost an unprecedented five straight losses. Apart from rugby the main sport in New Zealand is cricket, and although they haven't had much of an international team since Richard Hadlee retired in the '80s, they would <u>never</u> resort to bowling underarm to win a test match (unlike their neighbours Australia). The Aussies are the old sporting enemy, with whom the Kiwis compete passionately at all sports (the Kiwis also enjoy beating the Poms). Apart from rugby, cricket and a few other sports, most New Zealand 'sports' involve trying to commit suicide by hurling yourself off bridges, out of planes or into boiling rapids (you cannot accuse Kiwis of being wimps!).

New Zealand isn't noted for its cuisine (something else they inherited from the British) which largely consists of numerous ways of serving lamb, fish and chips, meat pies and the obligatory tomato sauce (which goes with anything), ice cream, kiwi fruit and pavlova (the national dish invented in Australia). Kiwis are voracious carnivores and among the biggest meat eaters in the world – in fact things haven't changed a lot since the first Polynesian settlers ate each other. Kiwis generally have an unhealthy diet of biscuits, cakes, fast food and take-aways, despite the country's abundance of fresh fruit and vegetables (in New Zealand a salad is haute cuisine). To compensate for their lack of culinary skills New Zealanders have been making some passable wines in recent years with 'catchy' names such as 'cat's pee on a gooseberry bush', although most Kiwis are beer drinkers. One of the secrets of enjoying a meal in New Zealand is to drink a lot (which the Kiwis do with gusto), as when you're drunk most food tastes okay.

The Kiwis are famous for their relaxed pace of life (except when motoring, when they are hell bent on reaching the next life as fast as possible), particularly in rural areas where a fast life consists of a brisk walk to the nearest pub (or a ride on a tractor). Outside of Auckland and Wellington, the night-life usually consists of watching TV or getting drunk (or both) and most Kiwis are tucked up in bed by 9pm (you would be also if you had to get up at 5am to milk the ewes). Kiwis go to extraordinary lengths to 'amuse' themselves (which is why they partake in all those death-defying sports) and a popular pastime in a pub in Napier (called 'bar-fly hopping') involves bouncing on a trampoline and trying to attach yourself to a wall with velcro! New Zealand is notorious as a cultural backwater (even neanderthal Australians make fun of it), although it isn't as (all) black as it's painted (at least in the major cities) and the Maoris have a thousand years of culture and history in New Zealand.

The Kiwis are slow to make changes, both individually and as a nation, and the country is often reckoned to be around 20 years behind the rest of the world (which isn't surprising as it used to take that long to get there from Europe or North America – assuming you could find it at all!). Not so long ago Kiwis were still wearing '60s fashions and driving around in Morris Minors and Ford Anglias. However, it isn't true that they don't have electricity, although it may sometimes appear that way when visiting Auckland. The country is so far from anywhere that it was one of the last places on earth to be inhabited by man (if you go any further south you'll fall off the end of the world) and although most people have heard of New Zealand, few actually know where it is. Sometimes you don't just feel as if you're in the most isolated country in the world, but on a different planet altogether (the end of the world will probably be a few weeks late reaching New Zealand). Not surprisingly, New Zealand can appear a little detached from the rest of the world and newspapers and news bulletins rarely mention 'overseas' unless something particularly dramatic happens (such as the world price of wool or lamb going through the floor).

New Zealand politics are deadly boring, even to Kiwis, although things have livened up in recent years with the introductions of proportional representation. Nowadays you never know which politicians will jump into bed with whom (metaphorically speaking) and how long they will remain bedfellows, which makes for a lively parliament but hardly adds to the stability of government. New Zealand has (surprisingly) always been at the forefront of social change and is something of an economic laboratory. It was the first self-governing country to give women the vote in 1893 (25 years before Britain) and in 1998 New Zealand's women were rated 4th in the world by the United Nations at gaining access to power. New Zealand was also one of the first countries (in 1938) to establish a system of social security (including a national health service), the first to introduce an old-age pension and the first to institute an eight-hour working day. Both sexes have equal rights and opportunities in law, and New Zealand is one of the few countries in the world to have had a woman prime minister. Nevertheless, like most democracies, Kiwis have a healthy disrespect (contempt) for their politicians.

Immigration has undeniably made New Zealand a culturally richer, more diverse and interesting country, although it's now closed to many of the sort of people (and sheep) who made it was it is today. However, if you're rejected, try to look on the bright side: the New Zealand Dream isn't always the paradise that it's cracked up to be and some newcomers cannot wait to go home. Despite its isolation from the real world, the country isn't completely detached from the problems that beset other countries. These include a spiralling crime rate (particularly youth crime and delinquency); high unemployment; homelessness; a worsening drug problem; welfare dependency; a burgeoning divorce rate; an horrific road accident-rate (aided by widespread drunken driving); many single-parent families (which make up almost a quarter of Kiwis); racial tensions; and an economy that's too dependent on crumbling Asian markets. These problems are no means unique to New Zealand in today's turbulent world and many are shared by other western countries. However, how New Zealand faces up to them and the challenges of the new millennium will shape its future for generations to come.

And now for the good news! New Zealand is one of the most open, liberal, stable and tolerant societies in the world. It has a strong economy, political stability, an excellent education system; a skilled workforce, a high standard of living, some of the most desirable cities to be found anywhere and one of the cleanest environments in the world (the country declared itself the world's first nuclear-free zone in 1985). New Zealand is also renowned for its wealth of natural beauty, outdoor lifestyle, wholesome food, friendly people, sports' prowess, freedom, healthcare, excellent local government and things that work. Although immigrants may occasionally criticise some aspects of New Zealand life, relatively few consider leaving and most are proud to call themselves Kiwis. In fact, immigrants from a vast range of backgrounds firmly believe that New Zealand (God's Own Country or 'godzone') is one of the best countries in the world. Put simply, New Zealand is a great place in which to live and raise a family.

A final few words of caution for newcomers – whatever you do don't make jokes about Kiwis and sheep, which are in bad taste and to be avoided at all costs.

Up the All Blacks! Long Live New Zealand!

20.

MOVING HOUSE
OR
LEAVING NEW ZEALAND

When moving house or leaving New Zealand there are many things to be considered and a 'million' people to be informed. The checklists contained in this chapter are designed to make the task easier and hopefully help prevent an ulcer or a nervous breakdown, providing of course you don't leave everything to the last minute (only divorce or a bereavement cause more stress than moving house). See also **Moving House** on page 88 and **Relocation Consultants** on page 77.

MOVING HOUSE

When moving house within New Zealand the following items should be considered:

- If you live in rented accommodation you must give your landlord notice (the period will depend on your contract). You may need to remain until a minimum period has elapsed and if you don't give your landlord sufficient notice, you'll be required to pay the rent until the end of your contract or for the full notice period. This will also apply if you have a separate contract for a garage or other rented property, e.g. a holiday home.
- Inform the following:
  - Your employer.
  - If you're a homeowner and are moving to a new area, you should inform your present council when you move and re-register in your new council area after arrival. When moving to a new area or state you may be entitled to a refund of a portion of your property taxes (rates).
  - Your electricity, gas and water companies.
  - Your telephone company (or companies).
  - Your insurance companies (for example health, car and home); banks, post office, stockbroker and other financial institutions; credit and charge card companies; hire purchase companies; solicitor and accountant; and local businesses where you have accounts.
  - Your family doctor, dentist and other health practitioners. Health records should be transferred to your new doctor and dentist, if applicable.
  - Your children's and your schools. If applicable, arrange for schooling in your new area. Try to give a term's notice and obtain a copy of any relevant school reports or records from your children's current schools.
  - All regular correspondents, subscriptions, social and sports clubs, professional and trade journals, and friends and relatives. Give or send them your new address and telephone number. Arrange to have your mail redirected by NZ Post.
  - If you have a New Zealand driving licence or a New Zealand registered car, give the authorities your new address as soon as possible after moving.
  - Your local consulate or embassy, if you're registered with them (see page 70).
- Return any library books or anything borrowed.

- Arrange removal of your furniture and belongings by booking a removal company (see page 88) well in advance. If you have only a few items of furniture to move, you may prefer to do your own move, in which case you could need to hire a van.

- Arrange for a cleaning company and/or decorating company for rented accommodation, if required.

- If you're renting, make sure that you get your bond returned.

- Cancel the milk and newspaper deliveries.

- Ask yourself (again): 'Is it really worth all this trouble?'

LEAVING NEW ZEALAND

Before leaving New Zealand permanently or for an indefinite period, the following items should be considered *in addition* to those listed above under **Moving House**:

- Give notice to your employer(s), if applicable.

- Check that your family's passports aren't out of date.

- Check whether any special requirements (e.g. visas, permits or inoculations) are necessary for entry into your country of destination by contacting the local embassy or consulate in New Zealand. An exit permit or visa isn't required to leave New Zealand.

- Book a shipping company (see page 88) well in advance. International shipping companies usually provide a wealth of information and may also be able to advise you on various matters concerning your relocation. Find out the exact procedure for shipping your belongings to your country of destination from the local embassy in New Zealand of the country to which you're moving (don't rely entirely on your shipping company). Special forms may need to be completed before arrival. If you've been living in New Zealand for less than a year, you're required to export all personal effects, including furniture and vehicles that were imported tax and duty free. Arrange to sell anything that you won't be taking with you, e.g. house, car and furniture.

- You may qualify for a rebate on your tax payments (see page 213). If you're leaving New Zealand permanently and have been a member of a company superannuation scheme, you may be entitled to a refund or may be able to have your fund transferred to a new employer's fund. Contact your company personnel office or superannuation company for information.

- If you have an New Zealand-registered car which you're permanently exporting, you should ask the New Zealand authorities to de-register the vehicle, and register it in your new country of residence on arrival.

- Depending on your destination, your pets may require special inoculations or may need to go into quarantine for a period (contact the embassy of your country of destination for information).

- Contact your telephone and other utility companies well in advance, particularly if you need to get deposits repaid.

- Arrange health, travel and other insurance as necessary (see **Chapter 13**).

- Depending on your destination, arrange health and dental checkups for your family before leaving New Zealand. Obtain a copy of all your health and dental records and a statement from your health insurance company noting your present level of cover.

- Terminate any outstanding loan, lease or hire purchase contracts and pay all outstanding bills (allow plenty of time as some companies may be slow to respond).

- Check whether you're entitled to a rebate on your car and other insurance. Obtain a letter from your New Zealand motor insurance company stating your number of years' no-claims' discount.

- Sell your house, apartment or other property, or arrange to let it through a friend or a letting agency (see **Chapter 5**).

- Check whether you need an international driving permit or a translation of your New Zealand or foreign driving licence for your country of destination.

- Give friends and business associates in New Zealand a temporary address and telephone number where you can be contacted overseas.

- If you're travelling by air, allow plenty of time to get to the airport, register your luggage, and clear security and immigration.

- Buy a copy of *Living and Working in ********* before leaving New Zealand. If we haven't written it yet, drop us a line and we'll get started on it right away!

Have a safe journey.

APPENDICES

APPENDIX A: USEFUL ADDRESSES

Embassies & Consulates

Most foreign embassies in New Zealand are located in the capital Wellington (as you would expect), although some countries have their missions in Auckland. Note that business hours vary considerably and all embassies close on their national holidays and on New Zealand's public holidays. Always telephone to check the business hours before visiting.

Argentina: Level 14, 142 Lambton Quay, Wellington (☎ (04) 472 8330).

Australia: 72 Hobson Street, Thorndon, Box 4036, Wellington (☎ (04) 473 6411).

Austria: 22 Garrett Street, PO Box 6016, Wellington (☎ (04) 801 9709).

Belgium: 12th Floor, 1-3 Willeston Street, Box 3841, Wellington (☎ (04) 472 9558).

Brazil: 10 Brandon Street, Wellington (☎ (04) 473 3516).

Canada: 61 Molesworth Street, Box 12049, Wellington (☎ (04) 473 9577).

Chile: 12/1 Willeston Street, Box 3861. Wellington (☎ (04) 471 6270).

China: 2-6 Glenmore Street, Kelburn, Wellington (☎ (04) 472 1382).

Costa Rica: 50 Lunn Avenue, Mount Wellington, Box 686, Auckland (☎ (09) 527 1523).

Czech Republic: 12 Anne Street, Wadestown, Box 2843, Wellington (☎ (04) 472 3142).

Finland: 25 Victoria Street, Box 1201, Wellington (☎ (04) 472 4924).

France: 34-42 Manners Street, Wellington (☎ (04) 384 2555).

Germany: 90-92 Hobson Street, Thorndon, Box 1687, Wellington (☎ (04) 473 6063/4).

Greece: 237 Willis Street, Box 27157, Wellington (☎ (04) 484 7556).

India: 180 Molesworth Street, Box 4045, Wellington (☎ (04) 473 6390/1).

Indonesia: 70 Glen Road, Kelburn, Box 3543, Wellington (☎ (04) 475 8697).

Iran: 151 Te Anau Road, Roseneath, Wellington (☎ (04) 386 2976).

Ireland: 87 Queen Street, Box 279, Auckland (☎ (09) 302 2867).

Israel: Plimmer City Centre, Box 2171, Wellington (☎ (04) 472 2362).

Italy: 34 Grant Road, Thorndon, PO Box 463, Wellington (☎ (04) 473 5339).

Japan: 3-11 Hunter Street, Box 6340, Wellington (☎ (04) 473 1540).

Korea: 11th Floor, ASB Bank Tower, 2 Hunter Street, Wellington (☎ (04) 473 9073).

Malaysia: 10 Washington Avenue, Brooklyn, Box 9422, Wellington (☎ (04) 485 2439).

Mexico: 150-154 Willis Street, Box 3029, Wellington (☎ (04) 485 2145).

Netherlands: Investment House, Cnr Ballance & Featherstone Streets, Box 840, Wellington (☎ (04) 471 6390).

Norway: 55 Molesworth Street, Wellington (☎ (04) 471 2503).

Pakistan: PO Box 3830, Auckland (☎ (09) 528 3526).

Papua New Guinea: 180 Molesworth Street, Box 197, Wellington (☎ (04) 473 1560).

Peru: Level 8, Cigna House, 40 Mercer Street, Wellington (☎ (04) 499 8087).

Philippines: 50 Hobson Street, Thorndon, Box 12042. Wellington (☎ (04) 472 9848).

Poland: 196 The Terrace, Box 10211, Wellington (☎ 471 2456).

Portugal: Southpac House, 1 Victoria Street, Wellington (☎ (04) 472 1677).

Russia: 57 Messines Road, Karori, Wellington (☎ (04) 476 6113).

Singapore: 17 Kabul Street, Khandallah, Box 29023, Wellington (☎ (04) 479 2076).

Spain: Box 71, Papakura, Auckland (☎ (09) 298 5176).

Sweden: Greenock House, 39 The Terrace, Box 5350, Wellington (☎ (04) 472 0909).

Switzerland: Panama House, 22 Panama Street, Wellington (☎ (04) 472 1593).

Thailand: 2 Cook Street, Karori, Box 17226, Wellington (☎ (04) 476 8618).

Turkey: 404 Khyber Pass Road, Newmarket, Auckland (☎ (09) 522 2281).

United Kingdom: Reserve Bank Building, 2 The Terrace, Box 1812, Wellington (☎ (04) 472 6049).

USA: 29 Fitzherbert Terrace, Box 1190, Wellington (☎ (04) 472 2068).

Government Departments

Department of Conservation, PO Box 10 420, Wellington (☎ (04) 471 0726, fax (04) 471 1082).

Department of Corrections, PO Box 1206, Wellington (☎ (04) 499 5620, fax (04) 499 5636).

Department for Courts, PO Box 2750, Wellington (☎ (04) 473 8800, fax (04) 473 4796).

Department of Internal Affairs, PO Box 805, Wellington (☎ (04) 495 7200, fax (04) 495 7222).

Department of Labour, PO Box 3705, Wellington (☎ (04) 915 4000, fax (04) 471 0012).

Department of Prime Minister & Cabinet, Parliament Building, Wellington (☎ (04) 471 9700, fax (04) 473 2508).

Department of Social Welfare, Private Bag 21, Wellington (☎ (04) 916 3884, fax (04) 916 3913).

Department of Survey and Land Information, Private Bag 1666, Wellington (☎ (04) 473 5022).

The Treasury, PO Box 3724, Wellington (☎ (04) 472 2733, fax (04) 473 0982).

Government Ministries

Ministry of Agriculture & Forestry, PO Box 2526, Wellington (☎ (04) 474 4100, fax (04) 474 4244).

Ministry of Agriculture & Forestry, Quarantine Services, PO Box 1254, Wellington (☎ (04) 256 8547, fax (04) 256 6410).

Ministry of Civil Defence, PO Box 5010, Wellington (☎ (04) 473 7363, fax (04) 473 7369).

Ministry of Commerce, PO Box 1473, Wellington (☎ (04) 472 0030, fax (04) 473 4638).

Ministry of Consumer Affairs, PO Box 1473, Wellington (☎ (04) 474 2750, fax (04) 473 9400).

Ministry of Cultural Affairs, PO Box 5364, Wellington (☎ (04) 499 4229, fax (04) 499 4490).

Ministry of Defence, PO Box 5347, Wellington (☎ (04) 496 0999, fax (04) 496 0856).

Ministry of Education, PO Box 1666, Wellington (☎ (04) 473 5544, fax (04) 499 1327).

Ministry for the Environment, PO Box 10 362, Wellington (☎ (04) 917 7400, fax (04) 917 7523).

Ministry of Fisheries, PO Box 1020, Wellington (☎ (04) 470 2600, fax (04) 470 2601).

Ministry of Foreign Affairs & Trade, PO Box 18 901, Wellington (☎ (04) 494 8500, fax (04) 494 8512).

Ministry of Health, PO Box 5013, Wellington (☎ (04) 496 2000, fax (04) 496 2340).

Ministry of Housing, PO Box 10 729, Wellington (☎ (04) 472 2753, fax (04) 499 4744).

Ministry of Justice, PO Box 180, Wellington (☎ (04) 494 9700, fax (04) 494 9701).

Ministry of Pacific Island Affairs, PO Box 833, Wellington (☎ (04) 473 4493, fax (04) 473 4301).

Ministry of Research, Science & Technology, PO Box 5336, Wellington (☎ (04) 472 6400, fax (04) 471 1284).

Ministry of Maori Development (*Te Puni Kokiri*), PO Box 3943, Wellington (☎ (04) 494 7000, fax (04) 494 7010).

Ministry of Transport, PO Box 3175, Wellington (☎ (04) 472 1253, fax (04) 473 3697).

Ministry of Women's Affairs, PO Box 10 049, Wellington (☎ (04) 473 4112, fax (04) 472 0961).

Ministry of Youth Affairs, PO Box 10 300, Wellington (☎ (04) 471 2158, fax (04) 471 2233).

Miscellaneous

Births, Deaths & Marriages, PO Box 5040, Wellington (☎ (04) 474 7580, fax (04) 474 7584).

Citizenship Office, PO Box 805, Wellington (☎ freephone (0800) 225151, fax (04) 474 8006).

Land Information New Zealand, Private Bag 5501, Wellington (☎ (04) 460 0110, fax (04) 472 2244).

National Archives of New Zealand, PO Box 12-050, Wellington (☎ (04) 499 5595, fax (04) 499 6210).

National Library of New Zealand, PO Box 1467, Wellington (☎ (04) 474 3000, fax (04) 474 3035).

New Zealand Children, Young Persons and their Families Service, Private Bag 21, Wellington (☎ (04) 916 3100, fax (04) 916 3137).

New Zealand Customs, PO Box 2218, Wellington (☎ freephone (0800) 428786, fax (09) 359 6730).

New Zealand Immigration Service, PO Box 27 149, Wellington (☎ (04) 384 7929, fax (04) 384 8243).

Statistics New Zealand, PO Box 2922, Wellington (☎ (04) 495 4600, fax (04) 495 4610).

TeachNZ, PO Box 1666, Wellington (☎ freephone (0800) 832 246, fax (04) 471 4432).

Magazines & Newspapers

Destination New Zealand, Outbound Newspapers, 1 Commercial Road, Eastbourne, East Sussex BN21 3XQ, UK (☎ 01323-412001).

New Zealand Outlook, Consyl Publishing, 3 Buckhurst Road, Bexhill-on-Sea, East Sussex TN40 1QF, UK (☎ 01424-223111).

TNT Magazine New Zealand, 14-15 Child's Place, London SW5 9RX, UK (☎ 0171-373 3377).

New Zealand News UK, Commonwealth Publishing Ltd., 3rd Floor, New Zealand House, Haymarket, London SW1Y 4TE, UK (☎ 0171-747 9200).

APPENDIX B: FURTHER READING

There are many useful reference books for those seeking general information about Australia including the *New Zealand Official Year Book* published annually by Statistics New Zealand. A selection of books about New Zealand are listed below (the publication title is followed by the name of the author and the publisher's name in brackets). Books prefixed with an asterisk (*) are recommended by the author. Some of the books listed are out of print, but you may still be able to find a copy in a bookshop or library.

Living & Working

Finding a Job in New Zealand, Joy Muirhead (How To Books)

Live & Work In Australia & New Zealand, Fiona McGregor & Charlotte Denny (Vacation Work)

Live & Work in New Zealand, Avril Harper (Dawson)

**Living and Working in New Zealand, Mark Hempshell (Survival Books)

Living and Working in New Zealand, Joy Muirhead (How To Books)

*The New Zealand Immigration Guide, Adam Starchild

The Small Business Book: A New Zealand Guide, Robert Hamlin & John English (Bridgit Williams)

Your Successful Small Business: A New Zealand Guide to Starting Out and Staying in Business, Judith Ashton (Viking Pacific)

Tourist Guides

*Australia & New Zealand Travel Planner (TNT Magazine)

*Baedeker's New Zealand (AA)

Berlitz Pocket Guide to New Zealand (Berlitz)

*Berlitz Travellers Guide New Zealand (Berlitz)

*Blue Guide New Zealand (A & C Black)

Destination New Zealand, Hildesuse Gaertner & Sue Bollans (Windsor)

Essential New Zealand (Automobile Association)

Fielding's New Zealand, Zeke & Joan Wigglesworth (Fielding)

*Fodor's New Zealand (Fodor)

*Frommers New Zealand from $50 a Day, Elizabeth Hanson & Richard Adams (Macmillan)

Insider's New Zealand Guide, Harry Blutstein (MPC)

*Insight Guides to New Zealand (APA Publications)

*Let's Go New Zealand (Macmillan)

*Maverick Guide to New Zealand, Robert W. Bone (Pelican)

Nelles Guide: New Zealand (Verlag Nelles)

New Zealand at Cost, Fay Smith

New Zealand Handbook, Jane King (Moon)

*New Zealand: A Travel Survival Kit, Tony Wheeler & Nancy Keller (Lonely Planet)

*New Zealand: The Rough Guide, Laura Harper (The Rough Guides)

Travellers Survival Kit: Australia and New Zealand, Susan Griffith & Simon Calder (Vacation Work)

Visitor's Guide to New Zealand, Grant Bourne & Sabine Korner-Bourne (Moorland)

Food & Wine

Fine Wines of New Zealand, Keith Stewart (Grub Street)

James Halliday's Australian and New Zealand Wine Companion, James Halliday

New Taste in New Zealand, Lauraine Jacobs & Stephen Robinson (Ten Speed Press)

Pocket Guide to the Wines of New Zealand, Michael Cooper (Mitchell Beazley)

Wines of New Zealand, Michael Cooper (Millers)

The Wines of New Zealand, Rosemary M. George (Faber & Faber)

Miscellaneous

Australia and New Zealand Contact Directory, Sheile Hare (Expat Network)

*Australia & New Zealand by Rail, Colin Taylor (Bradt)

Back Country New Zealand (Hodder)

Beautiful New Zealand, Peter Morath (Hale)

Culture Questions: New Zealand Identity in a Transitional Age, Ruth Brown (Kapako)

Dictionary of New Zealand English, H.W. Oarsman (Oxford University Press)

New Zealand in Pictures (Paperboards)

New Zealand Ways of Speaking English, Allan Bell & Janet Holmes (Multilingual Matters)

Oxford Illustrated History of New Zealand, Keith Sinclair (Oxford University Press)

A Personal Kiwi-Yankee Dictionary, Louis S. Leland Jr

Politics in New Zealand, Richard Mulgan (Auckland UP)

Smooth Ride Guide to Australia & New Zealand (FT Publishing)

Truth About New Zealand, A.N. Field (Veritas)

Wild New Zealand, B. Coffey (New Holland)

Wild New Zealand: Reader's Digest (Reader's Digest)

APPENDIX C: WEIGHTS & MEASURES

New Zealand uses the metric system of measurement. Nationals of a few countries (including the Americans and British) who are more familiar with the imperial system of measurement will find the tables on the following pages useful. Some comparisons shown are only approximate, but are close enough for most everyday uses. In addition to the variety of measurement systems used, clothes sizes often vary considerably depending on the manufacturer (as we all know only too well). Try all clothes on before buying and don't be afraid to return something if, when you try it on at home, you decide it doesn't fit (most shops will exchange goods or give a refund).

Women's clothes:

Continental	34	36	38	40	42	44	46	48	50	52
GB	8	10	12	14	16	18	20	22	24	26
USA	6	8	10	12	14	16	18	20	22	24

Pullovers:

	Women's						Men's					
Continental	40	42	44	46	48	50	44	46	48	50	52	54
GB	34	36	38	40	42	44	34	36	38	40	42	44
USA	34	36	38	40	42	44	sm	medium	large	exl		

Note: sm = small, exl = extra large

Men's Shirts

Continental	36	37	38	39	40	41	42	43	44	46
GB/USA	14	14	15	15	16	16	17	17	18	

Men's Underwear

Continental	5	6	7	8	9	10
GB	34	36	38	40	42	44
USA	small	medium		large	extra large	

Children's Clothes

Continental	92	104	116	128	140	152
GB	16/18	20/22	24/26	28/30	32/34	36/38
USA	24	6	8	10	12	

Children's Shoes

Continental	18	19	20	21	22	23	24	25	26	27	28
GB/USA	2	3	4	4	5	6	7	7	8	9	10

Continental	29	30	31	32	33	34	35	36	37	38
GB/USA	11	11	12	13	1	2	2	3	4	5

Shoes (Women's and Men's)

Continental	35	35	36	37	37	38	39	39	40	40
GB	2	3	3	4	4	5	5	6	6	7
USA	4	4	5	5	6	6	7	7	8	8

Continental	41	42	42	43	44	44
GB	7	8	8	9	9	10
USA	9	9	10	10	11	11

Weights:

Avoirdupois	Metric	Metric	Avoirdupois
1 oz	28.35g	1g	0.035oz
1 pound*	454g	100g	3.5oz
1 cwt	50.8kg	250g	9oz
1 ton	1,016kg	1kg	2.2 pounds
1 tonne	2,205 pounds		

* A metric 'pound' is 500g, g = gramme, kg = kilogramme

Length:

British/US	Metric	Metric	British/US
1 inch =	2.54 cm	1 cm	0.39 inch
1 foot =	30.48 cm	1 m3.	28 feet
1 yard =	91.44 cm	1 km	0.62 mile
1 mile =	1.6 km	8 km	5 miles

Note: cm = centimetre, m = metre, km = kilometre

Capacity:

Imperial	Metric	Metric	Imperial
1 pint (USA)	0.47l	1 l	1.76 GB pints
1 pint (GB)	0.568l	1 l	0.265 US gallons
1 gallon (USA)	3.78l	1 l	0.22 GB gallons
1 gallon (GB)	4.54l	1 l	35.211 fluid oz

Note: l = litre

Square Measure:

British/US	Metric	Metric	British/US
1 square inch	6.45 sq. cm	1 sq. cm	0.155 sq. inches
1 square foot	0.092 sq. m.	1 sq. m	10.764 sq. feet
1 square yard	0.836 sq. m.	1 sq. m.	1.196 sq. yards
1 acre	0.405 hect.	1 hectare	2.471 acres
1 square mile	259 hect.	1 sq. km	0.386 sq. mile

Temperature:

° Celsius	° Fahrenheit	
0	32	freezing point of water
5	41	
10	50	
15	59	
20	68	
25	77	
30	86	
35	95	
40	104	

The Boiling point of water is 100°C / 212°F.

Oven temperature:

Gas	Electric	
	°F	°C
-	225-250	110-120
1	275	140
2	300	150
3	325	160
4	350	180
5	375	190
6	400	200
7	425	220
8	450	230
9	475	240

For a quick conversion, the Celsius temperature is approximately half the Fahrenheit temperature (in the range shown above).

Temperature Conversion:

Celsius to Fahrenheit: multiply by 9, divide by 5 and add 32.
Fahrenheit to Celsius: subtract 32, multiply by 5 and divide by 9.

Body Temperature:

Normal body temperature (if you're alive and well) is 98.4° Fahrenheit, which equals 37° Celsius.

APPENDIX D: MAP OF NEW ZEALAND

The map below shows the major cities and geographical features of New Zealand.

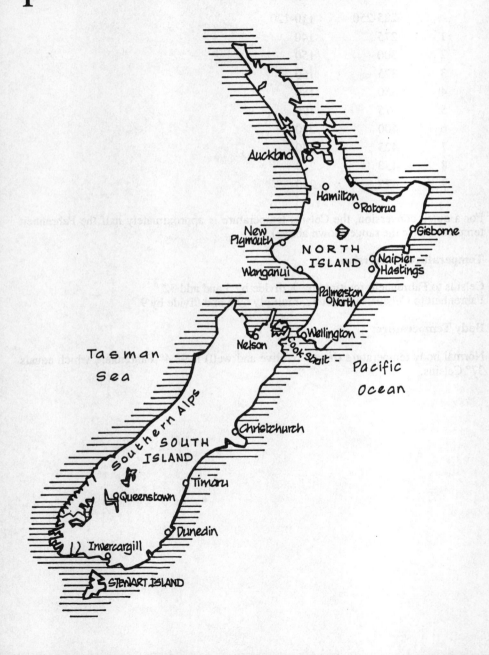

INDEX

N

O

P

SUGGESTIONS

Please write to us with any comments or suggestions you have regarding the contents of this book (preferably complimentary!). We are particularly interested in proposals for improvements that can be included in future editions. For example did you find any important subjects were omitted or weren't covered in sufficient detail? What difficulties or obstacles have you encountered which aren't covered here? What other subjects would you like to see included?

If your suggestions are used in the next edition of *Living and Working in New Zealand*, you'll receive a free copy of the Survival Book of your choice as a token of our appreciation.

NAME: _____

ADDRESS: _____

_____

_____

Send to: Survival Books, PO Box 146, Wetherby, West Yorks. LS23 6XZ, United Kingdom.

My suggestions are as follows (please use additional pages if necessary):

OTHER SURVIVAL BOOKS

There are other *Living and Working* books in this series including America, Australia, Britain, France, Spain and Switzerland, all of which represent the most comprehensive and up-to-date source of practical information available about everyday life in these countries. We also publish a best-selling series of 'Buying a Home' books including *Buying a Home Abroad* plus buying a home in Florida, France, Ireland, Italy, Portugal and Spain.

Survival Books are available from good bookshops throughout the world or direct from Survival Books. If you aren't entirely satisfied simply return them within 14 days for a full and unconditional refund. **Order your copies today by phone, fax, mail or e-mail from:** Survival Books, PO Box 146, Wetherby, West Yorks. LS23 6XZ, United Kingdom (tel/fax:44-1937-843523). E-mail: survivalbooks@computronx.com, Internet: computronx.com/survivalbooks.

WHY NOT AUSTRALIA?

ORDER FORM

Please rush me the following Survival Books:

Qty	Title	Price* UK	Europe	World	Total
	Buying a Home Abroad	£11.45	£12.95	£14.95	
	Buying a Home in Florida	£11.45	£12.95	£14.95	
	Buying a Home in France	£11.45	£12.95	£14.95	
	Buying a Home in Ireland	£11.45	£12.95	£14.95	
	Buying a Home in Italy	£11.45	£12.95	£14.95	
	Buying a Home in Portugal	£11.45	£12.95	£14.95	
	Buying a Home in Spain	£11.45	£12.95	£14.95	
	Living and Working in America	£14.95	£16.95	£20.45	
	Living and Working in Australia	£14.95	£16.95	£20.45	
	Living and Working in Britain	£14.95	£16.95	£20.45	
	Living and Working in France	£14.95	£16.95	£20.45	
	Living and Working in New Zealand	£14.95	£16.95	£20.45	
	Living and Working in Spain	£14.95	£16.95	£20.45	
	Living and Working in Switzerland	£14.95	£16.95	£20.45	
	The Alien's Guide to France (spring 1999)	£5.95	£6.95	£8.45	
				TOTAL	

Cheque enclosed/Please charge my Access/Delta/Mastercard/Switch/Visa* card,

Expiry date _____ No. __ __ __ __   __ __ __ __   __ __ __ __   __ __ __ __

Issue number (Switch only) _____ Signature: _____

* Delete as applicable (price for Europe/World includes airmail postage)

NAME: _____

ADDRESS: _____

_____

_____

Send to: Survival Books, PO Box 146, Wetherby, West Yorks. LS23 6XZ, United **Kingdom or tel/fax/e-mail credit card orders to 44-1937-843523.**